FROMMER'S EASYGUIDE TO

# Cancún & the Caribbean Coast

*By*

**Christine Delsol & Maribeth Mellin**

*Easy Guides are* • Quick To Read • Light To Carry • For Expert Advice • In All Price Ranges

Published by
**FROMMER MEDIA LLC**



ISBN 978-1-62887-158-6 (paper), 978-1-62887-159-3 (ebk)

Editorial Director: Pauline Frommer
Editor: Margaret Sanborn
Production Editor: Erin Geile
Cartographer: Liz Puhl
Cover Design: Howard Grossman

For information on our other products or services, see www.frommers.com.

Frommer Media LLC also publishes its books in a variety of electronic formats. Some content that appears in print may not be available in electronic formats.

Manufactured in the United States of America

5 4 3 2 1

## AN IMPORTANT NOTE

The world is a dynamic place. Hotels change ownership, restaurants hike their prices, museums alter their opening hours, and busses and trains change their routings. And all of this can occur in the several months after our authors have visited, inspected, and written about, these hotels, restaurants, museums and transportation services. Though we have made valiant efforts to keep all our information fresh and up-to-date, some few changes can inevitably occur in the periods before a revised edition of this guidebook is published. So please bear with us if a tiny number of the details in this book have changed. Please also note that we have no responsibility or liability for any inaccuracy or errors or omissions, or for inconvenience, loss, damage, or expenses suffered by anyone as a result of assertions in this guide.

# CONTENTS

## ABOUT THE AUTHORS

It took **Christine Delsol** nearly 20 years to recover from her first memory of Mexico—a bullfight during a childhood trip with her Mexican *Californio* grandmother—but since that first trepidatious experience she has logged about 10,000 miles in what she now considers her second home. She has spent most of her journalism career in newspapers, including eight years on the *San Francisco Chronicle's* travel section, where she won two Lowell Thomas awards. She wrote *Pauline Frommer's Guide to Cancún & the Yucatán* and co-authored four editions of *Frommer's Mexico* and *Frommer's Cancún & the Yucatán*. She writes frequently for the *Chronicle* as a freelancer, and contributes a monthly column on Mexico to its website, SFgate.com. Her work has also appeared in numerous magazines and travel websites. She lives in the San Francisco Bay Area with her husband and has an absurdly well-traveled 27-year-old daughter.

**Maribeth Mellin** is an award-wining journalist and photographer based in San Diego. She has received Mexico's prestigious Pluma de Plata as well as commendations from Cancún, Cozumel, Acapulco, and other destinations. In addition, her articles on medical, social, and legal issues have garnered numerous awards from journalism organizations. Mellin has authored several travel books, and her articles and photos have appeared in the U-T San Diego, Los Angeles Times, Dallas Morning News, Endless Vacation Magazine, the San Francisco Chronicle, and other publications. She also has contributed to multiple websites including Concierge.com and TravelCNN.com. When not traveling the globe, she enjoys time at home with her husband near the beach and border in San Diego.

## ABOUT THE FROMMER TRAVEL GUIDES

For most of the past 50 years, Frommer's has been the leading series of travel guides in North America, accounting for as many as 24% of all guidebooks sold. I think I know why.

Though we hope our books are entertaining, we nevertheless deal with travel in a serious fashion. Our guidebooks have never looked on such journeys as a mere recreation, but as a far more important human function, a time of learning and introspection, an essential part of a civilized life. We stress the culture, lifestyle, history and beliefs of the destinations we cover, and urge our readers to seek out people and new ideas as the chief rewards of travel.

We have never shied from controversy. We have, from the beginning, encouraged our authors to be intensely judgmental, critical—both pro and con—in their comments, and wholly independent. Our only clients are our readers, and we have triggered the ire of countless prominent sorts, from a tourist newspaper we called "practically worthless" (it unsuccessfully sued us) to the many rip-offs we've condemned.

And because we believe that travel should be available to everyone regardless of their incomes, we have always been cost-conscious at every level of expenditure. Though we have broadened our recommendations beyond the budget category, we insist that every lodging we include be sensibly priced. We use every form of media to assist our readers, and are particularly proud of our feisty daily website, the award-winning Frommers.com.

I have high hopes for the future of Frommer's. May these guidebooks, in all the years ahead, continue to reflect the joy of travel and the freedom that travel represents. May they always pursue a cost-conscious path, so that people of all incomes can enjoy the rewards of travel. And may they create, for both the traveler and the persons among whom we travel, a community of friends, where all human beings live in harmony and peace.

Arthur Frommer

# THE BEST OF CANCÚN & MEXICO'S CARIBBEAN COAST

1

by Christine Delsol & Maribeth Mellin

Yes, it's true—the aquamarine sea is astonishingly clear and warm, the sand is powder soft, and visitors are greeted with genuine hospitality along Mexico's Caribbean Coast. Just about everyone visiting the region gets a taste of Cancún, since its airport is the main entryway to the region. Those who linger in this famed resort city face endless delights, from flashy discos to gourmet restaurants, with archaeological sites and an excellent museum to give a sense of place. Visitors to the Riviera Maya find myriad water sports, jungle excursions, unforgettable walks through indigenous villages, and exhilarating eco-adventures. Tropical fish thrill divers and snorkelers visiting Cozumel, while Isla Mujeres pleases laid-back, beach-loving travelers. Costa Maya, extending to the Belize border in the south, remains tourism's last frontier, with long, empty beaches and a few villages only beginning to ramp up for tourists. We've logged thousands of miles in this beautiful region and have developed several personal favorites—always subject to change as we discover new delights.

## THE best AUTHENTIC EXPERIENCES

- **Going Downtown:** You might forget this is Mexico while you're in Cancún's Hotel Zone, but Ciudad Cancún, though just over 40 years old, is a real Mexican city where people live, work, speak Spanish, and pay in pesos. Hotels are small, inexpensive, and locally owned; restaurants serve traditional food unaltered for tourists' tastes; and buyers and sellers still bargain in the *mercados*. See p. 64.

- **Swimming in the Caribbean:** When you slip into the brilliant turquoise sea from a white sandy beach, it's entirely possible you'll feel you've entered paradise. Tropical fish may join you even in the shallowest coves, more interested in reefs and rocks than humans. There's no sensation quite like floating in the warm, welcoming waters of the Caribbean, watching puffy while clouds drift in the blue sky on a sunny day.
- **Catching Island Fever:** Cozumel and Isla Mujeres are two idyllic Caribbean islands far removed from the glitz and revelry of Cancún and the crowds in the Riviera Maya. Although only a mere 15 minutes from Cancún by ferry, sleepy Isla Mujeres feels worlds removed. Cozumel, just 45 minutes by boat from Playa del Carmen, has all the charms of an authentic Mexican town. See p. 123.
- **Dining Like a Local:** Municipal markets are perfect places to shop and dine like a local. On Isla Mujeres, join dozens of workers and schoolchildren at the *Mercado Municipal* (p. 124) for the *comida corrida,* a multi-course, low-cost lunch. The crowd is more varied at Cozumel's *Mercado Benito Juárez* (p. 146–147) where cruise-ship workers gather at food stands selling favorite dishes from the Philippines and Indonesia while islanders grab Yucatecan treats.
- **Floating in Sacred Canals:** The Sian Ka'an Biosphere Reserve protects a huge swath of lagoons, mangroves, sand, and sea, preserving the natural attributes that make this area so utterly gorgeous. The easiest way to explore the reserve is on a tour through canals constructed by the ancient Maya. You'll quickly see why the name means "The Place Where the Earth Meets the Sky" as your boat skims across a turquoise lagoon beneath billowing white clouds, and gain a sense of serenity as you don a lifejacket and bob along with the current past wild orchids and dense flowing vines. See p. 206.
- **Beyond Chichén Itzá:** The wonder of Mexico's marquee archaeological site (p. 100) can be lost in the hordes of tourists that crowd in. To genuinely grasp the grandeur of ancient Maya civilization, head to recently excavated and lightly visited Ek Balam (p. 114), the jungle paths of Cobá (p. 116), or the mysterious Río Bec archaeological sites (p. 220).
- **Kicking Back in the Jungle:** Skip that $200 treatment at the resort spa and put yourself in the hands of the Maya women at the Jungle Spa outside of Puerto Morelos. Their massages and wraps, administered in simple *palapa* buildings, are based on healing methods passed down from their elders. See p. 167.

## THE best HOTELS

- **Presidente InterContinental Cozumel:** An idyllic location on a secluded tranquil cove, understated yet luxurious suites with terraces by the sand, excellent restaurants, and the island's best spa are just the beginning. Add the incredible warmth of bellboys, housekeepers, and waiters who have pampered guests for decades and you have what could justifiably be called the most welcoming and soothing upscale resort in the region. See p. 146.
- **Fiesta Americana Grand Coral Beach:** Even among Cancún's plethora of luxury resorts, this recently remodeled beauty stands out, with gleaming marble, serene sand-and-sea hues, a multi-tiered cascading pool that goes on forever, and the most expansive panorama of land and sea on the island. See p. 69.
- **Beachscape Villas Kin-Ha:** Breaking up a line of massive high-rises, this cluster of low buildings set among palms and broad lawns offers resort-level services and

amenities in a down-to-earth atmosphere at surprisingly low rates. With a perch on one of Cancún's finest beaches, it's the best value on the island. See p. 75.

- **Marriott CasaMagna:** Acres of marble, classic columns, and crystal chandeliers aplenty attest to this family-oriented hotel's kinship with the adjacent JW Marriott, though it is warmer and more informal than its sumptuous, pricey sibling—and it goes all-out to cater to kids. See p. 76.
- **Esencia:** An Italian duchess wisely chose serene Playa Xpu-Ha for her private vacation villa in the 1980s, before the Riviera Maya became a huge tourism destination. She's since opened her estate, buried in acres of pristine jungle, to paying guests who find privacy, elegant simplicity, and sublime amenities—plus mouthwatering cuisine and talented, perceptive spa therapists. See p. 187.
- **Grand Velas:** Dispelling all preconceptions regarding all-inclusive resorts, this exclusive enclave on the Riviera Maya features multiple award-winning gourmet restaurants, sleek marble and polished wood suites, a heavenly hydrotherapy spa, glistening pools, and a fabulous beach—all included in a justifiably steep nightly rate. See p. 168.
- **Boca Paila Camps:** There's nothing glitzy or glamorous about these tent camps buried amid vines and bushes in the Sian Ka'an Biosphere Reserve, which pleases nature lovers thrilled to find a sacred place undisturbed by modern development. Shared bathrooms, compost toilets, and unreliable cell signals add to the joy of complete immersion in the real Mexican Caribbean. See p. 208.
- **Mayan Beach Garden Inn:** An off-grid hideaway in Costa Maya on a sparkling white beach at the ends of the earth—this is the very embodiment of Margaritaville, except that hot showers, king-size beds clad in soft linens, and a gourmet meal await after a day of exploring. And the owners make it look easy. See p. 213.

## THE best RESTAURANTS

- **The Club Grill:** Cancún's most celebrated restaurant feels like a dinner party at a European nobleman's manor, from cocktails in an opulent anteroom to foie gras and roast meat that would satisfy after a fox hunt. It pulls off old-world decadence without being stuffy, and the food approaches perfection. See p. 79.
- **Labná:** At this downtown Cancún temple to Yucatecan cuisine, you'll find *poc chuc, cochinita pibil,* and *sopa de lima* in their purest form, along with other intriguing local dishes you probably haven't heard of, such as *sikil-pak,* an addictive pumpkin-seed sauce—all prepared expertly and with great care. See p. 85.
- **Julia Mia:** Looking like it was lifted from the Hotel Zone and dropped downtown, this newcomer pushes traditional Mexican cuisine up a notch. From black bean soup to elaborate meat or seafood *molcajetes* (mixed grill), its recipes were handed down through generations and injected with contemporary zing. See p. 84.
- **The Leaky Palapa:** The two women who run this cozy restaurant in Xcalak, the coast's most remote village, are wizards of spontaneity, turning the best local ingredients they find fresh each day into masterpieces of traditional Mexican, Caribbean, and a smattering of Continental cuisine. See p. 214.
- **Cockteleria Justicia Social:** Seafood doesn't get any fresher than this Isla Mujeres find, thanks to the adjacent fisherman's collective. Overflowing seafood cocktails and platters of tangy ceviche and crispy fried whole snapper cover plastic tables in the outdoor dining area beside a pier. Arrive early, especially on weekends, or be prepared to wait as multi-generational families settle in for leisurely lunches. See p. 131.

- **La Cueva del Chango:** Living up to its name, the Monkey's Cave, this quirky, vine-draped hangout serves some of the healthiest and yummiest breakfast chow around, from eggs scrambled with *chaya* (like spinach) or chiles, to crepes with homemade yogurt and fresh fruit, and Yucatecan *huevos motuleños* (tortillas and black beans topped with fried eggs, cheese, ham, and peas). Lunch and dinner are delicious as well, served with an extensive selection of Mexican wines, tequilas, and mezcals. See p. 178.
- **Guido's:** This sentimental favorite on Cozumel went through a name change years back but has never lost its charm. Vines, trees, and fuchsia bougainvillea shade the back courtyard, where fans await the traditional puffy garlic bread, pizzas oozing with Oaxacan cheese, imaginative catch-of-the-day preparations, and irresistible homemade coconut ice cream. See p. 147.

## THE best FAMILY EXPERIENCES

- **Xcaret:** Admission is pricey and commercialization inevitable, but this all-in-one Riviera Maya eco park supplies full immersion in Maya and Mexican culture and regional flora and fauna in one exhausting and exhilarating experience. Highlights include macaws, jaguars, manatees, and butterflies, an underground river ride, one of the country's finest folk art museums, and a thrilling nightly folkloric music and dance show. The flourishing Xcaret operation includes the neighboring adventure park XPLOR. See p. 184.
- **CrocoCun:** Going nose to nose with iguanas, spider monkeys, surprisingly endearing baby crocodiles, and other native fauna is a surefire hit with kids and equally captivating for adults. Veterinary students, who volunteer as guides, share their knowledge and their passion for protecting these creatures. See p. 158.
- **Jungle Cruise:** Mixing thrills with a glimpse of the natural environment, this Cancún classic puts you at the helm of a small speedboat or WaveRunner to zip through Nichupté Lagoon and its wildlife-rich mangrove estuaries, ending up in the Caribbean for snorkeling at Punta Nizuc. See p. 95.
- **Selvática:** This adventure outfit along the Ruta de Cenotes, inland from Puerto Morelos, will get the whole family's adrenaline flowing on 12 of North America's longest and fastest zip lines; cool you off in a *cenote,* or sinkhole (which you can enter by still more zip lines); and feed you a hearty lunch. See p. 166.
- **Chankanaab National Park:** You can easily spend a full day snorkeling, diving, and paddling a see-through kayak with the fishes in this Cozumel park's lagoon. Landlubbers can explore the nature botanical garden, archaeological replicas, and Maya house, or simply swing in a hammock beneath a shady *palapa.* See p. 151.
- **Akumal:** You don't even need to snorkel to spot the sea turtles that swim year-round in the bays at this low-key vacation spot. A nearby reef protects the calm, shallow water, and it's easy for the smallest swimmers to splash about and catch a glimpse of graceful juvenile green turtles in their natural habitat. The adjacent museum has sea turtle exhibits and offers nighttime summer beach walks to watch lumbering mothers dig nests in the sand and lay their eggs. See p. 188.
- **Plaza Principal:** Head for the central plaza of just about any town in the evening as families gather to end their day with gossip, snacks, maybe a little music, and a chance for children to run out their excess energy. Especially on weekends, it may take on a carnival atmosphere, filling with food carts, balloon vendors, and street performers—or even puppet shows or trampolines.

# THE best BEACHES

- **Playa Norte:** Within a few minutes' walk of the main town, you can plant your toes on one of the region's most stunning swimming beaches at Playa Norte on Isla Mujeres. Whether you come for a day trip from Cancún or spend several nights here, be sure to float in the warm, calm water, lounge on the powder-soft white sand, and take in the sunset while sipping a cool one at a rustic beach bar. See p. 134.
- **Playa Paraíso:** The beaches along Tulum's busy hotel zone are gorgeous but crowded. On Playa Paraíso, away from the hotels and bars, you can actually take a long, leisurely stroll along the sand without feeling like you're parading in front of an audience. As a major plus, you can see the temples at the Tulum archaeological site if you swim out just a few feet from shore. You may encounter a tour group or two, especially on weekends, but they're only there around midday. For the ultimate seclusion, reserve a room at the small hotel on the sand. See p. 198.
- **Punta Sur:** The lonely Faro Celarain lighthouse overlooks a long beach that's usually virtually empty. If solitude's your thing, walk north along the sand until you reach an empty stretch, then spread your towel, don your snorkel and mask, and glide through calm, flat waters alongside queen angelfish. See p. 133.
- **Playa Delfines:** Cancún's longest, widest beach—free of the phalanx of resorts that claim so much of the Hotel Zone's sand—is a peaceful place for sunbathing under skies speckled with parasailers; surfers also find good waves here under the right conditions. In early morning, watch for the wild dolphins that give the beach its name. See p. 90.
- **Playa Langosta:** In the middle of Cancún's northern beaches, facing placid Bahía Mujeres, shallow waters here are ideal for swimming and snorkeling. The beach, made up of the powdery sand Cancún is famous for, is well supplied with *palapas,* restaurants, and bars. See p. 90.
- **Puerto Morelos:** The northern Caribbean coast's most pristine section of the Great Mesoamerican Reef rises close to the surface in this small fishing town, giving swimmers and snorkelers incomparable views of its sea life. Ojo de Agua, the best of its clean, rarely crowded beaches, lies north of the fishing pier. See p. 158.

# THE best OUTDOOR EXPERIENCES

- **Scuba Diving in Cozumel:** Crystal clear warm water nearly year-round and a series of protected reefs make Cozumel Mexico's premier scuba destination and one of the world's top dive spots. Mild currents along the reefs make for easy drift diving, while adventuresome types go for steep walls and spooky, beautiful night dives. Dozens of top-notch dive shops offer personalized service and dive classes. See p. 153.
- **Fly-Fishing off the Coasts of Punta Allen and Mahahual:** Serious anglers enjoy the challenge of fly-fishing for tarpon, snook, and other elusive fish in the saltwater flats and lagoons on the protected sides of these peninsulas. As an added attraction, the best spots are located near small beach towns free of crowds and bustle. See p. 207.
- **Underground Explorations:** Delve into the coast's caves and *cenotes* and discover dazzling caverns with sunlight streaming on crystalline stalactites and stalagmites and chilly pools of milky green water. The Maya considered the *cenotes* sacred—and their vivid colors and eerie echoes do indeed seem otherworldly. At Río Secreto,

guests don helmets and wetsuits and descend into partially submerged caves, then swim in an underground river. Certified cave divers submerge themselves in dark depths where bats cling to slippery rock walls. For tours and dive shops see p. 183.

- **Flamingos in Río Lagartos:** North America's largest flamingo population nests and lays its eggs in the shelter of a long, narrow estuary here, and local fishermen are more than happy to take you to their feeding grounds. There's nothing quite like the sight of great coral-pink clouds of flamingos taking flight over the turquoise waters. See p. 116.
- **Whale Sharks from Isla Holbox:** It's not the hot spot it used to be since the world's largest fish started congregating farther to the east in recent years (more boats depart from Isla Mujeres now). But with its smaller town, fewer tourists, and guides with long experience, this more remote island is still the best place to launch a trip to snorkel with the benign behemoths. See p. 181.
- **Costa Maya's Chinchorro Reef:** The Northern Hemisphere's largest atoll, part of the Great Mesoamerican Reef system, is a diver's holy grail, nurturing spectacular coral formations and kaleidoscopic sea life. Even snorkelers can explore its many shipwrecks and meet an abundance of manatees and rays from Mahahual or Xcalac. See p. 215.

# CANCÚN & MEXICO'S CARIBBEAN COAST IN CONTEXT

2

by Christine Delsol

In the space of a single generation, the Yucatán has been transformed from a forgotten backwater visited primarily by archaeologists, sports fishermen, and scuba divers into a major international destination and economic powerhouse. The changes wrought by Cancún's creation and growth are most visible on the coast, where fishing villages and coconut plantations have given way to huge resort developments, marching in lock step south to Tulum and inching toward the Costa Maya, which hunkers down next to the Belize border.

For the young Maya living in the interior villages, growth brought new work opportunities and their first close contact with the modern world—specifically, the modern world in vacation mode. The shift from village society to vacation paradise is the very definition of culture shock, which the implacable Maya meet with equanimity.

Less dramatically, tourism has also made its way to the peninsula's interior—first with the coronation of Chichén Itzá as a New World Wonder and then with the spotlight on all things Maya bestowed by the misguided end-of-days "prophecy" attributed to the Maya (who were, by the way, wholly innocent). More visitors are discovering the smaller, less-excavated ancient cities and the time-warp villages where today's Maya maintain ages-old traditions while adapting to contemporary demands.

Small-town life has changed surprisingly little in the face of all the excavation and renovation. Coastal natives not swept up in the tourism boom were relocated inland, where they continue their ancestors' ways. Families of many workers in the tourist palaces remain in the tropical forest, living in round thatch houses with no electricity, indoor plumbing, or paved roads, gathering plants for food and medicine, cooling off in hidden *cenotes,* and appealing to the gods for successful crops. To explore an older

## The Yucatán Peninsula

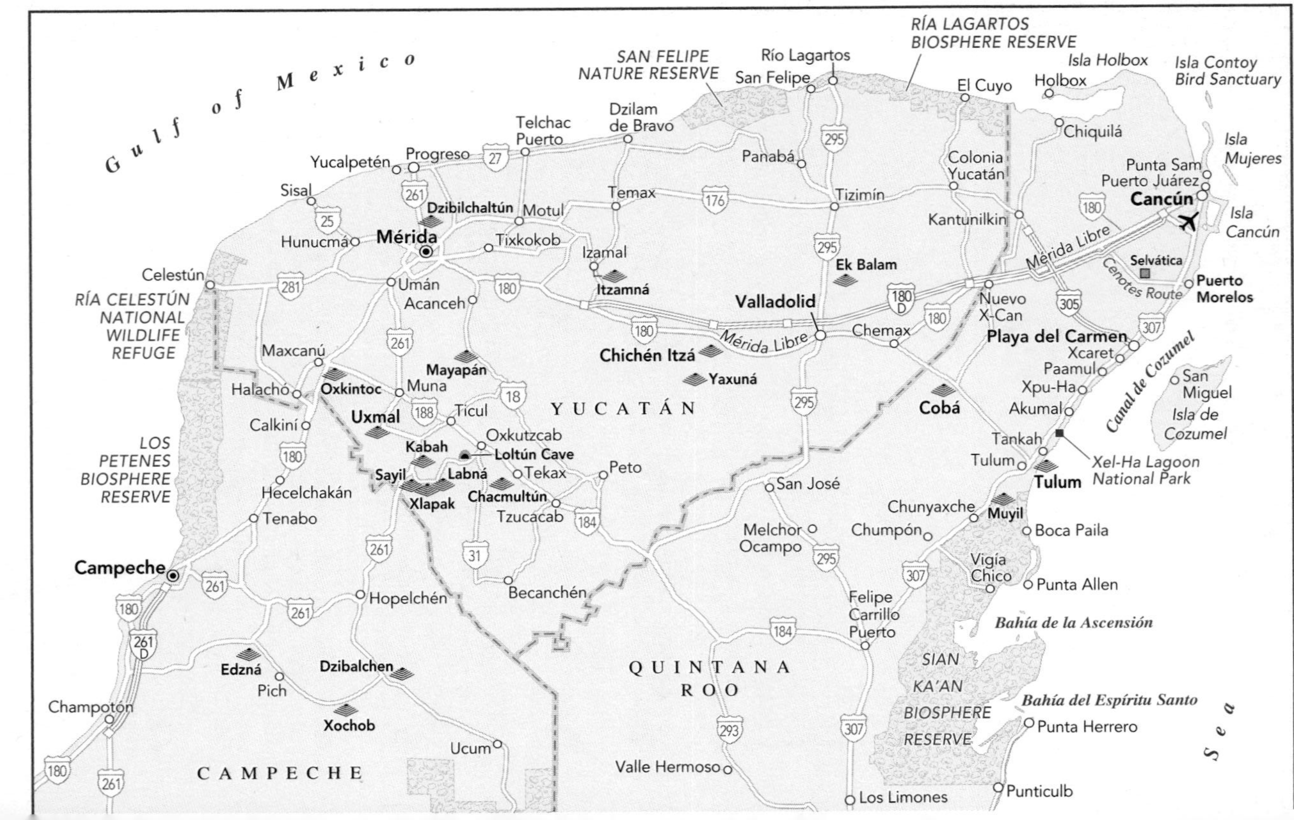

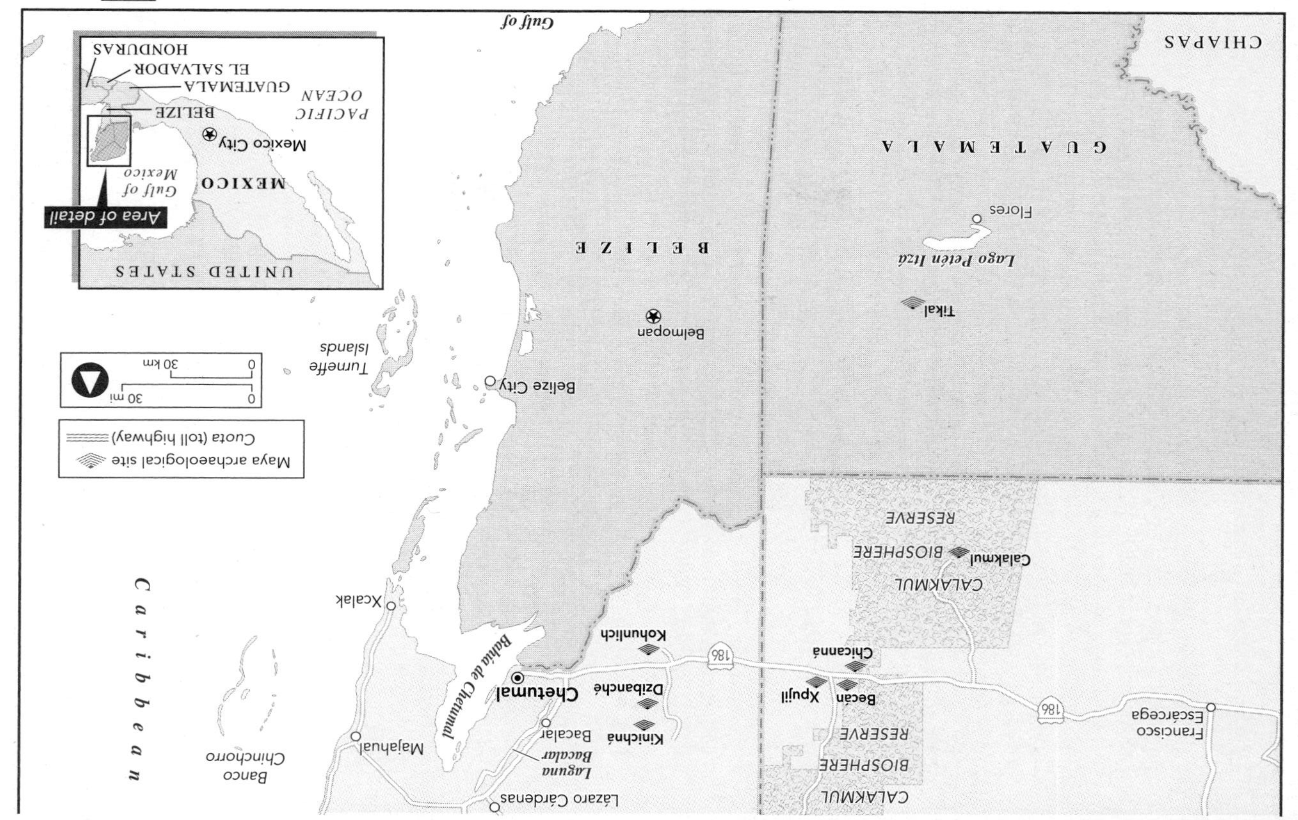
Caribbean
Banco Chinchorro
Maya archaeological site
Cuota (toll highway)
0 30 mi
0 30 km
UNITED STATES
Area of detail
Gulf of Mexico
MEXICO
Mexico City
PACIFIC OCEAN
BELIZE
GUATEMALA
EL SALVADOR
HONDURAS
Turneffe Islands
Xcalak
Majahual
Bahía de Chetumal
Lázaro Cárdenas
Laguna Bacalar
Bacalar
Chetumal
Belize City
Gulf of
Kinichná
Dzibanché
Kohunlich
Belmopan
BELIZE
186
CALAKMUL BIOSPHERE RESERVE
Xpujil
Becán
Chicanná
Calakmul
Tikal
Lago Petén Itzá
Flores
GUATEMALA
Francisco Escárcega
CHIAPAS

world where the Mayan tongue's distinctive intonations fill the air and centuries-old traditions endure, you have only to drive inland from the Caribbean coast and venture to Valladolid or to villages on the jungle side of the highway.

The turquoise waters and tropical climate may beckon first, but what will draw you back is the unique character of this land and its people.



# CANCÚN & MEXICO'S CARIBBEAN COAST TODAY

In the three states that make up the Yucatán Peninsula, great wealth lives alongside abject poverty. Paradoxically, the indexes of both wealth and poverty in this region surpass the national average. A tremendous amount of money flows into the area—from tourism in Yucatán and Quintana Roo and the oil industry in Campeche. Yet most residents reap little from this prosperity.

On the one hand, development has increased demand for local products and services. For example, *palaperos*—the native people who create the thatched roofs of palm leaves *(palapas)* that crown so many restaurants and hotels—are in high demand, not only for new construction but for repair whenever a hurricane brushes the coast. At the same time, development has destroyed the livelihood of other locals: Coastal coconut growers were wiped out when Cancún developers brought turf from Florida to build a golf course, unwittingly introducing a disease that killed the coconut palms; destruction of mangroves, crucial to the coastal food chain, has diminished fishermen's catches.

Although residents' incomes have not improved, tourism and oil money have brought indirect benefits. The government has paved most of the peninsula's roads and fitted out remote villages with electricity. Purified water is widely available. And in one of the most positive developments of recent years, an increasing emphasis on ecotourism has led to numerous villages forming partnerships with tour companies that allow them to profit from tourism while maintaining control over their own lives and environment.

## Today's Maya Culture & People

The Yucatán Peninsula often feels like a country apart from Mexico. The *jarana* music, sweetened by clarinets, and a cuisine redolent with capers, *achiote,* and saffron exude Caribbean sensuality. And the region's dignified, gentle people display little of the machismo or the relentless huckstering that tries visitors' patience in northern and central Mexico.

The sense of "otherness" grows partly from geographical isolation but even more from the Maya's fierce, centuries-long resistance to being absorbed into the Spanish spoils; some Maya refuse to recognize Mexican sovereignty even today. All of which makes their warm, generous natures as much a wonder as their ancestors' famous pyramids. Your simplest transaction with a local easily evolves into spirited conversation. In the peninsula's interior, where some Maya Indians are uneasy speaking Spanish, you are more likely to encounter initial reticence. Usually, it's quickly overcome with smiles and inventive gestures.

You don't need to leave Cancún to meet the Maya; thousands travel from the interior to jobs at hotels and restaurants. More than 350,000 Maya living on the peninsula speak Yucatec, the local Mayan language. Most, especially men, also speak Spanish, and workers in Cancún usually know at least basic English.

### In the Beginning

*The animals showed them the road. And then grinding the yellow corn and the white corn, Xmucané made nine drinks . . . and with it they created the muscles and the strength of man . . . After that they began to talk about the creation and the making of our first mother and father; of yellow corn and of white corn they made their flesh; of corn meal dough they made the arms and the legs of man.*

—from the *Popol Vuh*, the Maya "bible"

Though they held fast to their language through the Spanish conquest, the Maya lost virtually all written records of their pre-Hispanic history to a brutal *auto-da-fé* carried out by Diego de Landa, a rabid Catholic bishop intent on stamping out what he regarded as devil worship. What living memory was retained is cloaked in myth and worked into elements of Catholicism. That process of syncretism, as anthropologists call it, continues today in the many Maya communities that have native churches.

The question of their ancestors' rightful place among the world's ancient civilizations might be as much a mystery to today's Maya people as it is to scholars. But nearly every year, archaeological discoveries of the art and architecture of the ancients add to the growing picture of a complex urban culture that thrived where only sparsely populated jungle exists today.

## The Well-Lived Life

Despite economic inequities, Mexican society remains tremendously resilient and cohesive. Mexicans place paramount value on family and friends, social gatherings, and living in the present; worrying about the future takes a back seat. Mexicans always have time to meet with friends for a cup of coffee or attend a family get-together. The many spirited public celebrations Mexico is known for are simply another manifestation of this attitude. Visitors can summon the full measure of their natural gregariousness by being mindful of some social norms. Here's a start:

**SLOW DOWN** The stereotype of "mañana time" is mostly true. Life obeys slower rhythms, and "on time" is a flexible concept. Arriving 30 minutes to 2 hours late to a party in someone's home is acceptable—in fact, coming at the specified hour would be rude, for your hosts almost certainly will not be ready. Here's the "mostly" part: Dinner invitations are less flexible; arrive within 30 minutes of the appointed hour. And be on time for business appointments, public performances, weddings, and funerals.

**MEET & GREET** Don't skimp on the hellos and goodbyes; social values take precedence over efficiency. A Mexican must at least say "¡Buenos días!" even to strangers. An individual will greet each member of a group separately, no matter how long it takes. Handshakes, *abrazos* (embraces), and, among women, kisses abound. Stick to handshakes until your host initiates a more intimate greeting. But don't back away from an embrace—that would amount to a rejection of friendship.

**HAVE A LITTLE RESPECT** Mexicans are lavish with titles of respect, so dispense *señor, señora,* and *señorita* (Mr., Mrs., Miss) freely. Teachers, lawyers, architects, and other professionals have earned the right to a title: *licenciado* for lawyers (and some other professions requiring a college degree), *maestro* or *maestra* for elementary

> **Mayan Terms & Phrases**
>
> Hundreds of thousands of Maya living on the Yucatán Peninsula today speak at least some of their mother tongue. Most speak Yucatec Mayan (commonly called simply "Mayan"), one of more than 30 Mayan languages used today that can be traced back about 4,000 years to a single language believed to have originated in northwestern Guatemala. You will see numerous spelling variations around the peninsula. ***Note:*** The term "Mayan" is reserved for Mayan languages. The noun or the adjective for the people is "Maya." For a glossary of Mayan phrases, see "Spanish & Mayan Terms & Phrases," p. 237.

school teachers, *profesor* or *profesora* for secondary or college teachers, and so forth. Mexicans have two surnames, father's first and mother's second. Both appear on business cards (the mother's name might be abbreviated to an initial), but when addressing people, use just the first (paternal) surname.

**DON'T GET HUFFY** Mexicans are genuinely interested in foreign visitors. If they stare, it's friendly curiosity. They like to practice their English, and might ask about family, friends, money, and other intimate matters. If you are over 30 and have no children, they may express deep concern. Don't take it personally.

**SHOW SOME CULTURE** Mexicans tend to divide the world into the well-raised and cultured *(bien educado)* and the poorly raised *(mal educado)*. Don't be shy about trying out your rudimentary Spanish; even the most elementary attempt is appreciated because it shows your interest in the culture. To be categorized as a foreigner is no big deal. What's important in Mexico is to be categorized as a cultured foreigner and not one of the barbarians.

# LOOKING BACK: CARIBBEAN COAST & YUCATÁN HISTORY

## Pre-Hispanic Civilizations

The earliest "Mexicans" might have been Stone Age hunter-gatherers from the north, descendants of a race that crossed the Bering Strait and reached North America around 12,000 B.C. A more recent theory points to an earlier crossing of peoples from Asia to the New World. What we do know is that Mexico was populated by 10,000 B.C. Sometime between 5200 and 1500 B.C., these early people began practicing agriculture and domesticating animals.

### THE OLMEC & MAYA: THE PRE-CLASSIC PERIOD (1500 B.C.–A.D. 300)

Agriculture eventually supported large communities, with enough surplus to free some people from agricultural work. A civilization emerged that we call the **Olmec**—an enigmatic people who settled the Tabasco and Veracruz coasts. Anthropologists regard them as Mesoamerica's mother culture, because they established a pattern for later civilizations from northern Mexico to Central America. The Olmec developed basic calendar, writing, and numbering systems; established principles of urban layout and architecture; and originated the cult of the jaguar and reverence for jade. They probably also bequeathed the sacred ball game common to all Mesoamerican cultures.

A defining feature of the Olmec culture was its colossal carved stone heads, several of which reside today in the Parque-Museo La Venta in Villahermosa, Tabasco. Their significance remains a mystery, but they were immense projects, sculpted from basalt mined more than 80km (50 miles) inland and transported to the coast, probably by river raft. Their rounded, baby-faced look, marked by a peculiar, high-arched lip—a "jaguar mouth"—is an identifying mark of Olmec sculpture.

The **Maya** civilization, centered initially around Guatemala's lowland Petén region, began developing around 500 B.C. At least one large Maya city, Dzibilchaltún, Yucatán, developed during this time. The Caribbean coast is dotted with Maya archaeological sites, many still unexplored. Maya settlement spread north some time after 300 B.C. Archaeologists believe the migrants were hunter-gatherers who founded villages throughout the Yucatán and later turned to corn cultivation. The earliest surviving inscriptions are dated A.D. 564 in Tulum—one of a very few cities the Maya built on the water. Understanding of this period is sketchy, but Olmec influences show up everywhere. The Maya perfected the Olmec calendar and developed both their ornate system of hieroglyphic writing and their early architecture. The people of **Teotihuacán,** north of present-day Mexico City, and the **Zapotec** of Monte Albán, in the valley of Oaxaca, also emerged around this time.

## TEOTIHUACÁN, MONTE ALBÁN & PALENQUE: THE CLASSIC PERIOD (A.D. 300–900)

The rise and fall of these three city-states are bookends to the Classic period, the height of pre-Columbian Mesoamerican art and culture, which coincides with the decline of the Roman Empire. Achievements include the pyramids and palaces of Teotihuacán; the ceremonial center of Monte Albán; and the stelae and temples of Palenque, Bonampak, and Calakmul.

**Teotihuacán** (100 B.C.–A.D. 700), near present-day Mexico City, a well-organized city built on a grid, is thought to have had 100,000 or more inhabitants at its zenith, led by an industrious, literate, and cosmopolitan ruling class. The city exerted tremendous influence as far away as the Yucatán and Guatemala. Its feathered serpent god, Quetzalcóatl, joined the pantheon of many succeeding cultures, including the Maya, who called the god Kukulkán. Teotihuacán's refined aesthetics, evident in its beautiful, highly stylized sculpture and ceramics, show up in Maya and Zapotec objects. The city was abandoned some time around the 7th century, leaving the peoples' identity and ultimate fate shrouded in mystery.

**Cobá, Kohunlich, Dzibanché,** and **Muyil** in present-day Quintana Roo grew into important ceremonial cities during the Classic period, which saw the peak of the Maya empire of independent city-states. This era also produced the Maya's greatest intellectual and artistic achievements, such as development of hieroglyphic writing, use of the mathematical concept of zero, a complex calendar with which priests predicted eclipses and the movements of the stars, and grand architecture using the corbelled arch. The Classic period ended with the collapse of the southern lowland cities, the cause of which is still debated.

## TOLTEC & AZTEC INVASIONS: THE POSTCLASSIC PERIOD (A.D. 900–1521)

Warfare became more pervasive during this period, and these later civilizations were less sophisticated than those of the Classic. In Central Mexico, the **Toltec** established their capital at Tula in the 10th century. Originally one of the barbarous hordes that periodically migrated from the north, they were influenced by remnants of Teotihuacán

## IT'S ALL IN THE game

The ancient Maya played a ball game of such importance that ball courts appear in virtually every Maya city (Bonampak, in Chiapas, is a rare exception). They were laid out in a capital **I** shape with sloping walls in the center. Similar ball courts have been found as far south as Nicaragua and as far north as Arizona.

Though we know little about this sacred game, ancient depictions, early accounts by the Spanish, and the *Popol Vuh* (the Maya "bible") show that the solid rubber ball was heavy and could inflict injury. Wearing thick padding and protective gear, players formed teams of 2 to 10 members, the object being to propel the ball through a stone ring or other goal using mainly the hips.

We also know the game was part sport and part religious ritual based on the Maya's cosmological beliefs. It sometimes involved sacrifice, though we're not sure whether the winners, the losers, or perhaps prisoners of war were sacrificed. In the *Popol Vuh*, the hero twins Hunahpu and Xbalanque challenge the lords of the underworld to a ball game, played in part with the head of one brother. Eventually the twins win and are allowed to return to the world of the living. Playing the ball game, then, might have been one way to cheat the underworld.

culture at some point and adopted the feathered-serpent god Quetzalcóatl. The Toltec maintained a large military class, and Tula spread its influence across Mesoamerica. But their might was played out by the 13th century, probably because of civil war and battles with invaders from the north.

The Maya of the Yucatán, especially the **Xiu** and **Itzáes,** might have departed from the norm with their broad trading networks and multiple influences from the outside world. Tikal was abandoned in 899, though northern cities flourished during the Postclassic period (A.D. 900–1521). Quintana Roo's coastal cities of Tulum, Xcaret, Xaman-Há (now Playa del Carmen), and Xel-Há were important commercial and religious centers along an extensive Maya trade route, and Cobá became the biggest and most powerful Maya city in the northeastern Yucatán. Cancún's main activities appear to have been fishing and serving as a navigational and lookout point on trade routes between Chichén Itzá, Tulum, Cozumel, and Isla Mujeres. Cozumel was a center of navigation and trade—its salt and honey were more valuable than gold—while Isla Mujeres was not only a commercial corridor but a sacred pilgrimage site, bringing pilgrims from all over the Maya world to the small stone temple on the island's southern tip to pay homage to Ixchel, the Maya goddess of fertility and the moon.

Inland, beautiful cities rose in and around the Puuc hills, south of Mérida, the architecture characterized by elaborate exterior stonework above door frames and extending to the roofline. Impressive examples include the Codz Poop at Kabah and the palaces at Uxmal, Sayil, and Labná. Chichén Itzá, also ruled by Itzáes, was associated with the Puuc cities but shows strong Toltec influence in its architectural style and its cult of Quetzalcóatl/Kukulkán.

The exact nature of the Toltec influence on the Maya is a subject of debate. An intriguing myth in central Mexico tells of Quetzalcóatl quarreling with the god Tezcatlipoca and being tricked into leaving Tula. Quetzalcóatl heads east toward the morning star, vowing someday to return. In the language of myth, this could be a metaphor for a civil war between two factions in Tula, each led by the priesthood of a different god. Could the losing faction have migrated to the Yucatán and later ruled Chichén Itzá? Perhaps. What we do know is that this myth of Quetzalcóatl's eventual return became, in the hands of the Spanish, a devastating weapon of conquest.

## Cortez, Moctezuma & the Spanish Conquest

The first European reports of the Yucatán Peninsula were those of **Francisco de Córdoba,** leading an expedition from Cuba in 1517 that had stopped earlier at Isla Mujeres. As they were sailing close to shore on today's Campeche coast, Córdoba's party spotted the first large populated center in the Americas that Europeans had ever seen. The tall, solidly built pyramids and other buildings prompted them to call it *El Gran Cairo.* Córdoba stopped there to replenish his water supply but the hostile Maya killed him, along with his crew, when they didn't move on quickly enough.

Despite his discovery, Córdoba was not the first European to set foot in the Yucatán. In 1511, a ship on its way from Hispaniola to Cuba foundered off this same coast, shipwrecking sailors **Jerónimo de Aguilar** and **Gonzalo Guerrero.** At the time of Córdoba's arrival, they were among the Maya and speaking the local dialect.

Another Spanish expedition, under **Hernán Cortez**—looking for some excitement after nearly 15 years of the good life in Cuba, where he had risen to the post of *alcalde* (mayor) of the provincial capital of Santiago—landed on Cozumel in February 1519. The coastal Maya were happy to tell Cortez about the gold and riches of the Aztec empire in central Mexico. Disobeying his superior, the governor of Cuba, Cortez promptly sailed with his army to the mainland and embarked on one of history's most bizarre culture clashes.

Cortez encountered Aguilar and Guerrero and invited them to join him. Guerrero, who had married a Maya woman and appears to have been governing an indigenous community, chose to remain with the Maya; he died defending his adopted people and is still a hero to the Maya today. Aguilar joined Cortez, using his knowledge of the Mayan language and customs against them in what was to be the first strike in the conquest of Mexico.

Cortez landed in Tabasco, established a settlement in Veracruz, and worked his way up the Gulf Coast and inland, pillaging and ravaging along the way as he saw fit. The Aztec empire was at the height of its wealth and power. **Moctezuma II** ruled the central and southern highlands from Tenochtitlán, extracting tribute from lowland peoples; his greatest temples were plated with gold and encrusted with the blood of sacrificial captives. A fool, a mystic, and something of a coward, Moctezuma refused Cortez's repeated entreaties to be invited to the Aztec capital. As Cortez blustered and negotiated his way into the highlands, some reports portray Moctezuma as terrified and convinced that Cortez was the returning Quetzalcóatl. In any case, he opened his city and his home to the Spaniards. By now, Cortez had accumulated 6,000 indigenous allies who resented paying tribute to the Aztec ruler. In November 1519, he took Moctezuma hostage.

In the midst of Cortez's maneuverings, another Spanish expedition landed with orders to end Cortez's unauthorized mission. Cortez hastened to the coast, routed the rival force, and persuaded the vanquished to join him on his return to Tenochtitlán. Aztec forces chased his garrison out of the capital, and Moctezuma was killed during the attack—whether by his own people or the Spaniards is not clear. For the next year and a half, Cortez laid siege to Tenochtitlán, aided by a devastating smallpox epidemic. When the Aztec capital fell in 1521, all of central Mexico lay at the conquerors' feet, vastly expanding the Spanish empire. The king immediately legitimized his victorious rogue and ordered the forced conversion to Christianity of the acquired colony, to be called **New Spain.**

## Spanish Colonialism & the Rise of Mexico City

Though the ancient Maya civilization was already in decline by the beginning of the 16th century, it took the Spanish conquest to deal the death blow.

Fierce native resistance kept the Spanish at bay in the Yucatán until **Montejo the Younger** gained a foothold and founded today's city of **Campeche** in 1540, then **Mérida** two years later. New Spain now included possessions from Vancouver to Panama.

As the only populated harbor, and with easy inland access, Campeche fueled Spanish expansion into the Yucatán and soon became one of New Spain's richest ports, funneling timber, gold, silver, and other local products to Spain. This bounty did not escape the notice of Spain's rivals, and Campeche quickly became a favorite lair for English, French, Dutch, and other pirates. So, too, did **Isla Mujeres,** which served as a hideout and supply station during the 17th and 18th centuries for such sea dogs as Henry Morgan and Jean Lafitte.

With the Spanish entrenched, the Maya became second-class citizens on their own ancestral land. In the two centuries that followed, Franciscan and Augustinian friars converted millions of Indians to Christianity—of a sort—and Spanish lords built huge feudal estates using Indian farmers as serfs.

Cortez, meanwhile, set about building a new city atop the ruins of the Aztec capital, collecting the tributes that the Indians once paid to Moctezuma. Many paid in labor, which became the model for building the new colony.

Over the three centuries of the colonial period, Spain became the richest country in Europe from the influx of New World gold and silver chiseled out by Indian labor. The colony met the Crown's insatiable demand for taxes and contributions and still managed to support an extravagant lifestyle. The Spanish elite built lavish homes filled with ornate furniture and draped themselves in imported velvets, satins, and jewels. Under the new class system, those born in Spain were deemed superior to the *criollos,* or Spaniards born in Mexico. The mestizo population (Spanish-Indian, Spanish-African, or Indian-African mixes) and descendants of the native Maya occupied society's bottom rungs.

*Criollo* resentment of Spanish rule following the 1767 expulsion of the largely *criollo* Jesuit clergy simmered for years. In 1808, **Napoleon** invaded Spain, deposed Charles IV, and bestowed the crown on his brother **Joseph Bonaparte.** To many in Mexico, allegiance to France was unthinkable, and revolt was the only logical response.

## Hidalgo, Juárez & Mexico's Independence

In 1810, **Father Miguel Hidalgo** set off the rebellion in the town of Dolores, Guanajuato, with his *grito,* the fabled cry for independence. With **Ignacio Allende** and a citizen army, Hidalgo marched toward Mexico City. Although he ultimately failed and was executed, Hidalgo is honored as the "Father of Mexican Independence." Another priest, José María Morelos, kept the revolt alive with several successful campaigns before he, too, was captured and executed in 1815.

When the Spanish king who replaced Joseph Bonaparte decided to institute social reforms in the colonies, Mexico's conservative powers concluded they didn't need Spain

## A sticky HABIT

Cigar smoking and gum chewing are two pleasures we have the Maya to thank for. Gum, the more innocuous of the two, comes from the sap of a species of *zapote* tree that grows in the Yucatán and Guatemala. Chewing releases its natural sugars and a mild, agreeable taste. The chewing-gum habit spread from the Maya to other cultures and eventually to the non-Indian population. In the second half of the 19th century, a Mexican (said to have been General Santa Anna) introduced gum to the American Thomas Adams, who realized that it could be sweetened further and given other flavors. He marketed chewing gum in the U.S. with great success. Chemists have since figured out how to synthesize the gum, but the sap is still collected in parts of the Yucatán and Guatemala for making natural chewing gum. *Chicle* is the Spanish word, originally from the Nahuatl (Aztec) *tzictli,* and those who live in the forest and collect the sap are called *chicleros.* Because the tree takes so long to produce more sap, there is no way to cultivate it commercially, so it is still collected in the wild.

after all. Royalist **Agustín de Iturbide** defected in 1821 and conspired with the rebels to declare independence from Spain and install himself as emperor. However, internal dissension soon deposed Iturbide, and Mexico was instead proclaimed a republic.

The young, politically unstable republic ran through 36 presidents in 22 years, in the midst of which it lost half its territory in the disastrous **Mexican-American War (1846–48).** The central figure, **Antonio López de Santa Anna,** assumed the presidency no fewer than 11 times and just might hold the record for frequency of exile. He was ousted for good in 1855 and lived out his days in Venezuela.

Independence did not improve the lot of the native Maya, who were virtually enslaved in debt peonage to the landowners. They had merely exchanged one master for another—instead of the Franciscan missions, they now worked on large haciendas, cultivating tobacco, sugar cane, and *henequén* (the agave rope fiber we know today as sisal) on large haciendas. The plantations encroached on Maya communal land, and the workers were mistreated and underpaid.

In 1861, months after reform war hero **Benito Juárez,** a Zapotec Indian lawyer and former governor of Oaxaca, was elected president under Mexico's new constitution, France invaded Mexico, eyeing the country for a satellite state. Amid continuing political turmoil after rag-tag Mexican troops won a fleeting victory over well-equipped French forces in a battle near Puebla in 1862 (now celebrated as Cinco de Mayo), Napoleon III invited Archduke Maximilian of Austria to establish a Mexican monarchy. With the support of French troops and the blessing of Mexico's conservative elite, **Emperor Maximilian** and **Empress Carlota** arrived in 1864 and moved into Chapultepec Castle in the heart of Mexico City.

Maximilian, who turned out to be quite liberal, instituted a raft of reforms to improve living conditions and rights in Mexico and even offered Juárez the post of prime minister. Juárez, however, refused to recognize Maximilian's rule, and his Republican forces waged constant battle with the French troops. After 3 years of civil war, the French abandoned Maximilian, leaving him to be captured and executed in 1867. Juárez resumed his presidency and did his best to unify and strengthen his country before he died of a heart attack in 1872. His plans and visions bore fruit for decades, and he remains one of Mexico's most cherished heroes.

## Yucatecan Independence & the Caste War

In 1845, amid nationwide political turmoil, the Yucatán's landed oligarchy declared independence from Mexico. They armed the populace—including Indians who had slaved all their lives on the haciendas—to defend the territory from invasion. The Indians, resentful of their three centuries of serfdom, decided it didn't much matter whether their oppressors lived in Mexico City or Mérida. In 1847, they turned against the landowners in a bloody revolt known as the **War of the Castes.**

The rebel peasants soon controlled most of the countryside, capturing several towns and the city of Valladolid. Mérida, too, was on the verge of surrender when the Maya fighters suddenly laid down their weapons and returned to their cornfields. Their seemingly inexplicable act attests to the central importance of corn in Maya life, on a spiritual as well as physical level. Nothing took precedence over answering the call of planting season, and so they failed to press their advantage on the battlefront.

The Yucatecans regrouped, allied their territory with Mexico, and called for a government army. During more than 60 years of intermittent but often intense fighting that almost extinguished the Maya population, a great many fled the slaughter and settled in the dense jungle of today's Quintana Roo. They were largely left on their own, virtually a nation within a nation. Descendants of the first fugitives built a capital city called Chan Santa Cruz ("Small Holy Cross") on the site of today's Felipe Carrillo Puerto. The Mexicans didn't know about it for decades—none who ventured into the eastern jungle ever lived to tell about it. The city was the last rebel holdout, finally destroyed by a huge, well-equipped Mexican force that penetrated the region in 1901. The war was officially declared over, though sporadic fighting continued in settlements that refused to acknowledge Mexican control. Quintana Roo didn't come under government control for another 30 years, and some of today's Maya still do not recognize Mexican sovereignty.

## Díaz, Zapata, Pancho Villa & the Mexican Revolution

A few years after Juárez's death, one of his generals, **Porfirio Díaz,** seized power in a coup. He ruled Mexico from 1877 to 1911, a period now called the *Porfiriato,* maintaining power through repression and by courting favor with powerful nations. With foreign investment came the concentration of great wealth in few hands, and discontent deepened.

During the final days of the *Porfiriato,* citizens of Valladolid mounted a rebellion against the many injustices they had endured. Merchants, landowners, artisans, Maya leaders, and workers alike took up arms on June 3, 1910, and they had control of the city by dawn the next day. Four days later, Díaz pushed back with hundreds of well-equipped troops, leaving 200 rebels dead, 500 wounded, and 600 imprisoned. On June 25, three of the rebellion's leaders were executed by firing squad in the courtyard that is now Valladolid's Heroes Park. Despite Díaz's victory, that rebellion is known as ***La Chispa***—"the spark" that ignited the Mexican Revolution three months later.

In September 1910, **Francisco Madero** led an armed rebellion that became the Mexican revolution ("La Revolución"—as opposed to the revolution against Spain, which is known as the "Guerra de Independencia"). Díaz was exiled and is buried in Paris. Madero became president, but **Victoriano Huerta,** in collusion with the U.S. ambassador, betrayed and executed him in 1913. Those who had answered Madero's call rose up again—the great peasant hero **Emiliano Zapata** in the south, and the

## OF henequén & HACIENDAS

Commercial production of *henequén*, the thorny agave that yields the rope fiber we know as sisal, began in 1830. Demand reached fever pitch during World War I; with a virtual monopoly on the *oro verde* ("green gold"), Yucatán blossomed from one of Mexico's poorest states to one of its richest. In addition to their baronial homes along Mérida's Paseo de Montejo, landowners built plantations to meet their every comfort when they traveled to the countryside. Their haciendas were small, self-contained cities supporting hundreds of workers, and each had its own school, infirmary, store, church, cemetery, and even a jail.

Invention of synthetic fibers during World War II devastated the *henequén* industry; abandoned haciendas became grand derelicts until a new generation of wealthy Mexicans began turning them into hotels in the early 1990s.

seemingly invincible **Pancho Villa** in the central north, flanked by **Alvaro Obregón** and **Venustiano Carranza.** They eventually routed Huerta and began hashing out a new constitution.

For the next few years, Carranza, Obregón, and Villa fought among themselves; Zapata did not seek national power, though he fought tenaciously for land for the peasants. Carranza, during his tenure as president, betrayed and assassinated Zapata. Obregón finally consolidated power and probably had Carranza assassinated. He, in turn, was assassinated when he tried to break one of the tenets of the revolution—no re-election. Not until **Lázaro Cárdenas** was elected in 1934 did the revolution appear to have a chance. He implemented massive land redistribution, nationalized the oil industry, instituted many reforms, and gave shape to the ruling political party, which evolved into today's Partido Revolucionario Institucional, or **PRI.** Cárdenas is practically canonized by most Mexicans.

## Modern Mexico

The presidents who followed were noted more for graft than leadership, and the PRI's reform principles were abandoned. In 1968, the government quashed a democratic student demonstration in the **Tlatelolco** neighborhood of Mexico City, killing hundreds of people and arresting more than 1,000. Though the PRI maintained its grip on power, it lost its image as a progressive party. Economic progress, particularly in the form of large development projects, became the PRI's sole claim to legitimacy.

In 1974, the government decided to build a new coastal megaresort that would outshine Acapulco, the reigning beach destination. Computer analysis by Mexico's tourist development agency, FONATUR, determined the ideal location to be an island off the northeastern corner of the Caribbean coast, in what remained an isolated and undeveloped federal territory now called **Quintana Roo** (after Andrés Quintana Roo, a Mexican loyalist influential in the War of Independence). Though bits of ancient Maya ruins dotted the scrub jungle and deserted shore, the only real settlement was Puerto Juárez on the mainland, a fishing village with a few hundred residents.

**Cancún** ("nest of snakes" in Mayan) was an unlikely choice in some respects: hours away from the nearest city; almost no paved roads through rough terrain; lack of capital and manpower. But it was close to some of the world's most famous Maya sites,

## A TALE OF TWO hurricanes

By 1988, when Hurricane Gilbert swept through, Cancún had more than 200,000 residents, with more than 12,000 hotel rooms and another 11,000 on the drawing boards. The storm's destruction barely slowed the city's growth; existing resorts were promptly remodeled and reopened, followed by dozens of new ones. But the decision to slash hotel rates to lure tourists back, combined with the national drinking age of 18, had the unintended effect of making Cancún the spring-break capital of North America. Images of binge-drinking college hordes replaced idyllic scenes of couples and families playing tag with turquoise waves.

Ironically, an even more devastating hurricane reversed this image. On October 18, 2005, Hurricane Wilma parked on top of the region, battering it with 240kmph (150 mph) winds that knocked out bridges and left the city without electricity and water for 10 days. The world's most celebrated beaches were scoured down to rock. It was the most destructive natural disaster in Mexican history, surpassing even the 1985 Mexico City earthquake.

The government, insurance companies, and major resort hotel chains mobilized a massive recovery effort. Restoration of more than 11km (6¾ miles) of white-powder beach with sand pumped from the ocean bottom (a solution that proved to be temporary and was reprised in 2009 and 2010 to make the repairs more permanent) grabbed the headlines, but a more important transformation was under way. Within three months, 18,000 of the 22,000 hotel rooms were ready for guests. Crews built new roads, installed better street lamps, planted thousands of palms, and installed modern sculptures. In rebuilding, often from the ground up, resorts took pains to distance themselves from the spring-break crowd, going bigger, better, and more luxurious than ever—with price hikes to match.

and its white, powder-fine beaches were a certain draw. Its northern location made it an easy trip for snowbirds from the U.S. and Canada.

Construction began in 1970 on the bridges that now link **Isla Cancún,** then a deserted sandbar studded by coconut palms, to the mainland. The government filled in part of Nichupté Lagoon to make room for roads and hotels, then built a downtown and an airport on the mainland. The tourism zone—the Zona Hotelera—had no residential areas, just hotels, shopping centers, golf courses, and marinas. **Ciudad Cancún** was built on the mainland to house construction workers (and later hotel and restaurant employees) and provide residential and commercial areas, government services, schools, hospitals, and markets.

Quintana Roo became a state in 1974, not coincidentally the year Cancún's first resorts (Palacio Maya and Club Med) opened. By 1976, Cancún boasted 18,000 residents, 1,500 hotel rooms, and 100,000 visitors. Despite natural disasters, a national depression leading to the 1982 peso devaluation, and a tourism slump following the September 11, 2001, terrorist attacks in the U.S., Cancún has repeatedly bounced back to prosper anew.

Tourists seeking an alternative to the phalanx of megaresorts found their way down the coast in the 1980s, but it remained jungle backcountry until 1995. Faced with expensive repairs and sinking land prices in the wake of Hurricane Roxanne, the government opened the coastline to international development. Today's **Riviera Maya** rivals Cancún as a tourist destination, with sprawling resorts and gated communities commanding most beaches between Cancún and Tulum.

The largely inaccessible **Costa Maya** remained an enclave of fishing collectives and traditional Maya communities until Carnival Cruise Lines opened its port in Mahahual in 2002. Within three years, Puerto Costa Maya was drawing more port calls than Puerto Vallarta or Mazatlán. The expanding port gave the region its name when officials declared the region a bona fide destination in early 2007, with plans to expand the small tourism zone, build new roads, and excavate and open more of the southern coast's dozens of little-known Maya sites to tourism.

The government weathered several bouts of social unrest caused by periodic devaluations of the peso. But in 1985, the devastating Mexico City earthquake brought down many new, supposedly earthquake-proof buildings, exposing the widespread corruption that had fostered the shoddy construction, and triggering criticism of the government's relief efforts. Opposition parties gained strength; the two largest were the **PRD** (Partido de la Revolución Democrática) on the left and the **PAN** (Partido Acción Nacional) on the right. To ensure its candidate, Carlos Salinas de Gortari, would win the 1988 presidential election over the PRD's Cuauhtémoc Cárdenas (formerly of the PRI and son of former President Lázaro Cárdenas), the government simply unplugged election computers and declared a system failure.

Under pressure at home and abroad, the government moved to demonstrate a new commitment to democracy and even began to concede electoral defeats for state governorships and legislative seats. Power struggles between reformist factions and hardliners within the party led to several political assassinations, most notably of the PRI's next candidate, **Luis Donaldo Colosio,** in 1994.

After a crippling economic crisis the same year, Gortari's successor, **Ernesto Zedillo,** spent his 6 years in office trying to stabilize the economy and bring transparency to government. In 2000, he shepherded the first true elections in 70 years of one-party rule. The winner was PAN candidate **Vicente Fox,** a former businessman who garnered many votes from citizens who more than anything else wanted to see if the PRI would relinquish power. It did, but Fox wasn't an especially effective politician. His efforts to build a coalition with segments of the PRI failed, and he accomplished little during his last 3 years in office.

The whisker-close and bitterly disputed presidential election of 2006 tested Mexico's nascent pluralism. The elections tribunal's ruling, denying the PRD's request for a recount and declaring PAN's **Felipe Calderón** the winner, was profoundly unpopular. Losing candidate **Andrés Manuel López Obrador** provoked a constitutional crisis that only time managed to heal. Calderón, recognizing the PRD campaign's resonance with the poor, announced programs to boost employment, alleviate poverty, and stabilize the skyrocketing price of tortillas.

His biggest challenge, however, proved to be the alarming escalation of **drug-related violence**—a conflagration attributed to his crackdown on traffickers ferrying contraband through Mexico to the United States. The violence, directed at journalists and government officials as well as rival drug cartels, was concentrated in six states along the U.S.-Mexico border and parts of northern and central Mexico.

Calderón succeeded in capturing or killing several high-profile drug lords in 2010 and dismantling several cartel networks, but such victories further upset the balance of power as the gangs attempted to preserve their territory and grab turf from weakened

## DRUG-RELATED violence: BEYOND THE HEADLINES

I'm often accused of hopeless naiveté. Of being on the Mexico Tourism Board's payroll. Of having a latent death wish. All because whenever I get ready for a trip south of the border, I answer the inevitable "Aren't you afraid?" with a simple "No."

Those accusations, of course, stem from the escalation of horrific violence among the country's drug-trafficking organizations in the middle of the last decade, when a variety of events fractured formerly well-defined territories. The carnage mounted as a growing number of smaller groups jockeyed for a piece of formerly off-limits turf, increasingly employing military-grade weapons and tactics.

Media reports of spectacularly grisly incidents rarely provide useful information, such as exactly where they took place (usually in remote towns tourists have never heard of); if in Sinaloa, for example, was it in Mazatlán, or 200 miles away? If a foreigner was involved, was it a hapless tourist or someone buying or selling drugs? Nor has the small but significant decline in violence over the past few years made its way into many headlines.

So, how can you assess whether travel is safe? Information and common sense are your best tools. Here are some points to keep in mind.

**Mexico is a big country.** Avoiding the Yucatán Peninsula because of violence in Nuevo León would be about as logical as skipping the Grand Canyon because East St. Louis, Illinois, has the highest murder rate in the U.S. Location means more than overall numbers; while border states and other scattered hot spots have astronomical homicide rates, Yucatán state, for example, had 0.1 murders per 100,000 people in 2010, at the height of the violence—U.S. tourist destinations don't come close to matching that. Most of Mexico is at least as safe as your own hometown.

**They aren't after you.** The violence is fueled by a turf war over the lucrative drug trade channel between Asia or South America and the United States (Mexico itself isn't a major producer). The targets are rival drug gangs, law enforcement, journalists, and wealthy businessmen. Foreign victims of crime not involved in drugs themselves are usually caught in the wrong place at the wrong time.

**Information is your best protection.** The State Department travel warnings (www.travel.state.gov) have become much more specific in pinpointing places that require caution or should be avoided altogether. (No destination in the Yucatán or adjacent states has ever appeared on these lists.) Check the U.K. Foreign Office (www.fco.gov.uk; "Travel Advice") for another perspective.

**A little common sense goes a long way.** Leave your baubles at home, carry your money and passport in a money belt, and don't divulge travel plans to strangers; in general, avoid looking like a rich gringo tourist. Ask your hotel manager, taxi driver, or another local what areas to avoid. And do we really need to tell you not to get wasted and go stumbling around dark, unfamiliar streets at night?

**Don't get rattled** if you see armed soldiers patrolling a beach or manning highway checkpoints. They are young men doing a difficult job, and your safety is their concern. On the road, they'll usually ask where you're coming from and where you're going; occasionally they will inspect your trunk. I log about 1,500 rental-car miles in Mexico each year, and every soldier I've encountered has been cordial and glad for a smile or a brief conversation.

rivals. Turf wars boiled up in formerly quiet states such as Nuevo Leon, Morelos, Mexico, Colima, and Jalisco. Opposition to his strategy mounted, leading to new tactics. Highly trained and better-paid (therefore less susceptible to corruption) federal police were deployed to Ciudad Juárez and other key areas. The legislature approved harsher prison sentences for terrorist acts while classifying drug-related violence as terrorism.

Even so, the PRI returned to power in 2012 with victor **Enrique Peña Nieto,** former governor of the state of Mexico, promising a much more democratic and open government this time around. Departing from his predecessor's policy, he has focused on reducing violence more than arresting and killing drug lords or intercepting their shipments—although he does have several high-profile captures to his credit. Drug-related violence has declined around 15% annually since its peak in 2011, but whether Peña Nieto can fulfill his bold promise of slashing violence by 50% during his 6-year term remains to be seen.

The Yucatán remains largely removed from the fray, likely because most of it is undisputed territory. With some of the lowest casualty counts in the country, the region is a safer place to travel than many parts of the United States or Canada. Yet blaring headlines about the drug wars, combined with a tenacious worldwide tourism slump and wariness left over from the 2009 flu scare, kept travelers away until 2013, when tourism showed strong signs of recovery before breaking all previous records in 2014. Prices have started to recover as well, but they remain roughly comparable to levels seen before the tourism slump in 2007.

# ART & ARCHITECTURE

Mexico's art, architecture, politics, and religion were inextricably entwined for more than 3,000 years. The Maya were perhaps the most gifted artists in the Americas, producing fantastically lifelike stone sculptures, soaring temples clad in colors we can only guess at today, and delicately painted pottery. While the Spanish conquest in A.D. 1521 influenced the style and subject of Mexican art, it failed to stamp out its roots, which endure today.

## Pre-Hispanic Forms

Nowhere is the interplay of religion and art more striking than in Mexico's renowned pyramids—truncated platforms crowned by monumental temples. Maya structures also served as navigation aids, administrative and ceremonial centers, tombs, astronomical observatories, and artistic canvases.

Circular buildings such as Chichén Itzá's El Caracol and the observatory tower in Palenque, Chiapas, aided Maya priests' astral calculations which, although used primarily for astrological divination, were stunningly accurate by modern astronomical standards, surpassing what was being used anywhere else in the world at the time. Chichén Itzá's El Castillo itself is a massive calendar, with four staircases of 91 steps, equaling the 365 days of the solar year when the central platform step is added. The stairways also divide the nine terraces of each face of the pyramid into 18 segments, representing the Maya calendar's 18 months; the 52 panels on the terraces symbolize the 52-year cycle, when the solar calendar converged with their separate religious calendar. Architects aligned the temple precisely to produce the equinox phenomenon of the stairway's shadow snaking down a corner of the pyramid to join a giant serpent's head at the bottom.

Throughout the Yucatán, even though the layout of Maya cities seems to have been somewhat random and even haphazard compared with those in other parts of Mexico—following the forms of nature rather than adhering to orderly grids—building alignments were carefully plotted in accordance with the cardinal directions and the orbits of the stars and planets. As cities evolved, great plazas were added, surrounded by a royal acropolis, great pyramids, palaces, and usually ball courts; the plazas were connected by *sacbeob* (plural of *sacbé*), or limestone causeways. Immediately outside of these ritual centers were structures for lesser nobles, smaller temples, and individual shrines. The modest homes of common people were built outside this urban core.

The practice of building one pyramid on top of, and incorporating, earlier ones was widespread, if not universal, yet the architecture itself is quite varied, drawing elements from a wide geographical area. Chichén Itzá's strong Toltec influence, with its angular, stepped profiles, emphasizes war and human sacrifice; the alternating vertical and sloping panels of Toltec and Aztec architecture surfaces also in Dzibanché, a partially excavated site that opened in the early 1990s near Laguna Bacalar in southern Quintana Roo. South of Chichén Itzá, Uxmal's refined and more purely Maya geometry, using intricate stone mosaics and beautifully sloped and rounded sides, is an example of the Puuc style, which incorporates the varied elevations of the Puuc hills but also borrows geometric elements and techniques from such distant areas as Oaxaca, Veracruz, and the Valley of Mexico. Ek Balam's buildings show marked resemblances to the Petén style, with its elaborate roof combs and tall, steep pyramids and stucco masks associated with Guatemala's Tikal. Far to the south, Calakmul also displays Petén influences as well as the more local Río Bec style, characterized by giant monster-mouth doorways, mosaic masks, and towers topped by false temples.

The true arch was unknown in Mesoamerica, but the Maya devised the corbelled arch (or Maya arch) by stacking each successive stone to cantilever beyond the one below, until the two sides met at the top in an inverted V.

The Olmec, who reigned over the Gulf coastal plains, are considered Mesoamerica's parent culture. Little survives of their pyramids, which were built of clay. We still have their enormous sculptural legacy, from small, intricately carved pieces of jade to the 40-ton carved basalt rock heads found at La Venta, Tabasco (some of which are displayed in the Parque–Museo La Venta in Villahermosa).

More intact later cities, built of stone, give us a better glimpse of ancient Maya art, but their exuberant color is all but lost. The stones originally were covered with a layer of painted stucco that gleamed red, blue, and yellow through the jungle foliage. Most of the fantastic murals that adorned their buildings are also lost to time, though surprisingly well-preserved fragments survive at Ek Balam and Balamkú in Quintana Roo. Vestiges also remain at Mayapán (in Yucatán) and Cobá.

Artisans also crafted marvelous stone murals and mosaics from thousands of pieces of fitted stone, adorning façades with geometric designs or figures of warriors or snakes. Uxmal, in fact, evidently had not a single mural; all its artistry is in the intricate stonework.

Murals and stone carvings served a religious or historical, rather than ornamental, purpose. Deciphering the hieroglyphs—rich, elegant symbols etched in stone or painted on pottery—allows scholars to identify rulers and untangle dynastic history. Michael Coe's *Breaking the Maya Code* traces centuries-long efforts to decode Maya script and outlines recent breakthroughs that make it possible to decipher 90% of the glyphs. "Cracking the Maya Code," a *Nova* program based on Coe's book, is available for viewing on www.pbs.org and for rent on Netflix.

Good hieroglyphic examples appear in Palenque's site museum. Several stelae, the large, free-standing stone slabs on which the Maya etched their history, are in place at Cobá. Calakmul is known for its many stelae, and good examples are displayed in Mexico City's Museum of Anthropology and the archaeology museum in Villahermosa.

## Spanish Influence

The Spaniards brought new forms of architecture to Mexico; in many cases they razed Maya cities and reused the limestone to build their Catholic churches, public buildings, palaces, and homes. In the Yucatán, churches at Izamal, Tecoh, Santa Elena, and Muna rest atop former pyramids. Indian artisans recruited to build the new structures frequently implanted traditional bymbolism, such as a plaster angel swaddled in feathers, reminiscent of the god Quetzalcóatl; they determined how many florets to carve around church doorways based on the ancient cosmos's 13 steps of heaven and nine levels of the underworld.

Spanish priests and architects altered their teaching and building methods in order to convert native populations. Church adornment became more explicit to combat the language barrier; frescoes of biblical tales were splashed across church walls, and Christian symbols in stone supplanted pre-Hispanic figures.

Remnants of 16th-century missions, convents, monasteries, and parish churches dot almost every Yucatecan village. Examples worth visiting include the Mission of San Bernardino de Sisal in Valladolid; the cathedral of Mérida; the vast atrium and church at Izamal; and the *retablos* (altarpieces), altars, and crucifixes in churches along the Convent Route, between the Puuc Hills and Mérida.

Porfirio Díaz's 34-year rule (1877–1911) brought a new infusion of European sensibility. Díaz commissioned imposing European-style public buildings and provided European scholarships to artists who returned to paint Mexican subjects using techniques from abroad. Mérida is a veritable museum of opulent, European-style buildings constructed during the Díaz years; the most striking are the Palacio Cantón, now housing the Regional Anthropology Museum, and the Teatro Peón Contreras.

## The Advent of Mexican Muralism

The Mexican revolution that rent the country from 1910 to 1920 gave rise to a new social and cultural era. In 1923, as one way to reach the illiterate masses, Diego Rivera and other budding artists were invited to paint Mexican history on the walls of the Ministry of Education building and the National Preparatory School in Mexico City. Thus was born Mexico's tradition of public murals.

The courtyard and History Room of the Governor's Palace in Mérida display 31 works of Castro Pacheco, the Yucatán's most prominent muralist. Though he painted on large panels rather than directly on the walls, he aligned with other great muralists in his affinity for strong colors and the belief that art is meant for public enjoyment, not just private collectors. Pacheco's murals are a chilling depiction of the bloody subjugation of the Yucatán, including the *Popol Vuh* legend, a jaguar with fierce warriors in headdresses, a Maya *henequén* worker's hands, and portraits of such heroes as Felipe Carrillo Puerto, the martyred Yucatecan governor who instituted agrarian and other reforms.

# RELIGION, MYTH & FOLKLORE

Nearly 90% of Mexicans are Roman Catholics, but Mexican Catholicism is laced with pre-Hispanic spiritual tradition. You need only to visit the *curandero* section of a market (where you can buy such talismans as copal, an incense agreeable to the gods; rustic beeswax candles, a traditional offering; and native species of tobacco used to ward off evil) or watch pre-Hispanic dances performed at a village festival to sense the supernatural beliefs running parallel with Christian principles.

Spanish Catholicism was disseminated by pragmatic Jesuit missionaries who grafted Christian tradition onto indigenous ritual to make it palatable to their flock. Nearly 500 years after the conquest, a large minority of Mexicans—faithful Catholics every one—adhere to this hybrid religion, nowhere more so than in Chiapas and the Yucatán.

The *padres'* cause enjoyed a huge boost when a dark-skinned image of the Virgin Mary appeared to an Aztec potter near Mexico City in 1531. The Virgin of Guadalupe, fluent in the local language and acquainted with indigenous gods, provided a crucial link between Catholic and native spiritual traditions. She remains Mexico's most beloved religious figure, smiling from countless shrines, saloons, and kitchen walls. Millions of pilgrims walk and crawl to her Mexico City shrine on her December 12 feast day.

The equally pragmatic native people chose the path of least resistance, dressing their ancestral beliefs in Catholic garb. They gave their familiar gods the names of Christian saints and celebrated their old festivals on the nearest saint's day. Thus we find the Catholic feasts of All Saints' Day and All Souls' Day superimposed on the ancient Day of the Dead celebration, and the cult of the "Black Christ"—an amalgam of Jesus Christ and the cave-dwelling Maya god Ik'al—entrenched in the Yucatán, Chiapas, and Tabasco. In one of the most dramatic examples of this spiritual hybridization, the Tzotzil Maya of San Juan Chamula in highland Chiapas carpet their church with pine needles, kneeling among candles and Coke bottles to pray in an archaic dialect under the painted eyes of helpful saints. They bring offerings of flower petals, eggs, feathers, or live chickens prescribed by local *curanderos* (medicine men) in an effort to dispel the demons of disease.

Common themes in the Catholic and Maya belief systems also made the Jesuits' task easier. The Catholics had the Bible, the Maya had the *Popol Vuh.* Both had long oral and written traditions (although Bishop Diego de Landa burned the Maya codices of Maní in the infamous *auto-da-fé* of 1562, leaving only three known bark-paper books). Ceremonial processions with elaborate robes and incense were common to both religions, as were baptism by water and the symbol of the cross.

The differences, though, are what intrigue us today. The Maya's multitude of deities—166 by most counts—is just the beginning. The *Popol Vuh*'s creation myth, similar to Genesis in making man on the last day and striking down imperfect earlier creations with an apocalyptic flood, departs from the Genesis plot in striking ways. Not the least of these is fashioning man from corn after failed tries with mud and wood. Maya mythology is a collection of convoluted tales, full of images placing nature on a level equal to man, that attempt to make sense of the universe, geography, and seasons.

The tall, straight ceiba tree was revered as a symbol of the cosmos. Its leaves and branches represented the 13 levels of heaven, the tree trunk the world of humans, and its roots the nine-level underworld—not a hell but a cold, damp, dark place called Xibalba.

## THE MAYA pantheon

Every ancient culture had its gods and goddesses, and their characteristics or purposes, if not their names, often crossed cultures. Chaac, the hook-nosed rain god of the Maya, was Tlaloc, the squat Aztec rain god; Quetzalcóatl, the plumed-serpent Toltec man/god, became the Maya's Kukulkán. Sorting out the ancient deities and beliefs can become a life's work, but here are some of the most important gods of the Maya world.

**Itzamná** Often called the Supreme Deity; creator of mankind and inventor of corn, cacao, writing, and reading; patron of the arts and sciences.

**Chaac** God of rain, striking the clouds with a lightning ax; sometimes depicted as four separate gods based on the four cardinal directions.

**Kinich Ahau** Sun god, sometimes regarded as another manifestation of Itzamná; appeared in the shape of a firebird.

**Kukulkán** Mortal who took on godly virtues, sometimes symbolized as Venus, the morning star.

**Ixchel** Wife of Kinich Ahau; multitasking goddess of the moon, fertility and childbirth, water, medicine, and weaving.

**Bacab** Generic name for four brothers who guarded the four points of the compass; closely associated with the four Chaacs.

**Yumil Kaxob** God of maize, or corn, shown with a crown or headdress of corn and distinguished by his youth.

**Balam** One of numerous jaguar spirits; symbol of power and protector of fields and crops.

**Ixtab** Goddess of suicide; suicide was an honorable way to die, and Ixtab received those souls into heaven.

Foremost among the Maya pantheon were those who influenced the growth of corn. The Maya worked hard to please their gods through prayer, offerings, and sacrifices, which could be anything from a priest giving his own blood to human sacrifice. They were obsessed with time, maintaining both a 260-day religious calendar and a 365-day solar calendar that guided crop planting and other practicalities. In fact, religion, art, and science were so entwined that the Maya might not even have perceived them as separate pursuits. So from a kernel of corn grew some of civilization's earliest and greatest accomplishments.

# MEXICO'S CARIBBEAN COAST IN POP CULTURE

## Books

### HISTORY & CULTURE

For an overview of pre-Hispanic cultures, pick up **Michael D. Coe**'s *Mexico: From the Olmecs to the Aztecs,* or **Nigel Davies**'s *Ancient Kingdoms of Mexico.* Coe's *The Maya* is probably the best general account of the Maya. For a survey of Mexico's history through modern times, *A Short History of Mexico* by **J. Patrick McHenry** is thorough yet concise.

## THE DAY THE world DID NOT END

On December 21, 2012, the day Earth was predicted to succumb to cataclysmic solar storms, magnetic pole reversal, earthquakes, a galactic collision, or alien invasion, the Maya Long Count Calendar uneventfully turned a page to a new 5,125-year cycle, just as our contemporary calendar turned the page on a new day. The origins of the "Maya prophecy" are primarily a matter of speculation. One of the earliest proponents, José Argüelles, is also credited among the originators of the Earth Day concept. Quite a few others seem to have arrived at their epiphanies under the influence of the psychedelic drug DMT, widely found in plants and used primarily in South America for both divination and healing.

History and time have swallowed much of the ancient Maya's scripture, but their contemporary descendants had no part in such predictions, except to enjoy the benefits of the world's increased focus on their culture. The Long Count Calendar, one of three interfacing calendars employed by the ancient Maya, hasn't been used for thousands of years. Only two or three oblique references to the date coinciding with the December 2012 solstice survive, none presuming an apocalypse; what significance the Maya attached to the end of the Long Calendar cycle is uncertain. They believed an earlier long cycle ended before their time—bringing no mass destruction—and some inscriptions refer to future events to come after completion of their current cycle, which should have ruled out a prediction of the end of days.

Contemporary Maya who considered the date significant at all regarded it not with fear but as a new dawn, a time for reflection and perhaps a change in consciousness. In some interpretations, the new cycle was to bring a reawakening of the ancient Maya world—and that it has, in the sense that thousands of tourists have been inspired to learn more about the New World's most advanced civilization and to explore its monumental cities. One lasting legacy of the "prophecy" is the construction of two excellent museums on Maya civilization and culture, one in Mérida, and one in Cancún. For that, at least, we are in debt to the doomsayers.

**John L. Stephens**'s two-volume *Incidents of Travel in the Yucatán,* illustrated by Frederick Catherwood, is not only one of the great books of archaeological discovery but a travel classic as well. Before his expeditions, beginning in 1841, the world knew little about the region and nothing about the Maya. Stephens's account of 44 Maya sites is still the most authoritative.

**Ronald Wright**'s *Stolen Continents,* published in 1992 for the 500th anniversary of Christopher Columbus's voyage, recounts the story of the European conquest from the point of view of indigenous Americans—Aztec, Maya, Inca, Cherokee, and Iroquois—who had been largely left out of the history every child was taught until then.

**Allen Wells** and **Gilbert Joseph**'s *Summer of Discontent, Seasons of Upheaval: Elite Politics and Rural Insurgency in Yucatan, 1876–1915* chronicles the breakdown of the old order during the first years of the revolutionary era, a process that was resisted and therefore more protected in the Yucatán.

**Lesley Byrd Simpson**'s *Many Mexicos* is a comprehensive cultural history; *Distant Neighbor* by **Alan Riding** is a classic of cultural insight.

For contemporary culture, start with **Octavio Paz**'s classic, *The Labyrinth of Solitude,* filled with great insight even though it remains controversial because of some of its cultural generalizations. *Our Word Is Our Weapon,* a collection of articulate, often poetic writings by Zapatista leader **Subcomandante Marcos**, provides insight into the Maya peasantry's armed revolt in Chiapas in the 1990s.

In *Maya Roads,* former war correspondent **Mary Jo McConahay**'s three decades of living and traveling in Mexico and Central America inform evocative descriptions of ancient cities and moving accounts of archaeological discoveries, the Zapatista uprising, and violence wrought by drug trafficking—and the stoic people who adapt to these changes in their way of life with remarkable resolve.

## ART & ARCHITECTURE

*Art and Time in Mexico: From the Conquest to the Revolution,* by **Elizabeth Wilder Weismann,** covers religious, public, and private architecture. *Maya Art and Architecture* by **Mary Ellen Miller** showcases the best of Maya artistic expression.

## NATURE

*A Naturalist's Mexico* by **Roland H. Wauer,** out of print but still available used, is a journey of discovery across Mexico in the context of its plants and animals (primarily birds). *A Hiker's Guide to Mexico's Natural History* by **Jim Conrad** is one of the few field guides for hiking in Mexico. *Peterson Field Guides: Mexican Birds* by **Roger Tory Peterson** and **Edward L. Chalif** is predictably excellent. **Les Beletsky**'s enlightened *Southern Mexico* is a richly illustrated, engagingly written field guide to the region's wildlife, as well as an ecotourism manual.

## LITERATURE

**Jorge Ibargüengoitia,** one of Mexico's most famous modern writers, died in 1983 but remains popular in Mexico, and his works are available in translation. His novels *Estas Ruinas Que Ves (These Ruins You See)* and *The Dead Girls* (a fictional account of a famous 1970s crime) display deft characterization and a sardonic view of Mexican life.

**Juan Rulfo,** one of Mexico's most esteemed authors, wrote only three slim books before his death in 1986. His second, *Pedro Páramo,* is Mexico's equivalent of Shakespearean tragedy and has never been out of print since its publication in 1955. The short novel of a son's search for his abusive, tyrannical father had a major influence on the magical realism movement. It has been translated twice into English and been made into film several times.

The earlier novels of **Carlos Fuentes,** during his lifetime Mexico's preeminent writer, are easier to read than more recent works; try *The Death of Artemio Cruz.* **Angeles Mastretta**'s delightful *Arráncame la Vida (Tear Up My Life)* is a well-written novel about a young woman's life in post-revolutionary Puebla. **Laura Esquivel**'s *Like Water for Chocolate* (and the subsequent movie) covers roughly the same period through a lens of magical realism and helped to popularize Mexican food abroad.

*Hasta No Verte Jesús Mío* by **Elena Poniatowska** and anything by Pulitzer-winner **Luis Alberto Urrea** offer hard looks at third-world realities.

**Guillermo Arriaga,** screenwriter for *Amores Perros, 21 Grams,* and *Babel,* is also a brilliant novelist. *El Bufalo de la Noche,* about a young man reeling from his best friend's suicide, was made into a movie and is available in English.

## VIEWS FROM THE OUTSIDE: films STARRING MEXICO

Director John Huston and his father, Walter, who co-starred with Humphrey Bogart, won three Oscars between them for ***The Treasure of the Sierra Madre*** (1948), one of the first Hollywood films shot entirely on location. Elia Kazan's 1952 classic, ***Viva Zapata!***, written by John Steinbeck, stars Marlon Brando as revolutionary Emiliano Zapata. The same year, Luis Buñuel's first international box-office success, ***Los Olvidados,*** presented a disturbing picture of a ruthless but doomed young street gang in Mexico City's slums. Orson Welles's 1958 film-noir ***Touch of Evil,*** despite the preposterous casting of Charlton Heston as a Mexican narcotics agent, is an examination of drugs and corruption in Tijuana that remains compelling even though it feels sanitized compared with today's screaming headlines.

In 1964, Richard Burton played a defrocked priest trying to get straight in Puerto Vallarta in the film of Tennessee Williams' ***The Night of the Iguana*** (1989). The adaptation of Carlos Fuentes's novel ***The Old Gringo*** (1989), a love triangle set during the Mexican Revolution, was shot with Gregory Peck, Jane Fonda, and a young Jimmy Smits in numerous locations in five Mexican states.

Director Robert Rodriguez's breakout film, ***El Mariachi*** (1992), originally aimed at the Mexican home video market, is a somewhat cheesy but highly entertaining action flick set in a small central Mexican town. The first of his Mexican trilogy was followed by ***Desperado*** (1995), introducing Antonio Banderas as El Mariachi, and ***Once Upon a Time in Mexico*** (2003), with still more star power, including

## Film

### GOLDEN AGE & CLASSICS

During Mexico's "Golden Age of Cinema" in the 1940s, studios stopped trying to mimic Hollywood and started producing unabashedly Mexican black-and-white films whose stars are still cultural icons in Mexico. **Mario Moreno,** aka Cantinflas, was a comedic genius who personalized the *el pelado* archetype—a poor, picaresque, slightly naughty character trading on his wits alone and getting nowhere. Mexican beauty **Dolores del Río** played the steamy Latin babe in Hollywood. **Pedro Infante,** the singing cowboy, embodied the ideal of Mexican manhood.

**Luis Buñuel**'s dark *Los Olvidados* (1950) was the Spanish surrealist's third Mexican film, exploring the life of young hoodlums in Mexico City's slums.

### THE NEW CINEMA

After a long fallow period, a new generation of filmmakers emerged in the 1990s. The first big *El Nuevo Cine Mexicano* (The New Cinema) hit outside of Mexico was *Like Water for Chocolate* (1992), directed by **Alfonso Arau,** author Laura Esquivel's then husband. He continues to make films, mainly in Mexico. *Sexo, Pudor y Lágrimas* (1999), by director **Antonio Serrano,** is an unflinching look at the battle of the sexes in Mexico City.

After **Alfonso Cuarón**'s debut film, the mordant social satire *Sólo con tu Pareja* (1991), scored critical and commercial success in Mexico, he garnered international acclaim with his ironic *Y Tu Mamá También* (2001), which touches on class hypocrisy

Salma Hayek and Johnny Depp. These aren't great movies, but they are fun and feature great Mexican settings. Ditto for ***The Mexican*** (2001) with Brad Pitt and Julia Roberts.

Billy Bob Thornton directed an adaptation of the novel ***All the Pretty Horses*** (2000), with Matt Damon as a young Texan who finds work on a Mexican horse ranch. Stephen Soderbergh's Academy Award–winning ***Traffic*** (2000), with Benicio del Toro, focuses on Tijuana's drug war from multiple points of view. HBO's 2003 flick, ***And Starring Pancho Villa as Himself*** with Antonio Banderas, is the true story of how revolutionaries allowed Hollywood to film Pancho Villa in battle. ***Man on Fire*** (2004), with Denzel Washington as a bodyguard hired to protect a little girl, is full of great Mexico City scenes, though the plot is depressing and all too real. Dylan Verrechia's ***Tijuana Makes Me Happy*** (2005), focusing on Tijuana's humanity rather than its perceived sins, has won awards in Latin America and at U.S. film festivals.

Mel Gibson's controversial ***Apocalypto*** (2006) cast indigenous Maya to depict the waning days of their ancestor's empire, with Veracruz state's rain forests standing in for the ancient jungles of the Yucatán. Mexico, most notably an uglified Campeche, stood in for 1950s Cuba in Steven Soderbergh's ***Che*** (2008), a two-part epic focusing first on the Cuban revolution and then on its hero's attempt to bring revolution to Bolivia; it won the Cannes best actor award for Benicio del Toro.

while following a pair of teenage boys on an impromptu road trip with a sexy older woman. Cuarón is now hot in Hollywood, directing *Harry Potter and the Prisoner of Azkaban* (2004), and writing and directing the science-fiction thriller *Children of Men* (2006) and *Gravity* (2013).

In *Amores Perros* (2000), **Alejandro González Iñárritu** (director of *21 Grams*) presents a keen glimpse of contemporary Mexican society through three stories about different ways of life in Mexico City that converge at the scene of a horrific car accident. He is the first Mexican director to be nominated for a best director Oscar—for *Babel* (2006), another tour de force, featuring a Mexican border scene that is realistic, exhilarating, and frightening all at once. His *Biutiful* brought a best actor award for star Javier Bardem at the 2010 Cannes Film Festival; 2014's *Birdman,* starring Michael Keaton as a washed-up actor trying to redeem himself, won two Golden Globe awards and at press time had been nominated for nine Academy Awards.

**Guillermo del Toro**'s debut, the dark, atmospheric *Cronos* (1993), won critical acclaim in Mexico. Moving into the international arena, he has directed similarly moody films such as Oscar winner *Pan's Labyrinth* (2006) and *Don't Be Afraid of the Dark* (2010). He picked up writing credit on the Hobbit movies, and both co-wrote and directed the apocalyptic sci-fi movie *Pacific Rim* (2013).

**Julie Taymor**'s *Frida* (2002), with Mexican actress Salma Hayek producing and starring, is an enchanting biopic about Frida Kahlo's life and work, from her devastating accident to her relationships with Diego Rivera and Leon Trotsky. The exquisite cinematography captures the magic realism evinced in Kahlo's work.

## Music

### MARIMBA & SON

*Marimba* music flourishes in much of southern and central Mexico, whose bands travel to play in Mexico City, Oaxaca, and other Mexican states.

*Son,* a native art form in much of Mexico, employs a variety of stringed instruments. Ritchie Valens's "La Bamba" popularized one of the most famous forms, *son jarocho,* in the '50s. Often fast-paced, with lots of strumming and fancy string picking, it originated in southern Veracruz. *Jarana,* the Yucatán's principal dance music, is a form of *son jarocho* that adds woodwinds and a sensuous Caribbean beat. The dance was born as part of the haciendas' annual *vaquerías,* or country fiestas, and is still performed every week in Mérida's central plaza and smaller parks.

### DANZÓN & BOLERO

These musical forms came from Cuba in the late 19th century and gained great popularity. *Danzón* is stately orchestral music that incorporates Latin flavor.

The Yucatán's *son yucateca,* born of its strong ties to Cuba, probably influenced bolero and the related *trova,* or classical guitar trios. This soft, romantic, and often slightly melancholy music is a linchpin of Yucatecan tradition, and singers sometimes use Mayan lyrics. Mérida's free nightly cultural events include *trova yucateca,* and the city stages an annual *trova* festival.

### MARIACHI & RANCHERA

Mariachis, with their big sombreros, waist-length jackets, and tight pants, embody Mexican spirit. The music originated in post-revolutionary Mexico from Jalisco state's *son,* arranged for guitars, violins, string bass, and trumpets. Now heard across Mexico and much of the American Southwest, it is at its traditional best in Jalisco and its capital, Guadalajara. Mariachi is also common in the Yucatán, especially in cantinas and during national celebrations. Yucatecan *trova* music even has its own mariachi adaptations.

The national pride, individualism, and sentimentality expressed in mariachi's kin, *ranchera,* earn it favored status as drinking music. Drawing on traditional folklore, it originated on ranches and in other rural areas. Many Mexicans know the songs of famous composer **José Alfredo Jiménez** by heart. The *corrido* is a variation on the ranchero that tells a heroic story.

### ROCK EN ESPAÑOL

After following U.S. rock's lead in the early years, Mexican rock forged its own identity in the 1980s and exploded during the '90s with bands such as **Jaguares** and **Molotov,** out of Mexico City, and Guadalajara-based **Maná,** probably Latin rock's most popular band today. Named for the famous 1920s cafe in the capital, **Café Tacvba** (pronounced Tacuba) has been at it since 1989. Their music is influenced by indigenous Mexican music as much as folk, punk, bolero, and hip-hop. The fast-rising **Yucatán a Go Go**—hailing, despite the name, from central Mexico—fuses a bouncy pop beat to lyrics firmly rooted in cultural tradition. Some bands out of the northern city of Monterrey have had international success: The movie *Mr. & Mrs. Smith* (2005) opens with "Los Oxidados" by **Plastilina Mosh,** and **Kinky** performed at the Coachella music festival in 2004. Latin alternative music, an answer to the slickly produced Latin pop exemplified by **Ricky Martin** or **Paulina Rubio,** has become a genre in itself. Practitioners such as **Panda, División Minúscula,** and **Zoé** have achieved not-so-alternative success.

# EATING & DRINKING

The tacos and burritos familiar north of the border are mere appetizers on Mexico's vast and varied menu. Some staples have graced plates throughout the country, but long distances and two formidable mountain ranges gave rise to a wide variety of distinct regional cuisines that evolved independently. It is not only possible but also one of life's great pleasures to eat your way through Mexico without downing a single taco or burrito.

Because of its long isolation from the rest of Mexico, the Yucatán's cuisine is especially distinctive, characterized by earthy, piquant *achiote* (also called *annatto,* from the seeds of a native evergreen bush), tangy sour oranges and limes, rich pumpkin seeds, and pickled onions. Meat, nuts, fruits, cheese, and spices introduced by the Spanish provided new ways to prepare native dishes. The Spanish also brought sugar, which they discovered in the Caribbean. In more recent decades, immigration from the Middle East, Cuba, the U.S., and Europe have produced still more variations. As in most Mexican cooking, Yucatecan cuisine remains simple at its core, with most of the *picante* flavor added with the chile and salsa found on every table.

## The Staples

**TORTILLAS** The tortilla is Mexico's bread, and sometimes its fork and spoon, used to scoop up other food. Corn is cooked in water and lime, ground into grainy *masa* dough, patted and pressed into thin cakes, and cooked on a *comal* (hot griddle). Even restaurants that serve bread always have tortillas available. The flour tortilla was developed in northern Mexico and is less common in the south.

**ENCHILADAS** The most famous of numerous Mexican dishes based on the tortilla was originally called *tortilla enchilada,* meaning a tortilla dipped in a chile sauce; variations include *entomatada* (dipped in tomato sauce) and *enfrijolada* (in a bean sauce). The basic enchilada, still sold in food stands, is a tortilla dipped first in hot oil and then chile (usually ancho) sauce, folded or rolled on a plate, and sprinkled with chopped onions and *queso cotija* (crumbly white cheese). It's often served with fried potatoes and carrots. Restaurants serve more elaborate enchiladas filled with cheese, chicken, pork, or seafood. In Southern Mexico, enchiladas are often bathed in a rich mole sauce.

**TACOS** Anything folded or rolled into a tortilla—sometimes two, either soft or fried—is a taco. Flautas and quesadillas are species of tacos. This is the quintessential Mexican fast food, sold in *taquerías* everywhere.

**FRIJOLES** Most Mexican households eat beans daily. Pinto beans are predominant in northern Mexico, but black beans are the Yucatán's legumes of choice. Mexicans add only a little onion and garlic and a pinch of herbs, as beans are meant to be a counterpoint to spicy foods. They also may appear at the end of a meal with a spoonful of sour cream. Fried leftover beans often appear as *frijoles refritos,* a side dish commonly called "refried beans." In fact, they are fried just once; the prefix *re* means "well" (as in "thoroughly"), so a better translation might be "well-fried beans."

### Local Wisdom

"The chile runs in our veins."
—Laura Esquivel, author of *Like Water for Chocolate* (1989), in the introduction to *La Cocina del Chile* (2003)

## A DEBT OF gratitude

Lost among the laurels heaped upon the ancient Maya for their contributions to science, mathematics, architecture, astronomy, and writing is the wide array of foods they introduced. It's no exaggeration to say discovery of the Maya's food changed the world's eating habits in the 1500s. Just try to imagine life without:

**Avocado** From its origins in southern Mexico, where it was used as an aphrodisiac, the avocado spread to the Rio Grande and central Peru before the Europeans learned about it.

**Black Beans** Archaeological digs indicate the black bean originated in southern Mexico and Central America more than 7,000 years ago. Still the favorite in and around the Yucatán, it has spread widely throughout Latin America, the Caribbean, and the United States.

**Chiles** Chiles have been cultivated in the Americas for more than 6,000 years. Blame Christopher Columbus for calling them "peppers," but credit him for their worldwide reach. Southern Mexico's *Capsicum annuum* species, with its many cultivars, is crucial to nearly every fiery cuisine in the world.

**Chocolate** The Maya's "food of the gods," made from the toasted, fermented seeds of the cacao tree, is arguably the Maya's greatest gift to civilization. Though Cortez learned of chocolate from the Aztec, the Maya ate it many centuries earlier and used cacao beans as currency. When the Spanish added sugar to the ceremonial drink to counteract the bitterness, it became the basis for the chocolate we couldn't live without today.

**Corn** The creation myth in the *Popol Vuh*, the Maya "bible," attributes humankind's very existence to this domesticated strain of wild grass, easily the most important food in the Americas. Thousands of years after corn became a dietary staple, the Maya started cultivating it around 2,500 B.C. and abandoned their nomadic ways to settle in villages surrounded by cornfields.

**Papaya** The large, woody, fast-growing herb—commonly referred to as a tree—was used to treat cuts, burns, and rashes, as well as stomach ailments and other ills. After spreading from southern Mexico, it now grows in every tropical country.

**Tomatoes** Even the Italians had to make do without tomato sauce before discovery of the New World. Stunted precursors originated in Peru, but the tomato as we know it came from the Yucatán, where the Maya cultivated it long before the conquest.

**Vanilla** The elixir from the vine-like *Vanilla planifolia* orchid, which can grow no more than 20 degrees north or south of the equator, originally flavored Maya chocolate drinks. Southern Mexico's jungle is still the only place the orchid grows wild, pollinated by stingless *meliponia* bees that produce Maya honey. Tahiti's prized vanilla, which comes from Mexican stock, must be hand-pollinated. Mexico's vanilla is the smoothest, darkest, and richest available today.

**TAMALES** The ultimate take-out meal, tamales (singular: *tamal*) developed in pre-Hispanic Mexico and became more elaborate after the Spanish introduced pork and other ingredients. To make a tamal, you mix *masa* (short for *masa de maíz,* or corn dough) with lard, beat the batter, add a filling, wrap it, and cook it. Every region has its own specialty. The most popular *rellenos* (fillings) are pork and cheese, but they might be anything from fish to iguana, augmented by pumpkin, pineapple, rice, or peanuts, and tucked into a blanket of yellow, black, or purple *masa.* Tamales are usually steamed but may be baked or grilled; the jackets are most often dried corn husks or fresh corn or banana leaves, but may be fashioned from palm, avocado, or *chaya* (a spinach-like vegetable) leaves.

Yucatecan tamales have a distinctly Maya flavor, filled with pork or chicken marinated in *achiote* and cooked in an underground pit or oven that chars the banana leaf black. Neighboring Chiapas' eclectic assortment of tamales might be filled with mole, *chicharrón* (crispy, fried pork rind), or even flower buds; the best known are *tamales de bola,* with pork rib, a prune, and a small dried chile, all wrapped up in a corn husk tied on top to form a ball *(bola).* Tabasco makes liberal use of freshwater fish and seafood, rice, and an array of exotic produce.

**CHILES** Hardly a traditional dish in all of Mexico lacks chiles. Appearing in wondrous variety throughout Mexico, they bear different names depending on whether they are fresh or dried. Chiles range from blazing hot with little discernible taste to mild with a rich, complex flavor, and they can be pickled, smoked, stuffed, or stewed. Among the best-known are the pimiento, the large, harmless bell pepper familiar in the U.S.; the fist-size poblano, ranging from mild to very hot; the short, torpedo-shaped serrano; the skinny and seriously fiery *chile de árbol;* the stubby, hot jalapeño; the chipotle, a dried and smoked jalapeño usually served in *adobo* (vinegar and garlic paste); and the tiny, five-alarm *pequín.*

If you suffer from misadventure by chile, a drink of milk, a bite of banana or cucumber, a spoonful of yogurt, or—if all else fails—a bottle of beer will help extinguish the fire.

## Regional Specialties

The heady blend of native and worldwide flavors in Yucatecan cuisine is like nothing else in Mexico. Turkey *(pavo),* still the most common meat in Yucatecan homes, is prominent on most menus, though beef, pork, and chicken have also become staples. Fish and seafood reign along the coast.

*Achiote* and sour orange came to the Yucatán by way of the Caribbean, Edam cheese through historical trade with the Dutch, and peas likely from the English. A wave of Lebanese immigration around the turn of the 20th century also left its mark; the spit-broiled *tacos al pastor* is basically a Mexican gyro, and you might come across *kibbeh* made of beef or potatoes instead of lamb or *dolmas* wrapped in *chaya* instead of grape leaves.

The Yucatán's trademark dishes are *pollo* or *cochinita* (chicken or pork) *pibil,* meat marinated in *achiote,* bitter orange, and spices, wrapped in banana leaves and barbecued or baked in a pit; *poc chuc,* pork slices marinated in sour orange and garnished with pickled onions; and *sopa de lima* (lime soup), made of shredded, lime-marinated turkey or chicken and topped with sizzling tortilla strips.

Try starting your day with *huevos moluleños*—fried eggs over sliced plantains, beans, and fried tortillas, topped with a dusting of salty cheese, tomato sauce, and peas—but only if you're ravenous. *Cochinita pibil* is also served in the morning. The

### Food Hygiene

The days when you had to carry water purification tablets to return from a trip to Mexico with your intestines intact are long gone. Nearly all restaurants that serve middle-class Mexicans use filtered water, disinfect their vegetables, and buy ice made from purified water. If in doubt, look for ice with a rough cylindrical shape and a hollow center, produced by the same kind of machinery across the country. Street vendors and market stalls are less consistent; look for clean, busy places and stick with cooked foods and unpeeled fruit.

best place to have the former is in any reputable restaurant; the best place for the latter would be a major market.

Customary dishes for the afternoon meal, which is typically the largest of the day, include *pavo en relleno negro,* turkey cooked with a black *recado* (paste) flavored with charred chiles, *achiote,* cloves, allspice, peppercorns, and cumin, garnished with hard-boiled eggs; *escabeche blanco,* chicken or turkey cooked in a vinegar-based sauce; or *queso relleno,* mild Edam cheese stuffed with seasoned ground beef. The unique *tikin-xic* (or some variant of this name) is grilled fish that has been lightly marinated in an *achiote* paste. These also appear on the evening menu in restaurants in Cancún and on the coast. Traditional evening foods are based on turkey and include such finger foods as *salbutes* and *panuchos,* two dishes of tortillas or *masa* cakes layered with shredded turkey or chicken; *panuchos* add a layer of *frijoles.*

Campeche has its own culinary traditions, a marriage of Spanish cuisine, recipes brought by pirates from all over the world, and local fruits and vegetables. The signature dish is *pan de cazón* (baby shark casserole)—layers of tortillas, black beans, and shredded baby shark meat, smothered in tomato sauce.

Distinctive dishes and flavors from neighboring areas of Maya settlement have also become a part of Yucatecan cuisine. The Maya of Chiapas were great mathematicians and astronomers, like their kin throughout the Yucatán, but they also were particularly accomplished farmers. Though they depended above all on corn, native herbs such as *chipilin,* a fragrant, thin-leaved plant, and *hoja santa,* the large anise-scented leaves that characterize much of southern Mexico's cooking, flavor the many varieties of Chiapas' famous tamales, which are heavier and larger than most. With the introduction of European cattle, Chiapans also became expert ranchers and, as a corollary, cheese makers. Similar to neighboring Guatemala, Chiapas' cooking uses a lot of beef, either grilled or in a stew.

Lying on the Gulf Coast, Tabasco has more in common with the Caribbean flavors of Veracruz, which developed close ties to Cuba during colonial times. Fresh fish, meat, and seafood are often prepared *a la veracruzana,* in a lightly spiced blend of tomato and onion. The specialty is the fish *pejelagarto,* whose mild, nutty taste is enhanced by chile and lemon. *Camarón* (shrimp), *ostión* (oyster), and *pulpo* (octopus) are ubiquitous, delicious, and cheap.

See the food glossary (p. 240) to learn more about regional dishes.

## Drinks

Coca-Cola is nearly as entrenched in Mexico's drinking habits as tequila, having been a fixture since 1926. Pepsi is also sold in every city and town. These and other

American *refrescos* outsell Mexican brands such as Manzana, a carbonated apple juice. If you like your soft drinks cold, specify *frío,* or you may get them *clima* (room temperature).

Better yet, treat yourself to ***licuados***—refreshing smoothies of fresh fruit (or juice), milk, and ice, sold all over Mexico. ***Aguas frescas*** ("fresh waters") are lighter drinks made by adding a small amount of fresh fruit juice and sugar to water. Hibiscus, melon, tamarind, and lime are common, but rice, flowers, cactus fruit (*tuna* in Spanish), and other exotic ingredients find their way into these refreshments. In the Yucatán, the most popular of these is ***horchata,*** a drink made from rice, almonds, cinnamon, and sugar. And inexpensive, fresh-squeezed juices from every fruit you can name—and a few you can't—are one of Mexico's greatest pleasures.

**Coffee** is one of Mexico's most important exports, and Chiapas grows some of the best. Tarted-up coffee isn't Mexico's style. Your basic choices are *café Americano,* the familiar gringo-style brew; espresso and sometimes cappuccino, served in cafes; and the widely popular *café con leche,* translated as "coffee with milk" but more accurately described as milk with coffee. Potent, delicious *café de olla,* traditionally brewed in a clay pot with raw sugar and cinnamon, is harder to find but worth seeking out.

**Hot chocolate** is a traditional drink, usually made with cinnamon and often some crushed almonds. Another traditional hot drink is *atole,* made from cornmeal, milk, cinnamon, and puréed fresh fruit, often served for breakfast.

Mexican **beer** generally is light and well carbonated, all the better to tame the chile burn. Brands such as Bohemia, Corona, Dos Equis, Pacifica, Tecate, and Modelo are favorites around the world. Mérida's Cerveceria Yucateca, alas, was bought by Modelo in 1979 and closed in 2002, but its León Negra and Montejo beers are still produced in central Mexico.

**Tequila** has come a long way from its days as a stereotype of bad Westerns and frat-party shot contests. Tequila tasting is a sophisticated, and often expensive, pursuit at some of Mexico's finest restaurants and cocktail bars, as a growing coterie of connoisseurs spotlight coveted, top-quality varieties available only in Mexico. Sip and swirl these as you would with fine wine, Scotch, or Cognac.

Though tequila can be legally produced only in the state of Jalisco and specific regions of a few other states, agave spirits are produced in other states without being called tequila (just as sparkling wine is produced outside of the French region of Champagne), and some of these are every bit as fine as Jalisco's products. Mayapan Distillery in Valladolid is one of these.

### Tequila 101

Tequila is a variety of *mescal* produced from the *A. tequilana* agave species, or blue agave, in the Tequila area of Jalisco state. Its quality and popularity have soared in the past decade or so. Distillers—all but one still based in Jalisco—have formed an association to establish standards for labeling and denomination. The best tequilas are 100% agave, made with a set minimum of sugar to prime the fermentation process. Tequila comes in three categories based on how it was stored: *Blanco* is white tequila aged very little, usually in steel vats. *Reposado* (reposed) is aged in wooden casks for between 2 months and a year. The coveted *añejo* (aged) tequila is stored in oak barrels for a year or more.

## dining SERVICE TIPS

- The afternoon meal is the main meal of the day, and many restaurants offer a multicourse daily special called *comida corrida* or *menú del día.* This is the least expensive way to get a full dinner.
- In Mexico you need to ask for your check; it is considered rude to present the bill to someone who hasn't requested it. If you're in a hurry, ask for the check when your food arrives.
- Tips range from 10% to 15%. Restaurants sometimes include a service charge or *propina* (tip). You may augment that if you like, but check to be sure you're not tipping twice.
- To summon the waiter, wave or raise your hand, but don't motion with your index finger, which is a demeaning gesture. If you need your check, it's okay to summon any waiter and ask, *"La Cuenta, por favor"*—or simply catch someone's eye and pantomime a scribbling motion against the palm of your hand.

Tequila's poorer cousins, **pulque** and **mescal,** originated with *octli,* an Aztec agave drink produced strictly for feasts. Mexicans drank *pulque,* made from juice straight from the plant, for more than 5,000 years, but it has given way to more refined—and more palatable—spirits. The Spanish learned to create serious firepower by roasting the agave hearts, then extracting, fermenting, and distilling the liquids. Thus were born *mescal* and its most refined variety, tequila. *Mescal,* famous for the traditional worm at the bottom of the bottle, is more potent than *pulque* but easier to swallow. High-quality *mescal* is starting to find a place alongside tequila in bars and restaurants. *Pulque* is most commonly consumed in central Mexico's *pulquerías.* You may also see it sold in cans; those I've tried were undrinkable.

Don't overlook southern Mexico's **local spirits.** Kahlúa, the Arabica coffee-flavored liquor ubiquitous in U.S. bars, is the Yucatán's best-known product. Xtabentún, a honey-anisette liqueur, is based on the Maya's ceremonial drink, produced from a species of morning glory whose nectar fuels local honey production. It is a popular after-dinner cordial, often served in coffee. Xtabentún's best-known maker, D'Aristi of Mérida, also makes Caribe rum and the lesser-known Kalani, a coconut liqueur. Other after-dinner liqueurs are flavored with native flowers such as hibiscus *(jamaica)* or fruit such as bananas *(plátano)* and pomegranate *(granada).*

## Calendar of Events

Religious and secular festivals are a part of life in Mexico. Every town, city, and state holds its own specific festivals throughout the year commemorating religious and historic figures—sometimes it feels like the festivities never die down.

### JANUARY

**Año Nuevo (New Year's Day),** nationwide. This national holiday is perhaps the quietest day in all of Mexico. All businesses are closed, and most people stay home or attend church. In traditional indigenous communities, new tribal leaders are inaugurated with colorful ceremonies rooted in the pre-Hispanic past. January 1.

**Día de los Reyes (Three Kings' Day),** nationwide. This day commemorates the Three Kings presenting gifts to the Christ Child. On this day, children receive presents, much like they do at Christmas in the United States. Friends and families gather to share the *Rosca de Reyes,* a special cake. Inside the cake is a small doll representing the Christ Child; whoever receives the doll must host a tamales-and-*atole* (a warm drink made of *masa*) party on February 2. January 6.

FEBRUARY

**Día de la Candelaria (Candlemas),** nationwide. Music, dances, processions, food, and other festivities lead up to a blessing of seed and candles in a ceremony that mixes pre-Hispanic and European traditions marking the end of winter. Those who attended the Three Kings celebration reunite to share *atole* and tamales at a party hosted by the recipient of the doll found in the *Rosca.* February 2.

**Día de la Constitución (Constitution Day),** nationwide. This national holiday is in honor of the current Mexican constitution, signed in 1917 as a result of the revolutionary war of 1910. It's celebrated through small parades. February 5.

**Carnaval,** nationwide. Carnaval takes place the 3 days preceding Ash Wednesday and the beginning of Lent. In Cozumel, the celebration resembles New Orleans's Mardi Gras, with a festive atmosphere and parades. In Chamula, the event harks back to pre-Hispanic times, with ritualistic running on flaming branches. Cancún also celebrates with parade floats and street parties.

**Ash Wednesday,** nationwide. The start of Lent and time of abstinence, this is a day of reverence nationwide; some towns honor it with folk dancing and fairs.

MARCH

**Benito Juárez's Birthday,** nationwide. This national holiday celebrating one of Mexico's most beloved leaders is observed through small hometown celebrations, especially in Juárez's birthplace, Guelatao, Oaxaca. March 21.

**Cancún-Riviera Maya Wine & Food Festival,** throughout the region. The 4-year-old festival celebrates Mexican and Spanish cuisine with more than 20 events featuring prominent chefs, winemakers, academics, and journalists. The 2015 festival honored female chefs.

**Spring Equinox,** Chichén Itzá. On the first day of spring, the Temple of Kukulkán—Chichén Itzá's main pyramid—aligns with the sun, and the shadow of the plumed serpent moves slowly from the top of the building down. When the shadow reaches the bottom, the body joins the carved stone snake's head at the base of the pyramid. According to ancient legend, at the moment that the serpent is whole, the earth is fertilized. Visitors come from around the world to marvel at this sight, so advance arrangements are advisable. Elsewhere, equinox festivals and celebrations welcome spring, in the custom of the ancient Mexicans, with dances and prayers to the elements and the four cardinal points. It's customary to wear white with a red ribbon. March 21 (the shadow appears Mar 19–23).

APRIL

**Semana Santa (Holy Week),** nationwide. Mexico celebrates the last week in the life of Christ, from Palm Sunday to Easter Sunday, with somber religious processions, spoofing of Judas, and reenactments of biblical events, plus food and craft fairs. Some businesses close during this traditional week of Mexican national vacations, and almost all close on Maundy Thursday, Good Friday, Holy Saturday, and Easter Sunday.

If you plan to travel to Mexico during Holy Week, make your reservations early. Airline seats into Cancún in particular will be reserved months in advance. Planes and buses to towns across the Yucatán and to almost anywhere else in Mexico will be full, so try arriving on the Wednesday or Thursday before Good Friday. Easter Sunday is quiet, and the week following is a traditional vacation period. Early April.

MAY

**Labor Day,** nationwide. Workers' parades countrywide; everything closes. May 1.

**Cinco de Mayo,** nationwide. This holiday celebrates the defeat of the French at the Battle of Puebla, although it (ironically) tends to be a bigger celebration in the United States than in Mexico. May 5.

**Feast of San Isidro.** The patron saint of farmers is honored with a blessing of seeds and work animals. May 15.

**Cancún Jazz Festival.** Over Memorial Day weekend, the Parque de las Palapas, as well as the area around the Convention Center, has live performances from jazz musicians from around the world. To confirm dates and schedule information, check www.cancun.travel.

**International Gay Festival.** This 5-day event in Cancún kicks off with a welcome fiesta of food, drinks, and mariachi music. Additional festivities include a tequila party, tour of Cancún, sunset Caribbean cruise, bar and beach parties, and a final champagne breakfast. For schedule information, check www.cancun.eventguide.com.

## JUNE

**Navy Day (Día de la Marina).** All coastal towns celebrate with naval parades and fireworks. June 1.

**Corpus Christi,** nationwide. The day honors the Body of Christ (the Eucharist) with religious processions, Masses, and food. Dates vary.

**Día de San Pedro (St. Peter and St. Paul's Day),** nationwide. Celebrated wherever St. Peter is the patron saint, this holiday honors anyone named Pedro or Peter. June 26.

## AUGUST

**Assumption of the Virgin Mary,** nationwide. This is celebrated throughout the country with special Masses and in some places processions. August 15 to August 17.

## SEPTEMBER

**Independence Day,** nationwide. This day of parades, picnics, and family reunions throughout the country celebrates Mexico's independence from Spain. At 11pm on September 15, the president of Mexico gives the famous independence *grito* (shout) from the National Palace in Mexico City, and local mayors do the same in every town and municipality all over Mexico. On September 16, every city and town conducts a parade in which both government officials and civilians display their pride in being Mexican. For these celebrations, all important government buildings are draped in the national colors—red, green, and white—and the towns blaze with decorative lights. September 15 and 16; September 16 is a national holiday.

**Fall Equinox,** Chichén Itzá. The same shadow play that occurs during the spring equinox repeats at the fall equinox. September 21 to September 22.

## OCTOBER

**"Ethnicity Day" or Columbus Day (Día de la Raza),** nationwide. This commemorates the fusion of the Spanish and Mexican peoples. October 12.

## NOVEMBER

**Day of the Dead (Día de los Muertos),** nationwide. What's commonly called the Day of the Dead is actually 2 days: All Saints' Day, honoring saints and deceased children, and All Souls' Day, honoring deceased adults. Relatives gather at cemeteries countrywide, carrying candles and food to create an altar, and sometimes spend the night beside the graves of loved ones. Weeks before, bakers begin producing bread (called *pan de muerto*) formed in the shape of mummies or round loaves decorated with bread "bones." Decorated sugar skulls emblazoned with glittery names are sold everywhere. Many days ahead, homes and churches erect special altars laden with Day of the Dead bread, fruit, flowers, candles, favorite foods, and photographs of saints and of the deceased. On the 2 nights, children dress in costumes and masks, often carrying through the streets mock coffins and pumpkin lanterns, into which they expect money to be dropped. November 1 and 2; November 1 is a national holiday.

**Annual Yucatán Bird Festival (Festival de las Aves de Yucatán),** Mérida, Yucatán. Bird-watching sessions, workshops, and exhibits are the highlights of this festival, designed to illustrate the special role birds play in our environment and in the Yucatán territory. Check out www.festivalavesyucatan.com for details. Mid-November.

**Revolution Day,** nationwide. This commemorates the start of the Mexican Revolution in 1910 with parades, speeches, rodeos, and patriotic events. November 20.

DECEMBER

**Feast of the Virgin of Guadalupe,** nationwide. Throughout the country, religious processions, street fairs, dancing, fireworks, and Masses honor the patroness of Mexico. This is one of Mexico's most moving and beautiful displays of traditional culture. The Virgin of Guadalupe appeared to a young man, Juan Diego, in December 1531, on a hill near Mexico City. He convinced the bishop that he had seen the apparition by revealing his cloak, upon which the Virgin was emblazoned. It's customary for children to dress up as Juan Diego, wearing mustaches and red bandanas. One of the most famous and elaborate celebrations takes place at the Basílica of Guadalupe, north of Mexico City, where the Virgin appeared. Every village celebrates this day, though, often with processions of children carrying banners of the Virgin and with *charreadas* (rodeos), bicycle races, dancing, and fireworks. December 12.

**Festival of San Cristóbal de las Casas,** San Cristóbal de las Casas, Chiapas. This 10-day festival includes a procession by the Tzotzil and Tzetzal Indians, *marimba* music, and a parade of horses. December 12 to December 21.

**Christmas Posadas,** nationwide. On each of the 9 nights before Christmas, it's customary to reenact the Holy Family's search for an inn, with door-to-door candlelit processions in cities and villages nationwide. These are also hosted by most businesses and community organizations, taking the place of the northern tradition of a Christmas party. December 15 to December 24.

**Christmas.** Mexicans extend this celebration and often leave their jobs beginning 2 weeks before Christmas all the way through New Year's Day. Many businesses close, and resorts and hotels fill up. Significant celebrations take place on December 24.

**New Year's Eve.** As in the rest of the world, New Year's Eve in Mexico is celebrated with parties, fireworks, and plenty of noise. December 31.

# WILDLIFE WONDERLAND

Mexico's Caribbean coast is entirely in the state of **Quintana Roo,** the easternmost of three states that make up the Yucatán Peninsula. This peninsula is truly a freak of nature—a flat, nearly 134,400-sq.-km (51,900-sq.-mile) slab of limestone with almost 1,600km (1,000 miles) of shoreline that is virtually devoid of surface water. The peninsula's geology, found nowhere else on Earth, was shaped by the same meteor thought to have extinguished the dinosaurs 65 million years ago. The impact fractured the brittle limestone into an immense network of fissures that drain all rainwater down below the surface. You'll see no rivers, lakes, or streams in the northern and central Yucatán, but fresh rainwater courses through a vast underground river system stretching for hundreds of miles.

Breaches in the ceiling of this subterranean basin have created an estimated 3,000 *cenotes*—sinkholes that reveal the underground to the world above. The Maya called them *dzonots,* or sacred wells, and regarded them as gateways to the underworld. Precious stones, ceramics, and bones unearthed in *cenotes* suggest that they were ancient ceremonial sites.

Quiet, dark, and cool, *cenotes* offer respite from the bright, often steamy glare above. Some are underground, with only a small breach in a roof perforated by thirsty tree roots. Others open to the surface like a lake. Most tourists get their introduction to this subterranean world at **Chichén Itzá,** with its **Cenote Sagrada** (Sacred Cenote),

## THE YUCATÁN'S strangest ANIMALS

**MEXICAN CAECILIAN** (Dermophis mexicanus), also called *culebra de dos cabezas* "two-headed snake." This perfectly respectable (if primitive) amphibian looks startlingly like a 2-foot-long earthworm, with a gray or purplish body ringed by creases and a slightly flattened head barely distinguishable from its tail. Like earthworms, caecilians spend most of the day underground. Unlike worms, they have tiny retractable tentacles and give birth to live young.

**STRIPED BASILISK** (Basiliscus vittatus), or *lagartija jesucristo,* "Jesus Christ lizard." Yellow racing stripes along its brown body distinguish this nimble lizard from its larger, more lethargic cousin, the common green iguana. With a slimmer body and longer legs, its agility extends to running across the surface of water on its hind legs, earning it the biblical nickname. About 32 inches long, it lives on the ground, sometimes climbing trees, and likes to stay close to a body of water.

**VIOLACEOUS TROGON** (Trogon violaceus), or *trogón violáceo* in Spanish. This cousin to the quetzal of Maya legend has a larger population and more widespread habitat than its rapidly vanishing kin, boosting the chances of spotting one in deep-forest tree canopies. Lacking the quetzal's extravagant tail streamers, it is still showy, with a dark violet-blue head, gold breast, green back, and black-and-white striped tail.

**ROSEATE SPOONBILL** (Ajaia ajaja), or *espátula rosada* ("pink spatula") in Spanish. Looking like a duck trying to impersonate a flamingo, it is a bit smaller, with a white neck and head encumbered by a comically elongated, spoon-shaped bill. It is found primarily in marshy areas in the Yucatán, often hanging out in the flamingo colonies.

and **Hidden Worlds Cenotes Park,** with underground caverns and waterways north of Tulum. But thousands more *cenotes* lie at the ends of narrow dirt roads throughout the peninsula, the greatest concentration being inland from the Playa del Carmen–Tulum corridor. The largest is **Cenote Azul,** at the end of **Laguna de Bacalar** in southern Quintana Roo.

The thin layer of soil coating the Yucatán's limestone shelf supports a nearly uniform terrain of dense, scrubby jungle full of wild ginger and orchids, monkeys, and tropical birds. These are a fraction of southern Mexico's astounding diversity of wildlife. North America's only flamingo nesting and breeding grounds flank the northern Yucatán's **Gulf Coast,** and whale sharks convene off the peninsula's northeastern tip. Spider and howler monkeys, coatimundi, and hundreds of bird species might pop up as you roam ancient Maya cities or hike through mangrove thickets. Though seen less often, ocelots, margays, and other smaller wildcats roam the region's tropical forests. Crocodiles, sea turtles, and hundreds of bird species abound throughout the region. Reclusive and increasingly rare jaguars, revered by the ancient Maya, still prowl the **Sian Ka'an Biosphere Reserve** south of the Riviera Maya, in the sparsely populated reaches of the **Costa Maya,** and in the **Calakmul Biosphere Reserve** just to the west.

And those are just the animals you might have heard of. This region has numerous strange and marvelous creatures, the likes of which you might never have seen before. (See "The Yucatán's Strangest Animals," above.)

**JAGUARUNDI** (Herpailurus yaguarondi), called *leoncillo* ("little lion") in Spanish. Just over 2 feet long, excluding the tail, this reddish- or grayish-brown cat looks rather like a small puma with a flattened head, though its short legs and elongated body give it a weasel- or otter-like silhouette. Favoring dense tropical vegetation, jaguarundis hunt near water and are expert fishers. Your best chances for an encounter are in the Calakmul and Sian Ka'an biosphere reserves.

**PACA** (Agouti paca), also called *tepezcuintle* or *tuza real* ("royal tuza") in Spanish. Though smaller than a capybara, the world's largest rodent, the 2.5-foot-long paca is Mexico's rodent king, burrowing in rain forests, mangroves, and even in tree thickets in public parks. It's cute, with a squirrel-like head, delicate feet, and fawn-like speckled fur, but its fondness for yams, cassava (tapioca), and other food crops bedevil farmers.

**TAYRA** (Eira barbara), in Spanish, *cabeza de viejo* ("old man's head"). This weasel and otter kin looks like a yellowish dog's head grafted onto a mink's body with soft, dense fur. Reaching about 28 inches plus a luxurious tail, this tree-climber has adapted to the human population, popping up in gardens and orchards as well as its natural tropical forest habitat.

**KINKAJOU** (Potos flavus), called *micoleón* ("lion monkey") or *mico de noche* ("night monkey"), can easily be mistaken for a reddish-brown monkey when seen hanging from a tree by its long, prehensile tail, but it is actually related to the raccoon, the coatimundi, and the ring-tailed cat. Feeding primarily on fruit and flowers, it has a narrow, 5-inch tongue that helps it scoop pulp from fruit and lick nectar.



# RESPONSIBLE TRAVEL

Mexico's ecological diversity is among the broadest of any country in the world, with an abundance of ecosystems ranging from the northern deserts to the central conifer forests and the southern tropical rainforests. Mexico also supports more than 122 million people and welcomes more than 20 million visitors—14 million from foreign countries—each year. Tourism is one of the country's biggest and most lucrative industries, and while tourism has brought jobs and growth to much of Mexico, it has also created and accelerated ecological problems. **Cancún** might be the highest-profile example: Rapidly developed from a rural outpost to an international resort destination, Cancún imported turf from Florida for its golf courses, inadvertently introducing a disease that wiped out the local coconut palms. The region's mangroves, a key habitat for native species and vital to protecting the land from hurricanes and erosion, have also suffered.

However, tourism has also encouraged development of ecological conservation. Mexico is home to seven of the world's eight species of sea turtle, and the entire turtle population was decimated on both coasts as a result of tourism growth and local overfishing. A recent success story comes from the **Riviera Maya,** where marine biologists are working with hotels to guard nesting turtles and their eggs. Ecologically sensitive developments like **Mayakobá** have planted new mangroves that host more bird species

### Biodegradable Sunscreen

Recent scientific studies have shown that chemicals in commercial sunscreen can do long-term damage to coral reefs, collect in freshwater, and even build up in your body. The Riviera Maya receives more than 2.5 million visitors every year, many of them drawn to its rare marine environment—a unique combination of freshwater *cenotes* and the world's second-largest coral reef. A few ounces of sunscreen multiplied by 2.5 million equals a substantial amount of harmful chemicals in the ocean and freshwater. That's why tours to the **Sian Ka'an Biosphere Reserve** and water parks **Xcaret** and **Xel-Ha** ask that you use only biodegradable sunscreen or wear none at all when swimming in their ocean or *cenotes.*

The label of a biodegradable sunscreen should state that it is 100% biodegradable (and only 100% will do). You can buy it at the parks, but you'll get a better price at local markets. Tropical Sands, Badger, and Caribbean Solutions are good brands readily available at U.S. outlets such as Whole Foods, Amazon.com, and Drugstore.com. There are others. If the label doesn't say "biodegradable," it won't be allowed.

than were there before it was built. Community-based tourism companies such as **Alltournative,** based in Playa del Carmen, have helped struggling farm families divert at least part of their livelihood from agricultural practices that deplete the land to carefully managed, sustainable tourism.

Mexicans are proud of their land and culture, and through your travels, especially in rural areas, you will likely encounter ***ejidos*** and ***cooperativos,*** local cooperatives that offer small-scale tourism services. This may be as simple as taking visitors on a boat ride through a lagoon or as visible as controlling access to archaeological ruins. *Ejidos* will also run tours to popular ecotourism destinations similar to those offered by large travel agencies. When you travel with *ejidos,* everyone you encounter will be from the community, and you know that your money goes directly back to them. Quintana Roo, Yucatán, and Chiapas states have particularly strong cooperative networks.

The Mexican Caribbean supports the Great Mesoamerican Barrier Reef, the second-largest reef in the world, which extends down to Honduras. This reef and other marine ecosystems face increasing pressure from sedimentation, pollution, overfishing, and exploitative recreational activities, all newly associated with growing regional tourism. The **Coral Reef Alliance** (CORAL; www.coral.org) is an example of an organization that, by teaming up with the **World Wildlife Fund** (WWF; www.worldwildlife.org) and **United Nations Environmental Program** (UNEP; www.unep.org), has been working to address threats to the Mesoamerican Barrier Reef and improve environmental sustainability throughout the region. CORAL partners with Mexican Amigos de Sian Ka'an, Conservation International, and the Cozumel Reefs National Park in an effort to build sustainability into mass tourism (such as cruise ships and resorts). CORAL assists marine tourism operators in implementing a voluntary code of conduct for best environmental practices.

One of the best contributions a diver can make to support a healthy reef is to avoid physical contact with the reef during a dive. Talk to your scuba outfitter about proper buoyancy control and body position to avoid damaging these fragile ecosystems.

## Animal-Rights Issues

The Yucatán presents many opportunities to **swim with dolphins** and **whale sharks.** Although laws and regulations are in place to protect these animals (you can read more about these in the destination chapters), not all boat operators adhere to the rules. And even if every one did, questions remain about whether the very fact of captivity—keeping them confined and restricting their social and physical activities—is a form of abuse for dolphins. Tourists visit the whale sharks in their natural environment, so confinement is not the issue. Over the past several years, however, they have shifted substantially to the east of their original spot off the coast of Isla Holbox, raising the question of whether they are just following the food supply (and if so, has the influx of human intruders affected the micro-organisms they feed on?). Or are the sharks trying to find someplace to eat in peace? No definitive answer has emerged, but it's something to keep in mind. Respecting the animals' needs for a normal, healthy life goes beyond obeying the regulations yourself. At the very least, question any potential tour operator to be sure they follow the rules and are committed to the animals' welfare, and speak up if you see anyone harassing the animals. And give serious thought to whether you want to participate in the system that robs these animals of their natural lives.

For more information, see websites of the **Whale and Dolphin Conservation Society** (http://us.whales.org), the **American Cetacean Society** (www.acsonline.org), and the **Humane Society of the United States** (www.humanesociety.org).

**Bullfighting,** inherited from Spain, is a long-held tradition in Latin culture. Before you attend a *correo,* you should know that the bulls (at least four) will ultimately be killed in a drawn-out gore fest. Some argue that bullfights are an important portal into understanding Mexico's Spanish colonial past, but the fact is they have become more of a tourist attraction than a local pastime, especially in tourist-laden Cancún. In many cases, all that keeps them going is the attendance of tourists. To read more about the implications of attending a bullfight, visit **Friends of Animals** (www.friendsofanimals.org) or **People for the Ethical Treatment of Animals** (PETA; www.peta.org).

# ORGANIZED TOURS

## Academic Trips & Language Classes

For Spanish-language instruction, **IMAC** (www.spanish-school.com.mx; ✆ **866/306-5040**) offers programs in Playa del Carmen and other Mexican destinations. The **Spanish Institute** is affiliated with intensive Spanish language schools in Puebla (http://sipuebla.com; ✆ **800/554-2951**) and Mérida (www.simerida.com; ✆ **281/071-8157** in the U.S.). **123 Teach Me** (www.123teachme.com) can set you up with schools in Mérida or Playa del Carmen. **GoAbroad.com** (www.goabroad.com; ✆ **720/570-1702**) offers numerous programs in Playa del Carmen and other Yucatán locations.

**ATC Tours and Travel** (www.atctours.com; ✆ **967/678-2550,** -2557), a Mexico-based tour operator with an excellent reputation, offers specialist-led trips, primarily in southern Mexico. In addition to trips to the ruins of Palenque and Yaxchilán (extending into Belize and Guatemala by river, plane, and bus if desired), ATC runs horseback tours; day trips to ruins; birding in the rainforests of Chiapas and Guatemala; and hikes that sometimes include camping and canoeing. The company can also prepare custom itineraries.

## Adventure Trips & Eco-Tours

**Mexico Sagaz** (Asociación Mexicana de Turismo de Aventura y Ecoturismo; www.amtave.org; ✆ **800/654-4452** toll-free in Mexico or 55/5544-7567) is an association of ecotourism and adventure tour operators. It maintains a database of participating firms and their offerings, all of which must meet certain criteria for security, quality, and training of the guides, as well as for sustainability of natural and cultural environments.

**The California Native** (www.calnative.com; ✆ **800/926-1140** or 310/642-1140), offers small-group deluxe escorted tours of varying lengths through the Riviera Maya, the Yucatán, and Chiapas.

**Trek America** (www.trekamerica.com; ✆ **800/873-5872** in the U.S.; 0333/999-7951 in the U.K.), organizes a variety of active trips, some more than a month long and taking in several countries, that combine trekking, hiking, van transportation, and camping along the Maya Route and across the Yucatán.

The **Mesoamerican Ecotourism Alliance** (www.travelwithmea.org; ✆ **800/682-0584** in the U.S.) offers award-winning ecotours to the Yucatán, Chiapas, and Central America recognized by National Geographic. ***Note:*** For 2015, the company is focusing exclusively on Nicaragua.

**Maya Sites Travel Services** (www.mayasites.com; ✆ **877/620-8715**) is staffed with archaeologists and other experts to lead inexpensive tours of Maya lands in eastern Mexico, Guatemala, Belize, and Honduras. The focus is on archaeological sites, but special tours such as one exploring Carnival festivals in the region are also available.

## Food & Wine Trips

If you plan on eating your way through Mexico, sign up with **Culinary Adventures** (www.culinaryadventuresinc.com; ✆ **253/851-7676**). It runs a short but select list of cooking tours in Mexico. Culinary Adventures features well-known cooks such as Diana Kennedy and Rick Bayless, with travel to regions known for excellent cuisine. Destinations vary each year, though often include the Yucatán. The owner, Marilyn Tausend, is the author of *Cocinas de la Familia* (Family Kitchens), *Savoring Mexico,* and *Mexican,* and co-author of *Mexico the Beautiful Cookbook.*

# SUGGESTED ITINERARIES

3

by Christine Delsol & Maribeth Mellin

These itineraries assume you're flying in and out of Cancún, the most common, and least expensive, entry point for the Caribbean coast. Rental cars work well for travel in this area. The roads are straight, flat, and generally easy to figure out; most have been revamped in recent years with wide shoulders that make passing easier and safer. There's little traffic in most of the region, with Cancún and often the Riviera Maya being notable exceptions.

Although a less ambitious version of these itineraries by bus would be possible, buses won't take you down the narrow roads from the highway to the beaches; you'll need to flag a taxi at the highway or face a long, hot walk. It's a pretty good money-saving strategy for footloose travelers, but it is time-consuming—and it doesn't allow for stopping on a whim, which often leads to the best travel experiences.

Think of these itineraries as a starting point that you can adapt to your liking; see "The Caribbean Coast's Regions in Brief" (p. 61) and individual destination chapters for ideas. The 14-day highlights itinerary keeps you on the move but allows for some down time and avoids marathon drives. Still, you might want to skip a couple of stops and spend more time in other destinations. Be sure to check the full descriptions referenced in the itineraries to see if you need to make any reservations in advance.

Don't pack too much into a day, especially during the heat and humidity of summer and early fall. Also, keep in mind that the Yucatán Peninsula's proximity to the equator means short days year round. There's not much difference between the earliest winter sunset (6pm) and the latest in summer (7:30pm)—Quintana Roo's 2015 shift from Central to Eastern time gives you an extra hour of light at the end of the day. You really don't want to drive at night if you can avoid it, especially when trying to find a place for the first time.

## HIGHLIGHTS OF CANCÚN & THE CARIBBEAN COAST IN 2 WEEKS

This itinerary includes destinations up and down the coast, along with a sampling of the Yucatán's interior. While you're in the Riviera Maya, you can stay in one place anywhere from Playa del Carmen to Tulum and take day trips, or move your base as you travel south. Our aim was to keep down time and activities more or less in balance; adjust as necessary if you'd like more or less of either.

## Days 1 & 2: Cancún ★★

Relax in your hotel, go for a swim, then take a taxi to dinner in a waterfront restaurant. Cap the evening with some of Cancún's famous nightlife; it can be as sedate as cocktails at the Ritz-Carlton's **Lobby Lounge** (p. 99) or as over-the-top as **CoCo Bongo**'s (p. 98) wildly inventive shows. The next morning, visit the **Museo Maya de Cancún** (p. 87), where you'll learn about local Maya history and visit the adjacent **San Miguelito** ruins. In the afternoon, snorkel or dive the **Cancún Underwater Museum** (**Museo Subacuático de Arte [MUSA],** p. 89) in the waters between Cancún and Isla Mujeres. Spend a leisurely evening at **La Isla Shopping Village** (p. 97), dining in one of its fine restaurants, maybe catching a movie, or just strolling along the lagoon. And yes, you can even go shopping, if you are so moved.

## Day 3: Isla Mujeres ★★

The 15-minute **ferry ride** (p. 124) from Cancún to **Isla Mujeres** takes you to one of my favorite hideaways. Life moves at the slow pace of sandy flip-flops here, and most folks get around the island in pokey golf carts. Walk from the pier to **Playa Norte** for a lazy day on one of the most beautiful swimming beaches anywhere, and then explore the little town's **Avenida Hidalgo** for shopping bargains and a delicious meal. See chapter 5 (p. 135).

### Rooster ☕ ★★

As you head east on Hidalgo, escape the sun in the cool green interior at **Rooster** (p. 13). If you're ravenous, try the divine lobster Benedict (breakfast is served all day) or a brisket burger. Want just a snack? Go for the tangy tequila and lime chicken wings. Sit at an outdoor sidewalk table if the heat doesn't get you down and watch shoppers strolling languidly along the avenue.

## Day 4: Valladolid ★★★

This small, informal colonial city is a 2-hour drive and a world away from Cancún. Relax on a shady bench in the **Main Plaza** (p. 111) and walk to **Cenote Zací** (p. 112), a couple of blocks away—bring a suit and towel if you're inspired to take the plunge. Drive to the **Mayapán Distillery** (p. 113) on the edge of town to observe the tequila production process—from growing and harvesting the agave to fermenting and distilling the liquid—and sample the end results. Around sunset, walk from the plaza down beautifully restored **Calzada de los Frailes** (p. 113) to the 16th-century **San Bernardino monastery** (p. 111) before retiring to your hotel.

### Taberna de los Frailes ☕ ★★★

A fusion of traditional Maya cooking and colonial recipes contributes to unique gourmet treatment of seafood, pork, and meat at this exceptional restaurant (p. 111) with a cenote on the grounds and a view to the monastery. For something different from what you've had on the coast, try Pavo en Relleno Negro or Pipían de Pollo.

# Highlights of Cancún & the Caribbean Coast in 2 Weeks

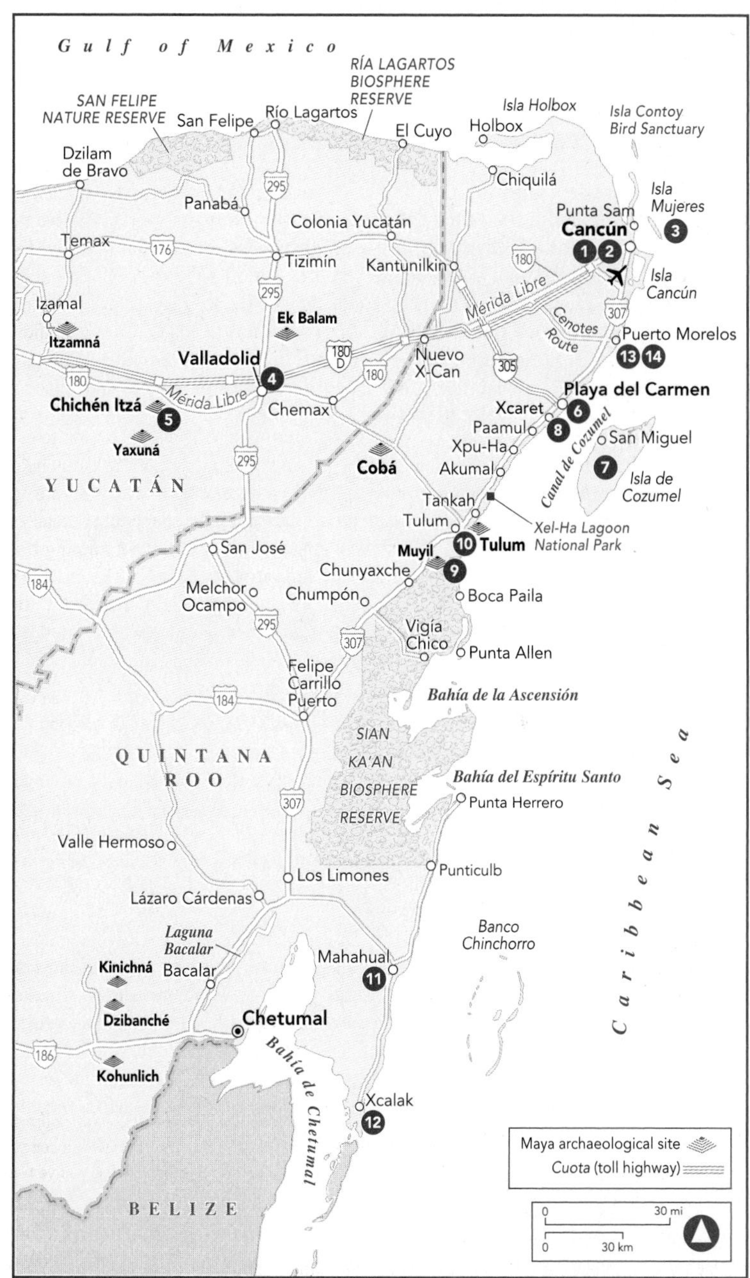

## Day 5: Chichén Itzá ★★

Get to the remarkable ruins of **Chichén Itzá** (p. 100) when they open. When the midday heat gets oppressive, head to the large, stunning **Cenote Ik-Kil** (p. 108) down the road to swim and relax for a few hours. Grab a bite there, or have a real dinner at the beautiful **Hacienda Chichén Resort** (p. 102) before returning to the ruins for the **Light and Sound Show,** brand new in 2014. ***Alternative:*** If you've seen Chichén Itzá before, visit **Ek Balam** (p. 114), north of Valladolid, and fill out the day exploring the city; you could also continue from Ek Balam to see the flamingos at **Ría Lagartos** (p. 116) and get back to Valladolid in time for dinner.



## Day 6: Playa del Carmen ★★

A brand-new toll road puts you less than 90 minutes' drive from "Playa," the preferred destination for youthful, hip visitors, with its vibrant beach-chic feel. Put on your tiniest swimsuit for people-watching on the long beaches dotted with casually sophisticated cafes and bars. After you've baked in the sun sufficiently, rinse off and head for **Quinta Avenida** (aka Fifth Avenue), the heart of Playa's shopping, dining, and nightlife action. Day-trippers pack the avenue and adjacent streets in daytime, while locals and visitors stroll more casually from classy restaurants to fun bars and clubs at night. See p. 170.

## Day 7: Cozumel ★★★

Hop on the jet ferry from Playa del Carmen to **Cozumel** and immerse yourself in the fish-filled waters around the island's many reefs. Combined, these coral stretches make up one part of the Great Mesoamerican Reef, the world's second-longest barrier reef. Snorkel and dive operators await potential customers at the ferry pier—if you're a serious diver, arrange your trip in advance with a reputable dive shop (p. 153). Back on dry land, rest a while at the main plaza, a block inland from the pier. Linger over a long lunch and explore shops along the side streets before returning to the mainland.

### Pancho's Backyard ☕ ★★★

With its marimba musicians, colorful tableware, and lush courtyard, **Pancho's Backyard** (p. 149) meets all the criteria for a fun Mexican restaurant. The menu features plentiful entrees, including fish tacos and chicken fajitas, along with perfectly mixed margaritas. Afterward, step inside and fulfill all souvenir needs at Los Cinco Soles, Cozumel's best folk art shop.

## Day 8: Xcaret ★★

An all-in-one attraction combining culture, nature, and adventure, **Xcaret** is worth a full day and evening visit. Begin your visit amid butterflies, tropical birds, turtles, and flamingoes in exhibits around the park, then float in an underground river ride or snorkel at a crystalline cove. Delve into culture by visiting the Maya village, folk art museum, Mexican cemetery, and Yucatecan hacienda. If you're feeling weary, snag a hammock on the beach for a siesta, and be sure to linger for the excellent nightly folkloric show. See p. 184.

## Day 9: Sian Ka'an Biosphere Reserve ★★★

This precious stretch of Caribbean coast is a natural wonder covering a great swath of coastline, mangroves, lagoons, and canals constructed by the Maya in centuries past. In the Maya language, **Sian Ka'an** (p. 205) means "where the sky is born," an apt description of the reserve's breathtaking beauty. **Community Tours Sian Ka'an** (p. 206) leads small groups on hikes through the jungle to a seemingly endless lagoon, where visitors board small boats and glide over glassy water to a long canal. After donning lifejackets, they float with the current in chilly freshwater past mangroves and wild orchids. The tour ends with lunch in a nearby Maya village, where locals describe their way of life.

## Day 10: Tulum ★★★

One of Mexico's most alluring Caribbean towns, **Tulum** (p. 193) is blessed with gorgeous beaches and one of the coast's most famous archaeological sites. Visit the **Tulum ruins** (p. 200) the minute they open at 8am to avoid overwhelming crowds, and consider taking a dip in the clear cove beneath the ancient **Castillo.** Plan to spend a night at a beach hotel here—the white sand beaches, crystalline water, and sea breezes are downright idyllic.

### El Camello ★★

For the freshest seafood, join the crowds at modest **El Camello** (p. 198) beside the highway in Tulum town. Fishermen bring their catch to the adjacent fish market, where it's cleaned and delivered to the kitchen. The skilled cooks prepare superb ceviche and seafood cocktails that taste like the sea, along with whole fried fish, octopus sautéed with chilies, and other local specialties. Don't be deterred if there's a line by the door, because tables open frequently and the food is well worth the wait.

## Day 11: Mahahual ★★

After a long drive, check into one of **Mahahual**'s inns (p. 212) along the beach road north or south of town and just kick back to savor the long, pristine swath of white sand, rhythmic sounds of nature, and blessed absence of crowds. If you're ambitious, do a little snorkeling off your hotel's beach. Have a leisurely dinner, then settle in for the best night's sleep of your life.

## Day 12: Xcalak & Mahahual ★★★

In the morning, visit **Xcalak** (p. 214), Mexico's last settlement before the Belize border. Take a diving or snorkeling excursion with **XTC** (p. 215) or **Costa de Cocos** (p. 215) dive centers for one of the best underwater shows on the Caribbean coast—this is your best chance to spot manatees and giant rays. Back in Mahahual, stroll the *malecón* and explore the shops and restaurants along **Yaya Beach** (p. 212). Before you call it a day, stop in at **Fernando's 100% Agave** (p. 214) for one of the tequila master's cocktails.

## Day 13 & 14: Puerto Morelos ★★★

After the long drive up the coast, ease in to Puerto Morelos's languid pace with a walk around the **central plaza** (p. 165) and along the neighboring seafront walk to the pier, with its landmark tipsy lighthouse. Have dinner at one of the many and various **restaurants** (p. 162) on and around the plaza before you turn in.

### La Buena Vida ★

On the way to Puerto Morelos, escape from the car in Akumal and dig your toes in the sand at **La Buena Vida** (p. 189) on beautiful Half Moon Bay. The menu covers the gamut from tacos and burritos to coconut shrimp and baby back ribs. A convivial group of neighborhood expats and frequent vacationers gather here day and night. Hang around long enough and you just might decide to spend the night—or a month—in a condo by the bay.

In the morning, get one last dose of the Caribbean with a swim at **Ojo de Agua** (p. 166) or a **snorkeling tour** (p. 165) in the north coast's most pristine waters. Amble down to the **Hunab Kú** market (p. 167) for top-notch handicrafts created and sold in a garden setting. An authentic Maya massage from the ladies at the **Jungle Spa** (p. 167) will help to preserve the sense of well-being for your trip home.

# A ROMANTIC CANCÚN WEEKEND

Whether you're sneaking away from an East Coast winter or fitting a few days of away-from-it-all bonding time into a longer trip, Cancún excels at romance for couples of all ages, interests, and sexual orientations. Languid mornings are a given, but when you emerge from your cocoon, there's plenty to do that will preserve the glow.

## Friday: Lazing on the Beach & a Dinner Cruise

First, the detox: Loll on a *palapa*-shaded day bed on the beach while a waiter delivers frosty drinks, play tag with the waves, and just talk together without a dozen other things on your mind. After a soak in your whirlpool for two, get ready for the **Columbus Lobster Dinner Cruise** (p. 85) on Nichupté Lagoon, either at sunset or in the moonlight. You'll sail the calm waters in a replica Spanish galleon while dining on fresh lobster or dry-aged steak, and snuggle as the Hotel Zone's sparkling lights float by to the mellow strains of a saxophone.

## Saturday: Fancy Fish, Culinary Creativity & Dinner on the Water

Slip away to **Puerto Morelos** (p. 161), where a pristine stretch of the **Great Mesoamerican Reef** rises to within a few feet of the surface just offshore so you can easily plunge into a kaleidoscope of swirling, brilliant fish. Afterward, learn all about modern Mexican cuisine at the **Little Mexican Cooking School** (p. 167) and take home some new skills and ideas for your next duo performance in the kitchen. Back in Cancún, head to **La Isla Shopping Village** (p. 97) in the evening for dinner at **Thai** (p. 82) in a private, lantern-lit cabaña set on stilts in the water, listening to the lagoon's gentle waves lapping below. Later, linger in the bar, watching dolphins frolic behind the glass wall shared with the adjacent aquarium, catch a movie, or just stroll along the lagoon in view of lights across the water.

## Sunday: A Dolphin Beach, Ruins & the Ritz

Hit **Playa Delfines** (p. 90) early in the morning and try to spot some of the wild dolphins that give Cancún's longest, widest beach its name; this is the only Hotel Zone beach that isn't hemmed in by mega-resorts. Then cross Bulevar Kukulcán to **Ruinas El Rey** (p. 89), a remnant of a Maya city whose tranquility allows an ancient presence to emerge from crumbling columns and stepped platforms. Close out your last day at the inimitable **Ritz-Carlton** (p. 74), starting with the ultimate in togetherness—a couples massage with aromatic oils at the **Kayantá Spa.** Stop by the serene **Lobby Lounge** (p. 99) for extraordinary cocktails before sitting down to dinner at **Casitas.** Your private beach cabaña is swaddled in mosquito netting, lit by candles and the moon, and serenaded by the whoosh of the waves as you say goodbye to Cancún.

# BEST OF COZUMEL IN 4 DAYS

If your perfect vacation includes superb diving and snorkeling in warm, clear water, great meals in casual cafes, and leisurely sightseeing in a traditional Mexican community, head for the blissful island of Cozumel. Stay at least 4 days so there's time for complete relaxation, or join the many return visitors spending weeks and even months on Mexico's idyllic island. Hit the water early in the day and choose from these possibilities for the afternoons and evenings—but be sure to fit in at least one nighttime session on the reefs.

## Day 1: San Miguel ★★★

You'll return again and again to Cozumel's main town, so it's worth taking a familiarization tour. Keep one caution in mind—if you see cruise ships looming over the waterfront, wait until they sail toward the horizon before getting to know **San Miguel** (p. 140). Evenings are best for strolling along the waterfront *malecón* past fishing skiffs, ferries, and young boys splashing and swimming by the pier. On weekends, don't miss the plaza, where grandmothers, teens, and toddlers gather to gossip, flirt, and chase balloons. Watch the action while sampling a cup of sliced mangoes or a papaya carved like a flower from the longtime vendor at the plaza's northwest corner.

### Guido's ★★★

Frequent Cozumel visitors gravitate to the vine-draped courtyard at **Guido's** (p. 147) like parrot fish munching on coral reefs. Dinner's my favorite meal, and I tend to choose Chef Yvonne Villiger's take on the catch of the day. The pastas and pizzas are superb as well, but it's the ambience that makes this venerable yet modern restaurant an enduring favorite. Settle back with a glass of wine, a fine meal, and your companions and ponder your vacation possibilities.

## Day 2: The Wild Side

Rent a car and drive along Cozumel's wild **windward coast** (p. 140), starting at Punta Sur on the southern tip. Stop at one of the stands along the road for coconut milk straight from the shell and souvenir shopping—hammocks are especially enticing when displayed swaying beneath palms on the beach. If families are playing at **Playa Chen Rio** (p. 154), it means the water's calm enough for swimming; if not, it's still a pretty spot for beachcombing and lingering over a whole-fried-fish lunch on the sand. Stick around for the sunset, and then head back to town before the sun completely disappears, as there are no streetlights on this side of the island, and it gets mighty dark at night.

## Day 3: Museum & Ruins ★

Far from stuffy and boring, the exhibits at the **Museo de la Isla de Cozumel** (p. 151) enhance your island adventures. Study the large relief map in the ground floor hall to get a sense of how much of the island has been protected in its natural state, with just a few ranches and ruins dotting the jungle. Experience that sense of wilderness while driving to **San Gervasio** (p. 151), the island's largest archaeological site, buried in dense low jungle. While exploring the structures, keep an eye out for photogenic giant iguanas sunning atop temples.

La Perlita ★★

San Gervasio is located in the island's interior, near busy local neighborhoods. Stop for a leisurely lunch at **La Perlita** (p. 149), where fishermen deliver the catch of the day and cooks prepare yummy seafood dishes, along with great guacamole and chips. Lionfish, a dreaded species that has invaded the reefs, is served grilled or covered with crisp coconut. All the food is prepared with purified water, a detail that attracts tourists as well as locals.

### Day 4: Chankanaab & Punta Sur Parks ★★

One of Mexico's oldest protected areas, **Chankanaab** (p. 151) is a great all-in-one park. The snorkeling and diving right off shore are superb, and underwater sights include caves and statues along with swarms of parrotfish. Don't miss the Maya house in the botanical garden, where ladies in traditional dress sometimes hand out freshly made tortillas. You could visit both Chankanaab and **Punta Sur** (p. 151), at the island's southern tip, though I'd advise whiling away leisurely hours at one or the other. Crocodiles lurk in dark lagoons at Punta Sur, which has a more natural, undisturbed feel. A lighthouse and small museum are the only attractions, other than miles of pristine, secluded white-sand beaches where sea turtles lay their eggs in summer.

## AN INTRODUCTION TO THE MAYA WORLD

The Yucatán's most important Maya archaeological sites lie in the peninsula's interior. This itinerary touches on a few of those but also covers lesser-known coastal sites—smaller and therefore easier to digest, and distinctive in their own right—and takes you into the world of today's Maya.

### Day 1: Cancún ★★

The small but beautifully put together **Museo Maya de Cancún** (p. 87), whose opening coincided with the 2012 end-of-days "prophecy," is an informative and very pleasant way to spend a few hours. You'll be surprised by how many traces of ancient Maya settlements survive in the coastal state of Quintana Roo. The museum incorporated adjacent **San Miguelito,** a small, previously inaccessible archaeological site, so you can experience some of what the museum conveys. Consider visiting **Ruinas El Rey** (p. 89), a peaceful oasis whose location next to a golf resort presents a thought-provoking juxtaposition of past and present.

### Day 2: Valladolid ★★★

Past and present are also intertwined in **Valladolid** (p. 108), a small colonial city full of handsome restored buildings. Contemporary Maya from nearby villages sell crafts and folk art around the **central plaza** (p. 111) or work in construction and celebrate finished projects by slow-cooking a cow's head in the ground for a feast of *tacos de cabeza.* Make the short trip north to **Ek Balam** (p. 114), a minimally excavated Maya city known for a beautifully sculpted sacred doorway on the northern Yucatán's tallest pyramid. Visit the ethereally beautiful (if slightly claustrophobic) **Cenotes Dzitnup** (p. 114), just west of town, or the more open **Cenote Zací** (p. 112) in the city center, and you'll know why the ancient Maya regarded these breaches in the earth's crust as sacred portals to the underworld.

## An Introduction to the Maya World

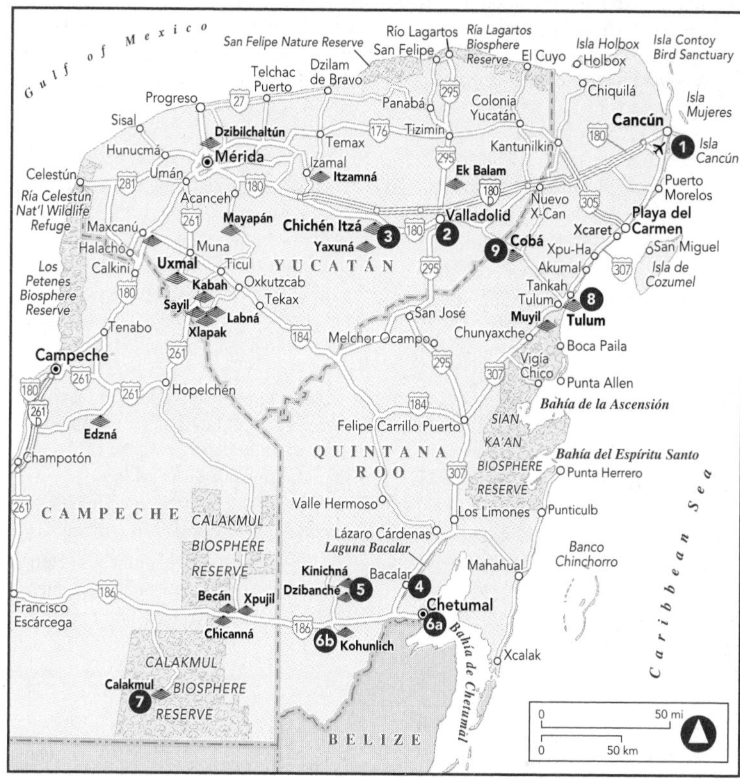


### Day 3: Chichén Itzá ★

Arriving when the ruins open is the key to enjoying this important and beautiful, but too often crowded, ancient Maya city. **Chichén Itzá**'s (p. 100) mix of architectural styles informed much of what we surmise about Maya civilization, and the great pyramid **El Castillo**—that symbol of Mexican tourism—embodies their mastery of astronomy and the calendar. When the caravan of tour buses reaches its peak, take a break and relax at **Cenote Ik-Kil** (p. 108) for a few hours, or fortify yourself at a restaurant in Pisté. Return to the ruins in the evening for the new **Light and Sound Show** (p. 104) before returning to Valladolid for the night.

### Days 4 & 5: Laguna Bacalar ★★

After several hours' drive, give yourself an easy afternoon in **Bacalar** (p. 216), a small, traditional city named for the "Lake of Seven Colors." Check in to one of the small hotels along the shore and visit the 18th-century **Fuerte San Felipe Bacalar** (p. 216). Cool off in **Cenote Azul** (p. 216), Mexico's largest; you can have dinner in the restaurant overlooking the water. The next day, drive to **Dzibanché** (p. 221), a good-size Classic period city. It's best known for its **Temple**

### Family Travel

Children are considered the national treasure of Mexico, and Mexicans will warmly welcome and cater to your children. I can't think of a better place to introduce children to the exciting adventure of exploring a different culture. The whole Mexican Caribbean region is the perfect area to begin introducing your kids to Mexico. Family-oriented attractions and facilities abound.

Before leaving home, ask your doctor which medications to take along. Disposable diapers cost about the same in Mexico but are of poorer quality. You can get brands identical to those sold in the United States at a higher price. Many stores sell familiar brands of baby foods. Dry cereals, powdered formulas, baby bottles, and purified water are easily available in midsize and large cities or resorts. Consider bringing your own car seat; they are not readily available for rent in Mexico.

Most hotels in the large resort areas have just about everything you need to keep your kids happy. Kids' clubs are common, and some offer evening hours so parents can have a few grown-up nights out. Babysitters are readily available as well, and are vetted by the hotels. Many properties offer special amenities for kids, including bath toys and bedtime cookies and milk. Cribs may present a problem except in the high-end resorts, but rollaway beds are often available. Restaurants are equally accommodating. Child seats or high chairs are common, as are children's menus. Plain cheese quesadillas are a good intro to Mexican food, and familiar boxed cereals are available at breakfast.

Be sure to bring your kids to the main plaza on weekend evenings. They'll find plenty of playmates running about and lots of goodies they absolutely must have immediately, including balloons and candies.

**of the Owl,** but continue beyond the temples and pyramid to the most recently excavated area—it's a bit of a climb—on a high vantage point that ensured any incursions would be spotted from miles away and that now provides stunning jungle views. The large, three-level acropolis at the smaller nearby site of **Kinichná** (p. 221) is also worth a stop before you return to Bacalar for the night.

## Day 6: Chetumal & the Río Bec Region ★★

Start the day at the terrific **Museo de la Cultura Maya** (p. 218) in Chetumal—until 2012, it was the only museum dedicated to the Maya—then head west on Highway 186. Before you cross into Campeche state, stop at the **Kohunlich** ruins (p. 222), famous for the **Pyramid of the Masks.** It's not far from the highway and is a delightful place to wander. Continue through **Xpujil** (p. 223), the Río Bec's only town, which has its own small archaeological site (spelled Xpuhil). Spend the night at one of the small lodges (p. 221) farther west.

## Day 7: Calakmul ★★★

Hire a guide to take you into **Calakmul** (p. 224), one of the prime city-states of the Maya's Classic age. It's well worth the cost—you avoid driving the long, challenging jungle road, leaving you free to look for wildlife, and you couldn't scratch the surface of Mexico's most extensive and mysterious ancient city without some expert help. The most exhilarating experience on this route is climbing to the top of **Structure II.** Guides often include a stop at **Becán** (p. 223), a large, fortified city with tall temples, before or after visiting Calakmul; you may also ask about visiting **Balamkú** (p. 225), on the highway near the Calakmul turnoff, for its beautiful sculptures and one of the largest stucco friezes yet discovered.

### Day 8: Tulum ★★★

If you haven't overdosed on ruins, visit **Chicanná** (p. 224), with its giant monster mouth doorway, before returning to Highway 307 and heading north to **Tulum** (p. 193). Tulum commands the most alluring setting of all Mexico's Maya sites, perched on a bluff overlooking the Caribbean. Bring a swimsuit and snorkel gear if you have them and clamber down to the beach in front of the ruins. Spend the night in Tulum. ***Alternative:*** If you've seen Tulum's ruins before—it's one of the coast's most-visited sites—stop instead at **Muyil** (p. 199), south of Tulum. You'll get not only an archaeological site but a tour of the northern end of the **Sian Ka'an Biosphere Reserve** (p. 205) and a visit with local Maya people in one fell swoop.

### Day 9: Cobá ★★★

The vast ruins of **Cobá** (p. 202), least developed of the major Maya sites, still keep most of the site's secrets hidden under a shroud of jungle growth. It's easy to visit on your own, but taking **Alltournative**'s (p. 183) Maya Encounter tour combines a few hours in the ruins with a visit to a Maya village. Although it limits the time for exploring the sprawling ancient city, that's a worthwhile tradeoff for the experience of following Maya villagers through their domain to identify plants and land formations, glide over one *cenote* on a zip line and rappel down into another, receive an elder's blessing, and have lunch with the villagers.

## AN ECO-ADVENTURE FOR FAMILIES

Outdoor activities and wildlife encounters on this itinerary will appeal to every member of the family. If you have your own snorkeling gear, bring it along; you can always get rentals, but you're better off with gear that fits well.

---

### Day 1: Puerto Morelos ★★★

On the highway north of the main **Puerto Morelos** (p. 161) turnoff, **CrocoCun** (p. 158) might remind mom and dad of the old roadside attractions of their youth, but meeting the Yucatán's native animals nose to nose is a delight, greatly enhanced by knowledgeable volunteer guides who are dedicated to conservation. The **Ya'ax Che** botanical garden (p. 160), just south of the same turnoff, is a preserved patch of jungle harboring native plants and animals. Its trails also lead to traces of an ancient Maya settlement and reconstructions of a traditional Maya home and a *chiclero* camp. Drive to the beach town to have dinner and spend the night.

### Day 2: Cenotes Route, Valladolid & Chichén Itzá ★★

Slightly south of the highway's main Puerto Morelos intersection, turn east off the highway at the yellow arch and follow the **"Ruta de Cenotes"** (p. 166). The jungle road passes through many of these sinkholes, some wild and others developed into parks. If you stop at **Selvática** (p. 166), with its adrenaline-pumping zip lines, aerial walkways, and parachute jumps, plan on at least half a day to get your money's worth. The jungle road meets Highway 180 *libre* in Leona Vicario; turn west and continue to **Valladolid** (p. 108) for a break or an early dinner, then pick up the faster toll road (Highway 180D) to **Chichén Itzá** (p. 100). Check into a hotel near the entrance (p. 102). Depending on timing and energy levels, you could catch the dazzling new evening **Light and Sound Show** at the ruins (through June 2015, check to see if your hotel has free passes for guests).

## Day 3: Chichén Itzá, Valladolid, & Ría Lagartos ★★★

Get to the archaeological site when it opens at 8am, and take your photos of the monumental pyramid **El Castillo** first thing. You'll be ready to leave not long after the tour buses start rolling in. If you return to Valladolid on the old free highway, you can stop at **Ik-Kil** (p. 108), just east of the ruins, or the **Balankanché Cave** (p. 108) and **Cenotes Dzitnup** (p. 114), just west of Valladolid. Otherwise, take the toll road for a quick trip to Valladolid and have a dip in **Cenote Zací** (p. 112) right in town. Either way, have lunch in Valladolid and head north to the coastal village of **Río Lagartos** (p. 116) at the Yucatán Peninsula's northern tip. Check into one of the inexpensive waterfront hotels and arrange an early morning boat tour of the flamingo sanctuary.

## Day 4: Ría Lagartos ★★

Start the day boating through mangrove and saltwater estuaries where great flocks of rosy flamingos share digs with hundreds of other bird species in the **Ría Lagartos** wildlife refuge (p. 116). And yes, the town is "Río," but the reserve is "Ría." On the way back to Valladolid, you could easily stop at **Ek Balam** (p. 114), just off the highway. But if the youngsters have had enough ruins for now, press on to town and spend the afternoon hanging out at the plaza, browsing the Maya ladies' embroidered dresses in the **Bazar Municipal** (p. 111) and other crafts at the **Mercado de Artesanías,** or wandering through the large **Mercado Municipal** (p. 114). Spend the night in one of the city's small hotels (p. 117).

## Day 5: Isla Holbox ★★★

After about three hours of driving and then the ferry crossing, you might not feel like doing much more than taking a spin around the plaza to scout restaurants (p. 119) for dinner prospects and walking on the beach. But if you're feeling ambitious and there's still time in the day, consider taking a boat tour around **Laguna Yalahau** (p. 121) to spot dolphins, flamingos, and the occasional manatee. You'll also get to swim in a freshwater *cenote* welling up in the salt water.

## Day 6: Whale Sharks of Isla Holbox ★★

Swimming with the largest fish in the sea (p. 120) is truly a bucket-list experience. Though Isla Mujeres has stolen some of Holbox's thunder since the sharks have gravitated farther east, the smaller town, lighter crowds, and experienced guides who respect regulations that protect the sharks make Holbox an ideal base for swimming with the benign behemoths. Reserve your spot in advance.

# An Eco-Adventure for Families

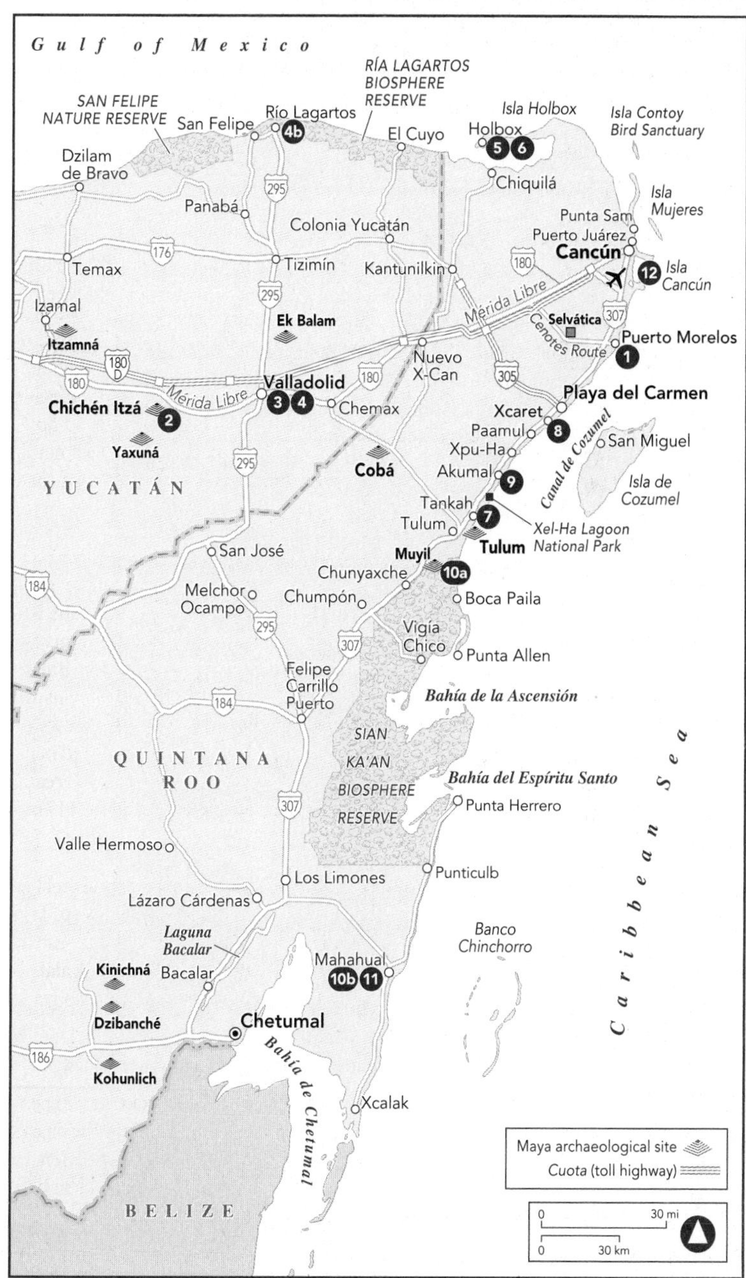

## Day 7: Tankah ★★

After several hours of travel, a dip in a cool *cenote* is just the thing to relieve stiff muscles and revive energy levels. **Cenote Manatí** (p. 185), down a dirt road in the small community of Tankah, is the perfect choice for all ages. You can swim, snorkel, and kayak in the *cenote*'s large green lagoon surrounded by vines and mangroves (gear is available at a small stand). The underground river feeding the lagoon rushes into the sea across the road, behind **Casa Cenote** restaurant (p. 192). Spend a few hours alternating among the *cenote,* shallow sea, and restaurant for a relaxing break before the following adventures.

## Day 8: Río Secreto ★★★

One of dozens of cave and caverns along the coast, **Río Secreto** (p. 183) remains my favorite for both adventure and education. Visitors don wetsuits and helmets before following a guide down the entrance into a dark, spooky cavern. A few steps along, sunlight streams through holes in the roof, illuminating a deep, green pool. Stalactites dripping with mineral-rich water glisten like icicles above walkways and pools, while bumpy stalagmites edge rocky paths. Guides keep up an informational banter as visitors alternately walk, float, and swim through the long cavern while learning about the Yucatán Peninsula's natural habitat.

## Day 9: Akumal ★★

One of the coast's most remarkable natural phenomena is the annual sea turtle migration, when mother turtles build nests and lay their eggs on the beaches. Most babies swim off to the deep sea, but many stay year-round in the bays along **Akumal's** (p. 188) shores. Start at the **Centro Ecológico Akumal** (p. 189) to learn about the turtles and their fragile ecosystem. Take a snorkeling tour (book in advance) with the **Akumal Dive Shop** (p. 188), the area's oldest operator, to see the turtles up close, swimming with rays and tropical fish. Guides take snorkelers and divers away from the crowds hovering over turtles near shore and teach clients how to swim with wild creatures responsibly. Newly minted turtle aficionados can find themed souvenirs in the shops at the **Hotel Akumal Caribe** (p. 189).

## Day 10: Muyil & Mahahual ★★

On your way south to the Costa Maya, stop to explore **Muyil** (p. 199), also called Chunyaxché, just south of Tulum. You might find yourselves alone in this sprawling archaeological site within the **Sian Ka'an Biosphere Reserve.** Well-marked paths to various structures wind through thick jungle (bring bug spray). The site's largest structure is the **Castillo,** one of the tallest Maya buildings on the coast. Note the rows of white rock between buildings; these are remnants of ancient roads called ***sacbeob.*** When you reach **Mahahual** (p. 211), stop in at **Doctor Dive** (p. 212) to confirm tomorrow's diving trip (booked in advance), then settle into your beach retreat and just relax.

## Day 11: Lionfish Hunting in Mahahual ★★★

We're all about conservation, but the more of these fish you can kill, the more applause you'll get. The **lionfish** (p. 216) is an invasive species from the South Pacific that has devastated great swaths of the Caribbean reef system because it has a voracious appetite and no natural predators—except humans. Fortunately, it's a tasty fish, and Doctor Dive guides will teach you how to snag them with

Hawaiian slings or miniature spear guns, and treat you to lionfish ceviche for your trouble.

### Day 12: Cancún

Your last day will be your longest travel day. Figure about 4½ hours of driving from Mahahual to the airport, but allow time to stop for lunch on the way.

#### Turtle Bay Cafe & Bakery ★★

This jack-of-all-trades cafe, a longtime favorite just inside Akumal's entrance arch, is quick to reach from the highway. Get a table in the lovely garden and choose from a hearty American-style breakfast (until noon), elaborate salads, wraps, a wondrous variety of tacos on fresh house-made corn tortillas, or comfort food such as sandwiches and burgers.



# THE CARIBBEAN COAST'S REGIONS IN BRIEF

Mexico's entire Caribbean coast lies within the state of Quintana Roo, one of three states that make up the Yucatán Peninsula. Some side trips in this book also venture into Yucatán state, a triangular territory occupying the upper middle portion of the peninsula, and Campeche, the western state along the Gulf of Mexico. Quintana Roo and Campeche broaden out as they reach southward and meet below Yucatán's southern tip. ("The Yucatán" refers to the entire peninsula, while "Yucatán" refers to just the state.)

The Yucatán's three states share their Maya heritage and a long history as Mexico's "outside lands," yet each has its own customs and personalities. Similarly, Quintana Roo has several distinct regions.

## North Coast

**Cancún** dominates this region, which includes the **Riviera Maya,** extending south to **Tulum.** In fact, Quintana Roo didn't become a state until Cancún opened for business in 1974, turning what had been an unknown string of fishing villages into a burgeoning vacation playground. Cancún's jurisdiction extends to **Isla Holbox** on the northeast tip of the Yucatán Peninsula, where Caribbean waters meet the Gulf of Mexico, and south to **Puerto Morelos,** which is popularly but not officially regarded as the gateway to the Riviera Maya. **Playa del Carmen,** its days as a sleepy fishing village long past, is the Riviera Maya's major city. A growing number of hotels on the coast between Cancún and Puerto Morelos are calling their location the Riviera Cancún, obscuring the fact that they are in neither Cancún nor the Riviera Maya.

## Sian Ka'an Biosphere Reserve

With 1.3 million acres of beaches, mangrove lagoons, and low jungle, including 120 kilometers (75 miles) of coastline, the **Sian Ka'an Biosphere Reserve** occupies nearly one-third of the Caribbean coast and is a region unto itself. Another 200,000 acres adjoining Sian Ka'an's southern border, designated the Uaymil Area for Protection of Flora and Fauna, further extends the continuous area of protected land—one of the largest in Mexico. More than half of its area is limited to scientific research, while a "buffer zone" on the periphery allows carefully managed tourism. About 2,000 people live inside the reserve; most are fishermen in the villages of **Punta Allen,** at the southern tip of a thread-like peninsula in the north, and **Punta Herrero,** on a spit of land in the south. The most popular entry point is at the end of **Tulum**'s hotel zone, but tours also run out of **Muyil,** off Highway 307 south of Tulum. Tourists almost never hear about the "secret" back entrance, reached by driving north from **Mahahual.**

## South Coast

In many ways, the region now known as the **Costa Maya** is much like the Riviera Maya of 20 years ago—sparsely populated, lightly traveled, and brimming with wildlife. But the Costa Maya is at least a 4½-hour drive from Cancún, and it might still be missing from the tourist map if Carnival Cruise Line had not built a port at the edge of **Mahahual** in 2001. Much of the area still runs on solar power, but now there are good roads and a variety of hotels and restaurants to meet any traveler's need, except the one seeking Cancún-style opulence. The term Costa Maya, taken from the Puerto Costa Maya cruise terminal, takes in **Mahahual** and **Xcalac** on the wide peninsula jutting out from the mainland under the **Sian Ka'an** reserve, and part of the reserve itself. On the mainland, the town of **Bacalar** and the state capital of **Chetumal**—a city not even half the size of Cancún—on the Mexico-Belize border are usually considered part of the Costa Maya as well.

## Highways & Byways

The main artery connecting northern and southern Quintana Roo is **Highway 307,** which follows the coastline from Cancún to Tulum, albeit several kilometers inland; narrow roads, not always paved, connect the highway to fishing villages and growing towns on the beach. The exception is Playa del Carmen, which has grown to meet and ultimately vault the highway in its eastward expansion. South of Tulum, Highway 307 veers inland to skirt the Sian Ka'an Biosphere Reserve and the peninsula that makes up most of the Costa Maya. At its end in the state capital of Chetumal, it meets **Highway 186,** which runs west into Campeche.

The major road coming into Quintana Roo is **Highway 180,** leading from Cancún to Mérida. A toll road *(cuota)* called **Highway 180D** (think *"dinero"*) runs roughly parallel to the original road for most of its length, ending at the turnoff to Izamal in Yucatán. From Felipe Carrillo Puerto, 96 kilometers (60 miles) south of Tulum on Highway 307, you can take **Highway 295** to Valladolid and up to Río Lagartos on the northern Yucatán coast, or **Highway 184** into Yucatán's Puuc Region. Just beyond Pedro Antonio Santos, 77 kilometers (49 miles) south of Carrillo Puerto, is the junction with **Highway 293,** which connects to Highway 184.

Local roads, narrow but mostly well-maintained, also branch off from Highway 307 to the west. Just south of the airport is a shortcut to Highway 180D. The *Ruta de Cenotes* ("Cenotes Route") out of Puerto Morelos traverses *cenote*-pocked jungle to meet Highway 180. In late 2014, a new **toll road** opened, following the path of the jungle road from Playa del Carmen to Highway 180D, greatly reducing travel time from the Riviera Maya to Valladolid and other parts of central Yucatán. The road leading from Tulum to the ruins of Cobá continues to meet the old Highway 180 at Chemax, east of Valladolid.

# CANCÚN

by Christine Delsol

4

Cancún, which generates about one-third of Mexico's tourism revenue, might be the least Mexican city in the country. You can spend your entire vacation without speaking a word of Spanish or exchanging a single dollar for pesos. Since the first three hotels opened in 1974 on a deserted spit of land visited only by local fishermen, Cancún's Hotel Zone has acquired a phalanx of massive resorts and megamalls, sprawling for 23km (14 miles) like the love child of Miami and Las Vegas. Yet no amount of change has tarnished the gift from nature that put it on the map 4 decades ago: an expanse of soft alabaster sand and a Caribbean sea the color of blue Curaçao. The brochures, in this case, don't lie.

Cancún today offers more than 32,000 rooms and has an estimated population of nearly 800,000. It is not only the Yucatán Peninsula's most prosperous city but one of the entire Caribbean's most-visited destinations. And its influence continues to grow. With precious little real estate left in the Zona Hotelera (Hotel Zone), the phalanx of luxury resorts marched relentlessly south down the coast, spurring an aftershock of luxury development along the Riviera Maya. A huge, upscale "city within a city" called Puerto Cancún is under development north of the Hotel Zone, with a marina, hotels and gated communities, a golf club, shopping center, and business complexes. Taking shape north of Ciudad Cancún (Cancún City, or "downtown") on the mainland is Playa Mujeres, a kind of mini–hotel zone with several hotels, a golf course, and more sublime beaches.

**ZONA HOTELERA:** So what do you experience in Cancún's *raison d'être*? Well, the narrow, dog-legged spit, barely wide enough for a single boulevard lined by imposing resorts that vaguely resemble pyramids, palaces, and Cubist sculptures, has nothing resembling the central plaza where so much of traditional Mexican life takes place. You won't stroll sleepy side streets, meet artisans who have been practicing their craft for generation after generation, or find a pristine, unmapped beach to call your own.

This Cancún is a culture unto itself, an idyllic Caribbean cocoon where life consists of sipping margaritas on those legendary sands, shopping in glittering retail palaces, gyrating in thumping, all-night discos, and seeking fortification in an array of fine restaurants so you can do it all again the next day. It's easy to get to, largely English-speaking, does business in dollars, and is well supplied with familiar international chains. It was designed from the ground up solely as an enclave of hotels, restaurants, shopping centers, golf courses, and marinas. The all-inclusive resorts that account for a large, and growing, percentage of Hotel Zone lodging eliminate the need to venture beyond their boundaries at all. This is vacationing at its purest.

The one demand Cancún makes is on your wallet. Tabs at the ever-more-luxurious resorts equal or surpass those at comparable U.S. properties.

**CIUDAD CANCÚN:** While the Zona Hotelera draws the tourists, Ciudad Cancún—El Centro (Downtown), as it is often called—is what makes it all work. Built on the mainland to house workers building the resorts and restaurants, it has no more history than the Zona Hotelera does, but it is a genuinely Mexican city that most foreign visitors overlooked until recent years. This is where Mexicans make their homes, conduct their business, do their shopping, and let off steam. With permanent homes, commercial areas, public buildings, parks, schools, hospitals and markets, it has evolved into a lively metropolis fusing Mexican, Yucatecan, Maya, Caribbean, and North American lifestyles. An ample supply of affordable hotels and restaurants that don't tone down their authentic flavors for tourists' palates makes it a reasonable alternative to the Hotel Zone for some travelers. Even Hotel Zone vacationers are venturing to the mainland in search of respite from sun-and-sand hangovers.



With downtown's increasing appeal, Cancún is achieving a balance as it matures, offering attractions for the adventurous spirit as well as the sybaritic vacationer. Though the Hotel Zone has perfected the art of relaxation and pampering in luxurious surroundings, you'll miss a lot if you don't venture past its alluring shores—you'll miss Mexico.

**AND BEYOND:** Because of its enormous popularity and resulting competition among airlines, Cancún's airfares are the lowest you'll find to Mexico outside of the capital. That, along with the good roads, sophisticated hotels, and enlightened tour companies make Cancún an ideal launch pad for forays to the Riviera Maya and fishing villages farther south, inland Maya ruins, and the splendid Yucatecan capital of Mérida to the west. Wherever you stay, make time to take advantage of perhaps Cancún's greatest virtue of all—its prime location in one of the most naturally blessed and culturally rich regions of Mexico.

# ESSENTIALS

## Getting There

### BY PLANE

Most international visitors arrive at **Cancún International Airport** (www.cancun-airport.com; ✆ **998/848-7200**), lying across Highway 307 from the southern tip of Cancún's Hotel Zone. The airport is 20km (12½ miles) from the heart of the Hotel Zone, about a 25-minute drive, and 19km (12 miles) from Ciudad Cancún, about 20 minutes away. See chapter 8 (p. 226) for more information.

**RENTAL CARS** Most major car-rental firms have outlets at the airport, so if you're renting a car, consider picking it up and dropping it off there to save on airport-transportation costs. Booking the rental online before you leave home will also save money compared with renting after you arrive. Major agencies include **Alamo, Avis, Budget, Dollar, Hertz, National,** and **Thrifty;** in my experience, National generally has the best cars at the lowest prices. The Zona Hotelera (Hotel Zone) lies 10km (6¼ miles)—a 20-minute drive—from the airport along wide, well-paved roads. ***Be prepared:*** Online quotes usually do not include taxes and insurance, which can bring the daily price to double what's initially quoted. (See p. 228 for more details.)

## THE BEST CANCÚN websites

- **All About Cancún: www.cancunmx.com** This site is a good place to start planning. It includes Cancún-specific information, bookings for regional tours, and a visitors' blog.
- **Cancún Convention & Visitors Bureau: www.cancun.travel** The official site of the Cancún Convention & Visitors Bureau lists excellent information on events and attractions. Its hotel guide is one of the most complete available (but does not include some very good hotels that are not CVB members) and includes events and news related to Cancún.
- **Cancún Online: www.cancun.com** This comprehensive guide has lots of information about things to do and see in and around Cancún, though most details come from paying advertisers. The site lets you reserve package trips, accommodations, activities, and tours.
- **Cancún Today: www.cancuntodaynews.com** Browse through this site for a look into cultural topics and ideas about off-the-tourist-track places to visit.
- **Cancún Tips: www.cancuntips.com.mx** This is the online version of the free tourist guide for information about Cancún and the Riviera, with pretty good maps.



**TAXIS** The rate for a **private taxi** from the airport is $40 one way or $70 round trip to Ciudad Cancún (downtown) or the Hotel Zone. The airport **shuttle service** to the Hotel Zone is $12 per person one way or $20 round trip; up to four people can book the "Economical Service" for $30 one way or $55 round trip for the entire group. **SuperShuttle** (www.supershuttle.com) began service in Cancún in 2014; rates range from $11 per person to Cancún (downtown or Hotel Zone) to $38 to Tulum. There is no shuttle service returning to the airport from Ciudad Cancún or the Hotel Zone, so you'll have to take a taxi, but the rate will be much less than for the trip from the airport. (Only federally chartered taxis may take fares *from* the airport, but any taxi may bring passengers *to* the airport.) Ask at your hotel what the fare should be.

**LOCAL BUSES** **ADO** runs a bus from the airport to its station in Ciudad Cancún for 64 pesos. From there, you can take another bus for less than a dollar to Puerto Juárez, where passenger ferries run to Isla Mujeres regularly. It also has a bus from the airport to Playa del Carmen for 156 pesos.

### BY CAR

From Mérida or Campeche, take **Highway 180** east to Cancún. This is mostly a winding, two-lane road that branches off into the express **toll road 180D** at Izamal. The toll road ends at the *libre* (free) Hwy. 180 in the outskirts of Cancún. At that point you can either continue on Hwy. 180 east into Cancún, or take the local road to the southeast to the airport and **Highway 307,** which will take you to Riviera Maya and points south. Mérida is about 320km (200 miles) from Cancún, about four hours' drive.

### BY BUS

Cancún's **ADO bus terminal** (www.ado.com.mx; ✆ **01-800/702-8000**) sits in downtown Ciudad Cancún at the intersection of avenidas Tulum and Uxmal. All out-of-town buses arrive here. Buses run to Playa del Carmen, Tulum, Chichén Itzá, other nearby beach and archaeological zones, and other points within Mexico. ADO buses also operate between the airport and downtown, as well as from the airport directly to Playa del Carmen (from where ferries depart for Cozumel). Schedules and fares are subject to change, so ask your hotel for current details or stop by the station before you plan your departure.

## Visitor Information

The **Cancún Municipal Tourism Office** is downtown at Avenida Nader at Avenida Cobá (✆ **998/887-3379**). It's open Monday through Friday from 9am to 4pm. The office lists hotels and their rates, as well as ferry schedules. In the Hotel Zone, the Cancún Convention & Visitors Bureau (www.cancun.travel; ✆ **998/881-2741**) is on the first floor of the Cancún Center at Bulevar Kukulcán Km 9. The state tourism website is in Spanish, at **sedetur.qroo.gob.mx**.

## City Layout



Cancún is really two cities: **Ciudad Cancún (Cancún City)**, also called **El Centro (Downtown)**, and **Isla Cancún (Cancún Island)**, also called **Zona Hotelera (Hotel Zone)**. Ciudad Cancún, on the mainland, is the original downtown area, where most of the local population lives. It's home to traditional restaurants, shops, and less expensive hotels, as well as pharmacies, dentists, automotive shops, banks, travel and airline agencies, and car-rental firms—all within about nine easily walkable square blocks. The main thoroughfare is **Avenida Tulum;** other major boulevards are named for the nearby archaeological sites Chichén Itzá, Tulum, and Uxmal. Many streets are named after famous Maya cities. Heading south, Avenida Tulum becomes Highway 307 to the airport, Tulum, and Chetumal; heading north, it intersects the highway to Mérida and the road to Puerto Juárez and the Isla Mujeres ferries.

Isla Cancún, with its grandiose resorts, actually is a thin strip 22km (14 miles) long that is separated by water from the mainland to the north but attached by a thread of land at the south end. It wraps like a "7" around Laguna Nichupté. Drivers reach the mainland via the Playa Linda Bridge at the north end and the Punta Nizuc Bridge at the south end. Ciudad Cancún's Avenida Cobá, after crossing Avenida Bonampak, becomes Bulevar Kukulcán, the Hotel Zone's main (and almost only) traffic artery. Cancún International Airport is just inland, across Highway 307 from the south end of the strip.

## Getting Around

### BY CAR

Driving is the quickest and most flexible way to see the Caribbean coast, especially if you plan to take some side trips (p. 100). But if you are based in Cancún, consider not renting a car or, if you've already rented one as part of a longer trip, leaving it parked while you explore Cancún. Traffic is maddeningly congested, and addresses can be hard to find. Also, Cancún is the only place in Mexico where I've been stopped by police in search of a *mordida,* literally a "bite," or bribe—just twice in two decades of frequent driving, but that's twice more than I've been hit anywhere else. You can take a shuttle to your hotel and easily get around on foot or by bus. Taxis can be hired by the hour, day, or half-day for less than the cost of renting a car, and many drivers turn

### Coming or Going?

Finding an address in Cancún can be a challenge, so study a map and get precise directions the first time you attempt to find a building.

Rather than the traditional Mexican city built around a central plaza, **downtown Cancún** is a collection of *supermanzanas* (groups of *manzanas*, or blocks) separated by large avenues, each with its own central park. Addresses often refer to the lot *(lote)* and the *manzana* or *supermanzana*, abbreviated SM. Even more confounding, many streets actually are two one-way streets with the same name.

Few **Hotel Zone** resorts or businesses have numbered addresses. Most are on Bulevar Kukulcán, and their location is described in relation to their distance, from 2 to 22 kilometers, from the boulevard's northern end. Fortunately, the central divider marks off nearly every kilometer. Unfortunately, several buildings may use the same number—and an address like Km 12.5 requires some guesswork.



out to be great tour guides as well. You can always rent a car for a day or two for an overnight excursion. See chapter 8 (p. 228) for more information.

## BY TAXI

Cancún's taxi prices are set by zone, though keeping track of what's in which zone can take some practice. Minimum fare within the Hotel Zone is high, at 100 pesos per ride. In addition, taxis in the Hotel Zone charge local residents about half of what tourists pay, and about twice as much for guests at high-priced resorts as those in budget hotels—all fares established by the taxi union. Rates should be posted in your hotel lobby, or you can ask the concierge. As always, confirm the price before you get in, and don't be shy about asking to see the official rate card (generally in Spanish), which all drivers are required to carry. Taxi drivers will accept dollars, though at an unfavorable (to you) exchange rate.

Within the downtown area, the cost is about 30 pesos per cab ride; within any other Ciudad Cancún zone, it's 30 to 60 pesos. Travel between the Hotel Zone and downtown will be about 200 pesos. Trips to the airport from most zones cost about 350 pesos (for up to four people). Taxis can also be rented by the hour for travel around the city and Hotel Zone, or for a full day for more distant excursions.

## BY BUS

Bus travel is a cheap, safe way to get up and down the Hotel Zone. In downtown Cancún, almost everything lies within walking distance. **Ruta 1, Ruta 2,** and **Ruta 15** city buses travel frequently between downtown and the Hotel Zone. Ruta 1 buses continue to Puerto Juárez for ferries to Isla Mujeres, while 2 and 15 go to Wal-Mart and Mercado 28 downtown. These city buses run 24 hours a day. Buses also go up and down the main strip of the Hotel Zone day and night. The public bus fare was 9.5 pesos at press time. The white **Bus One** also travels up and down the Hotel Zone for 9.5 pesos; it was once the route's only air-conditioned bus, but many public buses now have air-conditioning as well.

***Note:*** Rented scooters used to be a popular way to zip around Cancún, but they cost as much as renting a car and are extremely dangerous in the city's congested traffic. Stick to cars and buses if you value life and limb.

# [FastFACTS] CANCÚN

**Area Code** The telephone area code is **998.**

**ATMs & Banks** Most banks sit downtown along Avenida Tulum between avenidas Cobá and Uxmal and are usually open Monday through Friday from 9am to 4pm; some are also open half the day on Saturday. Many have ATMs. In the Hotel Zone, banks with ATMs can be found at Plaza Caracol (Bulevar Kukulcán Km 8.5) and Plaza Kukulcán (Km 12.5). They are generally open Monday through Saturday, 9am to 7pm. See p. 231 in chapter 8 for more information.

**Consulates** The United States, Canada, and England have consular agencies in Cancún; see chapter 8 (p. 232) for details. Irish, Australian, and New Zealand citizens should contact their embassies in Mexico City.

**Crime** Car break-ins are the most frequent crime, especially around shopping centers in the Hotel Zone. Sexual assaults sometimes occur, usually at night or in the early morning. Some bars and nightclubs in outlying downtown areas (rarely, if ever, visited by tourists) are havens for drug dealers and petty criminals. It is safest to travel in pairs or small groups; women should not walk alone at night.

**Currency Exchange** Cancún has many *casas de cambio* (exchange houses) with varying exchange rates. Hotels may change money for guests, usually at an awful exchange rate. Avoid changing money at the airport, especially at the first exchange booth you see—its rates are less favorable than those of any in town or others farther inside the airport. The easiest way to draw money is at an ATM, which will dispense money in pesos and charge a small transaction fee (usually around 35 pesos). ATMs also give you the best exchange rate, even considering the fee.

**Doctors** Several private hospitals, comparable to those in the U.S., are clustered in El Centro. **Galenia Hospital** (www.hospitalgalenia.com; ✆ **998/891-5200**) at Av. Tulum, SM 12, at Nizuc, is one of the city's most modern and provides excellent care. Also recommended: **Hospitén Cancún** (www.hospiten.com; ✆ **998/881-3700**) at Av. Bonampak south of Av. Nichupté; and **AmeriMed Hospital** (www.amerimedcancun.com; ✆ **998/881-3400**), at Av. Bonampak and Av. Nichupté (behind Las Americas mall). All are open 24 hours and staffed by English-speaking doctors and nurses (though not necessarily receptionists). ***Note:*** Mexican hospitals do not accept medical insurance from other countries; buy travelers' medical insurance if there's a chance you will need a hospital. **U.S. Air Ambulance** service (www.usairambulance.net; ✆ **800/948-1214**) is available around the clock.

**Drugstores** In the Hotel Zone at Bulevar Kukulcán Km 9.5, **Farmacías del Ahorro** (www.fahorro.com.mx; ✆ **998/892-7291** for call center offering deliveries) is open 24 hours. Plenty of drugstores sit in the major shopping malls in the Hotel Zone and are open until 10pm. **Farmacías del Ahorro** is also downtown, in front of El Rey del Caribe hotel at the corner of avs. Uxmal and Nadar. It's open daily from 7am to 11pm. **Farmacías Similares** (✆ **998/898-0190**), open 24 hours, is part of a well-regarded national chain, in Hotel RiveMar on Av. Tulum near Calle Crisantemos. Many prescription drugs are sold in Mexico without a prescription.

**Emergencies** Dial ✆ **065** to quickly reach the **Red Cross** (✆ **998/884-1616**), open 24 hours on Avenida Yaxchilán between avenidas Xcaret and Labná, next to the Telmex building. See also police and fire departments, below.

**Internet Access** Most hotels and many restaurants have Internet access, and five-star hotels have business centers. All of **Kukulcán Plaza,** Bulevar Kukulcán Km 13, offers free Wi-Fi. Pick up a password at Customer Services, near the main entrance.

**Newspapers & Magazines** Most hotel

gift shops and newsstands carry major U.S. newspapers and magazines, such as *USA Today*, and other English-language publications.

**Police & Fire Departments** Dial ✆ **060** or **066** to reach the police, fire station, or ambulance in an emergency. Cancún also has a fleet of tourist police to help travelers. Dial ✆ **998/885-2277.**

**Post Office** The main *correo* is on Avenida Sunyaxchen at the corner of Avenida Xel-Ha (✆ **998/884-1418**), in front of Mercado 28. It's open Monday through Friday from 9am to 4pm, and Saturday from 9am to noon for the purchase of stamps only.

# WHERE TO STAY

Isla Cancún hotels—almost all offering modern facilities and English-speaking staffs—line the beach like concrete dominoes, obscuring the sands and aquamarine waters from the view of those traveling Bulevar Kukulcán. Be aware that the farther south you go on the island, the longer it takes (20 to 30 minutes in traffic) to get back to the "action spots," which lie primarily between the Plaza Flamingo and Punta Cancún on the island and along Avenida Tulum on the mainland.

Hotels and resorts here have increasingly turned to all-inclusive concepts, as an option if not in full. The emphasis on quantity of consumption at lower prices sometimes compromises quality and sacrifices service, activities, and amenities. Some of the more expensive hotels have struggled to survive in this environment, even while a more recent trend of fantastically expensive, ultra-luxurious all-inclusives has emerged. As Cancún's hotel landscape continues to shift, resorts that are not all-inclusive—the Fiesta Americana Grand Coral Beach, the Marriott hotels, and the Ritz-Carlton—remain the best the Hotel Zone has to offer.

Many major hotel chains also have Hotel Zone properties. The reality is that Cancún is so popular as a **package destination** from the U.S. that prices and special deals are often visitors' deciding factor, rather than loyalty to any one brand.

You won't find much in the way of authentic Mexican charm in the Hotel Zone, but you can get a glimpse of it in Ciudad Cancún, where most of the local population lives. You'll find smaller, independently owned, inexpensive hotels (typically not all-inclusive), along with a number of outstanding traditional restaurants and some good-value shopping.

Hotel reviews in this chapter begin on Isla Cancún and finish in Ciudad Cancún ("downtown"). Stay in the Hotel Zone to be next to the stunning Caribbean beaches by day and the vibrant entertainment by night. If you prefer a more authentic Mexico and more affordable lodging, downtown Cancún is the better choice. Unless otherwise indicated, parking is free at Cancún's hotels.

## Isla Cancún (Hotel Zone)

### EXPENSIVE

**Fiesta Americana Grand Coral Beach ★★★** Grand in style as well as size, this all-suite luxury resort is the very definition of elegance. It also happens to command Cancún's best view, a marvelous 270-degree sweep of thrashing Caribbean waves meeting Bahía de Mujeres' placid waters, with Isla Mujeres visible in the distance. The blocky, salmon-colored exterior is a bit jarring among its more understated neighbors, but the expansive interior gleams with marble and is bathed in natural light. Suites, all remodeled in 2013, sport white marble floors and a serene blend of sand and sea tones. Junior suites, with king or two full-size beds, have sunken sitting areas, and

## PARSING packages

Vacation packages can save hundreds of dollars over booking hotels and flights separately; the tradeoff is that your choices are largely limited to chain hotels and all-inclusive mega-resorts, and you must stay put for the duration of your trip. Reliable, long-established package specialists include **Apple Vacations** (www.applevacations.com; ✆ **800/517-2000**), **BookIt.com** (www.bookit.com; ✆ **888/782-9722**), and **Funjet Vacations** (www.funjet.com; ✆ **888/558-6654**). **Best Day** (www.bestday.com; ✆ **800/593-6259**), based in Cancún, has competitive prices for the big resorts but also offers packages with smaller, lower-priced properties, including some in Ciudad Cancún. Most airlines also have a vacation package division (often run by a third party), and the Big Three (Expedia, Orbitz, and Travelocity) online booking sites also offer packages. Here are some tips to get the best deal.

- **Read the fine print.** Determine exactly what's included, and compare the cost *for the same features,* not only with other packages but with the price of booking the same travel separately.
- **Compare apples to apples.** You'll often have to go all the way through to the booking page to get the true price of a package. Prices that pop up on the initial search page usually don't include mandatory taxes and fees.
- **Think twice about upgrades and options.** Initial price quotes are for the most basic rooms and for specific flights. Choosing a different flight often increases the cost, and upgrading to a better room always does.
- **Double-check the total.** Some packages include airport transfers or travel insurance, but most don't. Some packagers insidiously add these or other extras to your choice by default; it's up to you to remove what you don't want.
- **Move quickly.** The price you see is good only for that instant in time. Because airfares and hotel occupancy rates can change in an instant, you could see a different price an hour later; it might update—or disappear—even as you are looking at it.

the 860-square-foot master suites, all with kings, have two vanities and a Jacuzzi. All have ocean views and balconies. Wi-Fi is now free throughout the resort. A multi-tiered pool stretches the length of the hotel, featuring waterfalls, fountains, and swim-up bars. The Gem Spa boasts Latin America's only complete 10-step hydrotherapy program, and a kids' club provides daily activities such as building sand castles, hunting seashells, crafts, and games.

Bulevar Kukulcán Km 9.5 (on Punta Cancún). www.fiestamericanagrand.com. ✆ **877/927-7666** in the U.S., or 998/881-3200. 602 units. High season $359–$669 junior and master suites; low season, $199–$453 junior and master suites. Governor suite, Presidential suite, and Grand Club level rooms also available. **Amenities:** 5 restaurants; 4 bars; babysitting; kids' club; concierge w/multilingual staff; concierge floor; fitness center; 1 indoor pool; 1 outdoor pool w/swim-up bars; children's pool; spa and sauna; business center; water sports; free Wi-Fi.

**Hyatt Zilara ★★** The former Royal Cancún was rebranded at the end of 2013, and though rooms now have a brighter look, the outstanding amenities and attention to

# Isla Cancún (Zona Hotelera)

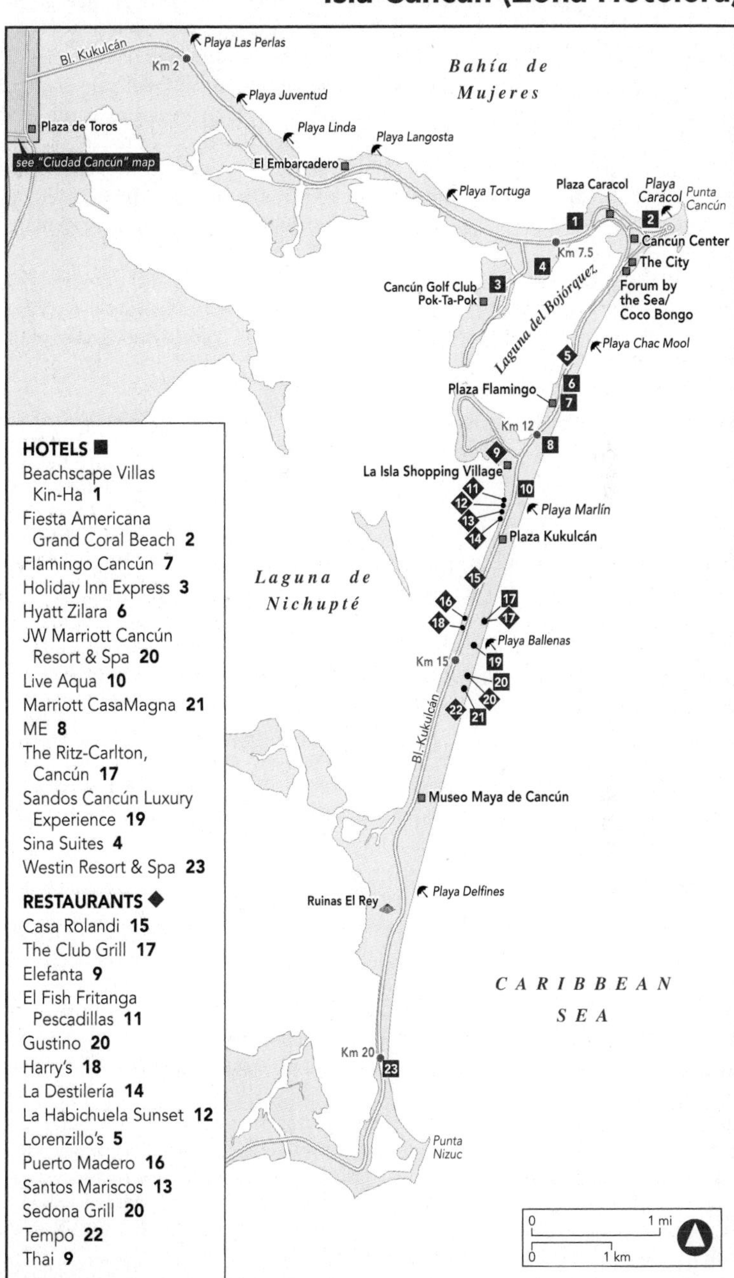

Bl. Kukulcán
Km 2
Playa Las Perlas
Bahía de Mujeres
Playa Juventud
Plaza de Toros
Playa Linda
Playa Langosta
see "Ciudad Cancún" map
El Embarcadero
Playa Tortuga
Plaza Caracol
Playa Caracol
Punta Cancún
Cancún Center
Km 7.5
The City
Forum by the Sea/ Coco Bongo
Cancún Golf Club
Pok-Ta-Pok
Laguna del Bojórquez
Playa Chac Mool
Plaza Flamingo
Km 12
La Isla Shopping Village
Playa Marlín
Plaza Kukulcán
Laguna de Nichupté
Playa Ballenas
Km 15
Bl. Kukulcán
Museo Maya de Cancún
Playa Delfines
Ruinas El Rey
CARIBBEAN SEA
Km 20
Punta Nizuc
0 1 mi
0 1 km
HOTELS
Beachscape Villas Kin-Ha 1
Fiesta Americana Grand Coral Beach 2
Flamingo Cancún 7
Holiday Inn Express 3
Hyatt Zilara 6
JW Marriott Cancún Resort & Spa 20
Live Aqua 10
Marriott CasaMagna 21
ME 8
The Ritz-Carlton, Cancún 17
Sandos Cancún Luxury Experience 19
Sina Suites 4
Westin Resort & Spa 23
RESTAURANTS
Casa Rolandi 15
The Club Grill 17
Elefanta 9
El Fish Fritanga Pescadillas 11
Gustino 20
Harry's 18
La Destilería 14
La Habichuela Sunset 12
Lorenzillo's 5
Puerto Madero 16
Santos Mariscos 13
Sedona Grill 20
Tempo 22
Thai 9

detail remain essentially unchanged and extraordinary for an all-inclusive. Dazzling infinity pools, a splendid beach, and an array of gourmet restaurants make staying at this adults-only, all-suites hotel a sybaritic pleasure. The elegant marble lobby has expansive views of the Caribbean on one side and the lagoon on the other. Each suite has a flatscreen TV with CD/DVD players, marble bathrooms with rain showers, double-jetted whirlpools, and balconies with hammocks for enjoying the ocean view. The Maya-inspired, oceanview spa offers a traditional *temazcal* steam hut, sauna, a cold plunge pool, massage waterfalls, and many treatment options. If for some inexplicable reason you should worry that you won't be sufficiently pampered, be assured the hotel employs "playadomos" who oversee the beach, as well as a dedicated romance concierge.

Bulevar Kukulcán Km 11.5. www.realresorts.com. ✆ **800/760-0944** in the U.S., or 998/881-5600. 307 units. High season from $240 per person; low season from $185 per person. Rates are all-inclusive. Minimum age 18. **Amenities:** 7 restaurants; 7 bars; concierge; expansive outdoor pool; oceanview spa w/steam room, sauna, whirlpool, fitness center; hair salon (for a fee); activities program; game room; tennis; business center; Wi-Fi and free wired Internet access.



**JW Marriott Cancún Resort & Spa ★★** JW is opulent without shouting about it, though the vaulted lobby's marble columns, chandeliers, and small forest of fresh flowers speak volumes. Guest rooms, while warm and staunchly top-caliber, seem understated by comparison; each has an oceanview terrace. With an unobtrusively efficient staff that remembers your name, the resort projects a sense of intimacy despite its towering 448 rooms. Its relatively narrow beach means you have to claim your *palapa* before breakfast in high season, but its two big meandering pools beyond a broad expanse of lawn feel sparsely populated even when it's hosting a convention. A separate 14-foot dive pool, just for scuba lessons, boasts an artificial reef. The resort opened the BeachWalk Game Center in 2013 to keep teens and 'tweens busy with ping-pong, air hockey, and football tables. Also getting a makeover was the three-level, 35,000-square-foot, Maya-inspired spa, which offers special men's and kids' services, an indoor pool, oceanview showers, and a fitness center where you can do your cardio facing the sunrise over the ocean or the sunset over the lagoon. **Gustino ★★★** (p. 80), the hotel's Italian restaurant, is extraordinary, while the more casual **Sedona Grill ★★** (p. 82) combines Southwestern and Caribbean flavors.

Bulevar Kukulcán Km 14.5 (5km south of convention center). www.jwmarriottcancun.com. ✆ **800/223-6388** in the U.S., or 998/848-9600. 448 units. High season $250–$450 double; low season $129–$350 double. **Amenities:** 3 restaurants; deli; lobby bar and pool bar; club floor; concierge; 2 expansive outdoor pools; dive pool w/waterfalls; indoor pool; 3 whirlpools; 24-hour room service; sauna; spa w/fitness center and aerobics studio; steam room; access to children's programs at Marriott CasaMagna; business center; Wi-Fi $15.

**Live Aqua ★★★** It's hard not to love a place that gives you a drink and a hand massage the minute you walk in. The entire resort feels like a spa, from the reflecting pool and seaview window wall in the lobby to the tranquil pale marble and muted beiges and grays in the spacious rooms (all with sea views, most with balconies), to aromatherapy scents and Zen music everywhere you turn. The actual spa offers a wide variety of international treatments, including aromavedic baths exclusive to Aqua. Outside, each pool is heated to a different temperature, offering a world of alternatives to the beach which, while beautiful, is subject to rough currents. Guests range from mid-20s into the 60s, but tend toward couples and families interested more in elegance than excess; spring breakers are discouraged. The resort became all-inclusive in 2010

## Ciudad Cancún

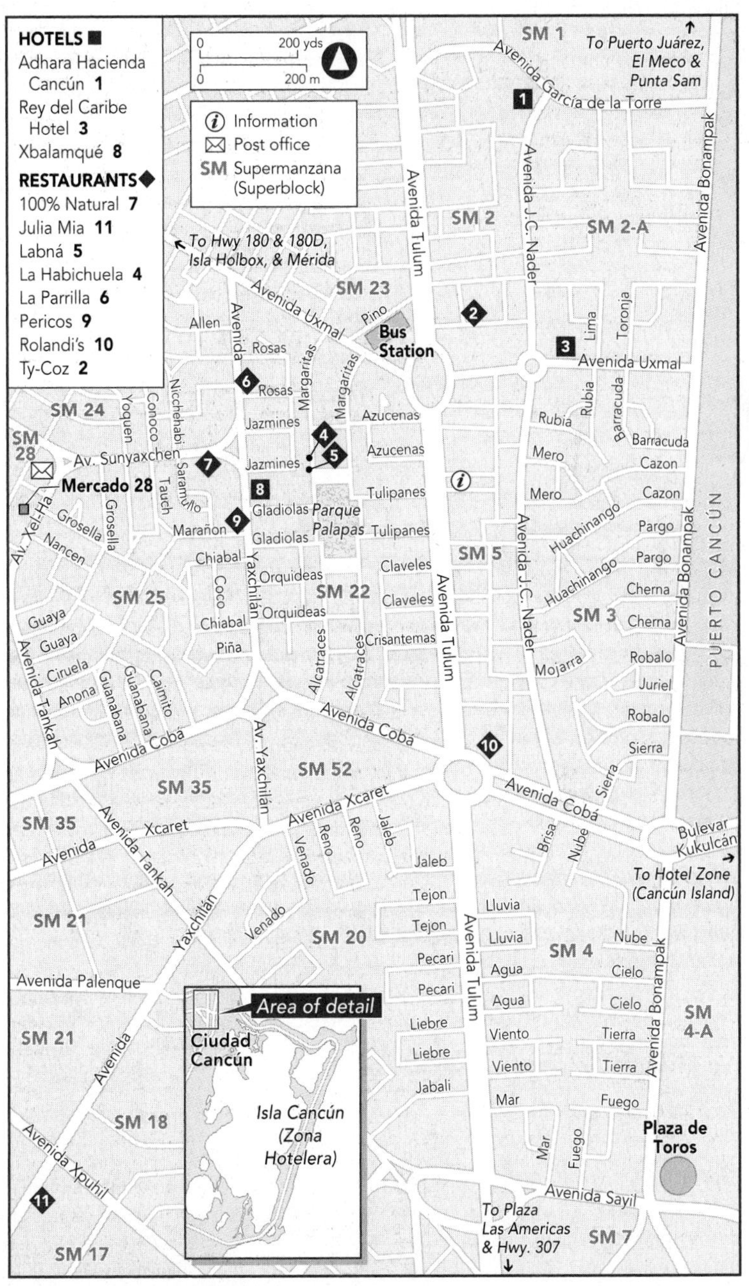

HOTELS ■
Adhara Hacienda Cancún 1
Rey del Caribe Hotel 3
Xbalamqué 8
RESTAURANTS ◆
100% Natural 7
Julia Mia 11
Labná 5
La Habichuela 4
La Parrilla 6
Pericos 9
Rolandi's 10
Ty-Coz 2
0 200 yds
0 200 m
Information
Post office
SM Supermanzana (Superblock)
To Puerto Juárez, El Meco & Punta Sam
To Hwy 180 & 180D, Isla Holbox, & Mérida
To Hotel Zone (Cancún Island)
To Plaza Las Americas & Hwy. 307
Bus Station
Mercado 28
Parque Palapas
Plaza de Toros
Area of detail
Ciudad Cancún
Isla Cancún (Zona Hotelera)
Avenida Tulum
Avenida Uxmal
Avenida García de la Torre
Avenida J.C. Nader
Avenida Bonampak
Avenida Cobá
Avenida Xcaret
Avenida Tankah
Avenida Yaxchilán
Avenida Palenque
Avenida Xpuhil
Avenida Sayil
Av. Sunyaxchen
Av. Xel-Ha
Bulevar Kukulcán
PUERTO CANCÚN

## Deciphering Hotel Prices

Most of Cancún's hotels set their rates in dollars, so they are immune to variations in the peso. Prices in this chapter are given in dollars except for hotels that set their rates in pesos. They do not include Christmas and Easter holiday periods, when rates can increase by as much as 100%. Note that the price quoted when you call a hotel's reservation number may not include Cancún's 16% tax. Prices can vary considerably throughout the year, so it pays to consult a travel agent or shop around.

and has been expanding its dining options ever since, most recently adding **Varenna** (brick-oven Italian) and secluded **Hidden Garden** (Asian) in 2013. The **Inlaa'kech Lobster & Grill** is the only one not included in the all-inclusive rate; fortunately, it's not among the best. Aqua's signature **Egos** bar offers mixology classes and employs its own DJ, who constantly researches and updates the playlist.

Bulevar Kukulcán Km 12.5 (across from La Isla Shopping Village). www.liveaqua.com. ✆ **800/343-7821** in the U.S., or 998/881-7600. 371 units. High season $490 and up double; low season $290 and up double. All-inclusive. **Amenities:** 7 restaurants included, 1 extra charge; 3 bars; club level; concierge; beach club; 8 outdoor pools; spa; fitness center; salon; 2 tennis courts; yoga and other classes; 24-hour room service; business center; free Wi-Fi.

**ME ★★** While the entire Hotel Zone inspires comparisons to Miami, this all-inclusive resort, commanding a quiet stretch of sublime beach, unabashedly promotes itself as "South Beach in the Mexican Caribbean." Unlike most all-inclusives, restaurants and bars are open to outside guests, and chic public spaces draw the bikini-and-stiletto set by day and local fashion boys and girls at night. The lobby features a reflecting pool, water-themed sculptures throughout the hotel, and chill music emanating from bars. The variety of food and drink is above average here, but "inclusive" extends to a fitness program, a foray into Playa del Carmen, and the spa's water ritual. Luxurious touches such as rain showers and MP3 players abound, though the minimalist rooms in black, white, and claret tones are a bit smaller than in many comparable properties. All have views of the ocean or the lagoon; only the high-priced suites have balconies. The oceanview spa offers facials, body treatments, massages, and purification rituals. Although children are welcome, ME is geared toward couples, with two pools and four suite levels reserved for adults and none of the activities that family-oriented resorts offer.

Bulevar Kukulcán Km 12 (about 2.5km south of club zone). www.melia.com. ✆ **877/954-8363** in the U.S., or 998/881-2500. 417 units. High season $180–$280 per person; low season $150–$250; adults-only suite levels from $400 per person. Rates are all-inclusive. **Amenities:** 4 restaurants; 2 bars; beach club (cover charge during weekends and events for guests in standard rooms); concierge; club level; 24-hour fitness center; Internet cafe; 3 outdoor pools (2 adults-only); whirlpool; spa; 24-hour room service; free airport transfers (one-way for standard rooms, round-trip for suites) with 48-hour advance notice; laptop rentals; free Wi-Fi.

**The Ritz-Carlton, Cancún ★★★** The reigning monarch of luxury resorts, while surrounded by an ever-growing cadre of worthy pretenders to the throne, is still the one to beat. With architectural lines borrowed from a European palace, the elegant but overwhelmingly beige guest rooms, little changed since the resort opened 20 years ago, underwent a renovation in 2014, trading staid carpets for a subtle but lively wave pattern in beachy sea and sand hues, the flared Victorian-style lampshades and curvy headboards for streamlined furnishings. Changes have also come to its famous Culinary Center, which has a new Bolivian chef, Carlos Garcia. Cooking classes now share the stage with a part exhibition/part dinner Chef's Table, team-building Extreme Chef competitions, and market tours that include directions on preparing your bounty. What hasn't changed is the impeccable service, the lineup of kids' activities and amenities, soothing spa treatments based on local ingredients, the sublime white beach, and the five-diamond awards for the resort—an unprecedented 16 years running—and two of its restaurants.

Retorno del Rey 36 (off Bulevar Kukulcán Km 13.5). www.ritzcarlton.com/Cancun. ✆ **800/241-3333** in the U.S. and Canada, or 998/881-0808. 363 units. High season $479–$679 double, suites and club level from $729; low season $249–$399 double, suites and club level from $499. **Amenities:** 6 restaurants; lounge/sushi bar; babysitting; Kids Camp; concierge; 2 club floors; culinary center; fitness center; 2 outdoor pools; spa; 3 lighted tennis courts; business center; Wi-Fi $20 per day.

**Sandos Cancún Luxury Experience ★★** Le Méridien, a longtime luxury favorite on the beach between the Caribbean and Laguna Nichupté, was taken over in 2012 by the Spanish Sandos chain, extensively renovated, and turned into a high-end all-inclusive resort oriented toward adults. Public spaces have taken on a pleasing mix of Art Deco and Maya motifs, while spacious guest rooms have a crisp, modern look in nearly monochromatic shades of ivory and white. Because of the resort's orientation, no rooms have full water views, but all have partial ocean or lagoon views. All but the least expensive rooms have balconies or terraces. Four revamped restaurants offer international fare, Caribbean dinners, upscale Asian cuisine, and molecular (experimental and science-based) cuisine. The European-style Spa del Mar is still the jewel of the property, with 12 treatment rooms, an outdoor whirlpool, steam rooms, and a wide array of treatments drawing on sea plants and marine algae. Also surviving are the three beautiful cascading infinity pools, although the pool area is now shaded in the afternoon by new construction next door.

Retorno del Rey Km 14 (off Bulevar Kukulcán on the same short street as the Ritz-Carlton). www.sandos.com. ✆ **866/336-4083** in the U.S., or 998/881-2200. 212 units. High season $409–$488 double, suites from $514; low season; $330–$463 double, suites from $439. Rates are all-inclusive for two people. **Amenities:** 4 restaurants; 2 bars (one for Premium level only); club levels; 24-hour room service; concierge; fitness center (minimum age 18); daily activities program; sauna and steam room; spa; salon; 3 outdoor pools; Jacuzzi; water sports center; 2 lighted tennis courts; business center; free Wi-Fi.

## MODERATE

**Beachscape Villas Kin-Ha ★★★** For my money, this is the best value in Cancún, offering a toned-down version of the service and amenities the resort area is known for in a small cluster of three-story buildings tucked between massive high-rises on one of Cancún's finest beaches. With arched doorways and balconies set among palm trees rising from acres of lawn, it's a breath of fresh air among the mega-resorts looming over the Hotel Zone. Guest quarters, ranging from standard rooms to three-bedroom suites, are among the largest on the island, bright with natural light and furnished in blond wood. All have either balconies or terraces, and all but the standard rooms have full kitchens and dining areas. The simple style holds up well, even though the hotel doesn't update every few years like bigger resorts do. It isn't perfect—Wi-Fi is reliable in the lobby but hit or miss in guest rooms, and restaurant service can be slow—but prices are moderate, dropping into the budget range during low season. The resort now offers an all-inclusive option; the food is good, but there's not a lot of variety. You'd do better with the room-only plan and taking advantage of some of Cancún's other fine restaurants. Beachscape is ideal for families, with its casual atmosphere, playground, ample wading section in the large, free-form pool, kids' activities, and wide, immaculate beach on protected Bahía de Mujeres.

Bulevar Kukulcán Km. 8.5 (1km west of Punta Cancun). www.beachscape.com.mx. ✆ **998/891-5400,** 998/891-5427, or 866/340-9082. 134 units. High season $97–$133 double, $183–$209 1-bedroom; low season $80–$94 double, $155–$170 1-bedroom. 2- and 3-bedroom units and all-inclusive meal plans available. **Amenities:** 2 restaurants; lobby bar; outdoor pool with shallow kids' section; gym; beauty salon; convenience store; Wi-Fi.

**Flamingo Cancún ★** One of Cancún's many buildings that echo the shape of a Maya pyramid, this is one of the Hotel Zone's best-known budget hotels, commanding a wide, beautiful white beach. Built in the 1980s and remodeled just once, it was beginning to show its age when incremental renovations began in 2011. That effort has opened up the bar area, created a new international restaurant, **La Fuente,** opened a wall with windows looking onto the main pool, added private day beds, and remodeled an entire floor of guest rooms, with bold colors contrasting with the white floors, walls, and bedding. Remaining rooms were remodeled in 2014. The reconfigured main interior courtyard feels less crowded than before, but the newer wing and pool on the ocean side are still the places to seek peace and quiet. Though its optional all-inclusive program is more in demand than ever, I recommend booking a room only and sampling the many flavors of Cancún, as the hotel's food is inconsistent and varies little from day to day.

Bulevar Kukulcán Km 11 (across from Plaza Flamingo shopping center). www.flamingocancun.com. ✆ **877/319-8464** in the U.S., or 998/848-8870. 260 units. High season $104 double/$141 all-inclusive; low season $92 double/$129 all-inclusive. **Amenities:** 2 restaurants; 2 bars; babysitting; fitness center; kids' club; 2 outdoor pools; Wi-Fi (in lobby).

**Marriott CasaMagna ★★★** If the grand entry through columns supporting a domed portico doesn't immediately dispel any notion of a cookie-cutter Marriott, a lobby longer than most city blocks—gleaming with marble, polished wood, and crystal chandeliers hanging between massive arches—will leave no doubt. This is a stellar family-oriented resort that delivers a taste of luxury without breaking the budget. I find it warmer and more approachable than its more sumptuous sister property, the adjacent JW Marriott, with which CasaMagna shares a kids' club and other amenities. The lobby opens onto a sprawling pool that curves out to an oversized whirlpool overlooking the beach. Rooms are smaller than in some of Cancún's newer luxury hotels—it was built in 1991—but are more than adequate, and feature traditional wooden furniture and warm red and gold tones. All have private balconies. The hotel remodeled **Mikado,** its Japanese restaurant, in 2013, while adding a new play structure to its kids' club and new oceanfront *palapas* and pool beds to the grounds.

Bulevar Kukulcán Km 15 (adjacent to JW Marriott). www.marriott.com. ✆ **800/228-9290** in the U.S., or 998/881-2000. 450 units. High season $250–$400 doubles; low season $99–$189 doubles. Family packages and all-inclusive options available. **Amenities:** 6 restaurants; lobby bar w/live music; babysitting; concierge; children's programs; fitness center and massage service; outdoor pool, children's pool, and whirlpool; 2 lighted tennis courts; business center; Wi-Fi $15 per day in rooms, $20 in public areas.

**Westin Resort & Spa ★★** Sitting at the very end of the Hotel Zone on a quiet strip separating the Caribbean from Nichupté Lagoon, which it shares with just two other resorts, this property offers water views from almost every room. This is as much seclusion as you'll find in the Hotel Zone, and its kids' club and variety of activities make it a great place for families. A subtle but thorough renovation in 2014 has refreshed everything from the marble floors to guest room furniture to the swimming pools. Spacious rooms, still bright and airy, have a warmer if more neutral feel with new sand-colored floor tiles, wooden furniture, and new artwork. Rooms offer views of either the ocean or the lagoon and have such luxurious touches as flatscreen TVs, iPod docks, and a spa with a choice of indoor or outdoor treatments and a *temazcal* for traditional Maya steam baths. Among its restaurants, all of which have ocean views, **Sea and Stones** is unique for providing hot volcanic stones for cooking your own meat, chicken, fish, or seafood under a beach *palapa.* A good 15-minute drive from nightclub central, this is not a place for party animals, but the waters here are the best in the Hotel Zone for snorkeling and one of the few spots viable for diving.

Bulevar Kukulcán Km 20 (south end of Zona Hotelera on Punta Nizuc). www.westin.com/cancun. ✆ **800/937-8461** in the U.S., or 998/848-7400. 379 units. High season $144–$235 double, from $256 suite; low season $115–$195 double, from $215 suite. **Amenities:** 4 restaurants; 3 bars; spa with *temazcal;* gym; 4 outdoor pools, 2 each on ocean and lagoon sides; kids' club; tennis courts; business center; 24-hour room service; Wi-Fi free in lobby and lobby bar, $15 a night in room.

## INEXPENSIVE

**Holiday Inn Express ★** This standard, somewhat older hotel is the least expensive lodging you can find in the Hotel Zone and still get clean, updated rooms—think lots of white, with beige accents—with extremely comfortable beds and pillows, along with such amenities as flatscreen TVs, toiletries, washcloths, irons and ironing boards, coffeemakers, safes, a business center with Internet computers, and a free breakfast buffet with varied offerings. The large, central outdoor pool—actually two pools connected by a bridge—is beautiful, with stone arches and a waterfall. Its location in a quiet residential area about a half-mile from Bulevar Kukulcán can be good or bad, depending on the kind of stay you had in mind. Mexican guests outnumber foreign tourists, a refreshing departure for Cancún; there always seems to be at least one staff member on duty who speaks English. On the downside, it doesn't have a full restaurant, bar, fitness center, or spa, and it's at least a 10- to 15-minute walk to the main drag. If you don't have a car, going out for dinner takes some planning, but there's a taxi stand right in the parking lot and a small grocery store across the street for snacks. Though it won't please the beach-and-party crowd, it's a great option for travelers on a budget.

Paseo Pok-Ta-Pok Lotes 21 & 22 (across the bridge south of Pok-Ta-Pok golf course). www.ihg.com. ✆ **998/883-2200.** 119 units. High season $64–$87 double; low season $51–$73 double. Rates include breakfast. **Amenities:** Outdoor pool; business center; free Wi-Fi.

**Sina Suites ★★** If you want to stay within quick reach of the Hotel Zone's clubs, restaurants, and beaches but don't want to be in the thick of it, this small hotel tucked away in a quiet, well-kept residential neighborhood on the Nichupté Lagoon side of Bulevar Kukulcán fits the bill. While basic but comfortable motel-type rooms along an upstairs corridor are an unbelievable deal for the Hotel Zone, most units are one-bedroom suites with kitchenettes and balconies or terraces opening onto a lovely garden and small marina. Furnishings might remind you of your grandma's house, but the clean, well-maintained rooms are huge, and the panoramic view of towering resort palaces across the water is spectacular at night. This calm refuge is about a 10 minutes' walk from Bulevar Kukulcán, and it provides daily transportation to beach clubs on the

Caribbean side. Wi-Fi is free, but spotty. The solicitous front-desk staff speaks English, and the owner lives on site, which always makes a difference.

Quetzal No. 33, Fracc Club de Golf (near Pok-Ta-Pok golf course). www.suitessinacancun.com. ✆ **998/883-1017,** 883-1018. 36 units. High season $95–$167 doubles; low season $65–$115 doubles; master suites for 4 to 6 people and monthly rates also available. **Amenities:** Restaurant; 2 bars; outdoor pool; marina; kitchenettes (in suites); free Wi-Fi.

## Ciudad Cancún (Downtown)

### MODERATE

**Adhara Hacienda Cancún ★★** The owners of downtown Cancún's top business hotel, which opened as a Holiday Inn and was most recently a Radisson, shed its franchise affiliation in 2014 and now operate it independently under a new name. Ensconced in a traditional hacienda-style building, the interior has been thoroughly remodeled, with work starting even before the name change. Guest rooms have new beds and linens, smart TVs with plasma screens, and larger bathrooms. Add a fresh coat of paint throughout, and the once humdrum hotel now feels rather sleek. With its four-story, circular onyx-and-teak lobby and lively bar, and a large, sparkling pool set among palms, it's also inviting for leisure travelers who don't need the Hotel Zone bustle or prices. It claims to be the only downtown hotel with a (distant) view of the ocean, but if you crave sand, a free shuttle will take you to the beach; admission to the Hotel Zone's Mandala Beach Club is also free. And praise be, the recent changes have not boosted prices.



Av. Nader 1, SM2 (at José García de la Torre). www.adharacancun.com. ✆ **998/881-6500** or 800/771-1531 toll-free in Mexico. 173 units. High season 1,124–1,185 pesos double, low season 950–1,110 pesos double. **Amenities:** Restaurant; lobby bar; small gym; outdoor pool with separate wading area; room service; business center; free transportation to beach and admission to beach club; free Wi-Fi.

### INEXPENSIVE

**Rey del Caribe Hotel ★★** The owners of Cancún's original eco-friendly hotel, Eduardo Rodriguez and Araceli Dominguez, live on site, overseeing a humming machine that employs solar collectors, a rooftop rainwater recovery system, composting toilets, and laundry-water recycling to ensure minimal environmental impact. Recycling and composting dispatch 75% to 85% of their garbage. The compost nurtures a luxuriant garden around a small pool, with hammocks and wrought-iron tables and chairs tucked into the foliage, turning a modest hotel into a tropical oasis. Large, sunny rooms with kitchenettes and either a king or two full-size beds are simple but cheerful. Thanks to continuous renovation, some rooms feel quite modern while others seem a bit dated; all received HDTV in 2014. Rates include a standard breakfast (*sincronizadas,* eggs with ham and cheese, hotcakes, *pain français,* cereal with yogurt and fruit) in the garden *palapa,* with more extensive choices available for an extra charge.

Av. Uxmal SM24 (at Nader). www.elreydelcaribe.com. ✆ **998/884-2028.** 31 units. High season 1,150 pesos double; low season 780 pesos double. Rates include breakfast. **Amenities:** Kitchenettes; outdoor pool; whirlpool; small spa; massage service; free Wi-Fi.

**Xbalamqué ★★** This unique hotel's public areas could be the entrance to a Disney "Maya Adventure" ride—stone block walls, replicas of Maya statues and stelae, murals of ancient myths and warriors, reliefs that could have been lifted from a Maya temple, stone archways (even in the sapphire-blue waterfall swimming pool). Guest rooms are more subdued, but most have been brightened by a 2014 remodel: Whitewashed walls contrast with dark wood furniture and blue or green cotton bed throws, while flatscreen TVs and efficient, whisper-quiet mini-split air-conditioning replaced older predecessors. Though hallways are still rather dim, and the location on a busy street known for its nightclubs makes asking for a courtyard room a wise choice, this is one of Cancún's best values. The hotel's spa offers Maya healing treatments, facials, and a traditional *temazcal* (Maya steam bath) at a fraction of Hotel Zone prices (guests get a 10% discount to boot). The "cafebreria" (coffee shop/bookstore) hosts live music in the evenings, and a small theater presents music, comedy, and Saturday-afternoon kids' shows. Don't miss the floor-to-ceiling city views from the third-floor corridor.

Av. Yaxchilán 31, SM22, Mza. 18 (btw. Jazmines and Gladiolas, 2 blocks west of Parque Las Palapas). www.xbalamque.com. ✆ **998/193-2720.** 91 units. High season 796–881 pesos double; low season 573–617 pesos double. American breakfast included. **Amenities:** Restaurant; bar; theater; beauty salon; travel agency; outdoor pool; spa; beach club discount; free Wi-Fi.

# WHERE TO EAT

Cancún claims some of Mexico's top restaurants, offering as wide a range of dining options as you'll find anywhere. Seafood is king, but most of the world's cuisines are represented here, from the U.S. to Europe, the Middle East to Asia. And, of course, Mexico—with scant heritage of its own, Cancún has adopted traditions from all over the country, and cuisine is no exception. Don't leave without sampling the Yucatán's own regional cooking (p. 80), with its unique Maya spices. A bonus: Mexican and particularly Yucatecan dishes are usually the least expensive items on the menu.

Cancún's restaurants fall into roughly three categories: expensive and international in resort hotels; independent establishments along the lagoon (with great sunset views); and small, inexpensive Mexican eateries in El Centro (Cancún City), where authenticity is not compromised to appeal to tourists. Restaurants reviewed below are typically locally owned, one-of-a-kind restaurants or exceptional selections at area hotels. Many schedule live music. Unless otherwise indicated, parking is free.

## Isla Cancún

### EXPENSIVE

**Casa Rolandi ★★** INTERNATIONAL Owned by the same family as Rolandi's downtown, but under different management, this more upscale waterfront restaurant bases its menu on Swiss-Italian cuisine, with forays into other international dishes. It excels at employing local seasonal ingredients in such dishes as jumbo shrimp baked in banana leaves with a Maya-style *achiote* sauce, while customer demand keeps stalwarts like osso bucco with Milanese risotto and rack of lamb on the menu. Items that could be afterthoughts, such as puff bread from a wood-fired oven and a salad and antipasto bar, contribute to making every meal a special occasion. Although the main dining room on the top floor (street level) of the two-story building provides lovely views of the lagoon, try for a seat on the alfresco terrace, right on the water, for a romantic sunset dinner. The Terrace Lounge on the large outdoor deck is a prime spot for a drink when it isn't being used for special events.

Bulevar Kukulcán Km 13.5 (across from the Royal Sands). www.casarolandirestaurants.com. ✆ **998/883-2557.** Reservations recommended. Main courses 172–499 pesos. Sun–Wed 1pm–midnight, Thurs–Sat 1pm–1am.

**The Club Grill ★★★** INTERNATIONAL After leading the pack for decades, the Ritz-Carlton's signature restaurant is still the one to beat. Dining is a theatrical experience, like being dropped into the set of a BBC historical drama. It begins in the opulent

## A taste OF THE YUCATÁN

When the first Spaniards landed in the Yucatán in 1519, they found native people cooking with corn, beans, chiles, tomatoes, and squash, along with wild game—primarily turkey. The conquerors introduced beef, pork, lamb, nuts, fruits, cheese, and sugar cane (by way of the Caribbean), fully expecting local women to adopt European cooking techniques. Imagine their dismay when Yucatecans incorporated the European ingredients to produce new versions of native food instead of replicating Spanish dishes.

Today's Yucatán boasts one of Mexico's most distinctive regional cuisines, a complex blend of European, Mexican, and Caribbean flavors and cooking techniques. Some of the most recognizable flavors are ***achiote*** (an earthy, mildly tangy paste made from the annatto seed), native **sour oranges, lime juice, pumpkin seeds,** and **pickled onions.** Turkey ***(pavo)*** is still the most common meat eaten in Yucatecan homes.

The region's trademark dishes are ***pollo*** or ***cochinita (chicken or pork) pibil,*** meat marinated in *achiote*, bitter orange, and spices, wrapped in banana leaves, then grilled or baked in a pit; ***poc chuc,*** thinly sliced pork marinated in sour orange juice, grilled, and garnished with pickled onions; and ***sopa de lima*** (lime soup), made with turkey broth, shredded chicken marinated in lime, and sizzling tortilla strips. Many other less-known local dishes are equally delicious.

In recent years, traditional Yucatecan cuisine has taken on flavors contributed by immigrants from Lebanon, Europe, Cuba, and even the United States. At the same time, restaurants serving international fare are adopting native Yucatecan ingredients. The evolution of new exotic flavors makes dining here a never-ending adventure.



anteroom with superb cocktails and a selection of wines, and continues into the candlelit dining room all the way through to caramel coconut soufflé or another divine dessert. The menu has a classic feel, with expertly prepared steak, lobster, and lamb. The frequently changing lineup is enlivened by contemporary flavors and combinations such as spicy blackened snapper, grouper, or other fish, roast duck with chipotle sweet potato puree and tequila sauce, and tuna loin with coconut foam. The exquisite five-course tasting menu introduces still more adventurous dishes and is reasonably priced for a restaurant of this caliber, and it can be ordered with or without wine pairing. The restaurant has a beautiful new patio with its own special menu. Smooth, live jazz is perfect for dining, and after dinner you can take a spin around the dance floor.

In the Ritz-Carlton (p. 74), Retorno del Rey 36 (off Bulevar Kukulcán Km 13.5). www.ritzcarlton.com/Cancun. ✆ **998/881-0808.** Reservations required. No sandals or tennis shoes; men must wear long pants and collared shirts. Main courses 380–640 pesos; tasting menu 580 pesos. Daily 6:30–11pm.

**Gustino ★★★** ITALIAN Cancún boasts many fine Italian restaurants, but none reaches the heights found at the JW Marriott's perpetual award-winner. The romantic dining room is a circular space surrounding a dramatic candle display, with views of the wine cellar and open kitchen; floor-to-ceiling windows look out on a man-made lagoon. It's a memorable meal from the basket of varied fresh Italian bread and focaccia to the appetizers and antipasti (try the breaded mozzarella with sautéed spinach, sundried tomatoes, and anchovies, or king crab with red cabbage and Granny Smith apples) to the entrees. Risotto, which may incorporate rib-eye stew, mushrooms, or sea scallops, is excellent, as is the house-made tagliatelle in truffle sauce. Lobster cooked in saffron with herbed chickpea puree is one of numerous standouts among the masterful *secondi piatti.* The menu changes seasonally but always features homemade pasta and extraordinary steak and seafood. The service, not surprisingly, approaches perfection, and the dress code is formal.

In the JW Marriott (p. 72), Bulevar Kukulcán Km 14.5. www.gustinocancun.com. ✆ **998/848-9600, Ext. 6637.** Reservations required. Dress code prohibits beachwear. Pizza and pasta 205–475 pesos, main courses 285-625 pesos. Daily 6–10pm.

**Harry's ★★** STEAK Cancún's top steakhouse, perched over the lagoon, is famous for its high prices and flashy environment worthy of the Vegas strip as much as for its Kobe beef, dry-aged in house. It's an institution that has bucked the trend toward sourcing locally. New York strips, rib-eyes, and other cuts are broiled to perfection in a super-heated oven, while an equally impressive array of fish and seafood, including king salmon and Maine lobster, is grilled on a *parrilla.* You can also choose shellfish from the raw bar, and fusion dishes such as tuna steak with jasmine rice and wasabi. Main courses are phenomenal, but the small things make the difference: a terrific chipotle lime and peppercorn sauce (one of a wide variety of butters and sauces to choose from), and the creamy garlic potato or sweet potato mashes could justify a trip all on their own. The wine list has nearly 500 international and domestic boutique wines. Portions are large, and service is impeccable, if a bit stuffy. The check comes with an uncharacteristically whimsical tower of cotton candy. The interior's preponderance of stone and marble creates an echo that makes conversation a challenge, so opt for outdoor seating if you can.

Bulevar Kukulcán Km 14.2. www.harrys.com.mx. ✆ **998/840-6550.** Reservations recommended. Main courses 450–1,100 pesos. Daily 1pm–1am.

**Lorenzillo's ★★** SEAFOOD This is Cancún's oldest restaurant, in business since 1979, and the crowds haven't thinned out yet. The romantic view of twinkly lights reflecting off the water from the adjacent dock has a lot to do with that, but ultimately it comes down to stellar seafood, and lobster in particular. The huge crustaceans you pluck from a big tank in the lagoon come from the restaurant's own lobster farm, and they prepare them broiled, grilled, with cilantro sauce or chile pepper vinaigrette, or any of 20 other ways. Of course there's also shrimp, fish, and combinations—*La Popa,* crepes stuffed with lobster and shrimp au gratin, is a decadent starter, and true seafood aficionados should try *El Temporal,* a rice *tumbada* ("tumbled") dish with calamari, shrimp, scallops, mussels, fish, clams, and crab meat. There are even a few beef and chicken dishes. Finish with an outrageous, oozing chocolate volcano cake, and if you can still walk consider a tasting in the larger walk-in wine cellar featuring hundreds of labels from more than a dozen countries.

Bulevar Kukulcán Km 10.5 (1.5km north of La Isla Shopping Village). www.lorenzillos.com.mx. ✆ **998/883-1254.** Reservations recommended. Main courses 305–790 pesos. Daily 1pm–12:30am.

**Puerto Madero ★★★** ARGENTINE/SEAFOOD/STEAK Modeled on the converted dock-warehouse restaurants in the famous Argentine port city, this is arguably the best of Cancún's many fine steakhouses. Poised at the edge of Nichupté Lagoon, its exposed brick and dark woods evoke the real thing while remaining contemporary and very urban. The extensive selection of beef is not Argentine but prime, including American Wagyu (at a price), and details like fresh bread served in leather baskets make it a memorable meal. Beef shares the spotlight with seafood, such as exceptional grilled Gulf of Mexico octopus seared in olive oil, and a small but inventive choice of pasta dishes. It may be sacrilegious to say so, but the appetizers and sides are some of the tastiest items; I could make a meal of the crispy empanadas with chimichurri dip, halibut casserole, soufflé potatoes, and creamed spinach with artichokes. The patio over the water, beyond the glass dining-room wall, is quieter than the bustling dining room, and smoking is allowed.

Marina Barracuda, Bulevar Kukulcán Km 14.1 (across from Ritz-Carlton). www.puertomaderorestaurantes.com. ✆ **998/885-2829,** -2830, -2831. Reservations recommended. Main courses 215–850 pesos. Daily 1pm–1am.

**Sedona Grill ★★** SOUTHWESTERN This less rarefied sibling to Gustino could serve nothing but the ambrosial *chiles en nogada* and earn my undying devotion. This heavenly cousin of the chile relleno was invented by nuns in Puebla state in 1821 to welcome Augustín de Iturbide, president of the newly independent Mexico: a poblano chile stuffed with ground beef and pork, onions, and various fresh and dried fruit, bathed in a creamy white walnut sauce, and topped with pomegranate seeds. Because of its history and its green, white, and red ingredients echoing the colors of the Mexican flag (and also because walnuts and pomegranates are in season), it became the country's traditional Independence Day dish. Complicated and time-consuming to prepare, it doesn't appear on many restaurant menus, but Iturbide would have rolled back his eyes in ecstasy after one bite of Sedona Grill's rendition. The menu is a blend of northern Mexico and U.S. Southwestern cuisine, but be ready for anything. Caesar salad gets a chipotle dressing, shrimp ceviche is served with Navajo fry bread, cioppino is heated up with green chiles, and pork tenderloin is paired with sweet potato mascarpone lasagna. The breakfast buffet is hugely popular, probably because every dish tastes like it was made to order, and it's reasonably priced at about $25.

In the JW Marriott, Bulevar Kukulcán Km 14.5. www.sedonagrillcancun.com. ✆ **998/848-9648.** Reservations required. Main courses 170–620 pesos. Daily 6:30am–11pm.

**Tempo ★★★** INTERNATIONAL When the all-inclusive Paradisus Cancún resort opened in the former Gran Meliá at the end of 2012, it lost no time bringing in Michelin-starred Spanish chef Martin Berasategui to open a new restaurant. His largely Basque-inspired Mexican and Caribbean cuisine reaches new heights for Cancún, drawing on fresh local market ingredients to create changing a la carte and six-course tasting menus. Something as seemingly simple as the smoked potato soup with octopus and parsley oil slows you down as you try to make each mouthful last. Veal tenderloin with Swiss chard, Camembert cheese and Iberian ham sauce is an a la carte standout. You never know what the tasting menu will bring, but give thanks if it includes the fresh seasonal fish with artichokes, fennel cream, and asparagus salad (also available a la carte). The ultra-modern setting, incorporating a mosaic mirror wall and a black baby grand piano, is more stunning than comfortable, though the linen-covered tables and white leather chairs set seemingly at random do allow more than the usual space from other diners.

Bulevar Kukulcán Km 16.5 (in the Paradisus Cancún, just south of Marriott CasaMagna). www.tempobymartinberasategui.com. ✆ **998/884 1086.** Main courses 315–495 pesos; tasting menu 637 pesos (987 pesos with wine pairing). Adults only. Mon–Sat 6pm–11pm; closed Sunday.

**Thai ★★★** THAI This open-air restaurant transports you to Thailand's coast, with lantern-lit dining cabanas rising on stilts from the water. The Thai chef, cooks, and waitresses serve fresh, authentic dishes that let underlying flavors shine through

### La Cuenta, Por Favor

If your previously attentive waiter seems to be ignoring you after the plates are cleared, it's not a lapse in service. By Mexico's rules of etiquette, it is rude to bring the check until you ask for it. It's okay to summon any waiter and say, "La cuenta, por favor," or to catch someone's eye and pantomime a scribbling motion against the palm of your hand. The standard tip for good service is 10% to 15% of the total bill, unless a service fee was included—although not common, this does happen, usually in upscale restaurants, so look before you tip.

perfectly balanced seasoning. The most popular dish is Pla De Phuket, a crispy fish filet in a tamarind chile sauce, but you'll find the gamut from satay to fresh Canadian salmon steak with garlic and chile sauce. Hearty curries and the rice and noodle dishes lend themselves to sharing, which takes some of the bite out of rather stiff (but worth it) prices. By 10pm, the bar fills with a younger crowd partying to DJ music against the backdrop of dolphins frolicking on the other side of a glass wall shared with the aquarium at La Isla Shopping Village.

La Isla Shopping Village (on southwest shore), Bulevar Kukulcán Km 12.5. www.thai.com.mx. ✆ **998/176-8070.** Reservations recommended during high season. Main courses 250–495 pesos. Daily 6pm–1am.

## MODERATE

**Elefanta ★★★** INDIAN This trendy restaurant on the lagoon borrows pointy archways and intricate tile work from Indian palace architecture to create an exotic setting for its fresh, tasty cuisine. Tables on stilted platforms right over the water afford views of the occasional ray or crocodile (at a safe distance) during the day and splendid sunsets in the evening. The chef, a native of northern India, manages two tandoors in open kitchens, producing rich dishes such as chicken marinated in spices and yogurt, and spicy shrimp curry with coconut. Potatoes in a tomato and cashew sauce is one among an impressive (and rare for Cancún) selection of flavorful vegetarian dishes. Although less expensive than Thai (above), its sister restaurant next door, prices do seem a bit high for the portion sizes, but the food is so flavorful that it's hard to complain. The bar offers more than two dozen types of exotic martinis, and a DJ is on duty on weekends.

La Isla Shopping Village (on southwest shore, near Thai), Bulevar Kukulcán 12.5. www.elefanta.com.mx. ✆ **998/176-8070.** Reservations recommended during high season. Main courses 145–540 pesos. Daily 6pm–11:30pm.

**La Destilería ★★** MEXICAN Inventive tweaks to traditional Mexican cooking, combined with superb tequilas and terrific sunset views over the lagoon, make this distinctive restaurant a good value for the Hotel Zone. More than 150 brands of tequila, many never found north of the border, go into the restaurant's mini-museum, which outlines the spirit's history and production process; ask about the afternoon tequila tours, which add tequila samples and appetizers to a guided museum tour. The dining room, surrounding a Herradura still, extends out onto the deck over Nichupté Lagoon. The hearty, affordable starters (quesadillas filled with mushrooms and squash blossoms, *sopes* covered with marinated, slow-roasted shredded pork) could make a light meal. But the main dishes, such as a goat-cheese chile relleno in a puff pastry crust, tamarind shrimp, or the signature *molcajetes* (a rich pot meal) of beef, chicken, or shrimp with grilled cheese, chorizo, beans, grilled cactus, and avocado served with tortillas for making fajitas, are hard to resist. Mariachis play from 8 to 9 each night, and kids can dine from their own menu in a playroom.

Bulevar Kukulcán Km 12.65 (across from Kukulcán Plaza). www.ladestileria.com.mx. ✆ **998/885-1086,** -1087. Reservations recommended for dinner. Main courses 159–460 pesos; tequila tour 85 pesos. Daily 1pm–midnight; Aug–Nov 1pm–11pm.

### INEXPENSIVE

**El Fish Fritanga Pescadillas ★★** MEXICAN/SEAFOOD Disguised as a little take-out dive on the lagoon side of Bulevar Kukulcán, this local favorite won't grab you unless you're looking for it. Head along the side to the stone steps in back, and descend to an oasis of *palapa*-sheltered tables under the palms on a small beach next to a marina. A few beef and chicken dishes are available, but this is a place for seafood lovers. You can satisfy any craving, from cheap *pescadillas* (deep-fried empanadas filled with whiting, a cod relative) to shrimp in orange sauce or seafood-stuffed fish filet. Try the signature Veracruz-style filet, or bring your own fresh catch to be prepared any way you like. Because it is seafood, some dishes veer into the expensive range, but just barely—since it caters to locals, prices are about 25% lower than other Hotel Zone restaurants. You won't hear much English here, but you will get a warm welcome, stellar service, and transcendent sunsets.



Bulevar Kukulcán Km 12.6 (across from and just south of Live Aqua). www.elfishfritanga.com. ✆ **998/840-6216.** Main courses 80–300 pesos. Daily 11am–10pm.

**Santos Mariscos ★★★** SEAFOOD This blink-and-you'll-miss-it place is a delightful, and delightfully low-priced, antidote to the Hotel Zone's hotel buffets and chain restaurants. A shrine to *lucha libre* with colorful retro furnishings, sculptures of the Virgin Mary, and plastic roses, it has just four tables on a patio adorned with Christmas lights throughout the year, plus a few booths inside. But it's everything a fish taco aficionado could wish for. Go with an open mind—one of the best dishes is a savory fish filling inside a taco shell made of fried shredded cheese. Some have pineapple in the filling, and the classic shrimp tacos come with seven sauces, including a strawberry jalapeño salsa. Chicken and beef tacos are available, too, and they do excellent *cazuelas* (spicy, slow-cooked seafood casseroles). Their tamarind margaritas are an unexpectedly perfect accompaniment.

Kukulcán Km 12.7 (just south of La Habichuela Sunset). ✆ **998/840-6300.** 55–170 pesos. Daily 11am–11pm.

## Ciudad Cancún

### EXPENSIVE

**Julia Mia ★★★** NEW MEXICAN With its white leather chairs, unexpected light sources, and creative cocktails, this chic, two-story restaurant is downtown's first Hotel Zone–style place. A local favorite since its opening in mid-2013, it is both devoted to Mexico's traditional flavors and fearless in fusing them with contemporary cuisine. Each ingredient gets its due, whether in crayfish tacos, roasted cream of corn soup with browned garlic and tomatoes, or salmon *al pastor* with roasted pineapple in a banana leaf. It's easy to be swayed by the *mocaljetes* and succulent meat dishes such as pork ribs in peanut and *pasilla* pepper sauce, but try to fit in the ravioli filled with *huitlacoche,* goat cheese, and grilled pumpkin flowers—if not as a main course, get an order to share with the table. Specials change every month, and the menu is revamped a

## Dinner & a Show

Pure kitsch—and pure fun, especially for families—the **Captain Hook Pirate Dinner Cruise** (www.pirateshipcancun.com; ✆ **998/849-4451**) combines a steak or lobster dinner with a cruise to Isla Mujeres and a pirate show, on two 98-foot replicas of 18th-century Spanish galleons launching from El Embarcadero at Playa Linda, Bulevar Kukulcán Km. 4). The steak option costs $87 per person; lobster or steak and lobster is $102. The additional dock fee is $12 per person. Up to two kids travel free and have a buffet meal; each kid beyond that pays half price. Open bar, pirate stories, wacky games, and swordfights included.

For a similar experience without the pirate antics, the **Columbus Lobster Dinner Cruise** (www.thelobsterdinner.com; ✆ **998/193-3360,** 866/393-5158 from the U.S., or 866/793-1905 from Canada) is designed for couples. It makes sunset and moonlight departures from the Marina Aquatours Pier (Bulevar Kukulcán 6.25). Passengers cruise Nichupté Lagoon's tranquil waters while dining on steak, surf-and-turf, or vegetarian dinners accompanied by wine and a saxophone serenade. Cost is $99 per person.

couple of times a year. More than 100 wines and 60 top-end tequilas, including the rare *tequila negro,* are featured in pairings and tastings. Lovely duets and trios perform each night, and mariachis play on Fridays.

Av. Prolongacion Yaxchilán (btw. avs. Xpuhil and Bacalar, north of Costco). www.juliamia.com.mx. ✆ **998/884-1086.** Reservations recommended. Main courses 90–375 pesos. Mon–Sat 7am–midnight, Sun 7am–7pm.

### MODERATE

**Labná ★★★** YUCATECAN/MEXICAN Entering through the Maya stone arch, whose shape is echoed in the dining room's vaulted ceiling, lets you know what you're in for: purely Yucatecan cuisine, though it also offers a selection of Mexican "haute cuisine" as well. The menu's authentic—and excellent—renditions of the region's signature *sopa de lima, poc chuc* (pork marinated in the local sour orange and then grilled), and pork or chicken *pibil* (seasoned with *achiote* and slow-baked in banana leaves) gets even more interesting when you get to the less familiar regional dishes, such as *papadzules* (tortillas stuffed with hard-boiled eggs and bathed in *pepián* (pumpkin-seed) and turkey in *escabeche* (roasted and then grilled, seasoned with chiles and smothered with pickled onion). Even the traditional pre-meal chips here are exotic, served with four killer sauces such as chile habanero with sour orange and the addictive *sikil-pak,* made of ground pumpkin seeds, roasted tomatoes, onions, and cilantro. A mural of ancient Maya pyramids and photos from the hacienda era boosts the nostalgia quotient; happiness is tucking into the Yucatecan Tour combo ($15) to the strains of a traditional *trova* (guitar trio) on Friday through Sunday afternoons (2:30pm–5pm).

Margaritas 29, a few steps north of Parque Las Palapas, next to Cristo Rey church and La Habichuela restaurant. www.labnaonline.com. ✆ **998/892-3056.** Reservations recommended. Main courses 115–260 pesos. Daily noon–10pm.

**La Habichuela ★★** SEAFOOD Couples flock to the impossibly romantic courtyard of "the Green Bean," where lacy wrought-iron chairs and tables stand incongruously among Maya sculpture reproductions, flowering hibiscus, and trees, in an atmosphere reminiscent of jungle-draped ruins. The focus is on Caribbean flavors, ranging from Yucatecan specialties such as cream of *habichuela* soup to the signature *cocobichuela,* a lobster-and-shrimp curry topped with tropical fruit served in a coconut shell. Grilled seafood and steaks are excellent, if that's what you hunger for, but they are hardly unique; go for the local specialties, such as chicken mole and marinated *tampiqueña*-style grilled beef. If you don't have room for the butterscotch crepe for dessert, try the Xtabentún, a Maya liqueur made from honey and anise. The newer Hotel Zone branch, the sleek, modern La Habichuela Sunset, has a two-story window wall overlooking the lagoon and a dance floor on the water; there, prices are about 20% higher for a similar menu, and the less expensive dishes are missing.

Margaritas 25 (1 block from Parque Las Palapas, next door to Labná). www.lahabichuela.com. ✆ **998/884-3158.** La Habichuela Sunset at Bulevar Kukulcán Km 12.6 (just south of La Isla Shopping Village in the Hotel Zone). ✆ **998/840-6240,** -6280. Reservations recommended in high season. Main courses 238–625 pesos. Daily noon–midnight.

**La Parrilla ★** MEXICAN As if trying to compensate for the overwhelmingly U.S.-centric Hotel Zone, this typical Mexican family restaurant evokes all the cherished traditions: a sculpture of a bull out front, a hostess in a colorful embroidered blouse, waiters bearing trays of drinks on their heads, and mariachis every night. The open-air dining room's arches, fountains, and balconies are reminiscent of an old hacienda, and the menu revives authentic traditional recipes from the Caribbean (salmon with coriander sauce) and Old Mexico (mole enchiladas, Yucatecan *poc chuc* pork), as well as sizzling *parrilladas* (mixed grill plates for two) and all manner of tacos. A tequila sampler is available for the asking.

Av. Yaxchilán 51 (at Rosas). www.laparrilla.com.mx. ✆ **998/287-8119.** Main courses 105–555 pesos. Daily noon–2am.

**Rolandi's ★★** ITALIAN Best known for its wood-fired pizzas, this patio restaurant/bar and pizzeria is a locals' as well as tourists' favorite that has been turning out consistently good Italian food downtown since 1979. In addition to 20 kinds of pizza, from a simple margarita to an exotic smoked salmon with pomodoro and formaggio; the menu offers calzones packed with fresh asparagus, mushrooms, ham, or seafood and coated in olive oil; homemade veal ravioli, and 14 other pastas. Tender chicken, rib-eye steak, and a variety of shrimp and seafood dishes also come out of the oven. Though veal cheeks and pizza piled high with seafood are expensive, the rest of the menu falls into the moderate range. Rolandi's also has branches in Cozumel, Isla Mujeres, and Playa del Carmen.

Av. Cobá 10 (just south of Av. Tulum traffic circle). www.rolandipizzeria.com. ✆ **998/884-4047.** 141-317 pesos. Daily 1pm–midnight.

## INEXPENSIVE

**100% Natural ★★** BREAKFAST/HEALTH FOOD The other downtown and Hotel Zone branches of this popular natural-foods restaurant closed during the tourism downturn of a few years ago, but the original downtown Cancún location is still going strong. Offering fresh, varied, and often inventive food at reasonable prices, it's known for seemingly infinite blends of tropical juices spiked with aloe vera, *nopal, chaya* (a spinach-like leafy vegetable), pollen, and other health boosters. A breakfast of tasty pancakes, omelets, or fruit plates here will provide a day's worth of fuel. Salads, sandwiches, wraps, pasta, seafood, and poultry offer plenty of lunch and dinner options, while variations on traditional Mexican fare add intriguing flavor as well as nutrition.

This is one Cancún's few restaurants in which vegetarians will have to spend some time pondering a wide range of choices. Locals and visitors alike linger through the morning in the serene, palm- and hibiscus-lined courtyard anchored by a stone fountain that sports fresh fruit instead of cherubs.

Av. Sunyaxchen 63 (corner of Av. Yaxchilan, 3 blocks from Parque Las Palapas). www.100natural.com.mx. ✆ **998/884-0102.** Breakfast 50–75 pesos; main courses 68–190 pesos. Daily 7am–11pm.

**Ty-Coz ★★★** CAFE Tucked behind the Comercial Mexicana Supermarket, this cafe greets you with a fresh, peppery scent. Huge vegetarian or classic deli combination sandwiches come on your choice of baguettes or croissants. Though the wooden wainscoting and walls covered with posters and photos of Paris impart a French coffeehouse feel that attracts students as well as local professionals, one of its specialties is a *Muy Aleman* ("Very German") plate of cold meats and cheeses, baguette or croissant, garlic mayo, and butter and jam. The 12-inch *baguette economica,* with ham, salami, and cheese, is a paltry 18 pesos (about $1.40 U.S.). The flaky *cuernos* (croissants), which have a devoted following, go well with the fresh coffee, espresso, or cappuccino.

Av. Tulum 33 (at Av. Uxmal, across from ADO bus station, behind Comercial Mexicana). www.tycozmexico.com.mx. ✆ **998/884-6060.** 18–80 pesos. Mon-Sat 8am–10pm, Sun 8am–8pm.



# EXPLORING CANCÚN

## Museums

**Museo Maya de Cancún ★★★** The end-of-the-world nonsense in 2012 had at least one beneficial side effect: two new museums dedicated to Maya culture, one in Mérida, Yucatán's state capital, and the other in Cancún. Cancún's museum is a beautiful space, built on pillars 30 feet above sea level to protect the artifacts in case of flooding. The clean, contemporary architecture includes wrap-around windows with a fantastic panorama of the Caribbean Sea and overbuilt shore, reminding you of your time and place even as you delve into the ancient world. It takes a fairly traditional approach, though technology does come into play: the reproduction of an Ice Age cave where one of the Americas' three oldest skeletons was recovered may have you scratching your head until you realize that the man, woman, and fire inside are holograms.

The Quintana Roo gallery progresses through development of the monumental cities to the south and the rise of the northern city-states such as Chichén Itzá, and into the colonial era and devastating Caste War of the 19th century. Displays of funeral rites, architectural elements, and domestic and ritual objects employ artifacts from familiar sites such as Chichén Itzá, Tulum, Cozumel, and Cobá, along with lesser-known sites such as Dzibanché, Oxkantah, and Chacchoben.

The second exhibition hall covers the broad sweep of Maya civilization. Eye-catching displays include a map of the Maya's distribution in Mexico and Central America, as well as models, bas-reliefs, and other decorative elements from temples throughout the Maya world. A reproduction of Tortuguero Monument No. 6 from Villahermosa, Tabasco, is especially fascinating: The stone's cryptic hieroglyphic reference to the end of the last 5,125-year cycle of the ancient Maya calendar was misguidedly cited as the source of 2012's doomsday proclamations. The third hall shows rotating temporary exhibits.

## A SLICE OF real LIFE

Cancún may not have Old World charm or a much of a history, but it does have **Parque de las Palapas ★★★**. Bounded by Margaritas, Gladiolas, Tulipanes, and Alcatraces streets downtown, this is Cancún's *zócalo*, the central plaza that serves as a communal front yard in every Mexican town. It was here that Cancún's first municipal president was inaugurated, and where antiglobalization protesters regrouped during actions that brought down the World Trade Organization talks here in 2003. Zapatista leader Subcomandante Marcos wound up his "other campaign" during the 2006 presidential race at Las Palapas. But mostly, it is a place where people rest in the shade during a busy day, meet friends, and celebrate fiestas.

Rebuilt in 2008, this is a modern plaza, with white canvas umbrellas replacing the original *palapas* that once shaded tables and vendors' stalls. It has no patina of the past. But it is a traditional *zócalo* all the same.

Stop by on a Sunday, or any day after the sun sets, and Las Palapas bustles with couples, families, food and balloon vendors, and gaggles of chattering teenagers. Grab a seat under an umbrella and sample the tacos, salty corn cob on a stick, fried bananas, or *cochinita pibíl* sandwiches from the food stalls. Kids dance, chase dogs, zip around on toy SUVs, and swarm the play structures. Artists hang their wares here and in the smaller, adjacent Parque Los Artesanos and Jardín del Arte. Most weekends bring live music and dance performances—jazz and salsa on Friday nights, the Cancún Municipal Orchestra on Sunday afternoons—but you can also get a great evening's entertainment from the impromptu and surprisingly polished efforts of young bongo drummers, guitarists, and singers.

Bienvenidos a México.



The museum incorporates the archaeological site of **San Miguelito,** previously accessible only by begging your way through the lobby of a nearby resort. It's a small site set among mangroves, with plenty of shade that makes it a pleasure to explore. San Miguelito and **El Rey** (see Maya Ruins, below) were part of a large complex of temples, palaces, and houses dating from about A.D. 1250 to 1550 that was abandoned soon after the Spanish arrived. It stretched along the dunes now occupied by resorts, and was part of a vast coastal trade network extending from Honduras to Campeche. San Miguelito's residents made their living fishing, farming, and producing salt, honey, and *copal*—an aromatic tree resin used for ceremonial incense, glue, chewing gum, medicine, and religious offerings. Foreign goods such as basalt artifacts, flint, and copper rings were also uncovered here.

Most buildings surviving at San Miguelito were residences. Be sure to walk all the way to the south end, where the site's tallest building stands. **The Pyramid,** with a portion of its temple surviving at the top, faces a group of buildings that actually appear to have been a part of El Rey. In the **North Complex,** where you enter from the museum, the main structure is **Chaak Palace,** now just a foundation dotted with stubs of columns. It encompassed four houses, two temples, and a large lobby. Near the **Dragon Complex,** a small square with four palatial buildings and two houses, a separate small structure contains a mural where fish, a turtle, and some mythical creature swimming in a stream are still visible. At the center of the **South Complex,** another residential group, is a palace that would have been used for receiving visitors and performing rituals. More of the walls and other features have survived in this area.

Most, but not all, signs in both the museum and the ruins are printed in English as well as Spanish. Although you could walk through both in a couple of hours, plan on half a day if you want to absorb much of the information they provide.

***Note:*** If you have a chance—perhaps on a side trip that includes Chichén Itzá—Mérida's larger **Gran Museo del Mundo Maya** (Calle 60/Mérida-Progreso Highway 299-E; www.granmuseodelmundomaya.com; ✆ **999/341-0435**) is also worth a visit. Though similar in subject to Cancún's museum, there isn't much overlap, and the experience is quite different.

Bulevar Kukulcán Km. 16.5, Zona Hotelera. www.inah.gob.mx/museums. ✆ **998/885-3842.** 59 pesos adults; free for age 60 and up and kids under 13. No credit cards or dollars. Tues–Sun 9am–6pm; last admission 5:30pm. San Miguelito archaeological site 9am–5pm.

**Museo Subacuático de Arte (MUSA) ★★** Also known as the Cancún Underwater Museum, this is one of the world's largest underwater sculpture museums. More than 500 life-size figures—some modeled on local residents, others depicting a VW bug, a dinner table, street scenes, and other tableaux—are made of a special concrete designed to be colonized by fish, coral, and other marine life. The sculptures form an artificial reef in a formerly barren seabed, intended to draw divers and snorkelers away from natural reefs degraded by visits from more than 750,000 people a year. Unfortunately, the museum is at that awkward age: Most sculptures have altered enough by now that their features are indistinguishable from a distance; at the same time, they haven't yet drawn large numbers of the colorful fish people want to see. Snorkelers, required to wear life vests, can't dive deep enough to see them up close, as divers can. Fortunately, the artwork is divided into two galleries. Arrecife Manchones, close to Isla Mujeres, is 6 to 9 meters (20–30 feet) deep and open to both divers and snorkelers, though snorkelers won't see much detail; Arrecife Nizuc, off Cancún's southern shore, is 4 meters (13-feet) deep and open only to snorkelers, who can get a closer look.

Entrance to MUSA is through local snorkeling and diving outfitters, the best known being **Aquaworld** (p. 92), a MUSA supporter from the early planning stages. A visitor's center on the second floor of Kukulcán Plaza (p. 96) features 26 replicas of the sculptures and exhibits outlining British artist Jason deCaires Taylor's process of creating the submerged figures. Mexican artists have contributed later installations.

www.musacancun.org/english. ✆ **998/848-8312.** $45 snorkeling, $59 diving with Aquaworld; other companies' prices vary.

## Maya Ruins

They won't put Chichén Itzá, Tulum, or Cobá out of business, but vestiges of pre-Columbian settlements scattered throughout Cancún are an intriguing reminder of the Maya coastal trade empire that once stretched from Honduras' Bay islands to the salt beds of northern Yucatán state. Remnants of ancient watchtowers and lighthouses suggest the Maya used Cancún as a Caribbean lookout on the route between Tulum, Cozumel, and Chichén Itzá. At the least, visiting them can be a rewarding break from the rigors of snorkeling, shopping, or chasing a tan.

Besides those listed below, bits of Maya ruins dot the island in unlikely places, such as the two that punctuate the grounds of the Pok-Ta-Pok golf course.

**Ruinas El Rey ★★** The collision of ancient and modern is at its most striking here, on Nichupté Lagoon in the middle of the Hotel Zone. With 16 buildings, it is the most complete archaeological zone on Isla Cancún. Standing among the broken

## GOING public

Beaches may be public, but access often is not. The following beaches, marked by signs, have public access points. Most offer sailboard rentals, parasailing, and various watersports lessons. These can fill quickly on Sundays and holidays, when local families traditionally enjoy a day out. From north to south:

**Playa Las Perlas,** Km 2.5, in front of Hotel Imperial Las Perlas. The water isn't as turquoise as that off the eastern beaches, but this beach offers some of Cancún's safest swimming and is popular with locals.

**Playa Linda,** Km 4, west of Nichupté Bridge. Park at El Embarcadero marina. Curving sands near the bridge offer excellent swimming, but it can be crowded and busy with Isla Mujeres ferries, pirate dinner cruises, and other tourist attractions.

**Playa Langosta,** Km 5, near Hotel Casa Maya. Dolphin Discovery and Isla Mujeres ferries dock here. The water is shallow—good for snorkeling—and generally safe for children. No facilities but plenty of beach restaurants and bars.

**Playa Tortugas,** Km 6.5, next to Oxxo. Deep turquoise water here is deeper than other northern beaches for grown-up swimming, but also has shallow areas good for children. This is another Isla Mujeres dock; sands to the right, past the rocks, are more secluded.

**Playa Caracol,** Km 8.5, next to Fiesta Americana Coral Beach or through the Xcaret bus terminal. Clear, placid water and a flat, shallow sand bed are ideal for children and inexperienced swimmers. If it gets crowded, walk to the left (west) for more space.

**Playa Gaviota Azul** (also called Forum Beach), Km 9, near Plaza Forum and the City Beach Club; **Playa Chac Mool,** Km 10, across from and 1 km south of Señor Frog's; **Playa Marlin,** Km 13, behind Kukulcán Plaza. The three northernmost Caribbean beaches aren't glamorous but offer space and expansive views. They are popular with windsurfers and parasailers; Chac Mool has decent surfing when conditions are right. Swimmers enjoy the waves, but keep an eye on the warning flags.

**Playa Ballenas,** Km 14.5, end of sidewalk north of Hard Rock Hotel. Amid some of Cancún's glitziest resorts, this beautiful, broad beach is known for panoramic sea views. It's great for sunbathing and chasing waves but has a dangerous undercurrent.

**Playa Delfines,** Km 18, south of Ibérostar Cancún. Parking on Bl. Kukulcán above beach. One of Cancún's largest and widest beaches, away from the phalanx of mega-resorts, it is more relaxing than most, with intense turquoise water and plenty of room for everyone. Stick to strolling and sunbathing; the current can be treacherous.

**Playa Punta Nizuc,** Km 24, around the corner of the Hotel Zone's southern tip. Cancún's most isolated beach is a broad white crescent with tranquil waters, bordered by mangrove jungle. It has stellar snorkeling, including the shallow gallery of the MUSA underwater museum (p. 89).



columns, stepped platforms, and stairways of a palace **(Structure 4),** you'll see the precisely engineered angles and crowning glass pyramid of the Ibérostar Cancún (formerly a Hilton) looming in stark juxtaposition beyond the piles of stone. This is one of the most peaceful spots on Bulevar Kukulcán; it's so quiet that you'll hear the scuttling before you see the well-camouflaged, plump iguanas that populate the ancient foundations.

Many structures are marked by plaques with information in Spanish, Mayan, and English. Though the Maya lived in Cancún as early as 200 B.C., El Rey ("The King") was built much later. Serving as a ceremonial center and possibly an astronomy lookout, the city reached its apex during the Postclassic period (A.D. 900–1521). Its two main plazas and two ceremonial walkways are unusual among Maya cities, which typically have one of each. Archaeologists theorize that the site was a royal burial ground; skeletons uncovered in the pyramid **(Structure 2)** appear to have been kings. Two small altars are all that remain of a temple that once topped the pyramid. The Maya typically built pyramids on top of older structures, and partially buried in the middle of the pyramid are a stairway and a balustrade from an earlier building. The best-preserved building is **Structure 3B,** a temple where you can make out traces of an original painting in what probably was a king's tomb.

Bulevar Kukulcán Km 17.5, across from Playa Delfines, Zona Hotelera. Daily 9am–5pm. 43 pesos.

**El Meco ★★** The northern Caribbean's tallest pyramid lies just outside of Ciudad Cancún. El Meco, about 6km (3½ miles) north on Bahía de Mujeres, opened to the public only in 2001 and is still sparsely visited, so wandering among the 14 buildings, vestigial columns, and stucco walls that protrude from the jungle makes a tranquil interlude. Its main pyramid is the 41-foot **El Castillo,** and like its famous Chichén Itzá namesake, it is closed to climbers. El Meco emerged late in the 10th century on the site of an abandoned fishing village between the coast and a large lagoon to become a major port, commercial center, and departure point for Isla Mujeres. With the top of El Castillo visible from the water, it was an important reference point for sailors. The site's name means "bow-legged," supposedly coming from a bow-legged coconut farmer who owned the land in the 19th century. The original Maya name is lost to history.

The section that is open to the public includes the large central plaza that served as the city's ceremonial heart. El Castillo, with snakes carved into its base and an outer staircase leading to the top, looks onto two smaller buildings believed to have been a temple and an administrative building. The best-preserved building is a small temple in the northern part of the park. Archaeologists are still exploring the region between the highway and the coast, which has the remains of an ancient dock.

Carretera Puerto Juárez-Punta Sam Km 2.7 (btw. Puerto Juárez ferry dock and Punta Sam), Ciudad Cancún. Daily 9am–5pm. 47 pesos.

**Yamil Lu'um ★** This small remnant of a site, about which little is known, is beguiling mostly for its lovely seaside setting (Tulum's boast of being the only Maya site on the ocean notwithstanding). The two lone structures are believed to be the remains of a temple—only two crumbling walls survive—and a lighthouse used in the late 13th or 14th century. It's tricky to get to, standing between the Westin Lagunamar and Park Royal resorts above the beach on Cancún's highest point (the name is Maya for "hilly land"). You'll have to ask the concierge at one of the hotels to let you through, or view it from the beach below; it's a short walk north of Playa Marlin.

Bulevar Kukulcán Km 12.5 (across from La Isla Shopping Village), Zona Hotelera. Daily 9am–5pm. Free.

**San Miguelito** See **Museo Maya de Cancún** in the Museums section, p. 87.

## Beaches

Isla Cancún's 22km (14 miles) of beaches are among the most beautiful in the world. All Mexican beaches are public by law, but most are commanded by resorts, so you'll have to walk through a hotel lobby (either unobtrusively or with permission) or go to a public-access beach and walk to your chosen spot—by no means a hardship. The island's northern leg, protected by Bahía de Mujeres, has placid water ideal for swimming. On east-facing beaches fronting the open Caribbean, the water is choppier and subject to strong undertow. Get to know Cancún's system of flag alerts before taking the plunge. Here's how it goes:

**White** Excellent

**Green** Normal conditions (safe)

**Yellow** Changeable, uncertain (use caution)

**Black** or **red** Unsafe—use the swimming pool!

Storms can move in and change conditions from safe to treacherous in a matter of minutes; make for the shore if you see dark clouds heading your way.

## Outdoor Activities & Attractions





**DIVING & SNORKELING** Known for its shallow reefs, dazzling color, and diversity of marine life, Cancún is ideal for beginning scuba divers. Punta Nizuc is the northern tip of the **Gran Arrecife Maya (Great Mesoamerican Reef),** the largest reef in the Western Hemisphere and second largest in the world. In addition to the sea life along this reef system, several sunken boats add a variety of dive options. Inland, a series of caverns and *cenotes* (wellsprings) are fascinating venues for more experienced divers. Drift diving is the norm here, with popular dives going to the reefs at **El Garrafón** and the **Cave of the Sleeping Sharks**—but be aware that most of the legendary sharks have departed, driven off by swarms people watching them snooze. Those that do still frequent the caves aren't there every day, so ask your guide about current conditions before you suit up.

Numerous hotels offer resort courses that teach diving basics—enough to make shallow dives and ease your way into this underwater world of unimaginable beauty. If you want to get serious about it, one preferred dive operator is **Scuba Cancún** at Bulevar Kukulcán Km 5 (www.scubacancun.com.mx; ✆ **998/849-7508**). A 3-day open-water PADI certification costs $442. A half-day "discover scuba diving" course for beginners with theory, pool practice, and a one-tank dive at a reef costs $95. Scuba Cancún is open daily from 7am to 8pm. For certified divers, Scuba Cancún also offers PADI specialty courses and diving trips in good weather to 18 nearby reefs, as well as to *cenotes* and Cozumel. Two-tank dives to reefs around Cancún cost $77; one-tank dives are $62. Excursions to Cozumel are two-tank dives and cost $180. Discounts apply if you bring your own gear. Snorkeling trips cost $39 and leave daily at 1:30 and 4pm for shallow reefs about a 20-minute boat ride away. A day of *cenote* snorkeling costs $92, while snorkeling trips to Cozumel are $125.

Cancún's largest dive operator is **Aquaworld,** across from the Paradisus Cancún at Bulevar Kukulcán Km 15.2 (www.aquaworld.com.mx; ✆ **998/848-8326**). It offers resort courses and diving to reefs, wrecks, or caverns—as well as snorkeling, parasailing, jet-ski "jungle tours," fishing, Isla Mujeres and Cozumel day trips, and other watersports activities. Aquaworld offers the unique, narrated **SubSee Explorer** tour, in a boat with passenger seating beneath the water's surface; picture windows afford a glimpse of undersea life without needing to dive or snorkel. The vessel itself doesn't submerge. The voyage costs $40 for adults, $20 for children under 12. Aquaworld also offers a snorkeling tour to the impressive **MUSA,** aka Cancun Underwater Museum (p. 89), for $45 per person.

The Great Mesoamerican Reef also offers exceptional snorkeling. In **Puerto Morelos** (p. 161) 37km (23 miles) south of Cancún, the reef hugs the coastline for 15km (9⅓ miles). It is so close to the shore (about 460m/1,509 ft.) that it forms a

## THE dolphin DILEMMA

The uproar over dolphin swim tours scheduled for attendees of TBEX in Cancún in August 2014 brought a long-simmering controversy to a boil. Cancún organizers ultimately canceled the dolphin swims, but the issues remain. Humans are utterly enchanted by these brainy, playful creatures, and the allure of getting into a pool to play with them is nearly impossible to resist. And with those perpetual smiles, the dolphins seem to be having such fun. What could be wrong?

After a dolphin swim some years ago, I felt privileged beyond words to have had close contact with a species I'd long been in awe of. Then the doubts set in. Playful as the dolphins seemed, they didn't carry me on their backs or "kiss" me because they chose to. They were performing according to script, because that's what they have to do. And let's say they *were* having fun during our encounter. Here's the thing: I love roller coasters, and I will happily ride them all day. But if I had to live in an amusement park—if I could never choose to do anything else—it would soon become torture.

Mexico outlawed the capture of wild dolphins in its waters in 2002, and extended the ban on the import and export of marine mammals in 2006. Only dolphins born in captivity have been added to swim programs since then—a very good thing, because less than half of the wild animals survive the brutal capture and culling process. But it doesn't change the fact that dolphins who swim 50 to 100 miles a day in the wild swim only a small fraction of that in captivity. Or that these highly social animals often become unnaturally submissive or aggressive when human interaction replaces lifetime bonds formed with their families and pods in the wild. Or that despite a steady food supply and lack of predators, dolphins die younger in captivity, and infant mortality is high.

Dolphin swim programs have proliferated in Mexico, and you won't have any trouble finding one on the Caribbean coast. Many are staffed by marine biologists who say the mammals thrive under human care. Some also conduct research, conservation, and education programs. After my dolphin encounter, I spent a couple of hours with the head trainer of **Dolphin Discovery** (www.dolphindiscovery.com; ✆ **998/193-3360**), which runs the majority of dolphin programs in this area. I was impressed by their knowledge of these animals, sensitivity to their needs, the conditions under which the dolphins are kept, and their commitment to conservation. This organization is frequently summoned to rescue sick and injured animals, and I am glad for the work they do. If I were to do a dolphin swim again, this is the outfit I would choose—but I can't contribute to a system that amounts to indentured servitude for these highly intelligent, complex creatures.

For more information on a thorny issue, visit the website of the **Whale and Dolphin Conservation Society** at http://us.whales.org or the **Humane Society of the United States,** www.humanesociety.org. For general information on related issues, see the **Center For Responsible Travel** (CREST), www.responsibletravel.org.

natural barrier and keeps waters calm along the village's beaches. The water here is shallow, from 1.5 to 9m (5–30 ft.), creating ideal snorkeling conditions. Stringent environmental regulations implemented by the local community keep this section of reef unspoiled. A limited number of companies are permitted to offer snorkel trips, observing guidelines to ensure the reef's preservation. Family-run tour company

**Cancún Mermaid** (www.cancunmermaid.com; ✆ **998/177-1107** or 998/155-1946), one of the best, offers a "Snorkeling in Puerto Morelos" excursion that typically takes snorkelers to two sections of the reef, spending about an hour at each. When conditions allow, the boat drops off snorkelers and then follows them along with the current. "Drift snorkeling," as it is called, enables snorkelers to see as much of the reef with as little effort as possible. The 5-hour Puerto Morelos trip, costing $80, includes round-trip transportation from Cancún hotels to Puerto Morelos, snorkeling gear, life jackets, lunch, beverages, and time for shopping in Puerto Morelos if participants wish. The $3 marine park fee is paid separately. Reservations are required at least a day in advance.

***Note:*** The "Boating Excursions" section, later in this section, includes day cruises that offer more snorkeling opportunities.

**FISHING** Shared or private deep-sea fishing charters are available at one of the numerous piers or travel agencies. Prices fluctuate widely depending on the length of the excursion (there's usually a 4-hour minimum), number of people, and quality of the boat. Marinas will sometimes assist in putting together a group. Charters include a captain, a first mate, bait, gear, and beverages. Rates are lower if you depart from Isla Mujeres or from Cozumel—and, frankly, the fishing is better closer to those departure points than out of Cancún.

Every season is fishing season in the Caribbean. Here's a general idea of what to look for:

- **Blue Marlin:** March through August
- **White Marlin:** March through August
- **Sailfish:** January through August
- **Grouper:** Most of the year, except July and August
- **Wahoo:** November through August
- **Amberjack:** August through March
- **Dolphin Fish:** March through September

For a comprehensive guide, go to www.deepseafishingcancun.com/season.htm.

**GOLF** The 18-hole **Cancún Golf Club at Pok-Ta-Pok** at Bulevar Kukulcán Km 7.5 (www.cancungolfclub.com; ✆ **998/883-1230** or 883-0871) is a Robert Trent Jones, Jr. design on the northern leg of the island. Greens fees run $115 to $160 for 18 holes, including shared golf cart, balls, snacks and beverages. Clubs rent for $45; a caddy costs $20 plus tip. The club is open daily from dawn to dusk.

Formerly part of the Hilton, the **Ibérostar Golf Club Cancún** (www.peninsulaconventioncenter.com/golf-and-spa; ✆ **998/881-8092**) has a championship 18-hole, par-72 course. Greens fees during high season for the public range from $149 to $199 for 18 holes, including a shared golf cart, snacks, and beverages; equipment rentals are available. The club is open daily from 6am to 6pm.

The **Moon Palace Spa & Golf Club** (www.palaceresorts.com; ✆ **998/881-6000**) is home to the first Jack Nicklaus Signature Golf Course along the Riviera Maya. Greens fees ranging from $187 to $303 include cart, snacks, and drinks.

**WATERSPORTS** Many beachside hotels offer watersports concessions that rent kayaks and snorkeling equipment. On the calm Nichupté Lagoon are outlets for renting small **sailboats, jet skis, windsurfing gear,** and **water skis.** Prices vary and are often negotiable, so check around. The private, nonprofit association of watersports and boating operators, **Asociados Nauticos Cancún** (Cancún Nautical Association) provides links to its 16 member companies at **www.nauticoscancun.org**. The site is in Spanish, but many of the operators have English sites.

## Boating Excursions

**WAVERUNNER/SPEEDBOAT TOURS** Several companies offer the thrilling **"jungle cruise,"** in which you drive your own *lancha* (small speedboat) or WaveRunner rapidly through Cancún's lagoon and mangrove estuaries out into the Caribbean Sea to a shallow reef. The excursion lasts about 2½ hours and costs $60 to $80, including snorkeling equipment. Many people prefer companies offering two-person boats rather than WaveRunners, since they can sit side by side rather than one behind the other.

Operators offering the jungle cruise change often and may call them by slightly different names. Check with a local travel agent or hotel tour desk to find out what's available. The popular **Aquaworld** (p. 92) calls its 2-hour trip the Jungle Tour and offers multiple daily departures for $60 ($30 children), including 30 minutes of snorkeling time. Seating is the WaveRunner-style, one-behind-the-other configuration. It also rents just the WaveRunners by the hour and half-hour. If you prefer a side-by-side boat so that you and your partner can talk or at least look at each other, try **Blue Ray,** Bulevar Kukulcán Km 13.5, across the street from the Ritz-Carlton, next to Oxxo (www.blueray.com.mx; ✆ **998/885-1108**). Its Jungle Tour costs $69. Wear plenty of sunscreen, and bring cash for the national park fee and tips.

**ISLA MUJERES** The island of **Isla Mujeres,** just 13km (8 miles) offshore, is one of the most pleasant day trips from Cancún. At one end is **El Garrafón Natural Park,** which is good for snorkeling. At the other end is the captivating village with small shops, restaurants, and hotels, and **Playa Norte,** the island's best beach. If you're looking for relaxation and can spare the time, it's worth several days. For complete information about the island, see chapter 5.

The easiest and least expensive way to get to Isla Mujeres is by **public ferry** from Puerto Juárez. Less frequent and more expensive ferries also depart from the Hotel Zone. **Water taxis** (more expensive, but faster) also run to the island from these departure points.

Puerto Juárez, a few kilometers north of downtown Cancún, is served by the Ruta 1 bus on Avenida Tulum. The air-conditioned **Ultramar** (www.granpuerto.com.mx; ✆ **998/881-5890**) boats cost 78 pesos per person (46 pesos child) each way or 146 pesos (46 pesos child) round trip. Crossings take 15 to 20 minutes. Daily departures are every half-hour from 5am to 8:30pm and then at 9:30, 10:30, and 11:30pm. Ultramar also runs ferries between Isla Mujeres and El Embarcadero (Playa Linda), Playa Tortuga, and Playa Caracol in the Hotel Zone. The cost is $14 ($8 child) one-way, $19 ($12 child) round-trip. Upon arrival, the ferry docks in downtown Isla Mujeres near all the shops, restaurants, hotels, and Playa Norte. You'll need a taxi to get to El Garrafón park at the other end of the island. You can stay as long as you like on the island, but be sure to confirm the time of the last return ferry.

**Pleasure-boat cruises** to Isla Mujeres are a favorite pastime. More than 25 boats a day—modern motorboats, yachts, sailboats (including the "Sea Passion" catamaran; www.seapassion.net), and even old-time sloops—take swimmers, sun lovers, snorkelers, and shoppers out on the translucent waters. Some tours include a snorkeling stop at El Garrafón, lunch on the beach, and a little time for shopping in downtown Isla Mujeres. Most leave at 9:30 or 10am, last about 5 or 6 hours, and include continental breakfast, lunch, and rental of snorkel gear. Others, particularly sunset and night cruises, go to beaches away from town for pseudo-pirate shows and include a lobster dinner (p. 85). If you want to actually see Isla Mujeres, go on a morning cruise, or travel on your own using the public ferry from Puerto Juárez. Most day cruises leave from El Embarcadero; prices vary depending on length and services included. Reservations aren't necessary.

**ISLA CONTOY** Travel agencies offer an all-day excursion to the natural wildlife habitat of **Isla Contoy,** which usually includes time for snorkeling. The island, 90 minutes past Isla Mujeres, is a major nesting area for birds and a treat for nature lovers. Call any travel agent or ask at your hotel tour desk for a selection of boat tours to Isla Contoy. Prices range from $70 to $110, depending on the length of the trip and additional activities, and generally include drinks and snorkeling equipment.

# SHOPPING

You can buy just about anything you can think of in Cancún, which is renowned for its huge, air-conditioned malls catering to international tourists. Most of the stores, the brands, and even the food will look pretty familiar. U.S. visitors may find **clothing** more expensive in Cancún, but the selection is broader than at other Mexican resorts. Numerous **duty-free shops** offer excellent value on European goods.

You won't find the more traditional Mexican shopping experience—haggling over prices and dodging hawkers in open markets—in the Hotel Zone. For that, you'll need to head downtown.

**Handicrafts** are more limited and more expensive in Cancún than other parts of Mexico, because they are not produced here. Most of what's available is in the downtown markets.

Mall hours generally are 8 or 9am to 9pm or later daily. Other shops and markets keep similar hours, but posted hours tend to be regarded merely as suggestions. Most retailers in the malls take major credit cards, but markets deal strictly in cash.

## Zona Hotelera

The closest thing the island has to a traditional market, and the only place you may be able to bargain, is the open-air **Coral Negro** (Bulevar Kukulcán Km 9.5, next to Plaza Dady'O; daily from 7am to 11pm). Vendors sell sombreros, traditional clothes, souvenir T-shirts, Mexican candies, tattoos both real and fake, and other merchandise geared mostly to tourists. You can find some decent items at reasonable prices, but for serious shopping, your time will be better spent downtown. **Plaza La Fiesta** (Bulevar Kukulcán Km. 9, across the street from Cancún Center; ✆ **998/883-2428**), is a large Mexican outlet store selling handicrafts, clothing, jewelry, tequila, silver, leather, spices, coffee, and thousands of other Mexican products. It also has a pharmacy, a liquor store, a mini market, and clean bathrooms. Prices are fixed, reasonable, and well-marked. It's typically open daily from 9am to 10pm or later. If you want Mexican souvenirs without leaving the Hotel Zone, this is your best bet.

For the most part, Cancún shopping is done in sophisticated, air-conditioned **malls**—not quite as grand as some of their U.S. counterparts, but close. Most stand along Bulevar Kukulcán between Km 7 and Km 12. Kukulcán Plaza and La Isla offer the most extensive parking.

**Kukulcán Plaza ★★** This large, upscale mall houses hundreds of shops, restaurants, and entertainment. It has a bank, a bowling alley, several handicrafts stores, a game arcade and play area for kids, a liquor and tobacco store, several swimwear shops, music stores, a drugstore, a leather-goods shop (including shoes and sandals), and a store specializing in silver from Taxco. The second floor has a free visitor center for the MUSA underwater museum (p. 89). There's an extensive food court as well. The adjacent Luxury Avenue complex features designer labels such as Cartier, Fendi, Louis Vuitton, Salvatore Ferragamo, Ultrafemme, and the Mexican designer Pineda Covalin. Assistance for those with disabilities is available upon request, and wheelchairs, strollers, and lockers are available at the information desk. This is the only mall that offers free Wi-Fi throughout the complex. Bulevar Kukulcán Km 13. www.luxuryavenue.com/store/cancun. ✆ **998/193-0161.** Daily 8am–10pm, until 11pm during high season.

**Forum by the Sea ★** It's more likely entertainment and people-watching than shopping that will lure you to The Forum, which you'll know by the giant neon guitar out in front. This is home to the Hard Rock Cafe and Chili's (both of which have a terrace with great Caribbean views), Carlos 'n' Charlie's, and CoCo Bongo, granddaddy of all Cancún nightclubs. It also has an extensive food court. It's busiest after dark, when there are often street performers on the main level, and it stays open late. The few shops sell swimwear, sunglasses, jewelry, and souvenirs. Bulevar Kukulcán Km 9. www.forumbythesea.com.mx. ✆ **998/883-4425.** Daily 10am–11pm or midnight (bars remain open later).

**La Isla Shopping Village ★★★** Easily Cancún's most appealing mall, this is a wonderful open-air complex bordering the lagoon. In the evening, locals treat it like a traditional central plaza, dressing up and meeting friends and neighbors for a contemporary version of Mexico's evening *paseo* (promenade). Though designed as a "Caribbean village," its fountains, mosaic floors, and maze of walkways with bridges crossing a network of canals call Venice to mind (if Venice had been built only in the past decade). When the rigors of shopping start to wear you down, relax on a boat ride through the canals or stroll the pleasant boardwalk along the lagoon. Yes, you can drop a fortune at Lladró, but you can also pick up a well-made cotton blouse for $15 at a modest boutique or find good-quality silver jewelry for less than $50 at one of the craft carts that line the walks. The duty-free shop Ultrafemme sells Lancôme, Chanel, Clinique, and similar brands of cosmetics, typically for 25% less than U.S. prices. Nighttime is the right time at La Isla, whether you join in the *paseo,* head for a thumping disco, catch a movie at the 10-screen cinema, or fortify yourself in any one of the fine restaurants here. And how many shopping centers have a well-respected aquarium in their midst? This is a mall even the retail-challenged can love. Bulevar Kukulcán Km 12.5. www.laislacancun.com.mx. ✆ **998/883-5025.** Daily 10am–10pm.

## Ciudad Cancún

**Ultrafemme ★** Specializing in imported cosmetics, perfumes, and fine jewelry and watches, this duty-free store has spawned many branches, including some in the Hotel Zone's most popular malls. This location in downtown Cancún's Plaza Las Americas, though, offers lower prices than those in the Hotel Zone. Plaza las Americas, Av. Tulum Sur 26 at Calle de Las Amercas. www.ultrafemme.com. ✆ **998/272-5476.** Mon–Sat 10am to 7pm.

**Mercado 28 ★★** Cancún's main open-air market sells many of the same items found in the Hotel Zone at a fraction of the price, plus a lot more. The dizzying array ranges from hammocks made in Mérida to silver from Taxco to *alebrijes* (carved wooden figures) from Oaxaca, along with the full complement of cheesy souvenirs. Locals do their daily shopping here, but be prepared: Tourists get the hard sell. The clean and orderly market also houses a couple of the city's best seafood restaurants, **El Cejas** and **Pescado con Limón.** Av. Xel-Ha at Sunyaxchen. ✆ **998/892-4303.** Daily 9am–7pm.

**Plaza Bonita ★** After stocking up on crafts and souvenirs at Mercado 28, browse the adjacent **Plaza Bonita** for shoes, clothing, imports, furnishings, and local restaurants. The colorful outdoor mall, designed like a little colonial street painted in typical Mexican colors and accented with wrought iron, also has boutiques, gold and silver stores, ice cream parlors, and kids' clothing shops. Prices are higher than in Mercado 28, but way below anything in the Hotel Zone. Av. Xel-Há at Sunyaxchen. www.plazabonita.mx. ✆ **998/884-6812.** Mon–Fri 10am–8pm, Sun 10am–6pm.

# ENTERTAINMENT & NIGHTLIFE

Cancún's party reputation is not confined to spring break—the action here continues year-round. While the revelry often begins by day at the beach, the sun-drenched crowd heads to happy hour at the rocking bars located along the Hotel Zone, which often serve two-for-one drinks at sunset. Hotels play a part in the happy hour scene, with drink specials to entice visitors and guests from other resorts. Come night, the hottest centers of action are also along Kukulcán, and include **Plaza Dady'O, Forum by the Sea,** and **La Isla Shopping Village.** These entertainment plazas transform into true spring break madness for most of March and April.



## The Club & Music Scene

Clubbing in Cancún is a hugely popular vacation pastime, often going on until the sun rises over that unbelievably blue sea. Several big hotels have nightclubs or schedule live music in their lobby bars. At the clubs, expect to stand in lines on weekends and pay a cover charge starting at about $40 with open bar ($15 to $25 without open bar, and about $10 per drink). Some of the higher-priced clubs include live entertainment. Those reviewed here are air-conditioned and accept major credit cards.

Numerous restaurants, such as **Carlos 'n' Charlie's, Hard Rock Cafe,** and **Señor Frog's,** double as nighttime party spots, offering wildish fun at a fraction of the price of more costly clubs. Many popular restaurants downtown also party hard as the evening wears on.

**Grupo Mandala** (www.shop.grupomandala.com.mx) offers "The Madness Tour," a package deal providing entry and open bar to three clubs in one night. Depending on the night, these may include La Vaquita, Dady'O, Mandala, MB, Palazzo, or The City. It costs 875 pesos (about $65) if booked online. ***Note:*** If you have been drinking when you're ready to call it a night, take public transportation or have someone with you rather than drive or get in a taxi alone.

**The City ★** Acrobats and brain-searing light shows are the trademarks of this nightclub, one of the world's largest. Its three floors hold nine bars and several VIP areas under roughly 100 rotating ceiling lights that rival Disney's Space Mountain ride, while international DJs man a booth that could be an airport control tower. It's been known as the go-to place for celebrity visitors ever since Paris Hilton partied very publicly here in the mid-2000s. If you just can't get enough, the club's Cabana Beach opens at 10am, offering a pool, beach cabañas, and food and bar service, along with frequent pool parties, bikini contests, and other activities. The City opens at 10:30pm. Bulevar Kukulcán Km 9.5. www.thecitycancun.com. ✆ **998/848-8380.** Cover $65 with open bar.

**CoCo Bongo ★★★** The spectacular shows at Cancún's hottest (and most expensive) dance club are legendary, but nothing will prepare you for your first time. Equal parts disco, Vegas revue, and Cirque du Soleil, it holds thousands of revelers on vertiginous tiers of bleachers. With no defined dance floor, you dance anywhere you can—on tables, on the bar, and sometimes on the stage, as performers impersonate pop culture icons and blend seamlessly into the film clips and music videos projected on huge screens. Trapeze artists gyrate overhead, jugglers wind through the seats, and bursts of confetti rain down upon you. Music runs the gamut, from Caribbean and salsa to 20th-century classics and techno. As in most clubs in the party zone, the crowd is young and energetic, but there's usually a respectable contingent of baby boomers. The cover charge is steep (go early in the week for lower prices), but for an all-night open bar and the equivalent of a 4-hour Broadway show, it's reasonable. Doors open at 10pm for 10:30pm shows. Plaza Forum by the Sea (2nd floor), Bulevar Kukulcán Km 9.5. www.cocobongo.com.mx. ✆ **998/883-5061.** Cover $80 ($75 online) Thurs–Sun, $70 ($65 online) Mon–Wed; includes open bar.

**Dady'O ★** Long lines of the young and the reckless form each night for this popular club, designed to evoke a deep-sea Caribbean cavern. With heavily advertised light shows and regular special events, it comes off as a second-string mash-up of CoCo Bongo and The City that promises bikini contests, lingerie carnivals, and "the hottest girls" for good measure. It does have a big dance floor and a state-of-the-art lighting system that produces terrific light and laser shows. Doors open at 10pm each night. Bulevar Kukulcán Km 9.5. www.dadyo.com. ✆ **998/883-3333.** Cover $50–$65 with open bar.

**La Madonna** An enormous reproduction of the Mona Lisa flanked by two-story Greek sculptures creates a surreally grandiose interior that is somehow perfect for enjoying a choice of more than 180 creative martinis and 2,000 labels of wine. Ambient music includes a lot of Bossa Nova and lounge tunes. The trendy restaurant/bar also turns out authentic Swiss-Italian fare and sinful desserts. Take your red mandarin, lychee, or green apple martini out to the patio and mingle with Cancún's hippest crowd, or head upstairs to sample cognac and cigars. La Madonna is open daily from noon to 1am. La Isla Shopping Village (south of the cinema), Bulevar Kukulcán Km 12.5. www.lamadonna.com.mx. ✆ **998/883-2222.**

**The Lobby Lounge at The Ritz-Carlton ★★** Five kilometers (3⅕ miles) and 180 degrees from the club zone, the Ritz-Carlton's intimate lounge is filled with vintage decor and overstuffed couches, where you can sip flavored margaritas, creative martinis, and single-malt whiskeys in complete serenity. Tequila tastings, available on request, sample from the hotel's collection of more than 100 varieties, and the Cigar Corner welcomes aficionados to enjoy a choice of Cuban and Mexican cigars on the terrace, Wednesdays through Saturdays. Guests inspired by the nightly live music can take to the small central dance floor. The Lobby Lounge is open daily from 5pm to midnight. The Ritz-Carlton Cancún, Retorno del Rey 36, off Bulevar Kukulcán Km 13.5. www.ritzcarlton.com. ✆ **998/881-0808.**

**Mandala** This unique, Asian-inspired club across from The City is impossible to miss: All three floors, bathed in red light, are open to the street. An auxiliary party is almost always in full rave on the sidewalk, feeding off the club's music and sexy vibe. It fills with slinky dancers partying into the wee hours, and the service is surprisingly attentive, considering how crowded it can get. Mandala is open daily from 9:30pm. Bulevar Kukulcán Km 9. www.mandalanightclub.com. ✆ **998/848-8380.** Cover $25–$50.

## Performing Arts

Several hotels host **Mexican fiesta nights,** including a buffet dinner and a folkloric dance show; admission with dinner and open bar costs about 600 pesos unless you're at an all-inclusive resort that includes this as part of the package. Check out the show at **Hacienda Sisal** (www.haciendasisal.com; ✆ **998/848-8220**), located at Bulevar Kukulcán Km 13.5, which is offered Tuesday nights starting at 7:15pm. **La Habichuela Sunset** (www.lahabichuela.com; ✆ **998/840-6240**), at Bulevar Kukulcán Km 12.6 in front of Kukulcán Plaza, offers a pre-Hispanic show with Maya influences Monday, Wednesday, and Friday nights at 8pm.

The hottest ticket in town these days is down the road, south of Puerto Morelos, where **Cirque Du Soleil** opened its first venue in the Mexican Caribbean in November 2014. See p. 167 for details.

**Moon Palace Concerts ★** If you could do without getting pummeled in Cancún's dance clubs, a good old-fashioned rock concert might be what you need. Moon Palace Golf & Spa Resort, just south of the Hotel Zone, has gotten into the entertainment business, with a concert lineup including Chicago, Shakira, Enrique Iglesias, Usher, and Ricky Martin in 2014. Kansas, REO Speedwagon, and Creedence Clearwater Revisited were on tap for early 2015. Though venues have included the resort's ballrooms and even the golf course, many of the big shows are now in the state-of-the-art Moon Palace Arena, which opened in 2014. Concerts are often a perk for guests, but many are available to the public through Ticketmaster (www.ticketmaster.com.mx). Carretera Cancún-Chetumal Km. 340. www.moonpalacecancun.com. ✆ **998/881-6000** or 888/327-0655 in the U.S. Prices vary; general range for most popular shows 441–1,174 pesos.

**Xoximilco ★★** The ever-expanding **Xcaret** (p. 184) empire, with four theme parks in the Riviera Maya, has made its way north to Cancún with the 2014 opening of **Xoximilco** in 2014. Much like Vegas casinos, Xcaret attempts to re-create other places. For its fifth park, it takes its inspiration (and name) from Xochimilco, the Mexico City neighborhood that occupies a remnant of the ancient lake that the Aztec capital was built on. Floating through the canals, having a long lunch and listening to mariachis is a treasured Sunday tradition in Mexico City. Cancún's Xoximilco also sends you through a series of canals on colorful, gondola-like *trajineras,* plying you with drink, food, and music, at about the same price as the real thing. While Xochimilco is busiest on weekend days, Xoximilco is strictly a nighttime activity; the park opens at 6:30pm daily. Carretera Cancún-Chetumal Km 338. www.xoximilco.com. ✆ **998/883-3143** or 855/332-2130 U.S. and Canada. $89 adult, $44 child. Online bookings discounted 10%.

# SIDE TRIPS FROM CANCÚN & RIVIERA MAYA

Of all Cancún's advantages, none is greater than its proximity to the natural and cultural riches that surround it. Any of these excursions could be done as a day trip from Cancún or the Riviera Maya if you leave before the rooster crows, but I recommend spending at least one night, or you'll be extremely limited in what you can see and do.

## The Ruins of Chichén Itzá ★★

179km (111 miles) W of Cancún; 120km (75 miles) E of Mérida; 138km (86 miles) NW of Tulum

The fabled ruins of Chichén Itzá (Chee-*chen* Eet-*zah*) are by far the Yucatán's best-known ancient monuments. Sadly, its coronation as a "New World Wonder" has made the great city harder to appreciate. Still, walking among these stone temples, pyramids, and ball courts gives you a feel for this civilization that books cannot approach, and there's no other way to comprehend the city's sheer scale; the ceremonial center's plazas would have been filled with thousands of people during one of the mass rituals that occurred here a millennium ago. And that is the saving grace for hordes of tourists that now flow through every day.

Much of what is said about the Maya (especially by tour guides) is merely educated guessing. We do know the area was settled by farmers as far back as the 4th century A.D. The first signs of an urban society appear in the 7th century in construction of stone temples and palaces in the Puuc Maya style, found in the "Old Chichén" section of the city. In the 10th century (the Postclassic Era), Chichén Itzá came under the rule of the Itzáes, who arrived from central Mexico by way of the Gulf Coast. They may have been a mix of highland Toltec Indians, who built the city of Tula in central Mexico, and lowland Putún Maya, a thriving population of traders. Following centuries brought Chichén Itzá's greatest growth. The style of the grand architecture built during this age clearly reveals Toltec influence.

The new rulers might have been refugees from Tula. A pre-Columbian myth from central Mexico tells of a fight between the gods Quetzalcóatl and Tezcatlipoca that forced Quetzalcóatl to leave his homeland and venture east. In another mythic tale, the losers of a war between Tula's religious factions fled to the Yucatán, where they were welcomed by the local Maya. Over time, the Itzáes adopted more and more the ways of the Maya. Sometime at the end of the 12th century, the city was captured by its rival, Mayapán, south of present-day Mérida.

Though it's possible to make a day trip from Cancún or the Riviera Maya, staying overnight here or in nearby Valladolid makes for a more relaxing trip. You can see the light show in the evening and return to see the ruins early the next morning when it is cool and before the tour buses start arriving.

## ESSENTIALS

### Getting There

**BY CAR** Chichén Itzá is on old Highway 180 between Mérida and Cancún. The fastest way to get there is to take the Highway 180D *cuota* west. Tolls from Cancún will total 326 pesos, and it will take about 2 hours, 15 minutes. From Playa del Carmen, take the new toll road from the end of Avenida Donaldo Colosio, follow it to Highway 180D, and turn west; tolls will add up to 283 pesos. From Tulum, take Route 109 west toward Cobá and Chemex; continue to Valladolid to pick up the Highway 180D toll road. You'll pay one 64-peso toll. Once on Highway 180D, take the Pisté exit and drive through the village. When you reach a T-junction at Highway 180 *libre,* turn left to the ruins; the entrance is well marked.

**BY BUS** Second-class buses leave Cancún's downtown station for Chichén Itzá (135 pesos) up to a dozen times a day, and at least one first-class bus (258 pesos) makes the trip daily. All leave between 2am and 1pm. Playa del Carmen also has at least one daily first-class bus (348 pesos) and one or two second-class buses (132 pesos). Tulum usually has one first-class bus (190 pesos) and one second-class bus (97 pesos) a day. Day trips to Chichén Itzá are also widely available from Cancún, Playa del Carmen, and most destinations in the Yucatán; any hotel can book these or provide information.

## AREA LAYOUT

The village of **Pisté,** where most of the budget hotels and restaurants are located, is about 2.5km (1½ miles) west of the ruins. Public buses can drop you off here. Another budget hotel, the Dolores Alba (p. 103), is on the old highway 2.5km (1½ miles) east of the ruins. Three luxury hotels are situated right at Chichén Itzá's entrance.

## WHERE TO STAY & EAT

The expensive hotels in Chichén occupy beautiful grounds, are close to the ruins, serve decent food, and have toll-free reservations numbers. They do a brisk business with tour operators—they can be empty one day and full the next. From these hotels, you can easily walk to the back entrance of the ruins, next to the Hotel Mayaland. **Hotel Chichén Itzá** (www.mayaland.com; ✆ **998/887-2495**) is the best of several inexpensive hotels in the village of Pisté, which has little else to recommend it. Another option is to stay in Valladolid (p. 108), 40 minutes away.

This area has no great food, but it has plenty of adequate food; simple choices are best. The ruins' visitor center serves decent snacks. Hotel restaurants do a fair job but are more expensive than they should be. In Pisté, try the Hotel Chichén Itzá or one of the restaurants along the highway that cater to bus tours (best during early lunch or regular supper hours, when the buses are gone).



### Expensive

**Hacienda Chichén Resort ★★★** The cottages here, connected by paths winding through lush vegetation, are named for the archaeologists who worked here when the Carnegie Institute set up camp in this former hacienda in 1923 to conduct excavations at the ruins. It's the quietest and most intimate of the upscale hotels bunched around the entrance to the ruins. Now those refurbished bungalows serve as guest quarters outfitted with air-conditioning, ceiling fans, and private porches. Set in a jungle-like tropical garden that harbors a small chapel and a sacred cave, the stucco bungalows with wood-beam ceilings seem inhabited by the ghosts of Stephens and Catherwood. The hotel's Yaxkin Spa, with a 99% Maya staff, has garnered international awards with its healing treatments using native *meliponia* honey, cacao, aloe, and tropical fruits.

Carretera Libre 180 Km 120. www.haciendachichen.com. ✆ **877/631-4005** in the U.S., or 999/920-8407. 28 units. High season $179–$215 double, from $269 suite; low season $119–$239 double, from $189 suite. Promotional rates often available. Free guarded parking. **Amenities:** Restaurant; 2 bars; large outdoor pool; spa; Wi-Fi (in lobby).



### Moderate

**Villas Arqueológicas Chichén Itzá ★★** Almost hidden behind the pricier hotels a little nearer to Chichén Itzá's entrance, this modest but quite attractive hotel is a great compromise between comfort and budget. Standing a 5- to 10-minute walk along a peaceful path to the ruins' side entrance, the contemporary rooms surround a pleasant courtyard and pool. The only drawback is that beds in standard rooms (a double and a twin in each) are tucked into niches with walls at the head and foot; travelers 6-foot-2 and taller should consider one of the suites, which have freestanding queen-size beds, as well as a double. Otherwise, standard rooms are smallish but comfortably furnished and more than adequate for a night or two. The spa offers relaxing and healing massages by a local Maya shaman. The exceedingly friendly, English-speaking staff can take care of guides, taxis, and any other needs you have. ***Note:*** Rates are the same all year, with no seasonal fluctuation.

Carretera Mérida–Valladolid Km 120. www.villasarqueologicas.com.mx. ✆ **985/851-0187.** 43 units. $65–$74 standard, $104–$118 suite. Rates include continental breakfast. Free parking. **Amenities:** Restaurant; bar; library; TV and game room; spa; large outdoor pool; Wi-Fi (in public areas).

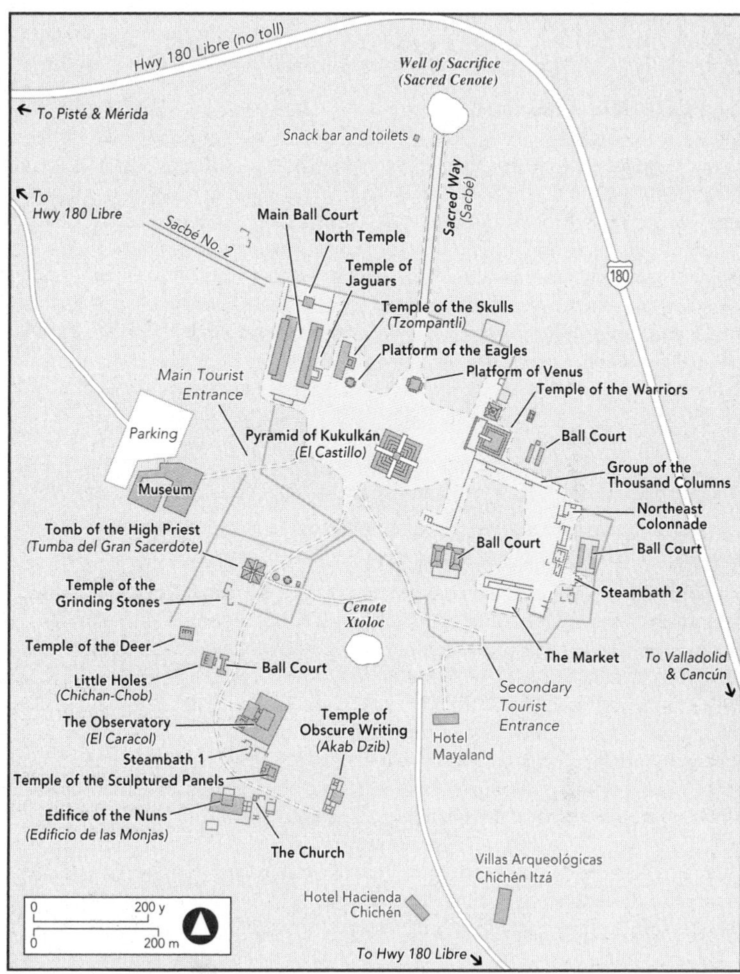


### Inexpensive

**Hotel Dolores Alba ★** Rooms in this perennial favorite of budget travelers are individual cottages reminiscent of a 1950s roadside motel, but the crisp, white rooms are embellished with colorful hacienda-style accents, and beds have divine pillow-top mattresses. Proximity to Chichén Itzá (though it's not really walking distance, except for athletes) is only one of the things the hotel has going for it: The Ik-Kil *cenote* (p. 108) is right across the road, and the hotel provides free transportation to the Balankanché cave as well as to the ruins. One of its two swimming pools is fed by a natural spring, and the lovely garden is frequented by birds. The poolside restaurant serves decent meals at moderate prices. This is a genuine bargain for what you get.

Carretera 180 libre, Km 122 (2.4km/1½ miles east of archaeological zone). www.doloresalba.com. ✆ **985/851-0117.** 35 units. 650 pesos double. Free parking. **Amenities:** Restaurant; bar; 2 outdoor pools; room service; shuttle to ruins; Wi-Fi (in public areas).

## EXPLORING THE RUINS

The site occupies 6.5 sq. km (2½ sq. miles), requiring most of a day to see it all. The ruins are open daily from 8am to 5pm. Admission for non-Mexicans is 216 pesos (split between state and federal agencies and purchased at separate windows); children 12 and younger are free. A video permit costs 45 pesos. A licensed guide costs 750 pesos (plus tip) and is now hired at a kiosk at the main entrance rather than by haggling with the cluster of contenders that used to approach. Parking costs 30 pesos. *You can use your ticket to re-enter on the same day.* At press time, the oft-delayed new, high-tech **Light and Sound Show**—which had been missing ever since lightning struck the original projection equipment in 2012—made its debut in December 2014. Admission is free until June 2015, when the price is expected (but not yet officially confirmed) to be 190 pesos. The large, modern visitor center at the main entrance consists of a museum, an auditorium, a restaurant, a bookstore, and bathrooms.

Chichén Itzá has two parts: the central (new) zone, which shows distinct Toltec influence, and the southern (old) zone, with mostly Puuc architecture. The most important structures are in New Chichén, but the older ones are also worth seeing. For more information, go to www.chichenitza.inah.gob.mx.

**EL CASTILLO** As you enter from the tourist center, the icon of Yucatán tourism, the magnificent 25m (82-foot) El Castillo (also called the **Pyramid of Kukulkán**), is straight ahead across a large, open grassy area. It was built with the Maya calendar in mind. The four stairways leading up to the central platform each have 91 steps, which, added to the platform, totals the 365 days of the solar year. The 18 terraces flanking the stairways on each face of the pyramid add up to the number of months in the Maya religious calendar. The terraces contain a total of 52 panels representing the 52-year cycle when the solar and religious calendars converge. The pyramid, now closed to climbers, is aligned so that the **spring** or **fall equinox** (Mar 21 or Sept 21) triggers an optical illusion: The setting sun casts the terraces' shadow onto the northern stairway, forming a diamond pattern suggestive of a snake's geometric designs. As it meets the giant serpent's head at the bottom, the shadow appears to slither down the pyramid as the sun sets, a phenomenon that brings hordes of visitors every year. (The effect is more conceptual than visual, and frankly, the ruins are much more enjoyable on other days when they are less crowded.)

Like most Maya pyramids, El Castillo was built over an earlier structure. A narrow stairway at the western edge of the north staircase leads inside to a sacrificial altar-throne—a red jaguar encrusted with jade. The stairway is open from 11am to 3pm and is cramped, usually crowded, humid, and uncomfortable. A visit early in the day is best. Photographing the jaguar figure is not allowed.

**JUEGO DE PELOTA (MAIN BALL COURT)** Northwest of El Castillo is Chichén's main ball court. The largest and best-preserved ball court known to exist anywhere, it's only one of nine built in this city. Carved on both walls are scenes showing Maya figures dressed as ball players and decked out in heavy protective padding. A headless player kneels with blood shooting from his neck while another player holding the head looks on.

Players on two teams would try to knock a hard rubber ball through one of the two stone rings placed high on either wall, using only their elbows, knees, and hips. According to legend, losers paid for defeat with their lives. However, some experts say the victors were the only appropriate sacrifices for the gods. Either way, the game, called *pok-ta-pok,* must have been riveting, heightened by the ball court's wonderful acoustics.

**THE NORTH TEMPLE** Temples stand at both ends of the ball court. The North Temple has sculpted pillars and more sculptures inside, as well as badly ruined murals. The ball court's acoustics are so good that someone speaking at the opposite end of the court, about 135m (443 feet) away, can be heard clearly at the North Temple.

**TEMPLE OF JAGUARS** Near the main ball court's southeastern corner is a small temple with serpent columns and carved panels showing warriors and jaguars. Up the steps and inside the temple, a mural chronicles a battle in a Maya village.

**TZOMPANTLI (TEMPLE OF THE SKULLS)** To the right of the ball court, the Temple of the Skulls obviously borrows from the Postclassic cities of central Mexico. Notice the rows of skulls carved into the stone platform; when a sacrificial victim's head was cut off, it was impaled on a pole and displayed with others in a tidy row. Also carved into the stone are pictures of eagles tearing hearts from human victims. The word "Tzompantli" is not Maya, but comes from central Mexico.

**PLATFORM OF THE EAGLES** Next to the Tzompantli, this small platform has reliefs showing eagles and jaguars clutching human hearts in their talons and claws, as well as a human head emerging from the mouth of a serpent.

**PLATFORM OF VENUS** East of the Tzompantli and north of El Castillo, near the road to the Sacred Cenote, is the Platform of Venus. In Maya and Toltec lore, a feathered monster or a feathered serpent with a human head in its mouth represented Venus. This is also called the tomb of Chaac-Mool, for the figure that was discovered "buried" within the structure.

**SACRED CENOTE** Follow the dirt road (actually an ancient *sacbé,* or causeway paved with limestone) north from the Platform of Venus for 5 minutes to get to the great natural well that may have given Chichén Itzá (the Well of the Itzáes) its name. The *cenote* was used for ceremonial purposes, and the bones of both children and adult sacrificial victims were found at the bottom.

Edward Thompson, who was the American consul in Mérida and a Harvard professor, purchased the ruins of Chichén early in the 20th century and explored the *cenote* with dredges and divers. He uncovered a fortune in gold and jade, most of which ended up in Harvard's Peabody Museum of Archaeology and Ethnology—a matter that disconcerts Mexican classicists to this day. Excavations in the 1960s yielded more treasure, and studies of the recovered objects show that the offerings came from throughout the Yucatán and beyond.

**TEMPLO DE LOS GUERREROS (TEMPLE OF THE WARRIORS)** Toltec influence is especially evident on the eastern edge of the plaza. Due east of El Castillo is one of Chichén Itzá's most impressive structures, the Temple of the Warriors, named for the carvings of warriors marching along its walls. The temple and the rows of almost Greco-Roman columns flanking it are also called the Group of the Thousand Columns, and it recalls the great Toltec site of Tula. A figure of Chaac-Mool sits at the top of the temple (visible only from a distance since the temple is closed to climbers), surrounded by columns carved in relief to look like enormous feathered serpents.

South of the temple was a square building that archaeologists named **El Mercado** (The Market), with a colonnade surrounding its central court.

The main Mérida–Cancún highway once ran straight through the ruins of Chichén. Though it has been diverted, you can still see the great swath it cut. South and west of the old highway's path are more impressive ruined buildings.

**TUMBA DEL GRAN SACERDOTE (TOMB OF THE HIGH PRIEST)** Past the refreshment stand to the right of the path, the Tomb of the High Priest shows both Toltec and Puuc influence. The 9m (30-foot) pyramid, with stairways on each side depicting feathered serpents, bears a distinct resemblance to El Castillo. Beneath its foundation is an ossuary (a communal graveyard) in a natural limestone cave, where skeletons and offerings have been found.

**CASA DE LOS METATES (TEMPLE OF THE GRINDING STONES)** This building, the next one on your right, is named after the Maya's concave corn-grinding stones.

**TEMPLO DEL VENADO (TEMPLE OF THE DEER)** Past Casa de los Metates is this fairly tall, though ruined, building. The relief of a stag that gave the temple its name is long gone.

**CHICHAN-CHOB (LITTLE HOLES)** This temple has a roof comb with little holes, three masks of the rain god Chaac, three rooms, and a good view of surrounding structures. It's one of Chichén's oldest buildings, built in the Puuc style during the late Classic period.

**EL CARACOL (THE OBSERVATORY)** One of Chichén Itzá's most intriguing structures is in the old part of the city. From a distance, the rounded tower of El Caracol ("The Snail," for its shape), sometimes called The Observatory, looks like any modern observatory. Construction of this complex building with its circular tower was carried out over centuries, acquiring additions and modifications as the Maya's careful celestial observations required increasingly exact measurements. Quite unlike other Maya buildings, the entrances, staircases, and angles are not aligned with one another. The tower's circular chamber has a spiral staircase leading to the upper level. The slits in the roof are aligned with the sun's equinoxes. Astronomers observed the cardinal directions and the approach of the all-important spring and autumn equinoxes, as well as the summer solstice.

On the east side of El Caracol, a path leads north into the bush to the **Cenote Xtoloc,** a natural limestone well that provided the city's daily water supply. If you see lizards sunning there, they may well be *xtoloc,* the species for which this *cenote* is named.

**TEMPLO DE LOS TABLEROS (TEMPLE OF THE SCULPTURED PANELS)** Just south of El Caracol are the ruins of a *temazcalli* (a steam bath) and the Temple of Panels, named for the carved panels on top. A few traces remain of the much larger structure that once covered the temple.

**EDIFICIO DE LAS MONJAS (EDIFICE OF THE NUNS)** This enormous nunnery is reminiscent of the palaces at sites along the Puuc route. The new edifice was built in the late Classic period over an older one. To prove this, an early 20th-century archaeologist put dynamite between the two and blew away part of the exterior, revealing the older structures within. Indelicate, perhaps, but effective.

On the east side of the Edifice of the Nuns is **Anexo Este** (East Annex), constructed in highly ornate Chenes style with Chaac masks and serpents.

## MORE OF THE maya INTERIOR

If your travels will take you deeper into the Yucatán's interior, here are two stops you shouldn't miss.

**Uxmal ★★★** This ceremonial city complex is one of the masterworks of Maya civilization, with expansive and intricate carved-stone facades that make it strikingly different from all other Maya cities. Also unusual is that Uxmal was built to incorporate hilly terrain, a rarity in the Yucatán. Standing about 30 meters (100 feet) above sea level, it has no *cenotes* to supply fresh water from the subterranean rivers, so the city depended on rainwater stored in *chultúnes*, or cisterns.

Evidence of the city's devotion to the rain god Chaac is everywhere; vertical repetitions of the long-nosed god masks appear so often on the corners of Uxmal's buildings that they are called "Chaac stacks." Twelve Chaac masks adorn the ornate doorway to the crowning temple of the strange and beautiful **Pirámide del Adivino** (Pyramid of the Magician), the city's tallest structure. Built over five earlier structures, the pyramid has an oval base and rounded sides, unique among the Maya.

Uxmal's great building period was A.D. 700 to 1000. Another notable structure is the **Nunnery Quadrangle,** an enormous plaza enclosed by elaborately carved stone buildings. No interior murals or stucco work have been found here; Uxmal's art is all in its exterior stonework.

Uxmal (www.mundomaya.travel/en/arqueologia/top-10.html) is on Highway 261 between Muna and Santa Elena. Admission is 199 pesos; hours are 10am–5pm.

Uxmal and four smaller sites close by—**Sayil, Kabah, Xlapak,** and **Labná**—make up the **Puuc Route.** Across from Uxmal's entrance is a marvelous museum that explores Maya culture through its reverence for chocolate.

**Choco-Story ★★★** In 2010, the makers of Mérida's Ki'Xocolatl chocolate and their business partners, all from Belgium, created the Ecomuseo del Cacao on their Tikul Plantation along the Puuc Route. It was renamed and moved to this new location in late 2014. The museum focuses as much on cocoa's mystical significance to the Maya as on the confection itself. A stone path leads to a series of traditional thatched-roof huts, each with its own theme: cocoa's sacred role in the Maya's spiritual world; daily Maya life (demonstrated in an outdoor kitchen, a wild orchid garden, and a colony of the native stingless bees that are crucial to cocoa's growth); the laborious chocolate-making process; and chocolate's introduction to Europe.

The huts are set in a botanical garden with signs in English and Spanish explaining the importance of such plants as vanilla, henequén, pomegranate, peppers, tamarind, lime, guava, and of course the cacao tree. Rescued spider monkeys and jaguars also live in the garden. The tour culminates in a demonstration of the preparation of a chocolate drink, to which you can add your own embellishments. Don't shy away from the chile—it was a Maya tradition, and once you try it, you'll find Hershey's unbearably dull.

The museum, on Highway 261 across from the Uxmal entrance, Yucatán (www.ecomuseodelcacao.com; ✆ **999/289-9914**), is open daily 9am to 7:30pm. Admission is 120 pesos adults, 90 pesos seniors, students, and children; children 6 and under are free. A Maya rain ceremony is performed hourly, and the site includes a craft store, playground, and cafeteria.

**LA IGLESIA (THE CHURCH)** Next to the annex is another of Chichén's oldest buildings, the Church. Masks of Chaac decorate two upper stories; a close look reveals armadillo, crab, snail, and tortoise symbols among the crowd of Chaacs. These represent the Maya gods, called *bacah,* whose job it was to hold up the sky.

**AKAB DZIB (TEMPLE OF OBSCURE WRITING)** Beloved of travel writers, this temple lies east of the Edifice of the Nuns. Above a door in one of the rooms are some Maya glyphs, which gave the temple its name because the writings are hard to make out. In other rooms, traces of red handprints are still visible. Reconstructed and expanded over the centuries, Akab Dzib might be the oldest building on the site.

**CHICHÉN VIEJO (OLD CHICHÉN)** For a look at more of Chichén's oldest buildings, constructed well before the time of Toltec influence, follow signs from the Edifice of the Nuns southwest into the bush to Old Chichén, about 1km (⅔ mile) away. Be prepared for this trek with long trousers, insect repellent, and a local guide. Attractions here include the **Templo de los Inscripciones Iniciales** (Temple of the First Inscriptions), with the oldest inscriptions discovered at Chichén, and the restored **Templo de los Dinteles** (Temple of the Lintels), a fine Puuc building. Some of these buildings are being restored.





## OTHER AREA ATTRACTIONS

**Ik-Kil** (79 pesos/35 pesos children; daily 8am–6pm) is a large, deep *cenote* in a private park on the highway across from the Hotel Dolores Alba, 2.5km (1½ miles) east of the main entrance to Chichén Itzá. Getting down to the water's edge requires navigating about 85 feet worth of stairs carved into the limestone, but they are easier to manage than those at Dzitnup. The view from both the top and the bottom is dramatic, with lots of tropical vegetation and hanging tree roots stretching to the water's surface. Go swimming before 11:30am, when bus tours begin to arrive. These tours are Ik-Kil's main source of income. It also has a mediocre restaurant and souvenir shops.

The **Cave of Balankanché** (105 pesos; kids 6 and under not permitted; 9am–4pm) is 5.5km (3½ miles) from Chichén Itzá on the road to Valladolid and Cancún. Taxis will make the trip and wait. The entire excursion takes about a half-hour, but the walk inside is hot and humid. This is the tamest of the Yucatán's cave tours, with good footing and the least amount of walking and climbing. It includes a cheesy and uninformative recorded tour. The highlight is a round chamber with a central column that resembles a large tree. The cave became a hideout during the War of the Castes, and you can still see traces of carving and incense burning, as well as an underground stream that supplied water to the refugees. You'll see jars, grinding stones, and incense burners once used in sacred rituals, discovered in the 1950s and returned to their original positions after they were studied. Outside, meander through the botanical gardens, where nearly everything is labeled with common and botanical names. Tours in English 11am and 1 and 3pm; in Spanish, 9am, noon, and 2 and 4pm. Double-check hours at Chichén Itzá's main entrance. Use of video camera 45 pesos (you can reuse a permit bought in Chichén the same day).

## Valladolid ★★★

40km (25 miles) E of Chichén Itzá; 160km (99 miles) SW of Cancún; 98km (61 miles) NW of Tulum

Valladolid (Bah-yah-doh-*leed*), a small colonial city halfway between Mérida and Cancún, was one of the first Spanish strongholds and crucible of the War of the Castes (p. 18). The city is graced by handsome colonial buildings and 19th-century

## Valladolid

structures that make it a pleasant place to get a taste of real life in the Yucatán. People are friendly and informal, and the only real challenge is the heat, which can be a serious energy drain in summer and early fall. The city's economy is based on commerce and small-scale manufacturing. It's close to a couple of famous *cenotes,* the intriguing ruins of Ek Balam, Ría Lagartos' nesting flamingos, and the sandy beaches of Isla Holbox (p. 117). It's closer to Chichén Itzá than Mérida is, and it is an inexpensive town, making it a good base for exploring.

## ESSENTIALS

### Getting There

**BY CAR** From Mérida or Cancún, you can take either the Highway 180D *cuota* (toll road; 262 pesos from Cancún) or Highway 180 *libre* (free). The toll road passes 2km (1¼ miles) north of the city; the exit is at the crossing of Highway 295 toward Tizimín. It takes somewhat less than two hours, depending on your starting point. Highway 180 *libre,* passing through a number of villages with their requisite *topes,* takes about an hour longer. Both 180 and 295 lead straight to downtown. Leaving is just as easy: From the main square, Calle 41 turns into 180 E. to Cancún; Calle 39 heads to 180 W.

to Chichén Itzá and Mérida. To take the toll road to Mérida or Cancún, take Calle 40 (see "City Layout," below).

**BY BUS** Buses leave Cancún throughout the day for Valladolid (134 pesos). You can also get several buses a day to and from Playa del Carmen (120–186 pesos) and Tulum (84–108 pesos). Second-class buses (26 pesos) leave Valladolid for Chichén Itzá every half hour or less. Valladolid's bus station is at the corner of calles 39 and 46.

### Orientation

**VISITOR INFORMATION** The small **tourism office** is in the Palacio Municipal, open Monday to Friday from 8am to 9pm, Saturday and Sunday 9am to 9pm.

**CITY LAYOUT** Valladolid's layout is standard for towns in the Yucatán: Streets running north–south are even numbers; those running east–west are odd numbers. The main plaza is bordered by Calle 39 on the north, 41 on the south, 40 on the east, and 42 on the west. The plaza is named Parque Francisco Cantón Rosado, but everyone calls it **El Centro.** Taxis are cheap and easy to come by.

### Where to Stay

Aside from lodging listed below, Valladolid's best budget hotels are **Hotel San Clemente,** on Calle 42 between calles 41 and 43 (www.hotelsanclemente.com.mx; ✆ **985/856-3161;** from 566 pesos double), and **Hotel Zací** (www.hotelzaci.com.mx; Calle 44 between calles 37 and 39; ✆ **985/856-2167;** 548 pesos).

For a change of pace, stay in a small ecohotel in the nearby village of Ek Balam, close to the ruins, at **Genesis Retreat Ek Balam** (www.genesisretreat.com; ✆ **985/101-0277;** 579–779 pesos). The Canadian owner takes guests on village tours that unveil the contemporary Maya's daily life. She rents simple cabañas (with shared or private bathrooms) surrounding a lovely pool and a restaurant.

**Casa Hamaca ★★★** A lovely house in a jungle-like garden ensconces guests in eight large rooms, each with its own theme. The house blends ancient Maya, Spanish colonial, and modern Mexican style in perfect, eye-pleasing harmony. All the comforts you could ask for are here, but the greatest asset is owner Denis Larsen. He is a serious student of his adopted culture and a serious gadabout in the community (he's president of the Valladolid English Library, housed on the property), and spending a little time with him will inevitably pull you deeper into local life.

Calle 49 no. 202-A (at Calle 40). www.casahamaca.com. ✆ **985/100-4270.** 8 units. High season $110 double; low season $80 double. Rates include full breakfast. Free secure parking. **Amenities:** Restaurant; bar; small outdoor pool; cooking and Spanish classes; massage and bodywork available; free Wi-Fi.

**Casa Quetzal ★★** The landlady, Judith Fernández, is a gracious Mexican woman who moved to Valladolid to slow down. She has created airy, attractive lodging in the refurbished Barrio Sisal, within walking distance of the main square. Emphasis is on comfort and service—good linens and mattresses, quiet air-conditioning, and a large and inviting central courtyard. English is spoken, and Sra. Fernández has lined up a good guide to take you to outlying areas.

Calle 51 no. 218 (btw. 50 and 52). www.casa-quetzal.com. ✆ **985/856-4796.** 8 units. 1,122–1,346 pesos double. Rates include full breakfast. No credit cards. Free secure parking. **Amenities:** Small outdoor pool; spa; room service; free Wi-Fi.

**El Mesón del Marqués ★★** Originally an early 17th-century house, the doyen of Valladolid's plaza has grown by adding new construction in back. All the rooms (most with two double beds) are quite comfortable, though the new buildings don't have the wow factor of the original porticoed courtyard, which drips with bougainvillea and hanging plants and is mostly occupied by the restaurant (below). The pretty, fairly large pool is another modern addition. The hotel is on the north side of the plaza, opposite the church.

Calle 39 no. 203 (btw. calles 40 and 42). www.mesondelmarques.com. ✆ **985/856-2073,** fax 985/856-2280. 90 units. 735–900 pesos double; 1,300 pesos junior suite. Free secure parking. **Amenities:** Restaurant; bar; outdoor pool; room service; free Wi-Fi.

### Where to Eat

Although not a hotbed of haute cuisine, Valladolid has some very flavorful local specialties, and everyone seems to do them well. This is cattle country, so they are based on meat—a distinct departure from the emphasis on seafood along the Caribbean. Look for *lomitos de Valladolid,* cubed pork cooked in fresh, chunky tomato sauce with local spices, stewed until meltingly tender, and garnished with chopped or sliced boiled egg. *Longaniza* is a local sausage that tastes somewhat like a cross between chorizo and linguica. Often found in tacos, it's also great with scrambled eggs or simply wrapped in a tortilla.

In a colonial building on the plaza, friendly, informal **Las Campanas ★** (www.lascampanas-valladolid.com; ✆ **985/856-2365**), at calles 41 and 42, serves tasty food at reasonable prices, including Mexican and international small plates and full dinners. Another good bet for casual dining is in Parque Candelaria, a few blocks north of the plaza. **Casa Italia ★** (www.casaitaliamexico.com; ✆ **985/856-5539**) is a small but popular restaurant at Calle 35 No. 202-J, between calles 42 and 44, that serves authentic, moderately priced Italian classics. The closest relative of fast food in Valladolid is found at the stalls in the **Bazar Municipal,** next door to the Mesón del Marqués. Locals like to meet over a quick meal here; I like it for a quick, cheap breakfast or a fresh-squeezed orange juice (which you can also take to go in a plastic bag with a straw).

The two finest restaurants in town specialize in regional cooking. **Hostería El Marqués ★★,** at the Hotel El Mesón del Marqués, occupies most of the achingly romantic courtyard in the original portion of the 17th-century mansion. It turns out a variety of wonderful Yucatecan classics and international dishes. Down near the San Bernardino monastery, **Taberna de Los Frailes ★★★** (www.tabernadelosfrailes.com; ✆ **985/856–0689**), on Calle 49 at Calle 41-A, arrived on the scene only a few years ago but has made a name for itself with excellent regional cuisine made from fresh local ingredients. Most dishes approach perfection, and the lush garden has its own *cenote.*

## EXPLORING VALLADOLID

**THE MAIN PLAZA** Valladolid's **main plaza** is the town's social center and a thriving market for Yucatecan artisans who come into the city each day to sell their wares. The lush old shade trees, thankfully, survived the square's renovation several years ago, and it remains the best place in town to wait out the heat of the day. Workers fortify themselves at food carts or stop for a shoeshine, couples nuzzle and friends chat in the S-shaped *confidenciales,* and little children stare up in awe at the statue, painted in bright colors, of a Maya woman pouring water.

On the plaza's south side, on Calle 41 at 42, is the imposing **Iglesia de San Gervasio** cathedral (sometimes called Parroquia de San Servacio), built in 1706 to replace the original church, built in 1545. Its thick stone walls weren't enough to stop the Maya rebels who sacked it in 1847, touching off the War of the Castes (p. 18), but you'll still find the impressive *retablo* (painting on carved wood) towering over the altar. Vallesoletanos, as residents are known, believe almost all cathedrals in Mexico point east, and they cherish a local legend to explain why theirs points north—don't believe a word of it.

On the east side, climb the worn steps of **El Ayuntamiento** (City Hall) on Calle 40 at 41, the repository for dramatic murals outlining the peninsula's history, including a wonderful depiction of a horrified Maya priest foreseeing the arrival of Spanish galleons. The second-floor gallery also provides a bird's-eye view of the plaza. On Sunday nights, beneath the stone arches of the Ayuntamiento, the municipal band plays *jaranas* and other traditional regional music under the arcade while locals waltz around the plaza's bandstand.

When is a museum not a museum? **Casa de los Venados** (www.casadelosvenados.com; ✆ **985/856-2289**) on Calle 40 at 41, is a private collection of Mexican folk art exhibited in the owners' 18,000-square-foot home, less than a half-block from the plaza's southeast corner. The house itself is a work of art, its 9-year renovation designed by the architect who resuscitated Mérida's exquisite Hacienda Xcanatún. But its highest purpose is to display the artwork that owners John and Dorianne Venator have collected over decades of travel. Outstanding examples of every kind of Mexican folk art I've seen in museums reside here—from miniatures and furniture to Day of the Dead skeletons and trees of life—all awaiting nose-to-nose inspection. Tours are given daily at 10am; no reservations are necessary.

**AROUND TOWN** Before it became Valladolid, the city was a Maya settlement called Zací (Zah-*kee*), which means "white hawk." The old name lives on in the *cenote* in a small park at the intersection of calles 39 and 36. The long but easily navigable stepped trail at **Cenote Zací** leads past caves, stalactites, and hanging vines that give the place a prehistoric feel, but the *cenote*'s partially open roof lightens the atmosphere. It's a fine place to cool off, whether you jump in for a swim, dangle your feet in the water and let the fish nibble your toes, or just walk down to escape city heat and noise. I find Zací more peaceful and just as pretty as the famous *cenotes* outside of town (p. 166). The park, which has a large *palapa* restaurant overlooking the *cenote,* is free; entry to the *cenote* is 25 pesos.

The pink, fortress-like building housing **Museo San Roque** (✆ **985/856-2529**), on Calle 41 between calles 38 and 40, is actually a former church, and it has a suitably cool, hushed atmosphere. This is a modest local museum that gives an interesting overview of the arts and crafts produced in the surrounding Maya villages; it also displays ancient stone masks, pottery, and bones unearthed at nearby Ek Balam (p. 114). A group of tiny infant bones found with jade offerings in an *olla* (pot) is particularly compelling. The museum is open daily 9am to 9pm. Entry is free.

Behind the museum, the quiet **Parque los Héroes** ★ is a good place for a break in the shade, but it's much more than that to the people of Valladolid. In a city with a long list of historical events of nationwide impact, none is more important than *La Chispa* (p. 18)—the local rebellion against President Porfirío Díaz's military dictatorship in 1810 that proved to be "the spark" for the Mexican Revolution. Díaz' forces executed three leaders of the uprising by firing squad in the courtyard that is now Heroes Park. The city put up an obelisk here in 1958 to commemorate their sacrifice, and on the

50th anniversary of the rebellion, in 1960, it moved the martyrs' bodies from the cemetery to be interred in a park wall. You can enter the park through Museo San Roque or through the gate on Calle 38.

Ten blocks southwest of the main square, at calles 49 and 41A, is the Franciscan monastery of **San Bernardino de Siena ★★,** looming over a vast grassy square surrounded by lovely colonial buildings. Built in 1552 by the same architect who built the city's original cathedral, the monastery complex was sacked during the War of the Castes, but a fine baroque altarpiece and some striking 17th-century paintings remain. A large underground river is believed to pass under the convent and surrounding neighborhood, which is called Barrio Sisal. ("Sisal," in this case, is a corruption of the Maya phrase *sis-ha,* meaning "cold water.") The entire *barrio* has been extensively restored and is one of Valladolid's most beautiful neighborhoods.

> **Cenote Etiquette**
>
> If you swim in a *cenote,* be sure you don't have creams or other chemicals on your skin, including deodorant. They damage the habitat of the small fish and other organisms living in the water. No alcohol, food, or smoking is allowed.

For a real treat, walk to the monastery just before sunset along the **Calzada de los Frailes (Walkway of the Monks) ★★.** From the corner of calles 41 and 46, follow Calle 41A, the cobblestone street running diagonally to the southwest, about 1km (⅔ mile) to the monastery. The road follows the route of one of the Maya's limestone causeways called a *sacbé,* in this case connecting the city of Zací with the village (now a Valladolid neighborhood) of Sisal, lined by huge clay planters, elegantly painted restored colonial homes, and intriguing shops.

The **Valladolid English Library,** Calle 49 at Calle 40 on Parque San Juan, has built up a collection of English-language books on all sorts of topics, including some rare titles on Maya history and culture. They are available for loan if you've run out of reading material, but the weekly Language Exchange Hour may be of even more interest; you can help Spanish speakers learn English and get help from them with your Spanish skills. The library also hosts talks on a wide variety of topics by local authors, teachers, environmentalists, and other experts. The library is in donated space adjacent to Casa Hamaca (p. 110), which you can contact for information.

**EDGES OF TOWN** Jalisco state, as we all know, has a lock on the word "tequila" for the seductive liquor made from blue agave. That doesn't mean it isn't made anywhere else—only that it can't be *called* tequila. Valladolid's **Mayapán Distillery** (www.mayapan.mx; ✆ **985/858-0246**) produces some very good . . . um, Mayapán from its own blue agave plants, imported from Jalisco. You can buy *blanco, reposado,* or aged versions of Mayapán as well as many other brands at the distillery's Tequila Store, which shares space with what might be the best gift shop in Valladolid. Visitors may take a tour (50 pesos) to follow the entire process from growth and harvest of the agave to cooking, crushing (by a horse pulling a 1-ton stone around a circular *molienda*), fermentation, and distilling. The capstone is sampling three shots, one each of *blanco, reposado,* and *añejo* (aged) liquor. The distillery, located north of town on the beltway at the intersection with the access road to the Highway 180 toll road, is open Monday to Saturday, 9am to 6pm, Sundays and holidays by request.

The **Cenotes Dzitnup** are 4km (2½ miles) west of Valladolid off Highway 180 toward Chichén Itzá. "Dzitnup" is the collective name for two *cenotes;* the larger, more popular one often referred to as Dzitnup is actually Xkekén, and it is reputed to be the most photographed *cenote* in the Yucatán. It's easy to see why: The deep, glassy blue water, beneath a thicket of stalactites and ropy tree roots straining for a drink, is a spectacle. The beautiful pictures, however, don't reveal the treacherous stone steps, the unrelenting humidity even on an otherwise comfortable day (wear contacts instead of glasses, which will be constantly fogged), and the danger of claustrophobia if you're down there with a crowd (and most of the time you will be). It's an awesome sight, and you should see it at least once. Bring a suit and take a swim; it will revive you for the climb back out. The *cenote* is open daily from 8am to 4:30pm; admission is 59 pesos. If it's crowded, you can go to the other *cenote,* called **Sammulá,** 90m (295 feet) down the road on the opposite side. It is smaller and less developed, but also beautiful—and you'll breathe easier.

For excursions farther afield, see Side Trips from Valladolid, below.





### SHOPPING

The **Mercado de Artesanías de Valladolid** (crafts market), at the corner of Calle 44 at Calle 39, gives you an overview of the local merchandise. Perhaps the town's primary handicraft is the brightly embroidered white Maya dresses called *huipiles,* which you can buy here or from women in the Bazar Municipal. Leather goods are a close second, because Valladolid is a major meat producer. This is a good place to buy inexpensive, locally made leather goods such as *huaraches* (sandals), bags, and belts. The **Mercado Municipal,** where you can find just about anything, is on Calle 32 between calles 35 and 37.

Regional goods and folk art are also very much present in Valladolid's upscale shops, such as **Yalat,** on Calle 39 at 40, owned by a member of one of Valladolid's oldest and most prominent families. It looks more like a gallery than a shop, but it sells unique creations from throughout Mexico, specializing in Yucatecan tapestries, ceramics, jewelry, black pottery, and, naturally, *huipiles.*

On Calzada de los Frailes, **Coqui Coqui** (www.coquicoquiperfumes.com; ✆ **985/856-5129**), at Calle 41a No. 207A between calles 48 and 50, is the first of hot Argentine model Nicolas Malleville's Mexican enterprises. He captures scents of the Yucatán in perfumes formulated from agave, vanilla, coconut, plumeria, citrus, and other regional plants. On the same block, **Dutzi Designs** (www.dutzishop.com; ✆ **985/856-1950**), at Calle 41A No. 209 between calles 48 and 50, sells burlap and raffia bags handmade by local Maya men and women working in a co-op.

## Side Trips from Valladolid

### EK BALAM: BLACK JAGUAR ★★★

About 29km (18 miles) north of Valladolid, off the highway to Río Lagartos, is the extraordinary archaeological site of **Ek Balam,** which means "black jaguar" or "star jaguar." Tourists are just starting to catch on to these ruins, which could prove to be more important than the discovery of Chichén Itzá. It has one of the northern Yucatán's longest records of human occupation, from as early as A.D. 100 until the Spanish invasion—hundreds of years longer than most Maya cities. Though it was surveyed in the 1980s, archaeologists began excavations only in the late '90s. Archaeological evidence indicates this previously unknown city was the center of a powerful regional kingdom named Talol. Built between 100 B.C. and A.D. 1200, Ek Balam has altered our picture of what happened to the ancient Maya civilization. Unlike the apparent collapse of southern lowland cities, the northern Yucatán saw the emergence of a new order, as Chichén Itzá overwhelmed the increasingly factionalized city-states and established itself as the center of a state whose influence extended throughout Mesoamerica—a scenario borne out by inscriptions at Ek Balam, which previously were scarce. Ek Balam reached its height in the late Classic period, as Chichén Itzá began its rise to power. Rather than eclipsing the former power, Chichén Itzá integrated Ek Balam's ruling elite into its government.

### Not Carved in Stone

Unlike Chichén Itzá and other ancient Maya cities whose buildings were decorated with stone carvings, Ek Balam's builders and artists worked in stucco and limestone mortar, a plaster-like material that was pliable enough to sculpt with fine detail. It also was smooth enough to paint over. Stone embellishments in Ek Balam are limited to small hoops at the corners of certain buildings.

Ek Balam is known primarily for the intricacy and uniqueness of its sculptures, but it is unusual in other aspects. Though designed primarily in the Petén style associated with northern Guatemala, it shows Chenes (Campeche) and Puuc (central Yucatán) influence as well. The buildings are among the largest in the Yucatán, and the city center was enclosed by two concentric walls; they likely were the boundaries of the city's ceremonial and administrative center rather than fortifications. Its vast network of ***sacbeob***—limestone causeways that connected Ek Balam with outlying settlements—is still visible. Although most Maya cities were linked by these roads, few are distinguishable today.

Of the 45 structures that have been mapped, only a few remarkably well-preserved buildings in the ceremonial center have been excavated. The ceremonial entrance arch deposits you in the **South Plaza,** where the first buildings you see are **The Twins** (Structure 17), holding two mirror-image temples on a one 40-meter (131-foot) foundation, and the splendid **Oval Palace** (Structure 15, sometimes called La Redonda or Caracol), which contained burial relics. The South Plaza buildings are the smallest in the site.

Two enormous platform structures form the east and west borders of the **Central Plaza:** Structure 2, on the west, has a temple in one corner, while Structure 3 remains unexcavated. Walking between them, you'll pass the **ball court** and a **steam bath** on your way to Structure 1, better known as **The Acropolis,** or El Torre (the tower).

No matter how many ruins you may have seen, Ek Balam's central pyramid is awe-inspiring in not only its size but its multilayered complexity. At about 160m (525-ft.) long, 60m (197-ft.) wide, and more than 30m (100-ft.) high, it easily surpasses El Castillo in Chichén Itzá. One of the most exciting discoveries is the **tomb,** often called La Trona ("the throne"), to the left of the main stairway midway to the top, with a large ceremonial doorway of perfectly preserved stucco work in the Chenes style. It forms an elaborate, toothy mouth representing the underworld god, surrounded by animal and human figures—including what appear to be winged warriors, referred to as "Mayan Angels"—all so finely detailed that you can see the strands of hair in their braids. About 85% of the friezes are original plaster, never retouched. Excavations inside the pyramid revealed a long burial chamber filled with pearls, jade, small bone masks, and other riches, as well as hieroglyphic writing that suggests the scribes came from Guatemala. The script revealed that the tomb was that of Ukit Kan Lek Tok, a king who ruled when Ek Balam was at its most powerful.

Unlike many Maya structures, Ek Balam's towering pyramid allows climbers. It's a long haul, best not attempted in the midday heat, and the descent is vertiginous. But the view from the top makes it all worthwhile: to the north, two large, untouched ruins rising like jungle-clad hills; to the southeast, an unfettered view stretches all the way to the tallest structures of **Cobá,** 50km (31 miles) distant. You can begin to appreciate the city's full reach when you make out the seemingly endless mounds of jungle vegetation that hide unrestored buildings, with *sacbeob* penetrating the forest in every direction. More than any of the better-known sites, Ek Balam imparts a sense of mystery and awe at the scale of Maya civilization and the utter ruin into which it fell.

To get to Ek Balam, take Calle 40 north out of Valladolid to Highway 295 and go 20km (12 miles) to a large marked turnoff. Ek Balam is 13km (8 miles) from the highway; admission is 130 pesos (split into two tickets, one for federal and one for state government), 45 pesos per video camera. You can hire a *triciclo* driver to take you to a *cenote* a couple of miles away in the village of X'Cachen for about 70 pesos, including entrance to the *cenote.* Ek Balam site is open daily from 8am to 5pm.

## RÍA LAGARTOS NATURE RESERVE ★★

About 80km (50 miles) north of Valladolid (40km/25 miles north of Tizimín) on Highway 295, Ría Lagartos is a 50,000-hectare (123,500-acre) refuge established in 1979 to protect the largest nesting flamingo population in North America. The nesting area is off-limits, but you can see plenty of flamingos, as well as many other species of waterfowl, on an enjoyable boat ride around the estuary.

Río Lagartos, at the west end of the estuary, is the place to get boats to the flamingos. Misnamed by Spaniards who mistook the long, narrow *ría* (estuary) for a *río* (river), it's a small fishing village of about 3,000 people who make their living from the sea and from the occasional tourists wanting to catch a glimpse of the flamingos. Colorful houses face the *malecón* (oceanfront street), and brightly painted boats dock here and there.

The nesting area, a good distance east of town, is off-limits, but boat tours allow you to see plenty of flamingos noshing at their many feeding sites and congregating on the sandy shores. You'll also see some of the nearly 400 other species of birds that frequent the estuary, including herons, ducks, spoonbills, and migratory wading birds from the United States and Canada. The guides also like to show you the evaporation pools used by the local salt producer at Las Coloradas (a good source of employment for the locals until it was mechanized) and a freshwater spring bubbling out from below the saltwater estuary.

You'll see flamingos any time of year (and probably ducks, hawks, cranes, cormorants, and osprey as well), but to see great rosy masses of them, go between April and September. After the birds complete their courtship rituals in Celestún, on the northwestern corner of the Yucatán, they fly to Ría Lagartos to nest, lay their eggs, and prepare their young for the return journey in October.

**Río Lagartos Adventures** (www.riolagartosnaturetours.com; ✆ **986/100-8390**), Calle 19 No. 134 (at Calle 14), offers 2-hour boat tours for $85 per boat (up to six people) plus the reserve's entrance fee of $2.50 per person.

> **In the Pink**
>
> The eye-catching pink plumage that makes such a spectacle when flamingos take flight isn't a birthright. There is no such thing as a pink flamingo chick—they are downy white when they hatch. As the babies grow, they feed on crab and shrimp larvae dredged from the shallows. Accumulated carotene from the crustaceans eventually gives the birds their characteristic coral color, becoming more vivid as they mature.

**WHERE TO STAY** The best time to see flamingos is in the early morning, so you might want to stay overnight in town. Río Lagartos has a few simple hotels. The best are **Hotel Villa de Pescadores** (www.hotelriolagartos.com.mx; ✆ **986/862-0020**) on Calle 14 at the waterfront, and **Hotel Tabasco Río** (www.hotelriolagartos.com; ✆ **986/862-0116**), on Calle 15 a block from the waterfront.

## Isla Holbox ★★

64km (40 miles) northwest of Cancún, 121km (75½ miles) northeast of Valladolid

A sandy strip of an island off the northeastern corner of the Yucatán Peninsula, Isla Holbox (Ohl-*bosh*) was a half-deserted fishing village in a remote corner of the world before tourists started showing up in search of a beach paradise. It is still populated by descendants of the families who settled the island in the 19th century, most of them fishermen who pull lobster, octopus, grouper, conch, and a variety of other fish from the rich waters where the Caribbean and the Gulf of Mexico mingle. The island is part of the Yum Balam protected area, established in 1994 to safeguard the dolphins, flamingos, pelicans, and other wildlife that flourish there.

Despite a measure of prosperity bestowed by increasing tourism, life goes on pretty much as it always has for the island's 2,000 residents, although the native fishing families have a lot of European expats among their neighbors now. Visitors can now find air-conditioning, Internet cafes, and TV. Palm-thatched cabañas, some of them rather luxurious, stand along the northern beach, and numerous small restaurants serve just-caught seafood and international fare. But the streets are still packed sand, lined with palm-thatched huts and brightly painted houses. Although the once ATM-less town now has a few machines, they work sporadically (as do credit-card machines; a pocketful of pesos is still a must). You can go for days without ever seeing a car; adults and children alike scoot around in golf carts. Outside of whale shark season, competition for a patch of paradise is almost nonexistent. This is one of Mexico's last best refuges for relaxing your body and clearing your mind.

### GETTING THERE

**BY CAR** The quickest way to get to Chiquilá, where ferries depart for Isla Holbox, is by car. Most websites, and probably many hotels, still admonish you to take Highway 180 *libre* east and avoid the Highway 180D toll road at all costs because there's no exit for Chiquilá. Until November 2014, that was true, as many travelers (including yours truly) learned to their dismay. Now, however, the toll road has a new exit, which leads to a new road, which takes a shortcut to Kantunilkin, where you pick up the old road straight into Chiquilá. Depending on your starting point, that shaves nearly an hour off the trip from Cancún to Chiquilá, which once took 2½ hours.

**From Cancún:** Take Highway 180 out of town as before, but now you can choose between the free road (to the right) or the *cuota* (toll road), which has new signs indicating that the road goes to Isla Holbox. Whether the time saved is worth the 136-peso toll will depend on your schedule and style of travel. Continue for about 80km/50 miles to the well-marked turnoff to Holbox/Chiquilá, then follow the new road to Kantunilkin, where you pick up the state road heading north to Chiquilá, about 44km/27½ miles.

***Note:*** If you're not sure you'll reach your destination by dark, I strongly recommend the toll road; *topes* (huge speed bumps), cars with bad headlights, chickens, cows and Maya-style tricycles all make driving on the narrow, two-lane roads at night an adventure only a fool could love.

**From Riviera Maya:** The new road from Highway 180 to Kantunilkin is actually an extension of a new toll road linking Playa del Carmen to Highway 180D. Because it eliminates so much backtracking, the new road can save up to 2 hours for travelers starting in Riviera Maya. To get to Chiquilá/Holbox, take Avenida Donaldo Colosio west until it turns into the toll road; when you meet Highway 180D, go straight across to the extension leading to Kantunilkin and continue as described for Cancún above. Here are some approximate drive times: **Puerto Morelos,** 2 hours; **Playa del Carmen,** 90 minutes; **Tulum,** 2 hours, 15 minutes. Toll is 92 pesos.

**From Valladolid:** Take Highway 180D east from Valladolid for 92km/57 miles to the Chiquilá turnoff. Total trip is less than 2 hours; toll is 160 pesos.

**BY BUS** If you aren't already traveling by rental car, it's not worth renting one just to get from Cancún to Chiquilá; you can't take it to the island. Second-class buses make the trip in about 3 hours from Cancún's main bus terminal four or five times a day and cost about 84 pesos; check with your hotel for current schedules.

**BY FERRY** If you drive to Chiquilá, you can park your car in a secure lot within a block or two of the ferry pier, generally charging 50 pesos per day. Two ferry companies, **Maritimo 9 Hermanos** in the blue ticket booth and **Holbox Express** in the red one, each make more than a dozen departures a day between 6am and 9:30pm. Tickets are 100 pesos one way, 180 pesos round trip. If you miss the last boat, water taxis and *lanchas* (fishing boats) will take you across the lagoon for 400 pesos (500 pesos at night).

When you land in Holbox, a golf-cart taxi to the beach hotels will cost about 40 pesos. The town is only about a dozen square blocks, and even the farthest hotels are no more than a half-hour's walk from town. But if you want to join the locals zipping around town, golf-cart rental companies are clustered around the ferry dock and scattered throughout town. You can also book a cart in advance through Holbox Island (www.holboxisland.com), the closest thing Holbox has to an official tourist site, for $12 an hour, $55 for 12 hours, or $70 for 24 hours.

## ORIENTATION

Isla Holbox is a narrow spit of land separated from the northwestern tip of the Yucatán Peninsula by 11km (7 miles) of water—the shallow Laguna Yalahau, domain of flamingos, pelicans, wild dolphins, and other exotic creatures. The island is about 11km (7 miles) long and about 3km (2 miles) across at its widest point. The northern shore is all beach, washed by warm Gulf waters, while the southern shores along the lagoon are mostly mangrove marshes.

Cabo Catoche, the cape at the northeastern tip of the island (and the Yucatán Peninsula), is where Gulf and Caribbean waters meet in a kaleidoscope of shifting turquoise and emerald hues. The village at the southeastern end is a tidy grid, simple to navigate: The main street from the lagoon-side ferry dock, Avenida Benito Juárez, runs north straight through town to the north-facing beach, where bungalow hotels line up to the left and right along Avenida Igualdad. The central plaza is 2 blocks from the beach at Benito Juárez between Igualdad and Porfirio Díaz. But the truth is, nobody uses street names, and street signs come and go. Mostly, people describe locations in relation to the main plaza.

## WHERE TO STAY

You can almost believe Holbox is your own private island when you stay at **Casa Takywara ★★★** (Paseo Carey sin numero, on the beach west of town; www.casatakywara.com; ✆ **984/875-2352**), only a 10-minute walk from town along the beach in a natural setting among mangroves The six huge units include doubles, suites, a bungalow, and a fantastic top-floor penthouse with 360-degree views; all have kitchenettes. Rates start at $165 in high season, $99 in low season. For a beach retreat closer to the center of town, the long-established **Hotel Mawimbi ★★★** (Avenida Igualdad; www.mawimbi.net; ✆ **984/875-2003**) with its garden of shady, hammock-strung palm trees, strikes a good balance between price and comfort. Airy and brightly decorated with locally hand-crafted furniture in a blend of European and Mexican styles, the 11 units are divided among doubles, studios, and oceanview suites, some with balconies and kitchenettes. Rates start at $90 in low season and $145 high.

Ideally located **La Palapa ★★** (Avenida Morelos 231, at the beach; www.hotellapalapa.com; ✆ **984/875-2185**) is a quiet haven just 2 blocks from the town square, with spacious, contemporary rooms. All have ocean views through the palm trees, and many have balconies. Larger top-floor rooms have a window wall providing a sea view visible from the bed. Doubles go for $100 to $150 in high season, $80 to $120 in low season. If you want real luxury (and are willing to pay for it) without sacrificing Holbox's down-to-earth atmosphere, you'll find it at **Casa Sandra** (www.casasandra.com; ✆ **984/875-2171**). With its grand yet rustic Caribbean architecture and interior decorated with original art, handmade Mexican furniture, and Cuban antiques, it has a sophisticated bohemian vibe. Doubles start at $299, suites at $390 in high season; doubles from $240, suites from $322 suites in low season.

Though I have yet to accept the idea of big resort-type hotels with pools and spas and turndown service in a place like this—even if they do have *palapa* roofs—there are two very good ones at the east end of the beach. If resort pampering is your style, look into **Villas Delfines** (Domicilio Conocido Playa Norte; www.villasdelfines.com; ✆ **998/875-2196**) and **Las Nubes** (Paseo Kuka at Calle Camaron, Playa Norte; www.hotellasnubesdeholbox.com; ✆ **984/875-2300**).

## WHERE TO EAT

Most of your gustatory needs can be met right on the main plaza. Possibly the most famous meal in town is the thin-crust lobster pizza at venerable **Pizzeria Edelyn** (✆ **984/875-2024**). The funky clapboard **Restaurant Colibri** (✆ **984/875-2162**), whose facade is an ever-changing canvas for murals and random art, turns out great breakfasts at great prices, especially for the smoothie and granola crowd; ceviche and fish dinners are also good but not as great a value. It has a rival in **El Limoncito** (✆ **984/875-2017**), across from the basketball court, which offers hearty traditional

## VISITING THE whale sharks OF ISLA HOLBOX

In 2002, Mexico's whale sharks were designated an endangered species. The government, along with environmental groups, closely monitors their activity and the tours that visit them off Isla Holbox. Captains and guides, most of whom are commercial fishermen, must be licensed by the government and pay large fines if they allow illegal activities. Restrictions limit the size and number of boats, their speed, and how closely they approach the animals. Whale shark tours are kept small; just two people at a time are allowed to snorkel with the sharks. Tourists must stay 2m (6 ft.) from the animals and use only biodegradable sunscreen; scuba diving and flash photography are not allowed.

Besides cooperating with those restrictions, you can help ensure the survival of these amazing animals by questioning an operator to be sure he takes the rules to heart. Unfortunately, since the greatest concentration of sharks has shifted to the east, making tours from Isla Mujeres more practical, not only has the number of tourists in the water increased, heightened competition has prompted many boat operators to ignore the rules in order to get a bigger piece of the pie.



Mexican breakfast dishes. For a change of pace, **La Tortilleria** (**© 984/875-2443**) specializes in Spanish tortillas (kind of like an omelet, but with potatoes replacing the eggs as a vessel) as well as pita rolls, croissants, and an array of Italian dishes. It's underneath the more prominently identified **Los Peleones** (**© 984/120-9685**), whose ample Italian menu with homemade pasta and excellent seafood provides room service to Casa Takywara. (That might be the best way to sample its food, unless you're a fan of *lucha libre,* which drives its decor.)

### EXPLORING

**BEACHES ★★** Next to spotting whale sharks, the primary activity for most visitors is lazing on Isla Holbox's broad, soft beaches. The north side of the island is fringed with beaches still unspoiled by the big resorts that have commandeered much of Mexico's coast. At the same time, these don't have that immaculate veneer of beaches constantly groomed by resort staff, nor do they get artificial deposits of sand dredged up from ocean floor to replenish beaches chewed up by a storm. Holbox's beaches, like most aspects of the island, are left in nature's hands. Depending on weather conditions and tourist numbers, they aren't always pristine. Since there's no reef offshore, it doesn't have the kaleidoscopic range of colorful fish found on the Caribbean side, so it's not an exciting snorkeling spot.

And yet . . . there may be no seaweed patrol here, but when the wind blows out to sea, Holbox's fine white sand is littered with nothing but seashells, and they are as dazzling as anything you'll see in Cancún or Playa del Carmen. The water, more green than Caribbean blue, is warm and placid, and so shallow in many places that you can wade out for hundreds of yards before being required to swim. And Holbox's beaches have a virtue that resort sands can't come close to matching: solitude. You'll often share your stretch of beach with no one but the birds.

**WHALE SHARK TOURS ★★★** Holbox is most popular with visitors from May to September, when more than a hundred whale sharks muster in nearby waters to feed on the plankton and krill churned up by the collision of Gulf and Caribbean waters. A shark the size of a mid-size whale might sound like a sci-fi nightmare—they can reach about 18m (59 feet)—but they are peaceable creatures, filtering their food much the way baleen whales do. The polka-dotted behemoths swim slowly along the surface of the water and seem to tolerate the boat tours and snorkelers that come for the thrill of swimming alongside them while they mill about, gulping thousands of gallons of water in their cavernous mouths to filter out microscopic organisms. That said, they can do some mischief if you annoy them.

Whale sharks frequent other parts of the world; the difference here is that they feed in shallow waters and stay close to the surface. Only a few arrive in May or stick around through September, but sightings from mid-June to early September are as close to a sure thing as you can get. Tour boats pull alongside a shark and let two swimmers at a time slip into the water, accompanied by a guide. The smaller the group, the more time each pair has to swim with the sharks. On the way to or from the sharks' feeding grounds, you might be treated to guest appearances from curious dolphins or manta rays (which can measure 6m/20 feet from wingtip to wingtip). Guides may anchor for impromptu swims or, if there is time, for snorkeling at Cabo Catoche.

Tours cost about 1,200 pesos per person, or up to 1,500 pesos if the sharks are in more distant waters. Tours typically last about four to six hours and include hotel transfers, snorkel gear, a life preserver, and a box lunch. Most hotels in town, and in Cancún and the Riviera Maya, can arrange a whale shark tour, though habitual Holbox visitors prefer to deal directly with their favorite operators. One of the most reputable is **Willy's** (www.holboxwhalesharktours.net; ✆ **984/875-2008**), a family operation run by lifelong Holbox residents. I can also recommend Fernando Rosado with **Xplore Holbox** (frg316@hotmail.com; ✆ **984/130-4009** or 984/876-2699).

***Note:*** Be wary of tours costing much less than 1,200 pesos; it could signal an unlicensed operator or one who routinely ignores regulations in an attempt to boost business.

**LAGUNA YALAHAU ★★** Whale sharks aren't the only game in town. A whole different landscape awaits in the shallow lagoon separating Isla Holbox from the mainland. The mangrove-fringed water is populated by wild dolphins and all manner of fish, while tens of thousands of nesting flamingoes visit from April to October. A 20-minute boat trip will take birders and nature lovers to **Isla Pájaros** (Bird Island), a wildlife sanctuary in the middle of the lagoon that harbors more than 150 species. Visitors can spot cranes, white ibis, brown and white pelicans, roseate spoonbills, and herons from the island's walkways and two observation towers; iguanas, horseshoe crabs, and other creatures scuttle around on the ground. Most boat trips also stop at **Ojo de Agua** (Eye of Water), a crystal-clear *cenote* in the mangroves that provided fresh water through the centuries for ancient Maya people, pirates, and, for many years, Holbox village residents. Today, the spring is a gorgeous swimming hole equipped with a large *palapa,* picnic area, and pier.

**ISLA DE LA PASIÓN** If Holbox hasn't gotten you far enough away from it all, tiny "Passion Island" is just 15 minutes away. The barren island, just 50m (164 feet) wide, is known for its white sand beach and emerald-green water, perfect for would-be

Robinson Crusoes. Trees and a large *palapa* provide some shade, but you'll need to bring your own water and snacks.

**Holbox Island Tours** (www.holboxislandtours.com; ✆ **984/875-2028**) will take you on a lagoon trip and to Isla de La Pasión and Punta Mosquito, a prime flamingo-viewing spot on the east side of the island, for 350 pesos per person, or 1,000 pesos for a private boat carrying up to five people. You can also ask about tours from the whale shark operators above or at your hotel, or try negotiating a better price from fishermen at the beach.

# ISLA MUJERES & COZUMEL

by Maribeth Mellin

These two Caribbean islands are among the most peaceful beach destinations in Mexico, both easy jaunts from Cancún and the Riviera Maya. Although day-trippers and cruise-ship visitors come ashore, the islands rarely feel overrun, and come evening the uncrowded streets and relaxed energy of the residents epitomize their enduring tranquility. Neither Isla Mujeres nor Cozumel is particularly large, and they each still have that small island feel—pristine beaches, bumpy roads that don't go far, and a seemingly timeless setting.

5

Fish-shaped **Isla Mujeres** lies 13km (8 miles) northeast of Cancún, a quick boat ride away. Despite this proximity, Isla Mujeres remains a little-known gem filled with regional and rustic charm, a world removed from its glittery neighbor. During pre-Hispanic times, Maya women would cross over to the island to make offerings to the goddess of fertility, Ixchel. Today's pilgrims arrive on passenger ferries from Cancún's Puerto Juárez and the Hotel Zone's Embarcadero at Playa Linda; car ferries arrive from Punta Sam. Hotels range from rustic to boutique, and the value of accommodations and dining are among the best one can find in this part of Mexico.

Larger than Isla Mujeres and farther from the mainland (19km/12 miles off the coast from Playa del Carmen), **Cozumel** has its own mini-international airport. Tourism revolves around two major activities: scuba diving and cruise ships making ports of call. Yet a strong sense of family and community continues to prevail here, luring travelers seeking gorgeous water and indigenous culture. There are fewer than 100,000 people on the island, a couple thousand of whom are Americans and the rest of whom are mostly Maya, Yucatecan, and Mexican from elsewhere in the country. There's just one town, San Miguel de Cozumel; to the north and south lie resorts. The rest of the shore is deserted and predominantly rocky, with a scattering of small sandy coves that you can have all to yourself. Because Cozumel remains a frequent stop on the cruise ship circuit, the town's waterfront *malecón* (boardwalk) is lined with jewelry stores and duty-free and souvenir shops. Savvy visitors walk inland to the main plaza and local neighborhoods. Unfortunately, there's no way to travel directly between Cozumel and Isla Mujeres, but you can get from one to the other by traveling via Cancún and Playa del Carmen.

# ISLA MUJERES ★★★

13km (8 miles) N of Cancún

Only a quick boat ride from the swarming beaches of Cancún, Isla Mujeres feels like a different world. Bathed in the warm waters of the Caribbean Sea, the sleepy island attracts visitors who prefer a laid-back lifestyle focused around the beach and watersports such as diving and snorkeling. The name translates as "the island of women," but few islanders agree on the origin. Although Isla Mujeres has a healthy nightlife, relaxed *isleños* frown upon spring break antics; if you're looking for parties, stick to Cancún.

## Essentials

### GETTING THERE

Isla Mujeres does not have a commercial airport. Travelers fly into Cancún and take the ferry to the island. Ferries depart from the "Gran Puerto" dock at Puerto Juárez, just north of Cancún, or from the Embarcadero in the Hotel Zone. **Ultramar** (www.ultramarferry.com; ✆ **998/881-5890**) runs fast boats leaving every half-hour between 5am and 8:30pm and hourly from 9:30-11:30pm from **Puerto Juárez,** making the trip in 15 minutes. There is storage space for luggage, and the fare is 78 pesos each way. From the Hotel Zone's **Embarcadero** at Playa Linda, located at Bulevar Kukulcán Km 4 on the northern tip of Cancún's Hotel Zone, Ultramar ferries to Isla Mujeres depart less frequently and cost $14 one way. There are up to six scheduled departures per day. Depending on the season, Ultramar also operates ferries to Isla Mujeres from the Hotel Zone's Playa Tortugas, at Bulevar Kukulcán Km 6.5, and from Playa Caracol at Bulevar Kukulcán Km 9.5. You don't need a car to get around on Isla, but if you're taking one to the island, you'll use the **Punta Sam** port a little beyond Puerto Juárez. The 40-minute car ferry (www.maritimaislamujeres.com; ✆ **998/877-0065**) runs five times daily between 7am and 8pm, Monday through Saturday, and four times on Sunday between 9am and 8pm, year-round except in bad weather. Always check online or by phone to verify the schedule. Cars should arrive an hour before the ferry departure to register for a place in line and pay the posted fee, which is 256 pesos per car. A gas pump is at Avenida Rueda Medina and Calle Abasolo, northwest of the ferry docks. To get to Puerto Juárez and Punta Sam from **Cancún,** take the Ruta 1 city bus.

### Visitor Information

The **City Tourist Office** (www.isla-mujeres.net/home.htm; ✆ **998/877-0307**) is located at Av. Rueda Medina 130, just across the street from the pier. It's open Monday through Friday from 9am to 4pm, closed on Saturday and Sunday.

### Island Layout

Isla Mujeres is about 8km (5 miles) long and 4km (2½ miles) wide, with the town at the northern tip. "Downtown" is a compact 4 blocks by 6 blocks, so it's very easy to get around. The **passenger ferry docks** are at the center of town, within walking distance of most hotels, restaurants, and shops. The street running along the waterfront and in front of the ferry docks is **Avenida Rueda Medina,** commonly called the ***malecón*** (boardwalk). The **Mercado Municipal** (town market) is by the post office on **Calle Guerrero,** an inland street at the north edge of town, which, like most streets in the town, is unmarked. The Carretera a Garrafón runs the length of the island southeast to Hacienda Mundaca, Parque Garrafón, and Punta Sur at the southern tip. The road

# Isla Mujeres

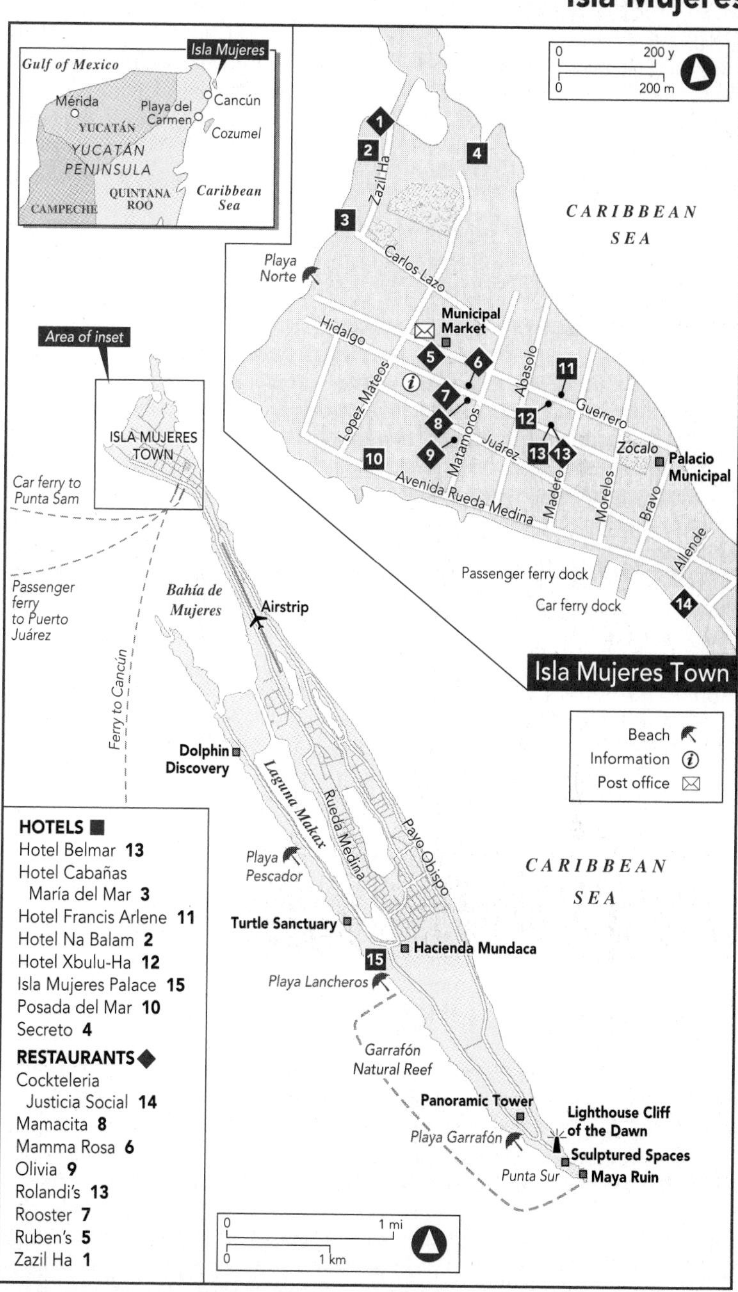

Gulf of Mexico
Isla Mujeres
Mérida
Playa del Carmen
Cancún
Cozumel
YUCATÁN
YUCATÁN PENINSULA
QUINTANA ROO
CAMPECHE
Caribbean Sea
Area of inset
ISLA MUJERES TOWN
Car ferry to Punta Sam
Passenger ferry to Puerto Juárez
Ferry to Cancún
Bahía de Mujeres
Airstrip
Dolphin Discovery
Laguna Makax
Rueda Medina
Payo Obispo
Playa Pescador
Turtle Sanctuary
Hacienda Mundaca
Playa Lancheros
Garrafón Natural Reef
Panoramic Tower
Lighthouse Cliff of the Dawn
Sculptured Spaces
Maya Ruin
Playa Garrafón
Punta Sur
CARIBBEAN SEA
0 1 mi
0 1 km
Zazil Ha
Carlos Lazo
Playa Norte
Hidalgo
Municipal Market
Lopez Mateos
Matamoros
Abasolo
Guerrero
Juárez
Zócalo
Palacio Municipal
Avenida Rueda Medina
Madero
Morelos
Bravo
Allende
Passenger ferry dock
Car ferry dock
0 200 y
0 200 m
Isla Mujeres Town
Beach
Information
Post office
HOTELS
Hotel Belmar 13
Hotel Cabañas María del Mar 3
Hotel Francis Arlene 11
Hotel Na Balam 2
Hotel Xbulu-Ha 12
Isla Mujeres Palace 15
Posada del Mar 10
Secreto 4
RESTAURANTS
Cockteleria Justicia Social 14
Mamacita 8
Mamma Rosa 6
Olivia 9
Rolandi's 13
Rooster 7
Ruben's 5
Zazil Ha 1

continues northwest along the island's windward side, past handsome homes and rugged coastline to town.

### Neighborhoods in Brief

The main neighborhood is the compact Centro, or downtown area, at the northwest end of the island. The few streets are lined with shops, restaurants, hotels, dive shops, and other businesses. Travelers, expats, and locals wander throughout this area during the day and night. The main plaza, church, and City Hall are located at Hidalgo and Morelos. Playa Norte, the most popular beach, is at the north end of downtown and is lined with beach bars and hotels. A sea wall runs along the northwest side of downtown. More hotels and attractions can be found in the Laguna Macax area southeast of town, the southern tip around Punta Sur, and the La Gloria neighborhood northeast of town.

### Getting Around

**BY GOLF CART, SCOOTER, & BICYCLE** There are no car rental agencies, but you won't need a car since the island is small and the pace leisurely. A popular form of transportation is the electric **golf cart,** available for rent at many hotels or rental shops for $49 per day for a cart seating four. Prices are the same at all rental locations. The golf carts don't go more than 30kmph (19 mph). **Ciro's Golf Car Rental** (Av. Guerrero 11; ✆ **987/877-0568**), copies Chevy fenders on their carts, giving them a fun flair. Many people enjoy touring the island by ***moto*** (motorized bike or scooter), though riding around on a scooter has several disadvantages. Sunburn tops the list—without shade you'll need to apply sunscreen constantly—and the risk of accidents is high. **Gomar** (✆ **998/877-0541**), at the corner of Madero and Hidalgo, rents reliable scooters. Fully automatic versions are available for 100 pesos per hour, 250 pesos for 8 hours, or 350 pesos for 24 hours. They come with helmets and seats for two people. There's only one main road with a couple of offshoots, so you won't get lost. Be aware that the rental price does not include insurance, and any injury to yourself or the vehicle will come out of your pocket. **Bicycles** are also available for rent at some hotels for about 35 pesos an hour or 200 pesos for 24 hours, usually including a basket and a lock.

**BY TAXI** Taxis await passengers at the ferry pier, by the plaza, and at popular beaches and attractions. Rates are about 40 to 54 pesos for trips within the downtown area and as far south as Hacienda Mundaca, and 78 pesos for a trip to the southern end of the island. You can also hire them for about 300 pesos per hour. **Triciclo** (three-wheeled bike) taxis are the least expensive and easiest way to get to your hotel if it's in town, though they're becoming scarce. From the ferry pier to any of the downtown hotels will cost about 30 to 40 pesos.

## [FastFACTS] ISLA MUJERES

**Area Code** The telephone area code is **998.**

**ATMs & Banks** Isla's main bank, HSBC Bank (✆ **998/877-0005**), is across from the ferry docks. It's open Monday through Friday from 8:30am to 6pm, and Saturday from 9am to 2pm. ATMs are popping up in hotels and restaurants and along Calle Hidalgo.

**Currency Exchange** Isla Mujeres has numerous *casas de cambio*, or currency exchanges, along the main streets. Most of the hotels listed here change money for their guests, although sometimes at less favorable rates than the commercial enterprises.

**Doctors & Hospital** The Centro de Salud health center is on Avenida Guerrero, a block before the beginning of the *malecón* (✆ **998/877-0117**).

**Drugstore** YZA Farmacía (✆ **998/877-1836**), located at the corner of Juárez and Morelos, stays open 24 hours.

**Emergency** Dial 006 for police, fire, and ambulance.

**Internet Access** Free Wi-Fi is available in the town plaza, many hotels, and downtown businesses including Cafe Mogauga at Juarez and Madero and Rooster restaurant at Plaza Isla Mujeres, Hidalgo 1. Europa Computer Internet, at Abasolo between Hidalgo and Juárez, offers Wi-Fi and computers for 20 pesos per hour. It's open Monday to Saturday from 9am to 10pm.

**Post Office** The *correo* is at Calle Guerrero 12 (✆ **998/877-0085**), at the corner of López Mateos, near the market. It's open Monday through Friday from 8am to 7pm, Saturday 9am to 1pm.

**Safety** The police station is on the main square (✆ **998/877-0882**). The emergency number is 066.

**Seasons** Isla Mujeres's tourist season (when hotel rates are higher) is a bit different from that of other places in Mexico. High season runs December through May. Some hotels raise their rates in August, and some raise their rates beginning in mid-November. Low season runs from June to mid-November.

## Where to Stay

You'll find plenty of hotels in all price ranges on Isla Mujeres. The rates listed below do not include the 19% room tax. They also do not necessarily apply to the brief Christmas/New Year's and Easter/Spring Break seasons, when many hotels charge extra. High season runs from December through March and sometimes includes August. Low season is the rest of the year.

If you're interested in private home rentals or longer-term stays, contact **Mundaca Travel and Real Estate** on Isla Mujeres (www.mundaca.com.mx; ✆ **866/646-0536** in the U.S., or 998/877-0025), or book online with **Isla Mujeres Vacation Rentals** (www.islamujeresvacationrentals.com; ✆ **770/438-3939** in the U.S., or 998/205-3003). More upscale vacation rentals are available through **Isla Home Services** (www.islahomeservices.com; ✆ **998/888-0948**). Looking for a quality all-inclusive resort near the town center? Consider **Privilege Aluxes** (www.privilegehotels.com; ✆ **866/947-6002** in the U.S., or 998/848-8470), located at Av. Adolfo Lopez Mateos. **VRBO** (www.vrbo.com) lists more than 144 units available for rent by owner.

### EXPENSIVE

**Isla Mujeres Palace ★★** I'm not usually fond of all-inclusive hotels, but the Palace hits all the right notes. First, and most important to me, it's small, with only 62 generously sized rooms with whirlpool tubs, stocked minibars, balconies, and small seating areas. ***Tip:*** Start filling the tub early—it takes a while. The whole place is spacious, with a soaring *palapa*—a palm-leaf roof—over the lobby and plenty of indoor and outdoor seating in the single restaurant. One flaw—the food needs improvement. Stick with omelets made to order, the salad bar, and the pizza served by the pool. The a la carte dinner is the best meal and the menu changes daily. Pastas are reliable choices. The pool area is small, but the swim-up bar is a friendly spot with good service. The beach is clean, but the sea grass in the shallow water by the shore makes swimming a less attractive option. The vibe is definitely couple oriented; unless you're accustomed to traveling alone, you'll feel out of place. You're a fair distance from town; a taxi costs about $5.

Carretera Garrafón. www.palaceresorts.com. ✆ **888/563-7804** in the U.S., or 998/999-2020. 62 units. $337 and up junior suite, $428 and up master suite. Rates include all food and beverages except premium wines and liquors. **Amenities:** Airport transfer via van and yacht (for a fee); fitness center; spa; pool, restaurant; bar; free Wi-Fi.

**Secreto ★★★** Though children are welcome, this sophisticated hideaway is more enjoyable for couples or adult friends. It's tucked away in a tiny cove facing the open Caribbean, a 10-minute walk from the more popular Playa Norte. A glass-walled shower sits between the featherbed and bath in some of the 12 suites—ask ahead if you prefer privacy. Extra pleasures include a living room area, Bose docking stations, and floor-to-ceiling glass doors leading to balconies with sunbeds. First-floor rooms open to the sleek infinity lap pool. In-room spa treatments are available. There is bar service but no restaurant; you'll find several good restaurants nearby for eating in or delivery.

Sección Rocas, Lote 1. www.hotelsecreto.com. ✆ **998/877-1039.** 12 units. $259–$289 double high and low season. **Amenities:** Bar; pool; fitness center; free Wi-Fi.

## MODERATE

**Hotel Na Balam ★★** A long-time favorite on Playa Norte with an artsy style has gone a bit downhill over the years. Still, the setting is lovely, with a white beach set against palms and flowering gardens. Some rooms face the beach, which sounds great but provides less privacy than those in the gardens by the swimming pool. The hotel's use of folk art has long been one of its best features. Hand-woven hammocks hang outside most rooms, which are decorated with embroidered textiles and carved statues of Maya royalty. Master suites include small pools with whirlpool. Yoga is emphasized here with daily classes, retreats, and workshops in an arrangement with a local yoga school. The restaurant, **Zazil Ha** (p. 131), and beach bar remain popular. Na Balam is a popular spot for destination weddings and is nearly always filled with large groups.

Zazil Ha 118. www.nabalam.com. ✆ **998/881-4770.** 32 units. High season $121–$145 double, $310 master suite; low season $114–$140 double, $267 master suite. **Amenities:** Restaurant; bar; diving and snorkeling trips available; massages; yoga classes; free Wi-Fi.

## INEXPENSIVE

**Hotel Belmar ★★** If you don't mind being constantly hungry thanks to the aroma of Italian cuisine drifting beneath your door, this centrally located hotel on pedestrian Avenida Hidalgo is one of the town's more pleasant retreats. The hotel rises three stories (no elevator) above wildly popular **Rolandi's** restaurant (see p. 130), and the rates are pleasingly low. The best room has a kitchen, dining area, and comfy orange couches all arranged in one large space. Tiled floors, ceiling fans, and doors opening to small balconies keep some rooms cool enough to skip the air conditioning (though noise from the restaurant can be a drawback). All rooms have a small desk and/or table and chairs. It's an easy walk to Playa Norte, and you're surrounded by restaurants, bars, and shops. A full breakfast is included.

Av. Hidalgo 110. www.rolandi.com. ✆ **998/877-0430.** 11 units. High season $68–$79 double, $100 suite; low season $44–$55 double, $117 suite. Full breakfast included. **Amenities:** Restaurant/bar; room service; free Wi-Fi.

**Hotel Cabañas María del Mar ★** An enduring favorite smack on Playa Norte, Cabañas María del Mar has enough variety in accommodations to please nearly anyone—though don't expect luxury. Rooms closest to the beach are located in the Tower section by reception; several have two double beds. The 31 Cabaña rooms face the pool and gardens and also have double beds. Couples prefer the Castle section with somewhat upgraded rooms with king-size beds, relatively quiet air conditioners, and balconies with partial ocean views. Avoid those in the floor above **Buho's** restaurant, where a free continental breakfast consisting of toast, coffee, and weak juice is served.

## THE BEST ISLA MUJERES websites

- **Isla Mujeres Tourist Information: www.isla-mujeres.net** The official site of the Isla Mujeres Tourism Board provides complete information on Isla, including places to eat, where to stay, and things to do.
- **My Isla Mujeres: www.islamujeres.info** Get a local's view of the island; check out the section called "My Isla Guide Book."

One of the great advantages here is the easy access to rental scooters, laundries, and bikes, and the clerks can answer just about any question. You can find erratic Wi-Fi by the reception area.

Av. Arq. Carlos Lazo 1. www.cabanasdelmar.com. ✆ **998/877-0179.** 73 units. High and low season $78–$119 double. Rates include continental breakfast. **Amenities:** Restaurant; bar; outdoor pool.

**Hotel Francis Arlene ★** Isla regulars ask for their favorite rooms at this small family-run inn, where various sons, daughters, and cousins staff the front desk and remember their returning guests. It's not fancy, but rooms meet all essential requirements, with decent beds with ruffled polyester covers, a couple of uncomfortable chairs, coffeemakers, fridges, and tiled baths with showers. Most have balconies overlooking a small courtyard. Ten rooms on the ground floor can be noisy as guests arrive and depart and lack air conditioning, but do have ceiling fans and are budget priced. Kitchenettes and ocean views keep top floor suites in high demand. Thoughtful touches include a water dispenser so you can fill your bottles for free.

Guerrero 7. www.francisarlene.com. ✆ **998/877-0310.** 24 units. High season $60–$75 double, $90 top-floor double; low season $50–$65 double, $80 top-floor double.

**Hotel Xbulu-Ha ★★** It's no wonder guests return annually to one of the best budget hotels I've seen in a long time. From the moment you enter the lobby you're treated with kindness and good cheer, and quickly become part of the family. The largest suite, which books early with guests staying a week or more, has a microwave, flatscreen TV, stove, full-size fridge, and a balcony with a partial sea view. Standard rooms have a small fridge and table. The bathrooms are so clean they look brand new. Extras include shelves of secondhand books for exchange and use of a small kitchen and lounge with microwave, coffeemaker, fridge, and other appliances. There's a rooftop terrace with views of the sea, and the hotel supplies beach towels and backpack chairs—it's just a 5-minute walk to Playa Norte.

Guerrero 4. www.xbuluha.islamujeres.biz. ✆ **998/877-1783.** 15 units. High season $47–$71 double, $73 suite; low season $37–$60 double, $60 suite. **Amenities:** Free Wi-Fi.

**Posada del Mar ★★** The staff at this popular hotel are among the island's most endearing characters. Kind and amiable Nacho, the general manager, knows just about everybody and everything on the island. Miguel, the bartender, inducts newcomers with a liquor-drenched flaming Mayan Sacrifice cocktail sure to encourage friendship among all. Omar handles tours, vehicle rentals, and general info with cheery aplomb. The location is ideal, at the west end of Medina across from the waterfront *malecón.* Playa Norte is a block west and the Centro's restaurants a couple of blocks north.

Three buildings with several types of rooms frame a restaurant, bar, lawns, and pool area. All rooms have individual air-conditioning units, ceiling fans, and patios or balconies. The newest are the best, of course, and have mini-fridges. Mini suites have king beds and sofas, fridges, and shower/bath combos. Most rooms have two double beds—ask for a king in advance. Quality and maintenance varies, but the location and room rates make this a good choice if you want to be close to, but not in the middle of, the action. Rates change six times during the year, based on holidays, seasons, and demand.

Medina 15. www. posadadelmar.com/index.php/en. ✆ **998/877-0044** or 800/544-3005 in the U.S. 78 units. High season $67–$81 double, $75 suite; low season $43–$57 double, $50 suite. **Amenities:** Restaurant; bar; pool; free Wi-Fi in lobby.

## Where to Eat

If you want to experience authentic Mexican food at local prices, head to the **Municipal Market,** next to the post office on Avenida Guerrero. Here hardworking women operate a row of outdoor food stands where working folk and students pay around $4 for the *comida corrida,* the meal of the day, with soup, entree, and drink. The menus posted behind the counter typically include tacos, enchiladas, and various meat and fish dishes. Place your order, wait to pick it up, and settle in a plastic chair at a table covered with bright, flowered oilcloth. ***Hint:*** Pick a stand with the most people chowing down for a great meal. I'm also fond of the *rotiscerias* scattered around town, where you can get half a roasted chicken, rice, beans, and tortillas for around $7.



### EXPENSIVE

**Olivia ★★** MEDITERRANEAN Locals are always thrilled to find alternatives to Isla's abundant Italian restaurants. Intimate Olivia hits the spot with its blend of Moroccan, Turkish, Greek and Bulgarian favorites. I like to start with the Greek appetizer sampler of feta, tzatziki, and olives, then segue into the classic salad of diced cucumbers, tomatoes, onions, and feta doused with olive oil. Choosing an entree is always difficult—shall I go for the flaky spanakopita or add a Mexican flair with *albondigas* (Mexican meatballs)? For a lighter meal consider the shawarma pita wrap with grilled chicken, hummus, and tahini. Romantic candlelight flickers on tables set beneath a palapa and throughout the tropical gardens, and lounge music blends with friendly conversations.



Av. Matamoros. www.olivia-isla-mujeres.com. ✆ **998/877-1765.** Main courses 110–190 pesos. No credit cards. Tues–Sat 5–9:30pm (also open Mon Jan–March).

**Rolandi's ★★** ITALIAN/SEAFOOD Everybody's happy at this island institution where you just might run into friends from previous visits. I can't possibly visit Isla without stopping by at least once, shunning the sidewalk tables for one in the interior courtyard with its twinkling white lights and friendly waiters rushing about. My favorite meal starts with Rolandi's signature puffy garlic bread and moves on to a simply perfect caprese salad followed by spinach cannelloni. I sometimes venture much further afield to veal scaloppini or shrimp sautéed with garlic and guajillo chiles, and will share a margarita pizza from the wood-burning oven with friends. But I always end with the homemade coconut ice cream drenched with Kahlua—a blend of flavors that always brings me back to my first island visit decades ago.

Av. Hidalgo 110. www.rolandirestaurants.com. ✆ **998/877-0430.** Reservations recommended in high season. Main courses 174–215 pesos. Daily 7am–midnight.

## MODERATE

**Cockteleria Justicia Social ★★★** SEAFOOD On my last visit to the island, I asked every cab driver, waiter, and bartender where I should go for the absolute freshest, yummiest ceviche. Every single person replied "Justicia Social." I stopped by one night only to find they closed at 7pm; I was the first customer at opening time—11:30am—the following morning. I settled at an outdoor table beneath an orange and white awning beside a fishing pier, ordered a Bohemia beer and ceviche *mixto* (fish, shrimp, and octopus), and just about swooned. Other white plastic tables filled as I lingered, with a family of 12 ordering bountiful seafood cocktails and platters of grilled fish. The restaurant is run by a fishermen's co-op, and you can watch the men work on their boats while you eat. I'm told the fish with ajillo chiles or simple garlic and butter is divine. And yes, if you shudder at the idea of fish, the menu includes beef and chicken fajitas.

Av. Medina. www.isla-mujeres.net/cockteleria. ✆ **998/274-0142.** Ceviche 110–150 pesos; main courses 100–120 pesos. Daily 11:30am–7pm.

**Mamacita ★** MEXICAN Italian food seems to prevail on Avenida Hidalgo; this colorful open-air restaurant at the street's north end satisfies cravings for *arrachera* (marinated beef) with rice, beans, and tortillas; generous sizzling fajitas; and standard comfort foods including tacos, burritos, and quesadillas. Fun is the focus here, with tequila as the main fuel. It's a happy, friendly place where diners tend to become friends, especially when service is slow and conversation fills the time.

Av. Hidalgo. ✆ **998/877-1811.** Main courses 105–175 pesos. Daily 4pm–midnight.

**Mamma Rosa ★** ITALIAN If the sight of diners sharing platters of pasta at the sidewalk tables doesn't catch your attention, the aromas of garlic and tomatoes surely will. The Diamante pizza topped with lobster goes well with the restaurant's wide range of Champagnes and Italian wines. Risotto choices include a vegetarian primavera version with broccoli and *calabacitas* (sautéed zucchini, squash, and garlic), and the portion of meat lasagna is so large you can easily order one salad and one entree to share. The cool interior is a welcome escape on sultry summer evenings, even if you just stop by for a glass of wine and crispy fried calamari.

Av. Hidalgo 10 (at Matamoros). ✆ **998/877-1811.** Main courses 155–250 pesos. Daily 3:30–11pm.

**Zazil Ha ★** SEAFOOD The fanciest restaurant on Playa Norte is a good place to stop for breakfast, lunch, or a romantic dinner. It's quieter than the beach bars, and has a lovely setting beside white sand and turquoise water scenes. Breakfast is the best meal, in my opinion, because there's a perfect yogurt, granola, and fruit plate and several vegetarian options including a goat cheese, tomato, and basil omelet, *chilaquiles* with salsa verde and fried eggs, and several healthy juices including the sometimes essential *detox verde* (green detox). Come night, candlelight sparkles underneath the open-air *palapa.* Specialties include panko-crusted fish with mango sauce, a bountiful seafood platter with scallops, shrimp, fish, octopus, and mussels, and a filet mignon

At the Hotel Na Balam. www.nabalam.com. ✆ **998/881-4770.** Main courses 130–200 pesos. Daily 7am–10pm.

## INEXPENSIVE

**Rooster ★★** CAFE There's no friendlier place to begin the day than at this casual eatery. Though most folks prefer mingling at the sidewalk tables, I'm fond of the delightfully air-conditioned, bright green indoor restaurant redolent with the fragrance of fresh cinnamon rolls and banana bread. No one minds if you settle in with a cappuccino and sweet treat while using the free Wi-Fi. Breakfasts are enormous and delicious, and it's hard to choose between the French toast with wild berry compote, waffles stuffed with ham, or more traditional huevos rancheros and *chilaquiles.* You must try the killer lobster Benedict at least once—it's so rich you may need to share, though you probably won't want to. Of course, you could skip all this and just go for that sticky, fluffy cinnamon roll. Some of the island's best burgers highlight the lunch and dinner menus. You can choose among beef, brisket, or chicken with assorted toppings, or go for the staggering selection of spicy chicken wings—I'm fond of the tequila and lime wings. Spinoff cafe Rooster On The Go pleases budget travelers at the nearby Poc Na Hostel with coffee, baked goods, and free Wi-Fi.

Calle Hidalgo 1, at Plaza Isla Mujeres. ✆ **998/274-0152.** Entrees 55–130 pesos. No credit cards. Daily 5:30am–10:30pm.

**Ruben's ★** CAFE Across the street from the market, this small, yellow-walled building holds Ruben Chavez's dream business, a simple cafe serving tasty, inexpensive meals that drew instant fans the moment it opened. The generous *comida corrida* includes a trip to the salad bar, soup, entree, and side dishes for 75 pesos. This isn't your usual inexpensive lunch, as the selection of entrees could include grilled fish with mango sauce, chicken with chipotle chiles, *carne asada,* and all sorts of creative preparations. Breakfast is a hit as well, with homemade sauces and tortillas making a big difference in quality.

Guerrero across from the market. No phone. Entrees 65–95 pesos. No credit cards. Mon–Sat 7am–8pm.



## Exploring

### ATTRACTIONS

**Dolphin Discovery ★** WATER PARK If you're turned off by the idea of dolphins in captivity see "The Dolphin Dilemma" box, p. 93), skip this park and go snorkeling or diving in the open sea. If the concept doesn't bother you, you'll find this long-established center (www.dolphindiscovery.com; ✆ **998/849-4748**) at the "Delfinario," midway along the island on the east side facing Cancún. The center appears to take good care of the dolphins, which reproduce frequently enough to keep the program going without adding new ones. The mothers and babies are kept in a separate enclosure without human contact for several months before trainers gradually introduce training. The Dolphin Royal Swim ($169 per person, $99 for kids) allows groups of up to eight people to swim with two dolphins and a trainer. Swimmers view an educational video and spend time in the water with the trainer and the dolphins before enjoying swimming time with the dolphins. Reservations are necessary. Less expensive programs allow you to learn about, touch, and hold the dolphins (but not swim with them), starting at $99 ($69 for kids). The Sea Life Discovery package includes encounters with dolphins, manatees, and sea lions. The price is $189 for adults and $129 for children. The center also offers snorkeling programs to El Farito reef; other packages include entry to both Garrafón (below) and Dolphin Discovery. Fees include food, an open bar, use of a freshwater swimming pool, lockers, and showers. The center is open daily from 9am to 5pm.

**Garrafón Natural Reef Park ★** NATURE RESERVE Garrafón (www.garrafon.com; ✆ **866/393-5158** or 998/849-4748) sits at the southern end of the island near Punta Sur. Once a public national underwater park, Garrafón is now operated by

Dolphin Discovery. Myriad water activities include snorkeling, kayaking, a dive platform, and swimming. Although there are some tropical fish in the snorkeling area, most of the reef has died. The pricey park also offers a swimming pool, zip line, bicycle tour, restaurant and bar, beach chairs, shaded hammocks, changing rooms with showers and lockers, and gift shop. It is only worth the cost if you spend the day here and take advantage of all the facilities. Admission costs $79 ($54 for children under 12); the all-inclusive package includes buffet lunch, domestic open bar, and use of snorkeling equipment and kayaks. Swimming with dolphin packages are also available, as are VIP packages that include a private, air-conditioned gourmet restaurant and bar. Round-trip transportation between Cancún and Isla Mujeres is also available if you're staying in Cancún. The park is open daily in high season from 10am to 5pm. In low season, it may close a couple of days per week.

**Hacienda Mundaca ★** HISTORIC SITE Almost in the middle of the island, a large park with several crumbling structures includes the ruins of a large hacienda constructed by the 19th-century pirate and slave trader Fermín Antonio Mundaca de Marecheaga. Mundaca is said to have constructed the hacienda for a local girl who'd captured his heart. She shunned him for a local boy and the pirate lived on his grand estate alone. The shaded grounds include a well-tended botanical garden and a lake; fortunately, the small zoo has been closed. It's a pleasant place for a walk but lacks picnic tables or seating areas. Stop at the entrance and visit with Caesar Espinosa, who crafts seashells into just about any sort of trinket you can imagine and sells them to support his family. The entrance fee is 20 pesos, and it's open daily 9am to 5pm.

**Isla Contoy ★★** NATURE RESERVE Visiting this gorgeous, isolated, uninhabited island, 30km (19 miles) by boat from Isla Mujeres, is like seeing the Mexican Caribbean in its most natural state. The 6km-long (3¾-mile) island, which became a national wildlife reserve in 1981, is covered in lush vegetation and harbors 70 species of birds, as well as a host of marine and animal life. Bird species that nest on the island include pelicans, brown boobies, frigates, egrets, terns, and cormorants. Flocks of flamingos arrive in April. Most excursions troll for fish (which will be your lunch), anchor en route for a snorkeling expedition, skirt the island at a leisurely pace for close viewing of the birds without disturbing the habitat, and then pull ashore. While the captain prepares lunch, visitors can swim, sun, follow the nature trails, and visit the nature museum, which has bathroom facilities. The trip from Isla Mujeres takes about 45 minutes each way and can be longer if the waves are choppy. Because of the tight-knit boatmen's cooperative, prices for this excursion are the same everywhere: $75. You can buy a ticket at the **Cooperativa Isla Mujeres** (no phone) on Avenida Rueda Medina, next to the gas station. Trips leave at 9am and return around 4pm. Boat captains should respect the cooperative's regulations regarding ecological sensitivity and boat safety, including the availability of life jackets for everyone on board. If you're not given a life jacket, ask for one. Sodas, beer, and snorkeling equipment are usually included in the price, but double-check before heading out. Bring extra water, a towel, a hat, and biodegradable sunscreen.

**Punta Sur ★★** NATURE RESERVE Walking or driving toward the southern tip of the island, you'll find a once-isolated natural point with a lighthouse and small Maya shrine. Today, the area includes a cluster of shops, a restaurant, and **Sculptured Spaces,** a sculpture garden with pieces donated to Isla Mujeres by internationally renowned sculptors including José Luis Cuevas and Vladimir Cora. A small

**Maya ruin** dedicated to the fertility goddess Ixchel lies here as well (**San Gervasio ★★,** p. 151). There's a 30-peso entrance fee for the garden and Maya ruin; a lighthouse is also located here. It's open daily from 9am to 5pm. The **Cliff of the Dawn ★★★**—the easternmost point of Mexico—lies just beyond the sculpture garden and offers extraordinary views from pathways leading nearly to the water's edge. The cafe and restrooms on-site are generally open from 9am to 5pm, but you can enter the walkways at any time.

**Tortugranja ★★** FARM Years ago, fishermen converged on the island nightly from May to September to capture turtles when they came ashore to lay eggs. Then a concerned fisherman, Gonzalo Chale Maldonado, began convincing others to spare the eggs, which he protected. Following his lead, the fishing ministry founded the **Centro de Investigaciones Pesqueras** to find ways to protect the species and increase the turtle populations. At the *Tortugranja,* as the Turtle Farm is called in Spanish, visitors walk through the indoor and outdoor turtle pool areas, where green, white, and loggerhead turtles paddle around. Turtles are separated by age, from newly hatched up to 1 year. Although the local government provides some assistance, most of the funding comes from private-sector donations. Turtle babies are released to the sea in August and September, and visitors are invited to take part. Inquire at the center. The sanctuary is on a spit of land jutting out from the island's west coast. The address is Carretera Sac Bajo no. 5; you'll need a taxi to get there. Admission costs 30 pesos; the shelter is open daily from 9am to 5pm. The small gift shop sells cold drinks and restrooms are available. For more information, call ✆ **998/877-0595.**

## OUTDOOR ACTIVITIES

### Beaches & Swimming

Isla Mujeres has no lifeguards on duty and does not use the system of water-safety flags employed in Cancún and Cozumel. The bay between Cancún and Isla Mujeres is calm, with warm, transparent waters ideal for swimming, snorkeling, and diving. The east side of the island facing the open Caribbean Sea is typically rougher, with much stronger currents.

**Playa Norte ★★★** Playa Norte, which extends around the northern tip of the island, is the island's best municipal beach—a gorgeous swath of fine white sand and calm, translucent turquoise-blue water that stays shallow far off the shore. It's just a short walk to the beach from the ferry and downtown hotels. Watersports equipment, beach umbrellas, and lounge chairs are widely available for rent. This is a terrific place for swimming and snorkeling. Tables, chairs, and umbrellas in front of restaurants usually cost nothing if you use the restaurant as your headquarters for drinks and food, and the best of them have hammocks and swings from which to sip your piña coladas.

**Playa Lancheros ★** On the Caribbean side of Laguna Makax is another lovely swimming beach with a restaurant. You must purchase food or drink to use the beach. Party boats from Cancún often unload dozens of rowdy passengers near here for day and night beach parties.

**Capitán Dulché ★★★** Most beach clubs along the east coast cater to day-trippers on booze cruises from Cancún. This lovely compound (www.capitandulche.com; ✆ **998/849-7594**) away from the noisy areas is the exception. Anchors, buoys, ship lanterns, and metal sculptures are scattered about park-like lawns leading to a restaurant serving seafood, pastas, and other fare far above the quality at most beach clubs.

A pristine, long beach is lined with small *palapas* and lounge chairs, and the water here is clear and calm. A museum dedicated to Capitán Dulché, who spearheaded the development of the island's first pier, displays historic photos, intricate model ships, and other nautical memorabilia; guided tours cost 50 pesos. The complex is sometimes closed for private functions and weddings, but is usually open daily from 10am to 6pm.

### Fishing

To arrange a day of fishing, ask at the **Cooperativa Isla Mujeres** (the boatmen's cooperative), a small shop on the right side of the pier off Avenida Rueda Medina, next to the gas station. Four hours of fishing costs $220 for up to eight people. Year-round you'll find bonito, mackerel, kingfish, and amberjack. Sailfish and sharks (hammerhead, bull, nurse, lemon, and tiger) are in good supply in April and May. In winter, larger grouper and jewfish are prevalent. The cooperative is open daily from 8am to 6:30pm. Other fishing companies offer half-day in-shore and full-day open water fishing, including the **Sport Fishing Center** (www.sportfishingcenter.net; ✆ **044-998-212-3592**) and **Sea Hawk Isla Mujeres** (www.seahawkislamujeres.com; ✆ **998/877-0296**).

### Scuba Diving & Snorkeling

Most of the dive shops on the island offer the same trips for similar prices, including reef, drift, deep, and night dives. One-tank dives cost about $55 to $75; two-tank dives about $65 to $90. **Aqua Adventures Eco Divers,** Av. Juarez at Morelos (www.diveislamujeres.com; ✆ **998/236-4316**) is a full-service shop that offers resort courses, dive packages, and certifications. Another respected dive shop is **Carey Dive Center,** at Matamoros 13A and Rueda Medina (www.careydivecenter.com; ✆ **998/877-0763**). Both also offer 2-hour snorkeling trips for around $35. Cuevas de los Tiburones (Caves of the Sleeping Sharks) is Isla's most renowned dive site—but the name is slightly misleading, as shark sightings are uncommon these days. Although sleeping shark sightings are rare, giant whale sharks by the hundreds migrate through these waters about 12 to 15 miles offshore between mid-June and mid-August. Other dive sites include a wreck 15km (9⅓ miles) offshore; Banderas reef, between Isla Mujeres and Cancún, where there's always a strong current; Tabos reef on the eastern shore; and Manchones reef, 1km (⅔ mile) off the southeastern tip of the island, where the water is 4.5 to 11m (15–36 feet) deep. The Cross of the Bay is close to Manchones reef. A bronze cross, weighing 1 ton and standing 12m (39 feet) high, was placed in the water between Manchones and Isla in 1994 as a memorial to those who have lost their lives at sea. At **La MUSA Underwater Museum of Art** (www.musacancun.com), more than 400 sunken life-size sculptures form an impressive artificial reef. Scuba and snorkeling trips are offered here. Diving is best if you want to examine the sculptures closely, but you can get a decent overview while snorkeling. There are few good snorkeling sites off Isla's shores, as the water by popular beaches is usually too shallow. The best offshore option is at Garrafón Natural Reef Park. Sea creature sightings are far better on boat trips to nearby reefs and Isla Contoy available through local dive shops and the Cooperativa Isla Mujeres.

## Shopping

Shopping is a casual activity on Isla Mujeres. Several shops, especially concentrated on Avenida Hidalgo, sell Saltillo rugs, onyx, silver, Guatemalan clothing, blown glassware, masks, folk art, crafts, beach paraphernalia, and T-shirts in abundance. Most sell

## LOCAL celebrities

The most famous visitors in Isla aren't movie stars or rock legends, but they are the biggest fish in the sea. I'm talking about the whale sharks that migrate to the waters off the northern Caribbean coast from May to September. Though Isla Holbox (p. 117) off the mainland's northern shores has been the center of whale shark sightings for years, Isla Mujeres can now claim more creatures appearing closer to shore. Nicknamed *ballenas dominos* (domino whales) for the white spots dotting their massive gray bodies, which can grow more than 50 feet long, whale sharks are impressively gentle and unthreatening. They're not the least bit interested in nibbling humans with their hundreds of teeth and much prefer filtering plankton for nourishment. Swimming with these docile leviathans is an absolutely incredible experience, one I've had the great fortune to enjoy several times. My first encounter was off Isla Holbox, on a small boat with a naturalist who filled me in on the do's and don'ts (first rule: no touching). As we approached the first huge shadow moving just below the sea's surface, I strapped on fins, snorkel, and mask and leaped into the water the minute the captain said, "Go!" Swimming madly, I reached the whale shark's gills as they gushed bubbling water in a natural whirlpool. Seconds later I dodged a swaying tail, amazed at how quickly a behemoth can disappear. I repeated the scene with about a dozen sharks, racing madly through the clear, warm water and holding my hands high to prove I wasn't touching them as they brushed my skin while swimming beneath me. Finally, the captain insisted I drag my weary, hyperventilating body back on the boat. I immediately mentally tallied the cost of returning the next day. The presence of whale sharks has boosted Isla's tourism numbers in the summer months, leading to a joyful annual Whale Shark Festival with a parade, costume contest, sand sculpture contest, and group beach cleanup session. For information on Isla's whale shark tour operators, see p. 120.



pretty much the same stuff. You'll find high quality masks, pottery, and other folk art at **Galería Aztlán** (Av. Hidalgo 5, no phone). Prices are lower than in Cancún or Cozumel.

## Entertainment & Nightlife

Those in a party mood by day's end may want to start out at the beach bars along Playa Norte, including **Buho's,** the beach bar of the Cabañas María del Mar (p. 128). This popular, low-key hangout features swinging seats under a giant *palapa* for super-casual sunset viewing. Also on the beach, the lounge of the **Na Balam** hotel serves tapas and creative cocktails to a cool crowd. **Jax Bar & Grill,** on Avenida Rueda Medina, close to Hotel Posada del Mar, is a Texas-style sports bar offering live music nightly. A rock-'n'-roll–loving set fueled by close to 100 tequila brands keeps the party going at **Fayne's,** located at Avenida Hidalgo 12 and open nightly from 7pm to midnight or later. It offers excellent live music starting at 8pm and dancing that usually gets going after 10pm. Also in the town center at Avenida Hidalgo 65, the super-casual **La Kokonuts** turns on the TVs for sporting events and cranks up the music for dancing. It's open from 8am to 4am—incredibly late for Isla. A DJ spins tunes at **Poc-Na** (essentially a beach party thrown by the youth hostel) on the waterfront off the end of Avenida Hidalgo, where a 20- and 30-something crowd dances on the sand until 4am.

# COZUMEL ★★★

70km (43 miles) S of Cancún; 19km (12 miles) SE of Playa del Carmen

If I moved to Mexico, I'd have no problem deciding where to go. Cozumel is my favorite place in the entire country. For one thing, the island is surrounded by clear, warm water and some of the finest reefs for diving and snorkeling in the world. More than that, however, is the terrific sense of community and tradition I feel every time I visit Cozumel. Family is important here—you won't find children selling trinkets on the sidewalk or vendors hassling passersby. Instead, families gather under feathery, flamboyant trees at the plaza and wander along the waterfront *malecón.* Children are an integral part of every island celebration. In the back neighborhoods, women dressed in traditional Maya *huipiles* (embroidered dresses) gossip on front porches as fishermen unload the catch of the day at humble restaurants serving extraordinary seafood creations.

Visitors are welcomed everywhere—I've never felt shunned or afraid here. In fact, safety is one of Cozumel's selling points, as is the healthy lifestyle. Chain restaurants and shops are nearly non-existent, and family businesses thrive. Granted, the waterfront has been taken over by jewelry and souvenir shops catering to the thousands of cruise ship passengers descending on the town almost daily. But wander a few streets inland and you're in the heart of a genuine Mexican community. Staying in the main town of San Miguel is fun and convenient, putting you in the center of everyday life. Alternatively, hotels and resorts line the western coast north and south of town. It's possible to travel on a small budget here, and easy to vacation comfortably without spending a fortune. If you're looking for a luxurious splurge, you'll find that as well, though minus any pretensions.

**The Coast** Cozumel is 45km (28 miles) long and 18km (11 miles) wide, and lies just 19km (12 miles) from the mainland. Most of the terrain is flat and clothed in a low tropical forest. Tall reefs line the **southwest coast,** creating towering walls that offer divers a fairytale seascape to explore. The water on the protected side, the **western shore,** stays as calm as an aquarium, unless a front is blowing through. The rougher, wild **eastern shore** remains more lightly traveled for those preferring to wander off the beaten path. **Chankanaab National Park,** along the southwestern shore of the island, offers beautiful sightseeing and sunning spots.

## Essentials

### GETTING THERE

#### By Plane

During high season, several international commercial flights fly in and out of Cozumel's airport (CZM). Airlines that might offer flights (this changes seasonally) include **American, Delta, Frontier, United,** and **US Airways.** There are few international flights in low season, but **Maya Air** (www.mayair.com.mx; ✆ **987/872-3609** or 314/669-6879 in the U.S.) runs several daily flights between Cozumel and Cancún, and connections are painless. Beware of weight limits, though, especially if you're carrying a lot of scuba gear.

#### By Ferry

Passenger ferries run to and from Playa del Carmen. **México Waterjets** (www.mexicowaterjets.com; ✆ **984/879-3112**) and **Ultramar** (www.granpuerto.com.mx; ✆ **998/881-5890**) offer departures almost every hour in the morning and about every

2 to 4 hours in the afternoon. The schedules change according to seasons but generally start at 7am and continue until 9 or 10pm. The trip takes 30 to 45 minutes, depending on conditions, and costs about 160 pesos each way. The boats are air-conditioned. In Playa del Carmen, the ferry dock is 1½ blocks from the main square. In Cozumel, the ferries use Muelle Fiscal, the town pier, a block from the main square. Luggage storage at the Cozumel dock costs 20 pesos per day.

The car ferry that used to operate from Puerto Morelos now uses the Calica pier just south of Playa del Carmen. The fare for a standard car is 683 pesos. **TransCaribe** (www.transcaribe.net; ✆ **987/872-7688**) has four departures daily, but only two on Sunday; check the website for exact scheduling. The ferry docks in Cozumel at the **Muelle Internacional** (the **International Pier,** which is south of town near El Cid La Ceiba Hotel).

### By Bus

**ADO** (www.ado.com.mx) makes a non-stop 1-hour trip (depending on traffic) from between the Cancún airport and Playa del Carmen from about noon to 11pm for 146 pesos; it's a 2-block walk from the ADO bus station to the pier in Playa del Carmen where you can easily catch the ferry to Cozumel.

## ORIENTATION

### Arriving

Cozumel's **airport** is just a 5-minute drive from downtown. **Transportes Terrestre** (✆ **987/872-1323**) provides hotel transportation in multi-passenger vans. Buy your ticket as you exit the terminal. To hotels downtown, the fare is 57 pesos per person; to hotels along the north and south shore, 96 pesos. A private taxi to downtown costs 134 pesos. Passenger ferries arrive at the Muelle Fiscal, the municipal pier, by the town's main square. Cruise ships dock at the **Punta Langosta** pier, several blocks south of the Muelle Fiscal, at the **International Pier,** which is at Km 4 of the southern coastal road, and **Puerta Maya** near the International Pier.

### Visitor Information

The **Municipal Tourism Office** (www.cozumel.gob.mx; ✆ **987/869-0212**), located at Plaza del Sol, also has information booths at the International Pier and Punta Langosta Pier. It's open 8am to 3pm Monday to Friday.

### City Layout

San Miguel's main waterfront street is **Avenida Melgar.** Running parallel to Melgar are avenidas numbered in multiples of five—5, 10, 15. **Avenida Juárez** runs perpendicular to these, heading inland from the ferry dock. Avenida Juárez divides the town into northern and southern halves. The calles (streets) that parallel Juárez to the north have even numbers. The ones to the south have odd numbers, except for Calle Rosado Salas, which runs between calles 1 and 3. Vehicles on the avenidas have the right of way.

### Island Layout

One road runs along the western coast of the island, which faces the Yucatán mainland. It has different names: **Santa Pilar** or **San Juan** north of town; **Avenida Rafael Melgar** in the city; and **Costera Sur** south of town. Hotels stretch along this road north and south of town. The road runs to the southern tip of the island (Punta Sur), passing **Chankanaab National Park. Avenida Juárez** (and its extension, the **Carretera Transversal**) runs east from the town across the island. After passing the airport and the turnoff to the ruins of San Gervasio, before reaching the undeveloped ocean side

# Cozumel

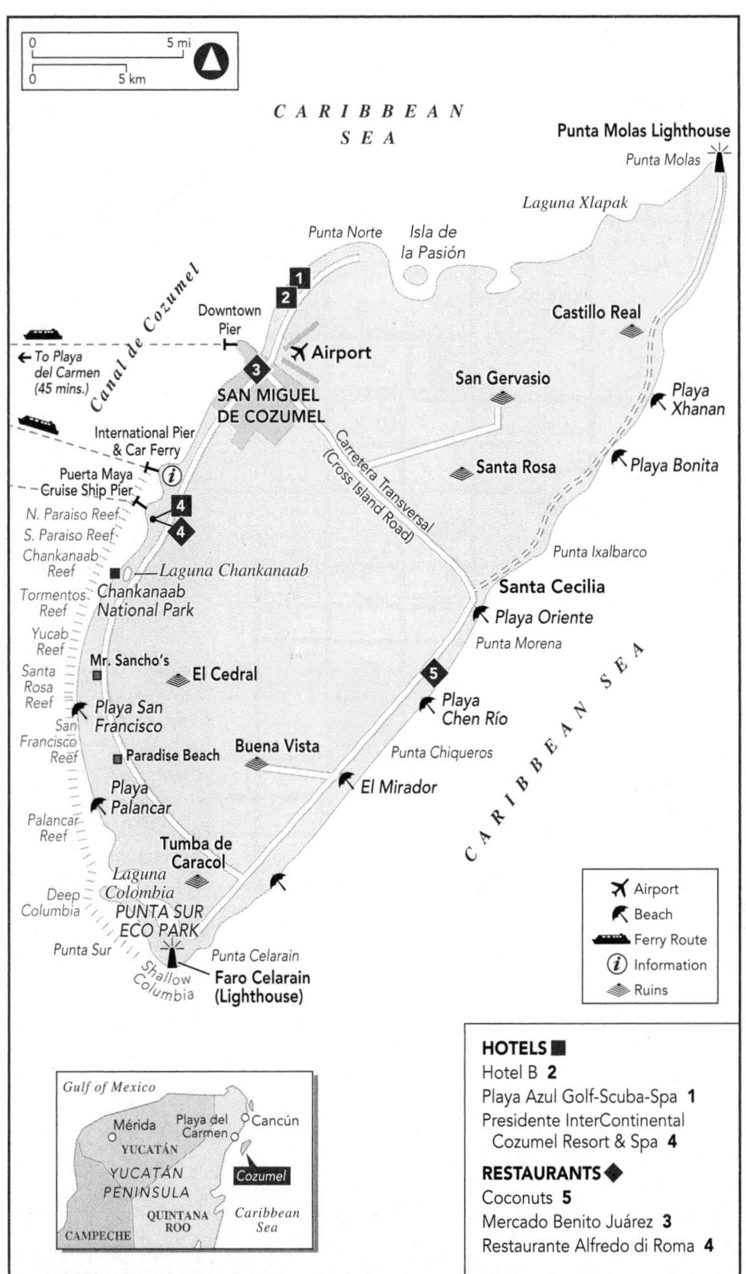

0 5 mi
0 5 km
CARIBBEAN SEA
Punta Molas Lighthouse
Punta Molas
Laguna Xlapak
Punta Norte
Isla de la Pasión
Canal de Cozumel
Downtown Pier
To Playa del Carmen (45 mins.)
Airport
SAN MIGUEL DE COZUMEL
Castillo Real
San Gervasio
Playa Xhanan
International Pier & Car Ferry
Carretera Transversal (Cross Island Road)
Santa Rosa
Playa Bonita
Puerta Maya Cruise Ship Pier
N. Paraiso Reef
S. Paraiso Reef
Chankanaab Reef
Laguna Chankanaab
Punta Ixalbarco
Santa Cecilia
Tormentos Reef
Chankanaab National Park
Playa Oriente
Punta Morena
Yucab Reef
Mr. Sancho's
El Cedral
Santa Rosa Reef
Playa San Francisco
Playa Chen Río
San Francisco Reef
Paradise Beach
Buena Vista
Punta Chiqueros
El Mirador
Playa Palancar
Palancar Reef
CARIBBEAN SEA
Tumba de Caracol
Laguna Colombia
Deep Columbia
PUNTA SUR ECO PARK
Punta Sur
Punta Celarain
Shallow Columbia
Faro Celarain (Lighthouse)
Airport
Beach
Ferry Route
Information
Ruins
Gulf of Mexico
Mérida
Playa del Carmen
Cancún
YUCATÁN
YUCATÁN PENINSULA
Cozumel
QUINTANA ROO
Caribbean Sea
CAMPECHE
HOTELS
Hotel B 2
Playa Azul Golf-Scuba-Spa 1
Presidente InterContinental Cozumel Resort & Spa 4
RESTAURANTS
Coconuts 5
Mercado Benito Juárez 3
Restaurante Alfredo di Roma 4

## HIGHLIGHTS ON THE wild SIDE

No trip to Cozumel is complete without a leisurely drive along Cozumel's eastern coast. Largely undeveloped, the craggy rock shoreline has been carved by winds and waves into a series of long beaches, small coves, and jagged points jutting into the sea. Traffic is usually light on the single road running along the coast, though tour buses sometimes mar the scenery. Allow at least four hours for a leisurely tour, including a leisurely lunch at one of the seafood restaurants on the sand.

A few minutes along the road, you'll spot palm-shaded stands with bright pink, green, and purple sarongs and hammocks waving in the wind at El Mirador. Stop here, watch a vendor hack a coconut in half with a machete and stick a straw inside, and pass over a few pesos for a refreshing coconut milk drink. Walk to the beach and, if the water's calm, climb onto the long black rock promontory for a perfect sky and sea photo op.

Moving along, you'll spot a tall limestone pillar at the side of the road. Erected to commemorate the December 21, 2012 dawning of a new cycle in the Maya calendar (as opposed to the popular, hysterical end of the world prophesy), the statue marks Playa San Martin, where hundreds gathered to celebrate the new era. Locals gather on weekends at this long beach with a manned lifeguard tower. As an added attraction, smoking is prohibited here.

You'll easily spot the next stop when you see children running in and out of a shallow pool sheltered by rocks at Playa Chen Rio, the best place for a swim if the water's calm. Coconuts, a popular tourist-oriented restaurant/bar atop a small hill by the beach is good for a cool drink and snack, but save your appetite for a seafood lunch on the sand at one of the *palapa*-shaded restaurants on the sand at Chen Rio and Punta Morena.

The road ends a bit farther along at Mezcalito's, one of the oldest bars along this coast with an all-day party scene. At this time, you're not allowed to enter the dirt road leading to a small archeological site on the island's northern tip. There have been jeep tours along this road in the past, and they just might start again.

***One important tip:*** Be especially careful where you walk on the beaches in summer, as sea turtles build their nests and lay their eggs all along the coast. Volunteers usually surround the nests with sticks and rope, or move the eggs to a more secure location. Still, stay away if you see a large hump in the sand.



of the island, the road then turns south and follows the coast to the southern tip, where it meets the Costera Sur.

### Neighborhoods in Brief

San Miguel is the island's dining, shopping, and business center, with endless choices in one-story buildings on streets branching off the main plaza. Avenida 5N and Avenida Juárez are closed to traffic for a couple of blocks around the plaza and are perfect for strolling and dining at sidewalk cafes. Residential neighborhoods and local businesses pack the streets from Avenida 15 inland.

South of town, the main road is lined with hotels and tourist-oriented businesses to the International and Puerto Maya piers. Buildings give way to undisturbed rocky coastline with a few businesses from here to the northern tip of the island. Shore diving and snorkeling is good in this area, but there are few sandy beaches. At the far south is a cluster of all-inclusive resorts. North of town, the coast is lined with more hotels facing shallow, clear water good for swimming and snorkeling.

The wild west coast is undeveloped except for a few rustic seafood restaurants and one hotel. Beautiful long beaches face rough seas—swimming is discouraged when the water is the least bit rough.

### Getting Around

You can walk to most destinations in town, and it's very safe. Getting to outlying hotels and beaches requires a rental car, moped, or taxi.

**Car rentals** are about $50 for a VW bug and $95 for a Jeep Wrangler. **Avis** (www.avis.mx; ✆ **987/872-0099**), **Dollar** (www.dollarmexico.com.mx; ✆ **987/869-2957**), and **Hertz** (www.hertz.com/rentacar/car-rental/mexico; ✆ **987/871-6783**) have counters in the airport, and a few other international companies have offices across the street. Most of the biggies have stands at the ferry pier as well. Other major rental companies have offices in town, including **Thrifty** (✆ **987/869-2957**) at Juárez 181, between avenidas 5 and 10 Norte. Rentals are easy to arrange through your hotel or at any of the many local rental offices. Some folks think it's fun to rent a topless jeep, but there are drawbacks, including brutal sunburns and the inability to lock possessions in the car.

> **Be Streetwise**
>
> North–south streets—the avenidas—have the right of way, and traffic doesn't slow down or stop.

**Scooters** are readily available and start at about $30 for a full day including a helmet but not insurance, which runs about $15 extra. **HTL Rentals** (✆ **987/869-3097**) at Av. 5 between calles 2 and 4 Norte is a reliable agency. You'll be amazed by the way locals pack their scooters with multiple families members and parcels. They scoot around traffic regularly, causing me to drive super cautiously. If you rent a scooter, be very careful: Scooter accidents easily rank as the greatest cause of injury in Cozumel, and first-timers often end up with road rash from sudden tumbles, if not more significant injuries. Before renting one, inspect it carefully to see that all the gizmos—horn, light, starter, seat, mirror—are in good shape. I've been offered scooters with unbalanced wheels, which made them unsteady at higher speeds, but the renter quickly exchanged them upon my request. You are required to stay on paved roads. It's illegal to ride a moped without a helmet outside of town (subject to a 500-peso fine).

Cozumel has lots of **taxis** and a strong drivers' union. Fares are standardized—there's no bargaining. Here are a few sample fares for two people (there is an additional charge for extra passengers to most destinations): island tour, 800 pesos; town to southern Hotel Zone, 80 to 200 pesos; town to northern hotels, 50 to 100 pesos; town to Chankanaab, 120 pesos for up to four people; in and around town, 50 pesos.

## [FastFACTS] COZUMEL

**Area Code** The telephone area code is **987.**

**ATMs, Banks & Currency Exchange** The island has several banks and *casas de cambio*, as well as ATMs. Most places accept dollars, but you usually get a better deal paying in pesos. **HSBC** has an ATM on the corner of the main plaza at Av. 5 Sur and Calle 1 Sur; the fee for withdrawing cash here is less than at other ATMs along Avenida Melgar.

**Climate** The weather is most pleasant from late October to December and March to June. January and February can bring strong winds and sudden rain. Hurricane season has become unpredictable; strong storms can occur any time between June and October.

**Consulates** The **U.S. Consular Agent** is in the Villa Mar Mall in the Plaza, Parque Juárez between Avenida Juárez and 5th Av. Norte (✆ **987/872-4574**); it's open Monday through Friday from noon to 2pm.

**Hospital** **Médica San Miguel** (✆ **987/872-0103**) works for most things and includes intensive-care facilities. It's on Calle 6 Norte between avenidas 5 and 10. **Centro Médico Cozumel** (✆ **987/872-9400**) is an alternative. It's at the intersection of Calle 1 Sur and Avenida 50.

**Internet Access** Several cybercafes are in and around the main square. If you go just a bit off Avenida Melgar and the main square, prices drop. Rates at **Mexatel,** between Av. Juárez 15 and Calle 2 Norte, are 10 pesos per hour. It's open daily from 9am to 10pm.

**Post Office** The *correo* is on Avenida Melgar at Calle 7 Sur (✆ **987/872-0106**), at the southern edge of town. It's open Monday through Friday from 9am to 3pm, Saturday from 9am to noon.

**Recompression Chamber** Cozumel has three *cámaras de recompresión.* The best are the **Hyperbaric Chamber and Clinic** (www.sssnetwork.com; ✆ **987/872-2387,** -1430), open daily 9am to 6pm, with a 24-hour emergency line, at Calle 5 Sur 21-B, between Avenida Melgar and Avenida 5 Sur; and the **Costamed Hyperbaric Center** (✆ **987/872-5050**), at Av. 25 Sur 50.

**Seasons** High season is from Christmas to Easter and August.

## Where to Stay

I've grouped Cozumel's hotels by location—**north** of town, **in town,** and **south** of town. The prices quoted are public rates and typically do not include the 19% tax. I've listed the lowest possible rate for high and low season, which typically means the smallest room without a view. High season is from December to Easter and August (when Mexican families go on vacation). Expect rates from Christmas to New Year's and around Carnival to be higher than the regular high-season rates quoted here. Most hotels have an arrangement with a dive shop and offer dive packages. These can be good deals, but if you don't buy a dive package, it's quite okay to stay at one hotel and dive with a third-party operator—any dive boat can pull up to any hotel pier to pick up customers, though many dive shops won't pick up from the hotels north of town. There's only one hotel on the island's windward side. The isolated, eco-friendly **Ventanas al Mar** (www.ventanasalmar cozumel.com; ✆ **987/564-4287**), which is ideal for those who want a pure escape. It sits beside a long, pristine beach; **Coconuts**, a popular restaurant, is on the other side and closes at dusk. As an alternative to a hotel, you can try **Cozumel Paradise Villas** (www.cozumelparadisevillas.com; ✆ **970/577-6153** in the U.S.), which rents villas and condos by the week. **VRBO** (www.vrbo.com) lists lavish vacation homes on the coast and smaller, more modest condos homes in town for rent by owner.

### NORTH OF TOWN

**Carretera San Juan** is the name of Avenida Melgar's northern extension. All the hotels lie close to each other on the beach side of the road a short distance from town and the airport.

#### Expensive

**Playa Azul Golf-Scuba-Spa ★★** Plenty of extras draw return guests to this boutique inn a 5-minute drive north of downtown. Complimentary breakfast and free golf at the Cozumel Country Club are big pluses, as are the ocean views from all

## THE BEST COZUMEL websites

- **Cozumel.net: www.cozumel.net** This site is a cut above the typical dining/lodging/activities sites. Click on "About Cozumel" to find weather, articles of interest, and links to services and events. There's also a comprehensive listing of B&Bs and vacation-home rentals.
- **Cozumel Insider: www.cozumelinsider.com** is an aptly named font of information.
- **Cozumel Hotel Association: www.islacozumel.com** Operated by the Cozumel Promotion Board, this site gives more than just listings of the member hotels. There's info on the island's history, culture, and ecology, plus useful descriptions of things to do and how to do them.

rooms. The smallest units have one or two beds, coffeemakers, air conditioning and fans, and balconies—the best views are from upper floors. Separate living rooms with sofa beds make the larger suites good for families, while the master suites with balcony or terrace hot tubs are popular with honeymooners and romantics. A garden house beside the hotel has a full kitchen, four bedrooms, and three baths. There's occasional live music at the onsite beach club, where lounge chairs beckon from beneath small *palapas*. An on-site dive shops offers dive lessons and trips, and snorkeling is good off the rocky shoreline.

Carretera San Juan Km 4. www.playa-azul.com. ✆ **987/869-5160.** 51 units. High season $200 double, $245 suite; low season $180 double, $205 suite. Rates include unlimited golf and full breakfast. All-inclusive option available. Free guarded parking. **Amenities:** 2 restaurants; 2 bars; dive shop; unlimited golf privileges at Cozumel Country Club; pool; room service; spa; free Wi-Fi.

### Moderate

**Hotel B ★★** General manager Beatriz Tinajero transformed the '70s-era Hotel Fontan into a chic boutique inn in 2011, and it's since become a favorite with international travelers seeking style, comfort, and reasonable room rates. Cheery lipstick-red umbrellas and turquoise wire chairs give the pool area a touch of South Beach and '50s-era Acapulco, though the background lounge music, beach beds, and mojitos are pure 21st century. Most rooms in the four-story building have ocean views from a wall of sliding glass doors and balconies with low-slung canvas chairs. The largest units have a low king-size bed facing the view, as well as a long countertop desk, small table and chair, vanity and sink area outside the bath (showers only), and a seating area with embroidered pillows on a shag carpet. Nearly every artsy accouterment is sold in the lobby shop, including the woven plastic wastebaskets, Oaxacan tapestries, and hand-painted Kleenex boxes. Fresh, healthy meals with lots of vegetarian options are served in the open-air bistro near the small pool. There's no beach, but hammocks beckon on a shaded deck where yoga classes are held each morning. Snorkeling is good right off the rocky shoreline and gear and dive trips are available from Scuba Du, one of the most reputable dive operations on the island. Occasional in-house workshops with talented artisans encourage guests to unleash their creativity.

Carretera Playa San Juan Km. 2.5. www.hotelbcozumel.com. ✆ **987/872-0300.** 45 units. High season $210 double; low season $184 double. **Amenities:** Restaurant; 2 bars; swimming pool; dive shop; spa services; free Wi-Fi in lobby.

## IN TOWN

The oceanfront in downtown San Miguel is too busy and unsightly for swimming, and there's no beach, only the *malecón*. There is a popular locals' beach just north of town, however, within easy walking distance from most hotels. Prices are considerably lower, and the main plaza, along with many restaurants and shops, is right in the neighborhood.

### Moderate

**Casa Mexicana ★★★** This modernistic building with an outdoor escalator rises above the sidewalk across from the downtown waterfront. A favorite with business travelers, the five-story hotel offers excellent free Wi-Fi, irons, desks, and shower-tub combos in the large rooms. Only 20 rooms have water views, while the others have a view of humble homes and clotheslines in a long-established neighborhood. Stay away from the rooms on the second floor above the breakfast area, as the noise is considerable all morning. Local execs and politicos huddle in privacy at the bountiful complimentary buffet breakfast, which includes eggs cooked to order, platters of fresh fruit, and serving dishes with sausages, beans, potatoes, and more. A small, shallow pool at the lobby's far end overlooking the waterfront pleases children but isn't large enough for actual swimming. Chairs by the pool looking out to the sea and street are the best front-row seats in town for watching Carnival parades and the daily procession of cruise ships and ferries.

Av. Melgar 457 (btw. calles 5 and 7 Sur). www.casamexicanacozumel.com. ✆ **987/872-9090.** 90 units. High season $76 double; low season $72 double. Complimentary full buffet breakfast. Limited street parking. **Amenities:** Small pool; bar; free Wi-Fi.

**Hacienda San Miguel ★** Guests feel as though they've entered a large Mexican home as they walk through flower-filled gardens to rooms in a two-story, sand-colored hacienda that looks like it belongs in the Yucatán countryside. The amiable staff members extend the kind of warm Mexican hospitality that makes guests return frequently. The low rates, which include continental breakfast and kitchens in all rooms, attract transplants vacationing for weeks and months, settling in suites with dining tables and chairs and separate living room areas. The beds are a bit hard, and some rooms may smell musty, especially when humidity is high. Second-floor rooms get a breeze. Summer is high season at this hotel.

Calle 10 Norte 500 (btw. Melgar and Av. 5). www.haciendasanmiguel.com. ✆ **866/712-6387** in the U.S., or 987/872-1986. 11 units. High season $95 double; low season $75 double. Rates include continental breakfast and free entrance to Mr. Sancho's beach club. Guarded parking on street. **Amenities:** Free Wi-Fi.

### Inexpensive

**La Casona Real ★** Dark ochre and gold walls are livened with stenciled birds above the beds in the simple rooms at this bargain find, a long 5 blocks inland from the downtown waterfront. Rooms have individual, sometimes noisy, air-conditioning units, roomy showers, and cable TV. Free Wi-Fi and continental breakfast enhance the deal, and you'd be hard put to find a pool in another hotel this inexpensive. Staff members are helpful and go the extra step to improve your stay with touches like towel swans and fresh flowers on the bed. A full kitchen, dining table and chairs, futon couch, and two full beds in the separate bedroom make the suite a perfect choice for families or anyone seeking the comforts of home.

Av. Juárez 501. www.hotel-la-casona-real-cozumel.com. ✆ **987/872-5471.** 14 units. $85 double year round. Limited street parking. **Amenities:** Restaurant; pool; free Wi-Fi.

# San Miguel de Cozumel

Information
Pedestrians only
Post office
0 200 yds
0 200 m
To Airport
Bulevar Aeropuerto Internacional
(Avenida Antonio Gonzáles Fernández)
Calle 14 Norte
To Hotels North
San Miguel de Cozumel
COZUMEL ISLAND
Avenida Rafael Melgar
Calle 12 Norte
Calle 10 Norte
20 Avenida Norte
25 Avenida Norte
Av. Pedro Joaquín Coldwell (30 Avenida Norte)
35 Avenida Norte
5 Avenida Norte
10 Avenida Norte
Calle 8 Norte
15 Avenida Norte
Calle 6 Norte
Museo de Cozumel
Calle 4 Norte
Cozumel Channel
Calle 2 Norte
Avenida Benito Juárez
To Carretera Transversal
Plaza del Sol
To Playa del Carmen
Calle 1 Sur
Market
Calle Dr. Adolfo Rosado Salas
Av. Pedro Joaquín Coldwell (30 Avenida Sur)
Calle 3 Sur
5 Av. Sur
10 Av. Sur
15 Avenida Sur
20 Avenida Sur
25 Avenida Sur
35 Avenida Sur
Calle Morelos
Recompression Chamber
Calle 5 Sur
Calle 7 Sur
Punta Langosta Mall
To El Caribeño
To Hotels South & Cruise/Car Pier
HOTELS
Casa Mexicana 15
Hacienda San Miguel 1
La Casona Real 10
Safari Inn 13
RESTAURANTS
El Amigo Mario 14
El Foco 16
El Moro 8
Guido's 5
Kinta 9
La Choza 11
La Cocay 4
La Perlita 2
Le Chef 12
Pancho's Backyard 3
Restaurant del Museo 6
Rock 'n Java 17
Zermatt 7

**Safari Inn ★** Amazing views of the downtown waterfront from some rooms enhance the benefits of staying in this immaculate budget hotel above the Aqua Safari Dive Shop. Up to five people can stay in one of four rooms with a king bed and three twins, perfect for dive groups who prefer to spend their money on multiple trips to Cozumel's world-famous reefs. Hot water for showers can be a bit sporadic, and TVs, phones, and other comforts are missing, but the air conditioning is good and mini-fridges are available. If you're looking for romance and fancy pools, stay elsewhere. But divers won't find a better bargain.

Av. Melgar Sur 429 between calles 5 and 7. www.aquasafariinn.com. ✆ **987/869-0610.** 12 units. $40 double year round. Limited off-street parking. **Amenities:** Dive packages.

### SOUTH OF TOWN

The hotels in this area tend to be more spread out and farther from town than hotels to the north. Some are on the inland side of the road; some are on the beach side, which means a difference in price. Those farthest from town are all-inclusive properties. The beaches tend to be slightly better than those to the north, and the boat trip to the reefs is shorter. Head south on Avenida Melgar, which becomes the coastal road **Costera Sur** (also called Carretera a Chankanaab).

#### Expensive

**Presidente InterContinental Cozumel Resort & Spa ★★★** One of Cozumel's earliest and loveliest hotels, the Presidente is by far the best resort on the island. A long driveway lined with towering palms leads to the open-air lobby and grounds with endless views of the sea. Three separate beach areas edge lawns around low-rise buildings; the single tower contains just five floors. The resort sits alone on a peaceful cove, with only a small marina to the north. With seven room categories, there's something for everyone, from the least expensive rooms facing quiet gardens and an adults-only pool; to oceanview rooms and suites, some with whirlpool tubs facing the sea; to beach-front rooms with large terraces equipped with hammocks, lounge chairs, and tables facing the sea. No matter the room, all are both elegant and comfortable, with marble baths, cushy beds with puffy pillows and duvets, flatscreen TV, and espresso coffeemakers. Beneath a giant *palapa* over the sea, **Caribeño** restaurant serves a buffet breakfast sure to keep you full long into the day, plus fresh guacamole made tableside at lunch and dinner. The **Alfredo di Roma** specialty restaurant serves authentic Italian food, and the **Napa Grill,** which opened in 2013, specializes in grilled lobster, steaks, and imaginative seafood dishes. Tapas and cocktails are served at the lobby bar **Bin K'iin** (Maya for sunset), another 2013 addition. The onsite Scuba Du dive shop is one of the island's most reputable, and the full-service **Mandara Spa**'s treatments include a Maya *temazcal* steam bath ritual. Attention to detail is so precise that the hotel even has pyramid-shaped refuges for the hoary iguanas who've been around for decades.

Costera Sur Km 6.5. www.ihg.com. ✆ **888/774-0040** in the U.S., or 987/872-9500. 220 units. High season $300 double; low season $242 double. Free valet and self-parking. **Amenities:** 4 restaurants; 3 bars; kids' club; concierge; dive shop; putting green; 2 pools, including adults-only pool; room service; full-service spa; fitness center; 2 lighted tennis courts; free Wi-Fi.

## Where to Eat

The island offers a number of tasty restaurants in all price ranges. The restaurants on the waterfront are tourist oriented for the most part; you'll find more Yucatecan and Mexican spots farther inland. The best spot for down home local food is the **Mercado**

**Benito Juárez** at Avenida 25 and Rosado Salas. Students and workers jam the lunch counters at midday for the inexpensive multi-course comida *corrida* (meal of the day with soup, entree, and beverage), *tortas* (sandwiches) stuffed with carne asada or beans and cheese, and other filling fare. The market also caters to the hundreds of cruise ship crew members in port most days with stands and cafes offering food from the Philippines, Indonesia, Japan, and other far-flung lands. It's also a good place to pick up goodies for your room or picnics. Look for fresh papayas and mangoes, crusty rolls called *bolillos,* and *pan dulce* (sweet baked goods).

Tiny taco restaurants and stands serve up cheap, tasty meals. Morning tacos of *cochinita pibil* are served at **El Amigo Mario** (✆ **987/872-0742**), on Av. 5 Sur, between Francisco Mújica and Avenida 35. The doors close at 12pm. **El Foco** ( ✆ **987/107-4108**), on Av. 5 Sur between calles 5 and 7 Sur, is the best spot for the late-night munchies—it's open daily 5pm to 2am. **Zermatt** (✆ **987/872-1384**), a long-standing little bakery selling homemade breads and desserts, is on Avenida 5 at Calle 4 Norte. It's open Monday to Saturday from 7am to 8:30pm. On the island's windward side, **Coconuts** on Carretera Oriente Km 43.5 serves decent Mexican and American dishes in a funky, rock-'n'-roll setting beneath a large *palapa;* it's open daily10am to dusk. Two restaurants at **Punta Bonita** on the windward side serve fresh ceviche, whole fried fish, and other seafood to tables on the sand.

## EXPENSIVE

**Guido's ★★★** SWISS/ITALIAN Long-time Cozumel visitors return to sit at their favorite tables in the vine-draped courtyard at this venerable restaurant, which opened as Rolandi's in 1979. Today, Chef Yvonne Villiger, daughter of the original owner, continues to please new and old customers with the restaurant's signature puffy garlic bread, homemade pastas, and irresistible coconut ice cream. There are a few tables near the wood-burning pizza oven by the restaurant's entrance, but you'd have to be mighty cold-blooded to withstand the heat. Far better for comfort and people watching are the polished wood tables scattered around the courtyard. You can dine on pasta or pizza with a moderate tab, or go all the way and feast on *Pulpo al la Gallega* (octopus with paprika and olive oil), scallops wrapped in prosciutto, or whatever catch-of-the-day creation Villiger has dreamt up. Reservations are recommended. She's also opened **Guido's Tiendita and Delicatessen** on Avenida 15 at Calle 10 (✆ **987/120-1827;** open Mon–Fri 9am–9pm, Sat 9am–1pm) with shelves stocked with imported olive oils, cheeses (like a tangy feta), quinoa, and other gourmet goodies. Savvy locals and travelers linger over coffee and yogurt in the courtyard or stop by for salads, baguette sandwiches, and a remarkable selection of wines and Belgian beers at lunch.

Av. Melgar (btw. calles 6 and 8 Norte). www.guidoscozumel.com. ✆ **987/872-0946.** Reservations recommended. Main courses $12–$24. Mon–Sat 11am–11pm; Sun 3–9:30pm.

**La Cocay ★★** MEDITERRANEAN/SEAFOOD Twinkling white lights draped across the eaves reflect this cozy restaurant's name, which means "firefly" in Maya. Early in the evening, locals gather for sangria and conversation while nibbling rich goat cheese *empanaditas* with mango chutney, savory sautéed calamari with *chile de arbol,* and other tapas. Informal dinner choices include lobster or shrimp pizza, though you're shortchanging yourself if you don't settle in for a lengthy romantic dinner at a linen-draped table in the courtyard. Share the tuna sashimi sprinkled with black sesame seed, then move on to the catch of the day Nicoise style or seared skirt steak with Manchego sauce. Be sure to save room for the palate-soothing ginger crème brûlée.

Owner Kathy Klein has developed a dedicated following, so be sure to make reservations.

Calle 8 Norte 208 (btw. avs. 10 and 15). www.lacocay.com. ✆ **987/872-5533.** Reservations recommended. Main courses 130–350 pesos. Mon–Sat 5:30–11pm.

**Restaurante Alfredo di Roma ★★★** ITALIAN Named for Alfredo Di Lelio, dubbed "La Maestosissime Fettuccine" for creating sublimely rich fettuccini Alfredo in 1908, this intimate, candlelit hotel dining room is the island's most elegant restaurant. A major change in 2013 improved the place immensely, when the formerly cavernous, characterless room was divided to create two separate restaurants (the other, called **Napa,** serves primo steaks and seafood). Waiters who've been at the hotel 30 years or more still deliver bowls of olives, bruschetta, and irresistible breads to the table as diners ponder their choices, including a divine beef carpaccio with black truffle mushrooms. Splurge on herb-crusted rack of lamb or Milanese-style veal chop, or, for a lighter meal, try the flaky Dover sole with lemon and capers. Ask for pasta instead of potatoes with your meal, or go Italian with lobster risotto. Dare you to finish a full order of the legendary fettuccini Alfredo—share with table mates as a side dish instead. The hotel's informal **Caribeño** restaurant has the best breakfast buffet on the island.

Costera Sur Km 6.5, in the Presidente Intercontinental. www.alfredodiroma.rest/cozumel. ✆ **987/872-9500.** Main courses 200–395 pesos. Daily 6–11pm.

## MODERATE



**Kinta ★★** CARIBBEAN/MEXICAN Nouvelle and regional Mexican cuisine is hard to find on Cozumel, but Chef Kris Wallenta is determined to fill that niche. His creativity starts with a twist on all names—Kinta for Quinta, Quekas for quesadillas, and so on. Though the names seem a bit gimmicky, the food reflects his sense of fun without sacrificing flavor. Melted Oaxaca cheese blends with poblano chile sauce and black *huitlacoche* (called the Mexican truffle by some) in the Quekas, and the Kamaron y Kallo estillo Kinta pairs grilled shrimp and scallops with tomato-corn salsa. The absolutely tummy pleasing (and filling) Porky Pasilla spices slow-roasted pork with pasilla chiles and cremini mushrooms, then tames the heat with fig marmalade. If you have any room left, share the Budin de Abuelita, Wallenta's take on the traditional tres leeches cake as a bread pudding with bananas, chocolate, and *canela* (caramelized goat milk). The setting is equally sophisticated, with original abstract paintings and clever, colorful crosses and animals decorating vivid yellow and orange walls. Wallenta has opened a second cheery spot called **Kondesa Cozumel,** named after one of Mexico City's chicest neighborhoods, at Av. 5 between calles 5 and 7 S, ✆ **987/869-1086.**



Av. 5 148B (btw. calles 2 and 4 Norte). www.kintarestaurante.com. ✆ **987/869-0544.** Main courses 120–165 pesos. Tues–Sun 6–11pm.

**La Choza ★** MEXICAN/YUCATECAN Before a disastrous fire in 2008, there was a distinct Mexican flair to the island's first fancy restaurant specializing in Yucatecan and regional Mexican cuisine. It has changed drastically in its new location, which looks like a white corridor with rows of wooden tables. An arched wall at the back frames a garden sans dining tables, and wicker lamps and Christmas decorations hang from the ceiling (even in March). Fortunately, the food's still good. The cooks whip up poblano chiles stuffed with shrimp, *pescado tikin-xic* (fish baked with sour orange and achiote spice), and *pollo en relleno negro* (chicken in a sauce of blackened chiles) in an open kitchen. The special dessert—cold avocado pie—is still on offer. It's the best thing on the menu, in my opinion.

Av 10 Sur (at Rosado Salas). ✆ **987/872-0958.** Main courses 120-230 pesos. Daily 7:30am–10pm.

**La Perlita ★★** SEAFOOD The seafood comes straight from the *pescadería* next door, where fishermen bring their catch each morning and vegetables and fruits are grown in the owner's garden. The staff pays meticulous attention to cleanliness—everything's cleaned with purified water. Fans have been going the extra distance to reach this neighborhood gem for nearly two decades and instantly feel at home after chatting with the cheery waiters. Start your feast with tangy ceviche, then move on to grilled octopus, whole fried fish, shrimp with garlic, or *pez león* (lion fish). This gorgeous specimen has become a huge problem for the local reefs, gobbling up all the pretty tropical fish and reproducing like rabbits on steroids. Several restaurants now serve the delicate white fish, and it's developed a local following. Inexpensive breakfasts include eggs scrambled with *panela* cheese and *chaya,* a healthy spinach-like green. Beware the fresh, crispy chips—eat too many and you won't have room for the main event.

Calle 10 at Av. 65. www.laperlitacozumel.com. ✆ **987/869-8343.** Main courses 100–200 pesos. Daily 8am–8pm.

**Le Chef ★★** CONTINENTAL Sipping a fine Cab while nibbling a perfectly prepared caprese salad at one of six sidewalk tables makes one want to linger for hours, as locals often do. The small bistro is best known for its legendary lobster and bacon sandwich, big enough for two though yummy enough to resist sharing. Watching the buff young men lift weights at the Power Gym across the street might inspire moderation, but you're on vacation, after all. You won't find corned beef and pastrami baguettes or smoked duck Carpaccio and roasted duck breast with tamarind and blue cheese anywhere else on the island. The reasonably priced pizzas and pastas are excellent as well. The bar is impressive, with Jameson, Drambuie, Campari, and other exotic imports along with 7 Lenguas and other fine tequilas.

398 Av. 5 (corner of Calle 5 Sur). ✆ **987/876-3437.** Main courses 95–179 pesos. Mon–Sat 8:30am–11pm.

**Pancho's Backyard ★★★** MEXICAN Marimba musicians play cheerful, melodic background tunes beneath bushy banana plants and palms, and fountains bubble as diners settle down in *equipale* (woven leather) chairs at tables set with painted Mexican tableware. Owners Pancho and Panchito (Pancho Jr.) Morales have designed the lovely restaurant to complement Los Cinco Soles, the waterfront's best folk art store, in a rambling, well-cared-for building, one of Cozumel's first hacienda-style homes. Waiters wearing traditional *guayabera* shirts serve fajitas and spaghetti for timid palates along with seafood with tropical salsa and chicken breast stuffed with spinach, cheese, and almonds in a poblano chile and cilantro sauce. Cameras flash as waiters set fire to the Camarones a la Naranja Flameados al Tequila (shrimp flambée with tequila). Cinco Soles now has a small lunch counter and tequila bar serving a wide range of tequilas along with tacos and other small meals near Pancho's entrance.

Av. Melgar 27 at Calle 8 Norte. www.panchosbackyard.com. ✆ **987/872-2141.** Main courses: $7–$19. Mon–Sat 10am–11pm; Sun 6–11pm.

## INEXPENSIVE

**El Moro ★★★** REGIONAL You don't often encounter waiters who call you "mi amor" (my love) and hug you as you enter and leave, but that's the norm at the Chacón family's outrageously orange establishment in a typical local neighborhood. The decor, with its stuffed (not real) lions, camels, and deer beside a nativity set and Santa (even during spring break) may be bizarre, but the food makes all oddities disappear. The meal starts with a basket of fresh chips and spicy pico de gallo, followed by crispy garlic bread and bodacious entrees. The *papillote* shrimp garners raves, but I've developed a fondness for the *filete Cubano,* a marinated thin, tender beef filet smothered in grilled onions, garlic, and cilantro served with beans and tortillas made by mom in the open kitchen. Linger long enough and the waiter just might bring a little glass of *Xtabentun* (a honey anise liquor). Local specialties including *queso relleno* and *cochinita pibil* draw crowds on Sundays.

75 Bis Norte 124 (btw. calles 2 and 4 Norte). ✆ **987/872-3029.** Main courses 85–145 pesos. Fri–Wed 1–11pm.

**Restaurant del Museo** ★ BREAKFAST/MEXICAN The rooftop restaurant and cafe of the **Museo de la Isla de Cozumel** ★★ (see below) remains my favorite place in San Miguel for breakfast or lunch (weather permitting). It offers a serene ocean view, removed from the traffic noise below and sheltered from the sun above. Breakfasts include huevos rancheros with corn tortillas, fried eggs, and salsa; Mexican and American omelets; fresh fruit platters; and pancakes. The Spanish menu offers even more choices than the English menu. Simple lunch dishes include sandwiches and enchiladas, while the Mexican platter for two, with chicken and beef tacos, enchiladas, nachos, quesadillas, and guacamole, ensures you won't go home hungry.

Av. Melgar (corner of Calle 6 Norte). ✆ **987/872-0838.** Main courses 55–110 pesos. Daily 7am–2pm.



**Rock 'n' Java** ★★ AMERICAN/MEXICAN Homesick gringos and local expats gather at this casual, friendly cafe with a water view and a wall of shelves filled with used books. Meals are meant to delight American palates while adding pleasing twists. Breakfasts include whole-wheat pancakes, steak and eggs, and open-faced biscuits topped with scrambled egg and bacon and smothered in cream gravy, along with healthy oatmeal and bountiful fruit plates. Burgers, wraps, garlic linguini, and walnut cilantro fish are highlights on the lunch and dinner menus, which also feature several salads including spinach and my personal favorite, a large Greek salad. Get here early for the gooey double-fudge brownies—they disappear quickly. The owner is a strong supporter of the local humane society and signs requesting donations are posted by the cash register and bookshelves. There's also an array of real estate brochures tempting Cozumel fans to put down a deposit on a dream vacation home.

Av. Melgar (between calles 7 and 11). www.rocknjavacozumel.com. ✆ **987/872-0455.** Main courses 85–140 pesos. Daily 6am–10pm.

## Exploring

### ATTRACTIONS

**El Cedral** ★ A side road leads inland off the Carretera Costera Sur at Km 17.5 to the island's oldest community, which existed before the Spaniards arrived in 1518. The town is a traditional agricultural center with a small church facing a central plaza and a few souvenir stands lining the road. Dirt roads lead away from the plaza to small ranches and homes, some used as "country" vacation homes by some of Cozumel's founding families. The annual Festival de Cedral, held in April, is a fascinating event with religious ceremonies, bullfights, horseraces, concerts, and other activities. The week-long fair culminates with the extraordinary traditional *Baile de las Cabezas de Cochino* (pig's head dance), when families wearing elaborate embroidered dresses and crisp *guayabera* shirts carry elaborately decorated trays with piles of bread or barbecued pigs on their head as sacrificial offerings to God. The parade is solemn at first; then the music gets faster and faster as children and adults twirl about in a frenzy.

**Chankanaab National Park ★★★** This park, off the Carretera Costera Sur at Km 9, is the pride of many islanders (www.cozumelparks.com). *Chankanaab,* the Maya word for "little sea," refers to a beautiful land-locked pool connected to the sea through an underwater tunnel. Admission includes a dolphin presentation and sea lion show, manatee exhibition, beach with facilities, and excellent snorkeling. Arrive before 9am to stake out a chair and *palapa* before the cruise-ship crowd arrives. The snorkeling is also best before noon. The park has bathrooms, lockers, a gift shop, several snack huts, a restaurant, and a *palapa* where you can rent snorkeling gear. The entrance fee is $21 for adults, $14 for children under 12.

You can also swim with dolphins here. **Dolphin Discovery** (www.dolphindiscovery.com; ✆ **800/293-9698**) offers several programs for interacting with these beautiful sea creatures. These are popular, so plan ahead and make reservations well in advance. The surest way is through the website—make sure to pick the Cozumel location, as there are a couple of others on this coast. The Dolphin Royal Swim costs $149 ($89 for kids) and features close interaction with the dolphins. The park is open Monday through Saturday from 8am to 4pm. Taxis run constantly between the park, the hotels, and town (about 120 pesos from town for up to four people).

**Museo de la Isla de Cozumel ★★** I always enjoy touring the small **Cozumel Island Museum,** housed in a pink building that served as the island's first hotel. A replica of a Maya dugout canoe carved from a single tree sits by the front steps. My favorite exhibit, on the first floor, covers the topography and plant and animal life of the island, and also offers an explanation of coral formation and displays of various types of coral. A large map shows how much of the island remains undeveloped—less than 10% is inhabited. The second-floor galleries feature the history of the town, photographs of leading families, artifacts from the island's pre-Hispanic sites, and Colonial-era cannons, swords, and ship paraphernalia. There's usually a temporary exhibit as well, featuring local artists, traditions, or history. The museum is located at Avenida Melgar between Calles 4 and 6 Norte (www.cozumelparks.com; ✆ **987/872-1475**). It's open Monday to Saturday from 9am to 4pm. Admission is $4. There's also a gift shop and a rooftop cafe (see above); you don't need to pay admission to eat here unless you plan to visit the museum, too.

**Punta Sur Eco Park ★★** This gorgeous ecological reserve at the southern tip of the island includes the Columbia Lagoon. A number of crocodiles make the lagoon their home, so swimming is not only a bad idea, it's not allowed. The only practical way of going out to the lighthouse and beaches, about 8km (5 miles) from the entrance, is to rent a car or hire a taxi in town to take you inside the park. Views from atop the Faro Celarain lighthouse are well worth the steep climb. The lovely beaches just in front are kept as natural as possible, but be cautious about swimming or snorkeling here depending on the winds and currents. Beaches extend for miles to north of the lighthouse, and it's easy to find a solitary spot. The park offers restrooms, showers, and water equipment rentals, but is blessedly free of motorized watersports. In summer, the park offers a turtle nesting tour for $55 per person. Regular hours are Monday to Saturday, 9am to 6pm. The entrance is $12 for adults, $8 for children under 12.

**San Gervasio ★★** Though it's nowhere near as impressive as the large archaeological sites on the mainland, this small Maya site (100 B.C.–A.D. 1600) was once an important ceremonial center, especially for women who paddled dugout canoes from the mainland to pay homage to Ixchel, the goddess of women, childbirth, pilgrims, the moon, and medicine. The most interesting building was the residence of a Maya leader and is called Las Manitas for the small red handprints still visible on the walls. A tall pyramid is thought by some to have been a temple to Ixchel. A limestone arch marks the entrance to a *sacbe,* one of the limestone roads that etched the land around Maya cities and ceremonial centers. To reach the site, follow the paved transversal road to Km 7.5 and you'll see the well-marked turnoff about halfway between town and the eastern coast. For what you see, it's a bit overpriced. Entrance is $9.50. A small tourist center sells handicrafts, cold drinks, and snacks. The ruins are open daily from 7am to 4pm. Guides charge about $35 for a tour for one to six people. Seeing it takes 30 to 60 minutes. Taxi drivers offer transportation for about $50, which includes the driver waiting for you outside the ruins.

## OUTDOOR ACTIVITIES

Cozumel's main tourism attraction has long been its proximity to the Great Maya Reef, the world's second-longest barrier reef. Diving and snorkeling are both excellent from the shore or by boat. For **island tours, ruins tours** on and off the island, **evening cruises,** and other activities, go to a travel agency such as **Proviajes,** Calle 2 Norte 365, between avenidas 15 and 20 (www.proviajescozumel.com; ✆ **987/869-0516**). Office hours are Monday through Saturday from 9am to 5pm, Saturday from 10am to 3pm.

### Boat Trips

Travel agencies and hotels can arrange boat trips, a popular pastime on Cozumel. Choose from evening cruises, cocktail cruises, glass-bottom boat cruises, and other options. A real submarine tour is offered by **Atlantis Submarines** (www.atlantis submarines.travel; ✆ **987/872-5671**). The tour includes 40 minutes at up to 30m (100 feet) beneath the surface of the Chankanaab protected marine park (total excursion time is 1½ hr.). It costs $105 per adult, $65 for kids ages 4 to 12; children under 4 are not allowed to take the tour.

### Fishing

The best months for fishing are March through June, when the catch includes blue and white marlin, sailfish, tarpon, and swordfish. The least expensive option would be to contact a boat owner directly and negotiate a price. A reliable operator offering flats bonefishing and deep-sea fishing in Cozumel is **Tres Hermanos** (www.cozumel fishing.com; ✆ **987/107-0655**). The cost for an 8-hour excursion is $450 for one to six anglers. Half-day trips are also available.

### Choosing a Dive Company

Cozumel has many excellent dive shops with experienced divemasters and high-quality gear. But, as in all popular dive destinations, some run "cattle boats," packing way too may divers on a boat and supplying sub-par gear. It pays to do a bit of research, checking out websites and recommendations. Try to stop by the shop before signing up for trips and check out the gear and boats. Most of my Cozumel dives have been fabulous, but I have been on unfortunate outings, made more disappointing by my experience with the island's excellent shops.

## Cenote Diving on the Mainland

A popular activity in the Yucatán is cave diving. The peninsula's underground ***cenotes*** (seh-*noh*-tehs)—sinkholes or wellsprings—lead to a vast system of underground caverns. The gently flowing water is so clear that divers seem to float on air through caves complete with stalactites and stalagmites. If you want to try this but didn't plan a trip to the mainland, contact **Germán Yañez** (www.germanyanez.com; ✆ **987/113-7044**), based at 60 Avenida 117, between Calles 2 and 4 North. He offers all-day *cenote* tours as well as cave dive training. The *cenotes* lie 30 to 45 minutes from Playa del Carmen, and a dive in each *cenote* lasts around 45 minutes. Dives happen within the daylight zone, about 40m (131 feet) into the caverns, and no more than 18m (59 feet) deep. Open water certification and at least five logged dives are required. For those without diving certifications, a *cenote* snorkeling tour is also offered.

### Scuba Diving

Cozumel is one of the finest dive destinations in the Western Hemisphere. The many dive locations include the famous **Palancar Reef,** with its caves and canyons, plentiful fish, and sea coral; the monstrous **Santa Rosa Wall,** famous for its depth, sea life, coral, and sponges; the **San Francisco Reef,** with a shallower drop-off wall and fascinating sea life; and the **Yucab Reef,** with its beautiful coral.

Diving in Cozumel is drift diving, which can be a little disconcerting for novices. The current that sweeps along Cozumel's reefs, pulling nutrients into them and making them as large as they are, also dictates how you dive here. The problem is that it pulls at different speeds at different depths and in different places. When it's pulling extremely strongly, it can quickly scatter a dive group. Generally, however, the current makes for an effortless diving experience if you just relax and let the scenery drift by. Photographers must adapt to the current and resist grabbing the coral in order to stop to take a photo—killing the coral in the process.

Don't forget your dive card and dive log, unless you're coming for just an introductory dive or beginner certification course. Dive shops will rent you scuba gear but won't take you out on a boat until you show your certification card. If you have a medical condition, bring a letter signed by a doctor stating that you've been cleared to dive. A two-tank dive trip costs about $70 to $90; some shops offer an additional one-tank dive for a modest additional fee. A lot of divers save some money by buying a dive package with a hotel. These usually include two dives a day.

Finding a dive shop in town is even easier than finding a jewelry store. Cozumel has more than 50 dive operators. **Aqua Safari,** which has a location on Av. Melgar 429 at Calle 5 (www.aquasafari.com; ✆ **987/872-0101**), is one of the oldest shops on the island. **Dive Paradise** (www.diveparadise.com; ✆ **987/872-1007**) has four locations in Cozumel, including the central facility between the Hotel Barracuda and Naval Base. It has been in business more than 25 years and offers dive training at all levels. **Liquid Blue Divers** (www.liquidbluedivers.com; ✆ **987/869-7794**) arranges tours by appointment and provides high-quality service to small groups. **Scuba Du** (www.scubadu.com; ✆ **987/872-9505**), is based at the Presidente InterContinental resort (p. 146), the **Hotel B** (p. 143), and other hotels. You needn't be a guest to use the company, which is one of the island's most reliable. Many shops offer certification courses. Shore diving is another option, and shops will rent you gear and direct you to the best places to enter the water.

### Snorkeling

Snorkeling is superb off Cozumel as well, even close to shore. The visibility is so good you can see many of the same creatures as the divers below. Even though you won't see a lot of the more delicate structures, such as fan coral, you will still see plenty of sea creatures and enjoy the clear, calm water of Cozumel's protected west side. Tropical fish swarm about high coral peaks and you could catch a glimpse of a sea turtle or ray on the horizon. ***Tip:*** Wear a life jacket even if you're a great swimmer. It will help you stay afloat and save energy.

Most hotels rent snorkeling gear and those beside the sea usually have sloping beaches or stairs leading to the best snorkeling areas. Be extra careful when entering the water from shore, as sections may be covered with rocks, coral, or stinging sea urchins. Stick to the designated areas, be careful with your hands and feet, and don't touch the coral.

There's also great shore diving off of many other beaches, at Chankanaab National Park, and at Punta Sur Eco Park. Snorkeling at many beach clubs is lousy, thanks to the thousands of humans splashing about. Most parks have boat trips to the reefs where sea creatures swim about relatively undisturbed. Some dive shops combine scuba divers and snorkelers, but you're better off with a snorkeling-only trip for maximum attention and time in the water. The reefs offer a far greater array of fish than you'll see close to shore, along with colorful coral formations. You could easily take several snorkeling tours and see something different every time. When contracting for a snorkel tour, stay away from the companies that cater to the cruise ships. Those tours are crowded and not a lot of fun.

## BEACHES

Along both the west and east sides of the island you'll see signs advertising beach clubs. A "beach club" in Cozumel can mean just a *palapa* hut that's open to the public and serves soft drinks, beer, and fried fish. It can also mean a recreational beach with the full gamut of offerings, from banana boats to parasailing. They also usually have locker rooms, a pool, and food. The biggest of these is **Mr. Sancho's** (www.mrsanchos.com; ✆ **987/120-2220**), south of downtown San Miguel at Km 15. It offers a restaurant, bar, massage service, and motorized and non-motorized watersports. Quieter versions of beach clubs are **Playa San Francisco** (no phone) and **Paradise Beach** (www.paradise-beach-cozumel.com), next to Playa San Francisco. All of these beaches are south of Chankanaab Park and easily visible from the road. Several have swimming pools with beach furniture, a restaurant, and snorkel rental. They cost about $12 to enter. If you're driving the coast looking for a club, stay away from those with large tour buses parked at the entrance—they're sure to be packed with day-trippers from the cruise ships.

Once you get to the end of the island, the beach clubs become simple places where you can eat, drink, and lie out on the beach. **Paradise Cafe** is on the southern tip of the island across from Punta Sur Nature Park, and as you go up the eastern side of the island you pass **Playa Bonita, Playa Chen Río,** and **Punta Morena.** Except on Sunday, when the locals head for the beaches, these places are practically deserted. Most of the east coast is unsafe for swimming because of the surf. The beaches tend to be small and occupy gaps in the rocky coast.

## ANATOMY OF THE CORAL reef

Corals are polyps, tiny animals with hollow, cylindrical bodies that attach by the thousands to hard surfaces of the sea floor. The polyps extract calcium carbonate from the seawater to create hard, cup-shaped skeletons that assume an endless variety of shapes and sizes. These massive limestone structures shelter nearly one-fourth of all marine life. The soft, delicate polyps retreat into their skeletons during the day, but their protruding tentacles can be seen when they feed at night.

Cozumel boasts the world's second largest reef (after Australia's Great Barrier Reef) with 26 classes of coral. Two distinct types of coral formations dominate its waters. Bases of the less developed platform reefs, such as Colombia Shallows, Paradise, and Yucab, are rarely more than 9 to 15m (30–49 feet) in depth. Edge reefs are more complex structures built up over many millennia, and their layered structures peak high above the edge of the drop-off, extending as much as 55m (180 feet) below the surface. These are found mostly in the south; examples include Palancar, Colombia Deep, Punta Sur, and Maracaibo.

### ISLAND TOURS

Travel agencies can arrange a variety of tours, including horseback, jeep, and ATV tours. Taxi drivers charge about 800 pesos for a 3-hour tour of the island, which most people would consider only mildly amusing, depending on the driver's personality.

### GOLF

Cozumel has an 18-hole course designed by Jack Nicklaus. It's at the **Cozumel Country Club** (www.cozumelcountryclub.com.mx; ✆ **987/872-9570**), north of San Miguel. Greens fees are $134 for a morning tee time, including cart rental and tax. Afternoon tee times cost $89. Tee times can be reserved 3 days in advance. A few hotels have special memberships with discounts for guests and advance tee times; guests at Playa Azul Golf and Beach Club pay no greens fees, but the cart costs $25. Look for online packages for reduced rates.

## Shopping

If you're looking for silver jewelry or other souvenirs, go no farther than the town's coastal avenue, Melgar. Along this road, you'll find one store after another selling jewelry, Mexican handicrafts, and other souvenirs and duty-free merchandise. The most impressive of these is **Los Cinco Soles** (www.loscincosoles.com; ✆ **987/872-9004**), on the waterfront at 8 Norte, fronting Pancho's Backyard restaurant (p. 149). It's open Monday to Saturday from 9am to 8pm and Sunday from 11am to 5pm. There are also some import/export stores in the Punta Langosta Shopping Center in the southern part of town in front of the cruise-ship pier. Prices for serapes, T-shirts, and the like are lower on the side streets off Avenida Melgar.

## Entertainment & Nightlife

Most of the music and dance venues are along Avenida Melgar. **Carlos 'n' Charlie's** (✆ **987/869-1648**), which is in the Punta Langosta shopping center, is practically next to **Señor Frog's** (✆ **987/869-1650**). Punta Langosta lies just south of Calle 7 Sur.

## AN all-inclusive VACATION IN COZUMEL

All-inclusives are becoming more common on Cozumel. Most are clustered near the island's southern tip, where the water can be full of sea grass—something to consider if snorkeling and diving from shore are important. On the other hand, these resorts are close to the best reef dive spots, making for quick boat rides. Check for packages including airfare and airport transfers—they often add up to a better deal than paying for everything separately. I include websites for you to find out more info about the properties. Check frequently before booking, as the game of setting rates with these hotels is complicated and always in flux.

Two all-inclusives are north of town: **El Cozumeleño** (www.elcozumeleno.com) and the **Meliá Cozumel** (www.solmelia.com). Both occupy multi-story modern buildings and have attractive rooms. El Cozumeleño is the larger of the two resorts and is best suited for active types. The Meliá is quieter and offers golf discounts for the nearby golf course. The Cozumeleño's small beach has to be replenished with sand periodically. The Meliá's beach is long, narrow, and pretty, but occasionally seaweed washes up, which doesn't happen on the rest of the island's coast. The advantages of staying in these two are the proximity to town, with its restaurants, clubs, movie theaters, and so on, and the fact that most rooms at these hotels come with views of the ocean.

The **Cozumel Palace** (www.palaceresorts.com) lies right on the water on the southern fringes of town. Despite the location, it doesn't have a beach. But that's not so bad. The water is usually so calm on Cozumel's west shore that swimming here is like swimming in a pool, and you can snorkel right out of the hotel.

Of the other all-inclusives to the south, my favorite is the **Iberostar Cozumel** (www.iberostar.com), followed by the **Occidental** resorts (**Grand Cozumel** and **Allegro Cozumel;** www.occidentalhotels.com). These are "village" style resorts with two- and three-story buildings, often with thatched roofs, spread over a large area at the center of which is the pool and activities area. Rooms at the Grand Cozumel are larger and more attractive than the all-inclusives in the south. The advantage to staying in these places is that you're close to a lot of dive sites; the disadvantage is that you're somewhat isolated from town, and you don't have many rooms with ocean views. The **Fiesta Americana Cozumel All-Inclusive** (www.fiestamericana.com), on a pristine stretch of beach off the road toward Chankanaab, features an excellent dive center. More centrally located, the **El Cid La Ceiba** (www.elcid.com/ceiba_beach) was one of my favorite Cozumel hotels until the Puerto Maya cruise ship port opened next door. It's still a great choice because of its large sea-facing rooms, great Mexican food, and excellent shore diving. The small pool area tends to fill up with day-trippers from the cruise ships in mid-day, but they clear out by late afternoon. The friendly **Hotel Cozumel & Resort** (www.hotelcozumel.com.mx) lies within short walking distance of the town and also offers diving packages. There's a tunnel under the road to their beach club.

In town, there are a few Latin music clubs. These open and close with every high season, prospering when people have cash in their pockets, but closing down when the flow of tourism stops bringing in money. Calle 1 Sur between avenidas 5 Sur and 10 Sur is a pedestrian street housing a number of local bars, some with live music. **Wet**

**Carnival**

*Carnival* (similar to Mardi Gras) is Cozumel's most colorful fiesta. It's a family-friendly weeklong celebration, with multiple parades along the waterfront, dance and music performances along the streets day and night, and a general sense of merriment that takes over the city. The plaza is the center of the action, with stands selling traditional foods and gathering for award ceremonies. It begins the Thursday before Ash Wednesday, with daytime street dancing and nighttime parades on Saturday, Sunday, and Monday (the best).

**Wendy's,** at 53 Av. 5 Norte between Calle 2 and Juarez (✆ **987/872-4970**), is a spirited open-air bar with a fun crowd toasting margaritas and other tequila cocktails. **La Rumba,** 121 Av. 10 between Salas and Calle 1 S (✆ **987/872-4970**), is the best spot for live Cuban and Latin music. **Dubai Cozumel,** Calle 11 Sur at Av. Melgar (✆ **987/119-9691**), is the latest dance club at this corner, where some sort of disco has existed for decades. It's the classiest dance club in town, and is open until 5am.

San Miguel's **movie theater** is Cinépolis, the modern multicinema in the Chedraui Plaza Shopping Center at the south end of town. It mainly shows Hollywood movies. Most of these are in English with Spanish subtitles *(película subtitulada)*; before buying your tickets, make sure the movie hasn't been dubbed *(doblada)*.

## Day Trips from Cozumel

### CHICHÉN ITZÁ, TULUM & COBÁ

Travel agencies can arrange day trips to the ruins of **Chichén Itzá.** The ruins of **Tulum,** overlooking the Caribbean, and **Cobá,** in a dense jungle setting, are closer and cost less to visit. A trip to both Cobá and Tulum begins at 8am and returns around 6pm. A shorter, more relaxing excursion goes to Tulum and the nearby nature park of **Xel-Ha.**

### PLAYA DEL CARMEN & XCARET

Going on your own to the nearby seaside town of **Playa del Carmen** and the **Xcaret** nature park is as easy as a quick ferry ride from Cozumel (for ferry information, see "Getting There," p. 124 in this chapter). While at Xcaret, visit their newest park, **Xplor** (www.xplor.travel; ✆ **998/849-5275**), next door. For information on Playa, Xcaret, and Xplor, see chapter 6. Cozumel travel agencies offer an Xcaret tour that includes the ferry ride, transportation to the park, and the admission fee.

# 6 THE RIVIERA MAYA

by Christine Delsol & Maribeth Mellin

The name is vague and the distances far greater than one might expect, yet the Riviera Maya has become one of Mexico's top tourism destinations. The region included under this marketing moniker stretches 182km (113 miles) south of Cancún to Playa del Carmen, Tulum, and the Punta Allen peninsula, including part of the vast Sian Ka'an Biosphere Reserve. The region's greatest natural asset is the Great Mesoamerican Reef sheltering the shoreline and providing endless opportunities for fabulous snorkeling and diving. The reef protects much of the shore from currents and waves, creating clear, blue coves and soft white sand beaches. Cultural attributes include the archaeological sites of Tulum and Cobá. Most famous of all is Playa del Carmen, the coast's commercial center, filled with hip hotels, eclectic restaurants, and a youthful, energetic vibe.

## PUERTO MORELOS & VICINITY

### Between Cancún & Playa del Carmen

The coast directly south of the Cancún airport has several roadside attractions, small cabaña and boutique hotels, and astonishingly luxurious all-inclusive resorts. The agreeable town of **Puerto Morelos** lies midway along this 51km (32 mile) stretch of coast between the airport and Playa del Carmen.

#### ROADSIDE ATTRACTIONS

**CrocoCun** ★★ ZOO This interactive zoo is especially captivating for children, but the up-close and sometimes hands-on encounters with iguanas, spider monkeys, a boa constrictor, immense tarantulas, native deer, and crocs of all ages and sizes disarm visitors of every age. Once a crocodile farm, CrocoCun now runs a breeding program that has helped replenish the toothy reptiles' local population and extends its protection to all animals native to the Yucatán. It even has some Xoloitzcuintles, the native "hairless" dog revered by the Maya, Aztec, and Toltec civilizations at least 3,000 years ago. A guided tour with one of the knowledgeable and

# The Yucatán's Upper Caribbean Coast

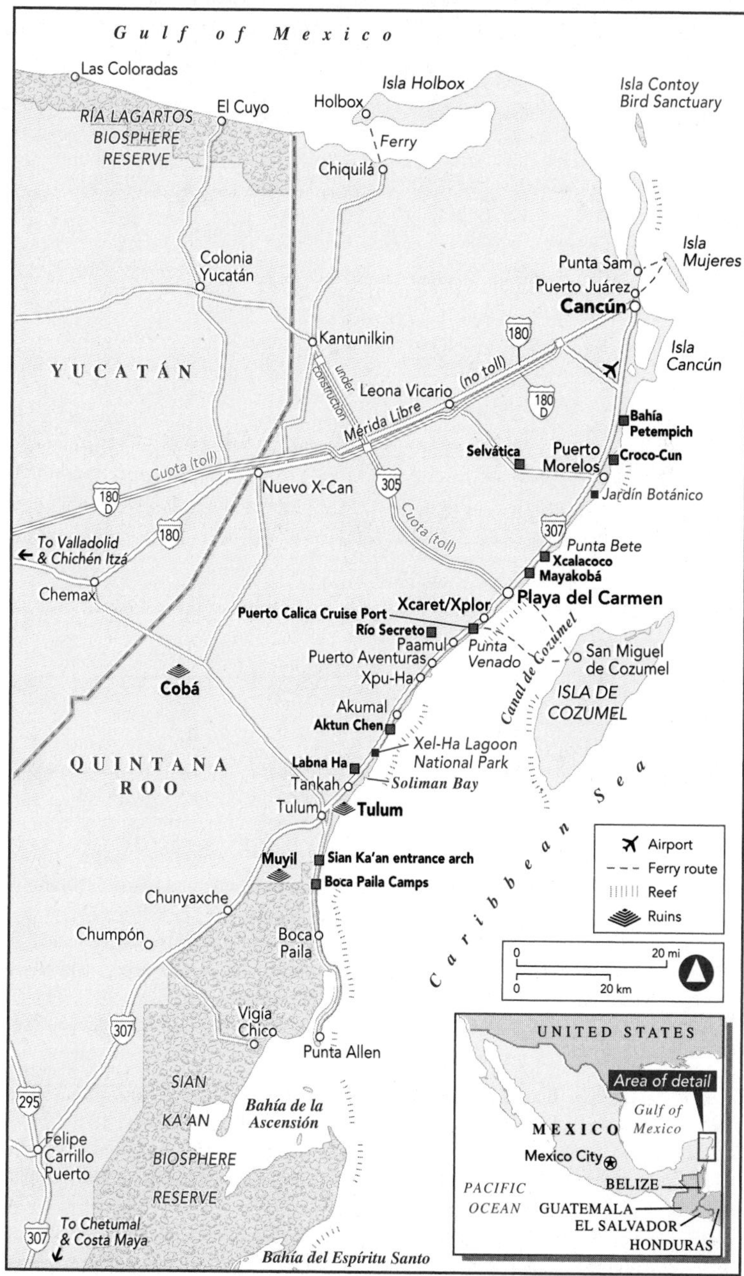

## driving THE RIVIERA MAYA

Driving along this coast isn't difficult, but it takes eagle-eyed attention, especially for first-timers. With only one highway, you can't get too lost unless you miss the signs for your hotel. Highway 307 traces the coastline for 380km (236 miles) from Cancún to the border with Belize at Chetumal, a 4½-hour trip by car. The section between Cancún's airport and Tulum is now a four-lane divided highway with speed limits up to 110kmph (68 mph). It takes about 2 hours to drive the 130km (81 miles) from Cancún airport to Tulum.

Turnoffs can be from either the right or left lane; if you miss the one you want, go a bit farther and circle back. You're not allowed to stop on the highway to make a left turn, but there are several short left-turn lanes at many points across the road from major resorts. It is impossible to overemphasize just how dangerous this highway can be, especially during high season when you've got locals speeding to work, tour buses clogging the lanes, truck and bus drivers barreling along, and confused or distracted tourists changing lanes on a whim. Speed limits are clearly posted and seem to change every few kilometers. Keep an eye out for speed signs, especially around towns and resorts. The police have become ever more sophisticated at ticketing speeders and are especially vigilant around stoplights and one-way streets. Several overpasses now carry you over the busiest intersections at Puerto Morelos, Puerto Aventuras, and Playa del Carmen, which greatly reduce the danger and traffic congestion.

All that said, it's hard to imagine traveling around the Riviera Maya without a rental car. So many wonderful places to explore are right beside the highway and along side roads leading to the beach and jungle. First-class gas station plazas with minimarts and fast-food spots are becoming a common sight. Attendants pump the gas (be sure they don't overfill the tank) and will check your oil. Make sure you receive the right change, and tip attendants if they provide extra services. As long as you study your maps in advance and keep your wits about you, driving allows freedom for serendipitous discoveries.

Always carry plenty of drinking water when driving along the coast. Some hotels supply a couple of bottles in your room upon arrival, while others charge $3 or more for each bottle. Have at least one half-gallon bottle in the car and a reusable water bottle with you at all times.

enthusiastic veterinary students who volunteer here lasts 60 to 75 minutes. Entrance fees are high, but the memories will last. Take bug repellant.

Highway 307, 1.6 km/1 mile north of Puerto Morelos. www.crococunzoo.com. ✆ **998/850-3719.** $30 adults, $20 children 6–12, free for children 5 and younger. Daily 9am–5pm.

**Ya'ax Che Jardín Botánico Dr. Alfredo Barrera Marín ★★** PARK/GARDEN This fecund 161-acre jungle is one of Mexico's largest botanical gardens and the last patch of protected forest between Cancún and Playa del Carmen. The Maya's sacred Ceiba trees stand tall amid palms, bromeliads, ferns, orchids, and medicinal plants. In addition to protecting threatened native species, 4km (2.5 miles) of trails demonstrate the Maya's use of natural resources. You'll also see a small archaeological site, a reconstructed Maya home, and a *chiclero* camp. Biology students working here eagerly share details (it helps to know some Spanish). Spider monkeys, nearly extinct elsewhere on the coast, frolic along with abundant tropical birds. This is more a jungle trek than a stroll in the park; wear sturdy walking shoes—I recommend closed toes to avoid bug-bitten feet—and insect repellent.

Highway 307, 2km (1⅕ miles) south of Puerto Morelos turnoff. www.ecosur.mx/jb/YaaxChe. ✆ **998/206-9223.** Admission 120 pesos. Mon–Fri 8am–4pm, Sat 8am–1pm.

## Puerto Morelos ★★

36km (22 miles) S of Cancún; 26km (16 miles) S of airport; 32km (20 miles) N of Playa del Carmen

Even though it's the closest town to Cancún, Puerto Morelos resembles the sleepy Playa del Carmen of old, when that now-burgeoning city first lured tourists away from the clamor of Cancún. Despite the enclaves of all-inclusive resorts rising on its flanks, as well as a new Chedraui supermarket by the highway and a shopping center going up at the edge of town, this has remained the northern Caribbean coast's last real fishing village, largely through the vigilance of locals. It's ideal for lazing on a white-sand beach, with occasional forays into snorkeling, diving, windsurfing, or kayaking. This was the coast's boomtown 100 years ago, when its port shipped hardwood and *chicle* to the U.S. and Europe. Today, the main lure is its friendly, small-town atmosphere and easy pace. It may brim with tourists in high season, but low season is slow enough that many businesses close temporarily.

The townspeople succeeded in protecting Puerto Morelos' section of the Great Maya Reef with a national marine park designation in 1998. The underwater coral mountain rises to within a few feet of the surface and is easy to snorkel. The water is shallow, calm, and clear, and the beaches are clean and rarely crowded.

### ESSENTIALS

#### Getting There

**BY CAR** Puerto Morelos is at Km 31, about a half hour from either Cancún or Playa del Carmen. From Cancún, you'll need to exit the highway onto the frontage road, then turn left under the overpass.

**BY BUS** Buses from Cancún to Tulum and Playa del Carmen usually stop at the highway here, but be sure to ask before buying a ticket. A taxi for the 2.5km (1½ mile) ride from the highway to the center of town costs 25 pesos.

#### Getting Around

Puerto Morelos consists of the beach area and the inland "urban zone" west of the highway popular called "La Colonia." The compact beach town is best explored on foot for the most part. Taxis charge 25 to 40 pesos around town and up to 80 pesos to the edges of town or the Colonia. Trips to the large resorts outside of town may cost 100 to 250 pesos. The taxi stand is on the northwest corner of the central plaza.

### WHERE TO STAY

For vacation rentals, see the website of Alma Libre Bookstore (www.almalibrebooks.com; p. 166), or contact Mayan Riviera Properties (www.mayanrivieraproperties.com; ✆ **248/275-5556** in the U.S. or 998/871-0716). Casa Caribe (below) also has several houses for rent.

**Casa Caribe ★★★** Sharing one of Puerto Morelos' oldest buildings with the Little Mexican Cooking School (p. 167), this reasonably priced B&B offers low-key luxury in five bright rooms. The four upstairs rooms have terrific views of the ocean just a block away, which can be savored from private balconies furnished with hammocks. The simple decor is enlivened by splashes of color, eclectic furniture, and tiled bathrooms with hand-painted basins. Upstairs rooms are cooled by fresh ocean breezes, while the downstairs room is air-conditioned. All have coffeemakers and fridges. The cooking school's chef oversees the breakfast menu, which offers four options.

Av. Javier Rojo Gómez (north of Ejército, 3 blocks from plaza). www.casacaribepuertomorelos.com. ✆ **998/251-8060** or 159-8890 (cell); U.S. number 512/410-8146. 5 units. High season $135 double, low season $85; weekly and monthly rates also available. Rates include full breakfast. **Amenities:** Terrace lounge; kitchen shop; beach chairs and umbrellas; free Wi-Fi.

**Hacienda Morelos★** This beachfront hotel in the middle of town delivers the sand at your feet and the sound of ocean waves wafting in your window without the frills or high prices of the nearby all-inclusive resorts. New owners who took over in 2014 (and restored its original name) have been making gradual but steady improvements. The good-size rooms are still basic but feel bright and contemporary. The hotel's primary virtues remain its ocean views from every room, the expansive beachfront patio and pool, and the location 1½ blocks from the main square, but the restaurant now offers a full menu, and the bar keeps regular hours with amicable bartenders.

Av. Rafael E. Melgar no. 5 (south of plaza). www.haciendamorelos.com. ✆ **998/871-0448** or 407/992-2503 in the U.S. 31 units. High season $113–$125 double; low season $80–$97. Free off-street parking. **Amenities:** Restaurant; outdoor beachfront pool; beach cabanas, towels, and umbrellas; watersports (for a fee); Wi-Fi.

**Posada El Moro ★★★** The appeal of this traditional hotel, just off the plaza, goes beyond its comfortable rooms and convenient location. The accommodating manager, Miguel, and his family and staff go out of their way to make every guest feel at home. The colorful, simply furnished rooms are filled with natural light. Doubles (called "singles," indicating one bed) have queen beds with good mattresses, plus a futon; deluxe rooms also have air-conditioning and TV. Junior suites, the newest units, have an additional single bed and a mini-fridge, while full suites have two doubles and a kitchen and dining room. All have contemporary tiled bathrooms, and most have patios or balconies. The compact grounds include a small pool in a tropical garden, and a recently added rooftop *palapa* offers sweeping ocean views.

Av. Javier Rojo Gómez, SM2, M 5, Lote 17 (1/2 block north of José Morelos). www.posadaelmoro.com. ✆ **998/871-0159** or 998/206-9005. 31 units. High season $72–$78 double, $95–$106 suite; low season $56–$72 double, $84–$89 suite. Rates include continental breakfast. **Amenities:** Restaurant; outdoor pool; rooftop terrace; room service; free Wi-Fi.

## WHERE TO EAT

The Puerto Morelos restaurant scene undergoes major churn during low season every year, but the one thing you can count on is a greater number and variety of good restaurants than you'd expect of a small town. Enduring favorites around the main square include **Doña Triny's** for Mexican and Yucatecan standards; **Los Pelícanos** for seafood; and **Café d'Amancia** for coffee, pastries, and smoothies. New restaurants worth a try (not reviewed here because they haven't had a chance to hit their stride) include **Chicken Itza** and **My Little Italy,** both just off the plaza on Rojo Gómez south of Posada el Moro, and **La Sirena** on the north side of the plaza.

**Al Chimichurri ★★** URUGUAYAN A carnivore's nirvana in a seafood-centric region, this family-run place cooks tender, richly flavored meat over a hot charcoal fire. A flank steak here takes on sublime qualities usually reserved for loftier cuts, and it is

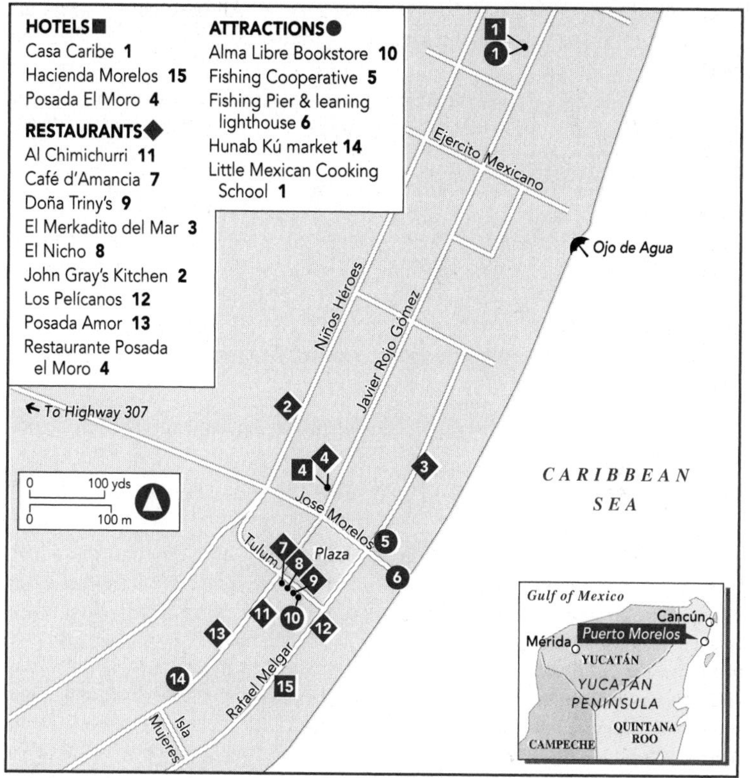


served with a simple salad and homemade bread. Portions are huge; try adding an order of grilled vegetables and splitting the two. The varied menu includes chicken, pizza, and salads. All are excellent, but don't miss the empanadas, a light, crispy Uruguayan version filled with meat, cheese, tomatoes, mushrooms, spinach, or corn. The friendly, hard-working staff can get bogged down on busy nights, which are more and more frequent as the restaurant's popularity grows. Avoid going at dusk; the restaurant is as popular with mosquitos as with people.

Av. Javier Rojo Gómez (1 block south of plaza). www.alchimichurri.com. ✆ **998/192-1129.** Main courses 110–250 pesos. Reservations recommended in high season. Tues–Sun 5pm–1am.

**El Merkadito del Mar ★★** MEXICAN/SEAFOOD This beachfront restaurant is usually called simply El Merkadito, but you might be saying Margaritaville after sipping one of their perfect margaritas or mojitos from a chilled tin cup while gazing at the turquoise water. Shrimp, tuna, mussels, salmon, octopus, calamari, and whatever else local fishermen deliver on any given day fill an array of tostadas, tacos, ceviches, grills, and pastas. While the shrimp tacos are a runaway everyday favorite, sea bass steak and Jack Daniels salmon are genuine standouts. Bring a bathing suit, and you can

## DAY TRIPS AND beyond

The Riviera Maya is an ideal base for exploring much of the Mexican Caribbean. Choosing a hotel north of Playa del Carmen gives easy access to Cancún for daytime exploring or nighttime dining and clubbing. You can also visit Chichén Itzá in a day, though it's always best to spend a night near the ruins so you can explore sans crowds in early morning. Playa del Carmen is a logical base for travelers without cars or those who want easy access to public transportation and abundant diversions. It serves as a great base for exploring the Riviera Maya's central coast, including Tulum and Cobá. A short ferry ride to the nearby island of Cozumel puts you alongside some of the finest scuba diving in the world. Tulum is an excellent midway point between the Cancún airport and the Costa Maya, allowing you to reach the Río Bec archaeological sites in a few hours' drive—though not in a one-day journey.



jump into the Caribbean waters you've been ogling throughout your meal; El Merkadito provides the beach chairs.

Rafael Melgar Lote 8-B (on the beach, north of lighthouse). www.elmerkadito.mx. ✆ **998/871-0774.** Tacos and tostadas 45–55 pesos; main courses 110–250 pesos. Daily noon–9pm.

**El Nicho ★★★** BREAKFAST The only complaint you'll hear about this unfailingly accommodating restaurant, opened in 2012 by the former teaching chef at the Little Mexican Cooking School (p. 167), is that it isn't open for dinner. Breakfast is delectable, from the Maya-style granola (with natural yogurt, Maya honey, and bee pollen), to the egg dishes, to typical Mexican breakfasts such as *molletes* and *chilaquiles.* Try the outstanding egg scramble with *chaya* (a leafy spinach-like plant), goat cheese, and toasted pumpkin seeds. Eggs Benedict may include avocados, cilantro sauce, *chaya,* lox, or crab cakes. The signature dish among the paninis and tortas is "The Bun," with ham or bacon, scrambled eggs, tomato, and cheese on an English muffin.

Avs. Tulum and Javier Rojo Gómez (across from plaza). www.elnicho.com.mx. ✆ **998/201-0992.** Breakfast and lunch 35–85 pesos. Daily 8am–2pm.

**John Gray's Kitchen ★★★** INTERNATIONAL Puerto Morelos' most upscale restaurant was opened by chef John Gray in 2002 after leaving the Ritz-Carlton Cancún, where he was responsible for the now-iconic Club Grill. Gray, whose restaurant feels more Manhattan than Mexico, decamped in late 2013 to become executive chef for Hilton Worldwide in Panama, but he still consults on the menu. Each day's offering depends on available local fruits and vegetables and what local fishermen have just pulled out of the sea, but the mouthwatering roasted duck breast with tequila-chipotle-honey sauce, pork loin in a Roquefort crust, and mac and cheese with shrimp and truffle oil are usually available. It's absolutely worth the splurge, but a bargain meal for two can be had by sharing three appetizers or sides, such as crab cakes, roasted red chile cauliflower, or artichoke salad.

Av. Niños Heroes, Lote 6 (north of Av. José Morelos). ✆ **998/871-0665.** Reservations recommended. Main courses 175–400 pesos. Daily 8am–10pm.

**Posada Amor** ★★ BREAKFAST/YUCATECAN Loyal patrons have frequented Puerto Morelos's oldest bar/restaurant, now in the capable hands of the founder's family, for 30 years. You can sit in the simple whitewashed *palapa*-roofed dining room, in the shady garden, or on sidewalk tables. The Sunday breakfast buffet is especially popular. The dinner menu focuses on fresh seafood and Yucatecan-influenced dishes; the ceviche is justly famous, and the grilled fish is stellar. Delicious fish, corn, and other vegetable soups, accompanied by tortillas, are hearty enough to make a meal.

Avs. Javier Rojo Gómez and Tulum (½-block southwest of plaza). www.posada-amor.wix.com/puertom. ✆ **998/871-0033.** Main courses 90–250 pesos. Daily 7am–10pm.

**Restaurante Posada el Moro** ★★★ MEXICAN/GRILL Posada el Moro, which previously provided breakfast only for guests, expanded service in 2014 to a full restaurant open to the public for breakfast and dinner. The wide-ranging menu includes grilled seafood, meats and vegetables, as well as pastas and *antojitos* (snacks). The specialty is a *mocaljete* (mixed grill in a traditional stone bowl with baked potato, grilled *nopal* cactus and vegetables) for two. Chile rellenos, my benchmark for Mexican food, are exceptional here, with batter that stays crispy and a chunky, mildly spicy tomato sauce. Service is outstanding; if you've scored on a fishing trip, the restaurant will prepare your catch any way you like, and you can even ask them to whip up regional dishes that aren't on the menu. Indoor seating is quite pleasant, but the shaded outdoor tables, on a patio that removes you from sidewalk traffic, offer the best of all possible worlds.

Av. Javier Rojo Gómez, SM2, M 5, Lote 17 (in Posada El Moro). ✆ **998/206-9005.** Main courses 85–350 pesos. Daily 7–10:30am and 5–9pm.

## EXPLORING IN & AROUND PUERTO MORELOS

The main attraction here is the **coral reef** ★★★ rising in front of town about half a kilometer offshore. It tops out so close to the surface that divers have nothing over snorkelers here; everyone gets a close-up of the convoluted passages and caverns burgeoning with fish and sea flora. Fishing and boating restrictions make this the most pristine stretch of reef on the north coast. Dive shops in town offer snorkeling tours for $30 to $45, but one of the best is the local **Fishing Cooperative** (✆ **998/121-1524**) at the foot of the pier. Its members are national park–certified guides who rotate tour gigs to supplement their fishing income. The 2-hour trip visits two snorkeling sites and costs 350 pesos. Tours leave approximately every half-hour Monday through Saturday from 9am to 3pm.

The excellent dive shops around town charge $50 to $75 for one-tank dives; basic two-day PADI certification courses cost $285 to $300. Enrique Juárez of the long-established **Almost Heaven Adventures,** on Javier Rojo Gómez a block north of the plaza (www.almostheavenadventures.com; ✆ **998/871-0230**), limits groups to five divers and is known for thorough briefings and attentive boat crews. Also recommended: **Aquanauts** (www.aquanautsdiveadventures.com; ✆ **998/206-9365**), **Dive In Puerto Morelos** (www.diveinpuertomorelos.com; ✆ **998/206-9084**), and **Wet Set Diving Adventure** (www.wetset.com; ✆ **998/206 9204** or 646/736-7726 from the U.S.). These outfits will also book fishing excursions.

**Central Plaza** ★ PARK/LANDMARK The modern, once-austere plaza around which local life revolves has been refurbed with new paint, attractive signs, landscaping, and a better play structure. The east side is just steps away from a lovely **sea walk**

## RUTA DE cenotes

The road heading inland from Highway 307, across from the Jardín Botanico (p. 160), is lined by *cenotes*, or natural swimming holes, along the 17km (10½-mile) stretch between Puerto Morelos and the village of Central Vallarta. An enormous arch marks the turnoff, and the *cenotes* are also well marked along a paved section of the road. Some have been turned into "adventure parks," with ATV tours, zip lines, aerial walkways, and parachute jumps that draw streams of tour groups from Cancún. **Selvática,** at Km. 19 (www.selvatica.com.mx; ✆ **998/898-4312** or 866/552-8825 (U.S.), is the most popular and expensive (starting at $99 adults/$49 children); **Boca del Puma,** at Km. 16 (www.bocadelpuma.com; ✆ **998/241-2855**), not only costs less (from $75 adults/$39 kids), but its ATV and zip line tours place greater emphasis on the environment and local culture. Facilities include a *chicle* camp and history museum.

Some truly beautiful, remote *cenotes* lie farther off the main road. The well-tended **Cenote Las Mojarras** (www.facebook.com/ParqueCenoteLasMojarras; ✆ **998/848-2831;** half day 150 pesos, full day 300 pesos), at Km. 12.2, looks like a large pond, and the park has a double zip line and double tower to jump from, as well as restrooms, hammocks, a picnic area, and a campground. It added horses, ATVs and a new zip line in 2014. Among the less developed *cenotes* is **Siete Bocas** at Km. 15.5, consisting of seven "mouths" to an underground river. Three are large enough for stairways straight down into the cool, clear water, and the others funnel light into the underground chamber—the effects are especially dramatic around midday. At Km. 18 is the gorgeous **Cenote Verde Lucero.** Jagged rock walls scored by massive tree roots enclose a crater holding clear, seemingly bottomless turquoise water. There's a zip line and a safety rope across its 100-foot diameter. You can descend a stairway or plunge about 20 feet into the water from a rock ledge, but there are no services.

that passes the fishing pier with its old landmark **lighthouse,** whose tilt, courtesy of Hurricane Beulah's 1967 rampage, makes the Leaning Tower of Pisa look downright upright. Residents wouldn't hear of tearing it down, even though a larger beacon took over its duties. While the **beach** here is often rocky and strewn with seaweed, a stroll north leads to finer beaches; the best is at **Ojo de Agua,** easily recognized by the hotel/restaurant of the same name.

Bounded by Calle Jose Maria Morelos, Av. Rafael E. Melgar, Av. Tulum and Av. Javier Rojo Gómez.

**Alma Libre Bookstore** ★★ SHOP This jam-packed shop sells more English-language titles than any other bookstore in the Yucatán. Canadians Joanne and Rob Birce stock everything from beach reads and English classics to cookbooks and volumes on Maya culture. The store also serves as a book exchange, tourist information center, and vacation rental agency; they now carry regional maps, locally made specialty foods, textiles, and gifts from all over Mexico. Opening dates and store hours seem to change each season; check the website for the latest info.

Av. Tulum, on south side of plaza. www.almalibrebooks.com. ✆ **998/252-2207.** Daily late Nov–late April 10am–6pm.

**Hunab Kú** ★MARKET The local Maya artisans' cooperative runs this collection of *palapa* stands selling hammocks, hand-embroidered clothes, jewelry, blankets, ceramics, and other handicrafts. The quality is high, and there are some bargains. Vendors don't hustle you, so it's worth a stroll just for the parklike setting; if you have time, watch some of the artisans at work in their shops.

Javier Rojo Gómez, a block south of plaza. Daily 9am–8pm.

**Jungle Spa** ★★SPA Authentic Maya massage, in several variations—including a special hangover treatment—is the specialty here, but you can also try an aloe vera/banana leaf or chocolate body wrap, all for a fraction of what you'd pay at resort spas. The women in this nonprofit cooperative have been trained to incorporate contemporary spa techniques into the traditional Maya healing massages they grew up with. The spa directly supports local Maya families. The women also perform a traditional Maya dance and sell unique handicrafts at their **Sunday Jungle Market,** held from mid-December to Easter Sunday. If you're not familiar with the Colonia, read the directions on the website carefully; better yet, take a taxi.

Calle Dos, Zona Urbana (just outside La Colonia, west of Hwy. 307). www.mayaecho.com. ✆**998/208-9148.** $40–$80. Tues–Sat by appointment.

**The Little Mexican Cooking School** ★★★SCHOOL Classes at this delightful cooking school, which shares a hacienda-style mansion with Casa Caribe (p. 161), begin with continental breakfast and an introduction to traditional ingredients and modern Mexican cuisine; each day of the week features food from a different region. Chef Cristóbal Tamariz is as entertaining as he is knowledgeable, combining demonstrations with hands-on preparation of seven to eight dishes—all of which will make up your *comida fuerte,* or full Mexican late lunch, to end the day.

Av. Rojo Gómez 768 (3 blocks north of plaza). www.thelittlemexicancookingschool.com. ✆**998/251-8060**.or 512/410-8146 (U.S.). $128. Reservations recommended. Tues–Fri. (some Sat) 9:45am–3:30pm.

# SOUTH OF PUERTO MORELOS

The beaches, bays, mangrove lagoons, and jungles between Puerto Morelos and Tulum are constantly undergoing transformation. Punta Maroma, home to the coast's first exclusive hideaway, now has several resort and residential compounds. Massive all-inclusives loom above beaches where campgrounds once thrived. Mayakobá, a master-planned resort just north of Playa del Carmen, is a fine example of an ecologically responsible development, though some other resorts use the land without much thought to conservation.

## Exploring South of Puerto Morelos

**Cirque Du Soleil** ★★ The Riviera Maya meets Las Vegas in Cirque du Soleil's UFO-like 600-seat theater, which opened in November 2014 beside the lavish 750-room Grand Mayan Resort. In true Cirque style, the show, called Joya, features swirling music based on Latin rhythms and performers in flowing butterfly costumes creating surrealistic, mesmerizing scenes. There is a story line about the journey of an alchemist and his granddaughter as they search for the meaning of life. But you needn't follow the plot to get caught up in the troupe's dazzling acrobatics. Tickets are available for the show alone, with the least expensive seats consisting of high stools ringing the back of the theater; the $80 seats are more comfortable. Packages include a combination ticket for the show, dinner, and Champagne.

Hwy 307 Km 48. www.cirquedusoleil.com/joya. ✆ **844/247-7837** in the U.S. and Canada. Tickets start at $65 for show only, and $165 for the show, dinner, and Champagne. Tues 9pm, Wed–Thurs 7pm, Fri-Sat 7 and 10:15pm.



## Where to Stay

### EXPENSIVE

**Grand Velas ★★★** Staying at an all-inclusive property makes sense in the Riviera Maya, especially if you don't have a car. Distances between resorts and the nearest towns are significant and taxi rates high. Not all such properties are the same, however. This aptly named grand property wows guests with award-winning restaurants, an outstanding spa, and suites worthy of a world-class hotel. Suites in the Grand Class section, for adults and teens only, have hot tubs, plunge pools, and stunning ocean views. Family suites in the Ambassador section are located near the kids' and teens' clubs and the main pool; those in the Zen Jungle Section are a 5-minute walk away from the beach and near the spa and meeting areas. Though you lose out on the sea views here, the jungle setting adds a sense of peaceful seclusion. Sleek marble floors, dark wood furnishings, and cream-colored walls all create an air of uncluttered sophistication. The spa's elaborate hydrotherapy area's jets, bubbles, pounding waterspouts, and waterfalls enhance superb treatments, and you can easily spend a full morning here. The restaurants have garnered numerous prestigious accolades—at no time do you feel like you're eating typical all-inclusive fare.

Hwy. 307 Km 62. www.rivieramaya.grandvelas.com. ✆ **866/335-4640** in the U.S. and Canada, or 984/877-4414. 481 units. High season $787–$1203 double; low season $625–$1107 double. Rates include meals, drinks, and many activities. Free valet parking. **Amenities:** 8 restaurants; 3 bars; butler service; children's programs; spa; watersports; free Wi-Fi.

**Hacienda Tres Rios ★★** This ecofriendly, all-inclusive property serves as proof that a hotel can be both comfortable and kind to the environment. Rooms sit atop raised pilings to reduce impact on the vegetation and allow the natural flow of surface and underground water. Air-conditioning, lighting, and hot water are all custom designed to reduce consumption. As a result, you won't get powerful, chilly air or strong showers in your rooms, but it's a small price to pay when you consider the tremendous damage this coast endures. The hotel is surrounded by a 132-hectare (326-acre) nature park incorporating jungle, mangroves, and coastal dunes. Tours within the property explore the vast plant and vegetable nurseries, 10 *cenotes*, three rivers, and vast untrammeled spaces. It's a long walk from some rooms to the beach and pool. Buffet meals reflect the concern over conservation, and most food items are arranged in individual portions rather than large communal trays. Tres Rios has received numerous accolades including Green Globe certification as a World Heritage Alliance for Sustainable Tourism site, and hosts yoga and meditation retreats and other special events.

Hwy. 307 Km 54. www.haciendatresrios.com. ✆ **800/494-9173** in the U.S. and Canada, or 998/287-4115. 273 units. $320 and up double. Rates include meals, drinks, and gratuities. Free valet parking. **Amenities:** 5 restaurants; 4 bars; children's programs; 2 pools; spa; watersports; free Wi-Fi.

**Viceroy Riviera Maya ★★★** Once completely isolated in the jungle, this small luxury hotel now has neighbors, including a large all-inclusive property. But it remains secluded and serene, thanks to dense vegetation and a thoughtful layout over

## MAYAKOBÁ RESIDENTIAL GOLF & SPA resort

One of the most impressive ecologically sensitive developments, **Mayakobá** (www.mayakoba.com) incorporates three upscale hotels (including the Fairmont Mayakobá reviewed below) and a championship golf course into more than 607 hectares (1,500 acres) of healthy mangroves, lagoons, *cenotes,* and beaches. In 2011, the resort's developers were awarded a Sustainable Standard-Setter Award from the Rainforest Alliance and the Ulysses Award for responsible, sustainable tourism projects from the United Nations World Tourism Organization. The compound's concept is unusual—it's a beach resort with precious few oceanview rooms. Instead, the hotels line a series of freshwater canals.

Guests travel about in electric boats and golf carts, and may use the restaurants, spas, and other facilities in all three hotels. Some have trouble with the jungle setting—bug repellent is a must, especially at dusk—and swimming is forbidden in the canals. I've spotted small crocodiles in the canals and have been assured they're removed to more suitable homes on Mayakobá's wild side. The **El Camaleón** golf course, designed by Greg Norman, is an Audubon-certified bird reserve—and a challenge for the pros competing in Mexico's only PGA tournament, usually scheduled for late February/early March. You must have a reservation to get past the gates of this extremely private development. Consider booking a meal or spa treatment at one of the hotels to take a look around.

2.5 hectares (6¼ acres) of waterfront property. The original 30 villas are so thoroughly buried in vegetation that you could skinny dip in your private pool or splash in your outdoor shower without worrying about your neighbors. Louvered wooden shutters block out light in the cool white rooms, with large bathrooms and closets and white gauze draped around the beds. The property's been expanded to include 11 villas either on the beach or with ocean views (original rooms are spread along winding paths away from the beach). Maya-inspired treatments are offered in the circular spa with a large whirlpool in the center, and the hotel is a popular spot for destination weddings conducted by a shaman. The restaurant's menu is suitably sophisticated, and the selection of high-quality sipping tequilas is outstanding. Children 17 and older are welcome.

Playa Xcalacoco, Hwy.307. www.viceroyrivieramaya.com. ✆ **866/332-1672** in the U.S. and Canada, or 984/877-3000. 41 units. High season $648 and up double; low season $393 and up double. Rates include full breakfast. Free secure parking. No children 16 and under except during some holidays. **Amenities:** Restaurant; 2 bars; concierge; 2 Jacuzzis; pool; spa; watersports; free Wi-Fi.

### MODERATE

**Fairmont Mayakobá ★★** The first resort to open in Mayakobá, the Fairmont takes full advantage of the natural setting. You don't even miss seeing the sea once you've spent an early morning watching cormorants and herons in the canals while sipping coffee on your overwater balcony. It's as if you'd lucked upon a luxurious home in the Amazon. Granted, there are a few high-end suites by the sand, but the juxtaposition of sleeping in the jungle and playing at the beach is quite alluring. Rooms are spacious, with large, uncluttered desks, big bathtubs with windows or shutters facing the outdoors, great thick mattresses, and large closets. The hotel is popular with families and groups, and the sprawling pool area can actually feel crowded at times despite its size, as can the main restaurant. The Willow Stream Spa's rooftop pool is a great escape and perfect for disciplined laps.

Hwy. 307 Km 298. www.fairmont.com/mayakoba. ✆ **800/540-6088** in the U.S. and Canada, or 984/206-3000. 401 units. High season $320 and up double; low season $225 and up. Free valet parking. **Amenities:** 3 restaurants; 3 bars; fitness center; 5 pools; spa; watersports; free Wi-Fi.

**Petit Lafitte Hotel ★** Another reincarnated original from the '90s era, this small hotel sits one kilometer (⅔ mile) south of the original, venerable Posada Lafitte. Longtimers have fond memories of the Posada and its adjacent spiffy campground, Kailuum, and the current hotel has maintained the same friendly, homey ambiance of the originals. Most rooms are in a three-story building on the sand, while bungalows are buried in coconut groves. Many rooms and bungalows lack ocean views, but are close enough to the sea for guests to hear the swishing surf. Some of the original staff members have stayed with the company, and many longtime guests now are accompanied by their children and grandchildren.

Hwy. 307 Km 63 (Punta Bete). www.petitlafitte.com. ✆ **984/877-4000.** 47 units. High season $189–$359 double; low season $181–$307 double. Free guarded parking. **Amenities:** Restaurant; bar; pool; free Wi-Fi.

# PLAYA DEL CARMEN ★★★

32km (20 miles) S of Puerto Morelos; 70km (43 miles) S of Cancún; 10km (6¼ miles) N of Xcaret; 13km (8 miles) N of Puerto Calica

Young, adventuresome travelers have long been attracted to the eclectic Playa del Carmen beach scene, but it's no longer a budget haven with seaside campgrounds and inexpensive eateries. In fact, Playa del Carmen is one of Mexico's fastest growing cities, with sprawling neighborhoods on both sides of the highway and nearly every big-box store you can imagine. Fortunately, Playa still retains a beach vibe, which combines with a cosmopolitan ethos to create a distinctly European feel. Many of the earliest hotel and restaurant owners moved to Playa from Italy, so there's no shortage of great pasta and vino. These days, restaurants serve everything from sushi to foie gras, and shops carry Balinese figurines and Brazilian bikinis. Playa's La Quinta (Fifth Avenue) is the coast's social magnet, with browse-worthy shops and plenty of bars and restaurants studding the pedestrian promenade.

## Essentials

### ARRIVING

**BY PLANE** Fly into Cancún and take a bus directly from the airport (see "By Bus," below), or fly into Cozumel and take the passenger ferry.

**BY CAR** **Highway 307** is the only highway that passes through Playa. A soaring overpass bypasses the busy city traffic—stay off it unless you're traveling south of Playa. Stick to the main highway and the two main arteries into town. Avenida Constituyentes works well for destinations in northern Playa, while Avenida Juárez leads to the town's main square and ferry pier. Keep to the inside lanes that permit turning left at any of the traffic lights. Don't panic if you miss your turn; just keep going south until you get to the highway's turnaround, then double back, staying to your right.

**BY BUS** **Autobuses Riviera** offers service from the Cancún airport about 10 times a day between 10:30am and 9:30pm. Cost is about 146 pesos one way. Ticket counters are located outside customs at Terminals 2 and 3. At either terminal, you can also pay

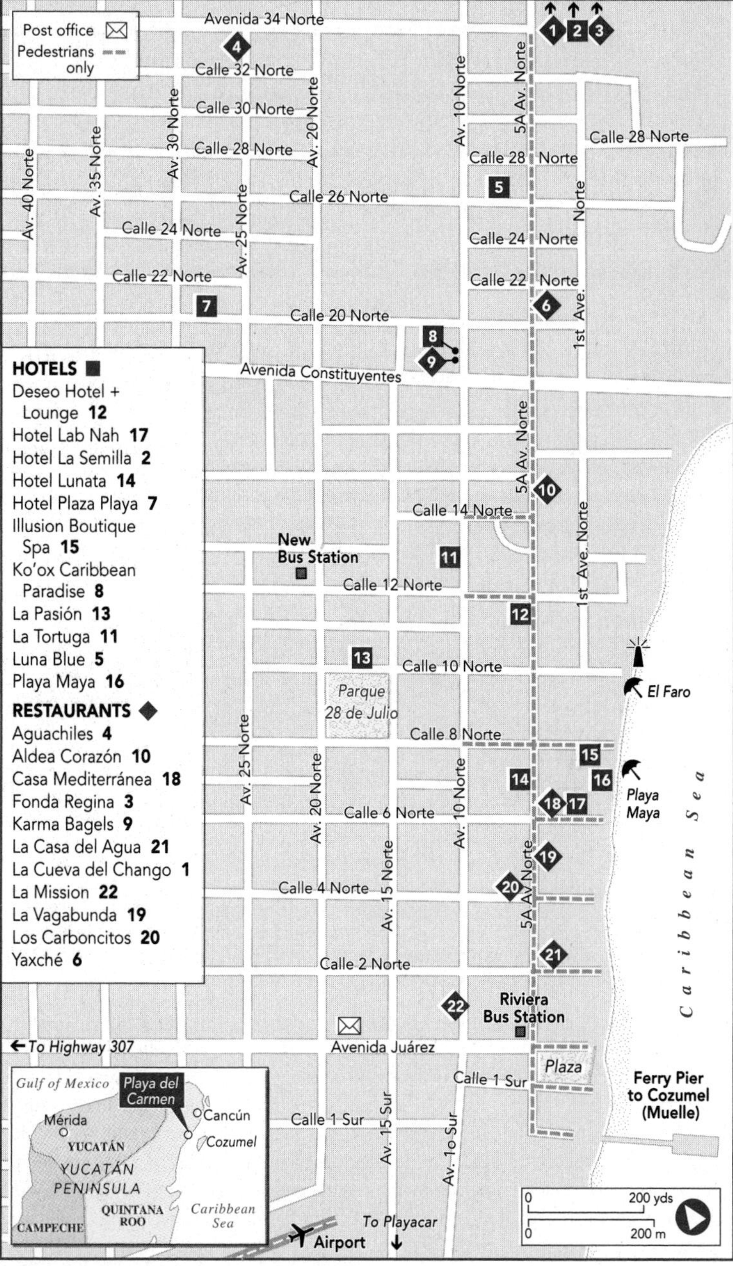
Post office
Pedestrians only
HOTELS
Deseo Hotel + Lounge 12
Hotel Lab Nah 17
Hotel La Semilla 2
Hotel Lunata 14
Hotel Plaza Playa 7
Illusion Boutique Spa 15
Ko'ox Caribbean Paradise 8
La Pasión 13
La Tortuga 11
Luna Blue 5
Playa Maya 16
RESTAURANTS
Aguachiles 4
Aldea Corazón 10
Casa Mediterránea 18
Fonda Regina 3
Karma Bagels 9
La Casa del Agua 21
La Cueva del Chango 1
La Mission 22
La Vagabunda 19
Los Carboncitos 20
Yaxché 6
Avenida 34 Norte
Calle 32 Norte
Calle 30 Norte
Calle 28 Norte
Calle 26 Norte
Calle 24 Norte
Calle 22 Norte
Calle 20 Norte
Avenida Constituyentes
Calle 14 Norte
Calle 12 Norte
Calle 10 Norte
Calle 8 Norte
Calle 6 Norte
Calle 4 Norte
Calle 2 Norte
Avenida Juárez
Calle 1 Sur
Av. 40 Norte
Av. 35 Norte
Av. 30 Norte
Av. 25 Norte
Av. 20 Norte
Av. 15 Norte
Av. 10 Norte
5A Av. Norte
1st Ave. Norte
Av. 15 Sur
Av. 10 Sur
New Bus Station
Parque 28 de Julio
Riviera Bus Station
Plaza
El Faro
Playa Maya
Caribbean Sea
Ferry Pier to Cozumel (Muelle)
To Highway 307
To Playacar
Airport
200 yds
200 m
Gulf of Mexico
Playa del Carmen
Mérida
Cancún
Cozumel
YUCATÁN
YUCATÁN PENINSULA
QUINTANA ROO
CAMPECHE
Caribbean Sea

## A new HIGHWAY

Side trips to the peninsula's far-flung destinations have become far easier with the opening of Highway 305, a new toll road linking Playa with Highway 180D (also a toll road). This link is particularly exciting for those wishing to swim with whale sharks off Isla Holbox. Many Playa dive companies offer Holbox tours with at least five hours of driving time back and forth. The new highway cuts that time nearly in half, making Holbox an easy day trip. Highway 305 also links to the toll road to Valladolid and Chichén Itzá, again greatly decreasing travel time. To reach Highway 305, drive west on Avenida Colosio about 8km (4½ miles) until it becomes 305. There are also exit signs off Highway 307 for Highway 305.

the driver, in either pesos or U.S. dollars. From the downtown Cancún bus station, buses depart almost every 30 minutes and cost 40 pesos.

**BY FERRY** Air-conditioned passenger ferries from Cozumel arrive at the pier 1 block from the main square. There is also a car ferry from Cozumel from the Calica pier just south of Playacar. The schedule changes with demand. You can usually count on hourly departures in the morning and late afternoon—just like rush hour on land. Ferries typically depart every 2 hours around midday. For more information about both ferries, see "Getting There" in the Cozumel section of chapter 5, p. 137.

**BY TAXI** Taxi fares from the Cancún airport are about $75 one-way.

**VISITOR INFORMATION** The Riviera Maya Tourism Board's website, www.riviera maya.com, is an excellent source of overall info and practical details.

**CITY LAYOUT** The main street, Avenida Juárez, leads to the town square from Highway 307. On the way, it crosses several numbered avenues running parallel to the beach, all of which are multiples of five. The east-west streets parallel to Juárez are in multiples of two. A wonderful bike path along Avenida 10 provides fairly safe passage for *tricilcos* (bike taxis) and cyclists. Quinta Avenida (Fifth Avenue) runs 1 to 2 blocks inland from the beach and is the most popular street in the Riviera Maya. It's closed to traffic from Avenida Juárez to Calle 12 (and some blocks beyond, in the evening). However, taxis and drivers are allowed to access hotels on side streets. Hotels, restaurants, shops, and clubs line La Quinta and its side streets. Avenida Constituyentes delineates the northern part of rapidly growing Playa. Several excellent international restaurants and pricey condo developments are located north of this intersection in Playa's most sophisticated neighborhood. Playacar, a golf-course development with private residences and several resort hotels, is located just south of Avenida Juárez.

## Getting Around

Playa has two bus stations. Buses from Cancún and places along the coast, such as Tulum, arrive at the Riviera bus station at the corner of Juárez and Quinta Avenida, by the town square. Buses from interior destinations arrive at the ADO station on Avenida 20 between calles 12 and 14. Taxi fares around central Playa run between $3 to $10, depending on the destination and time (taxis are usually more expensive after midnight). You can easily walk to the beaches, shops, and restaurants from central hotels. Driving in Playa is a hassle. Several streets are one-way, though signs are hard to come by; others simply end without warning, and traffic is usually heavy and disorganized.

## [FastFACTS] PLAYA DEL CARMEN

**Area Code** 984.

**ATMs, Banks, and Currency Exchange** All available along Quinta Avenida.

**Doctor** For serious medical attention, go to Hospiten (✆ **984/803-1002**) on Hwy. 307 at the second Playacar exit. Contact the hyperbaric chamber at ✆ **984/873-1365.**

**Drugstore** The Farmacía del Carmen, Avenida Juárez between avenidas 5 and 10 (✆ **984/873-2330**), is open 24 hours.

**Internet Access** Most hotels have Wi-Fi, at least in public areas, and Wi-Fi is available at many restaurants and bars on nearly every block around Quinta Avenida. Several public parks also have free Wi-Fi. Power outlets are harder to find, so charge up before heading out.

**Parking** Estacionamiento México, at avenidas Juárez and 10, is open daily 24 hours. Ask your hotel about parking. Few have on-site parking, but some can get you reduced rates at nearby lots.

**Post Office** Avenida Juárez at Calle 15.

**Safety** Call (✆ **060** for emergencies. Contact tourist security at ✆ **800/987-8224,** toll free in Mexico. For police call ✆ **984/872-8224.** The Red Cross is at ✆ **984/873-1233.**

**Seasons** The main high season is from mid-December to Easter. Mini high seasons are in August and around Thanksgiving. Low season is all other months, though many hotels further divide these into several micro seasons.

**Special Events** The Riviera Maya Jazz Festival, held in November, attracts international headliners for 3 days of music on the beach.

## Where to Stay

### EXPENSIVE

**Deseo Hotel + Lounge ★★** The second venture of the trendsetting Habita Hotel group set the tone for the South Beach aesthetic that has overtaken Playa over the past decade. This small, adults-only hotel creates a cool sensation with its white geometric shape, accented by horizontal wood railings and light blue day beds. Rooms wrap around the central pool and lounge area, which morphs into a trendy nightspot with its play of ever-changing colors. The multilingual staff is one of the friendliest in town, and the breezy, minimalist white-on-white rooms have unexpected touches such as random amenities (a banana, a straw hat) hanging from the ceiling. It all looks very restful—beds are quite comfortable—but don't expect to get much of that rest until the partying in the lounge area wanes in the wee hours.

Av. 5 (at Calle 12). www.hoteldeseo.com. ✆ **984/879-3620.** 15 units. High season $220–$360 double; low season $135–$290 double. Rates include expanded continental breakfast. No parking. No children 17 and under. **Amenities:** Bar; Jacuzzi; 24-hour front desk; small rooftop pool; room service; free Wi-Fi.

**Hotel La Semilla ★★★** A thin, sleek, poured concrete cubist facade hides a fanciful inn that could have been created by an *alux* (Maya sprite). Native woods and rocks complement a tiny stream running beside a miniscule Maya *na* (wooden hut) in a manicured courtyard, while gathered objects from cartoonish lottery cards to antique typewriters and sewing machines decorate enchanting guestrooms. The owners both put in years at international five-star hotels before creating their pièce de résistance, where thoughtful, clever design complements comfortable, sensible accommodations. A gourmet breakfast is served in the ground floor lounge, and sunrise meditation is available on the rooftop deck. Bikes await guests by the front door, and Playa's most popular beach is a block away.

Calle 38N at Ave 5. www.hotellasemilla.com. ✆ **984/147-3234.** 9 units. High season $190–$260 double; low season $170–$205 double. Rates include breakfast. Small parking lot. **Amenities:** Free Wi-Fi.

## MODERATE

**Hotel Lunata ★★** This hacienda-style hotel oozes so much Old World character that it almost looks out of place—in a good way—on Quinta Avenida. Colonial style reigns here, with limestone arches, wrought-iron railings, and hand-hewn wood beams creating a soothing envelope for contemporary comforts, including double-paned windows to combat street noise on the Quinta Avenida side. Midsize standard rooms have queen or two double beds; large deluxe rooms have kings or two doubles. All have balconies and mini-fridges. Hand-painted Talavera tile brightens the bathrooms, which have terrific water pressure.

Av. 5 (btw. calles 6 and 8). www.lunata.com. ✆ **984/873-0884.** 10 units. High season $139–$169 double; low season $105–$139 double. On-site parking. Rates include continental breakfast. No children 10 and under. **Amenities:** Bikes; watersports; free Wi-Fi.

**Illusion Boutique Hotel & Spa ★★** This five-story Mediterranean-style hotel packs a lot of luxury touches into its spacious rooms, from marble floors and large bathrooms in marble and native stone to work desks, mini-fridges, cable TV, and robes and slippers. The small rooftop pool has fantastic ocean views. The location couldn't be better, a half-block from either the beach or Quinta Avenida, and an easy walk from the bus station or Cozumel ferry. It isn't perfect—the pool bar keeps limited hours, it's devoid of the greenery that adorns many hotels in the area, and it does get some noise from nearby discos—but the value is hard to beat. Lower-level rooms, the least expensive, don't get nearly the light and air that rooms on higher floors do; an upgrade is well worth the money.

Calle 8 Norte (btw. Av. 5 and the beach). www.xperiencehotelsresorts.com/illusion. ✆ **984/803-3980** or 984/803-3018. 41 units. High season $121–$201 double, from $174 cabana; low season $60–$206 double, from $113 cabana. Rates include continental breakfast. No children under 14. **Amenities:** Restaurant; outdoor pool; spa; sun deck, terrace; restaurant; room service; ATM; beach club discounts; free Wi-Fi.

**Ko'ox Caribbean Paradise ★** Clean, comfortable, basic rooms right in a central location are the main draw at this modest budget hotel next to Ah Cacao. Since Ko'ox took over management in 2013, maintenance has improved and flatscreen TVs have been added. The amiable staff is eager to please. Rooms are small but very clean, and superior rooms have balconies, though Wi-Fi can be temperamental. The sparkling pool has good views. Opt for the pool side if you're an early-to-bed type; rooms overlooking Quinta get noise from nearby bars until about 1am. This is a terrific bargain for the location during low and mid seasons, but the high-season rate spike puts it in the same range with other hotels offering more amenities.

Av. 5 Norte (at Constituyentes). www.kooxcaribbeanparadisehotel.com. ✆ **984/803-2032.** 40 units. High season $124–$150 double; low season $46–$66 double. $5 charge for use of in-room safe. **Amenities:** Pool; massage room; beach club discount; free Wi-Fi.

**La Pasión Hotel Boutique ★★** This appealing three-story hotel across from Playa's town square started with eight rooms in mid-2012 and had grown to 30 by 2014, with plans to add 10 more. It's ideal for visitors who want to be within an easy 3-block walk of the beach and Quinta's party action but want a quiet retreat at the end

## PLAYA'S hip HOOD

As glitzy malls, chain restaurants, and familiar designer stores gobble up Avenida Quinta, crafty entrepreneurs have invested in the beachside neighborhood north of Avenida Constituyentes. Paved streets have replaced dirt paths and fancy condos line the sidewalks, interspersed with wine bars and trendy cafes. Stylish hotels including **Hotel La Semilla** (p. 173) are attracting sophisticates weary of the more mainstream scene on the south side of Playa's main tourism area. The late 2014 arrival of **Hotel Cacao** on Av. 5 at Calle 32 (www.hotelcacao.com.mx; ✆ **984/206-4199**) increased the hip factor even more, thanks to its cutting-edge design and amenities. The 60-room property is the second venture from the developers of San Miguel de Allende's much-lauded Hotel Matilda, the darling of Mexico City elite on weekend getaways. A stunning jungle mural, flowing water walls, hyacinth lily pond, and travertine limestone wall panels add an organic sense to public spaces. Rooms reflect a sense of place as well, with tree trunks topped with glass tabletops, walls paneled in wood and limestone, and stone sinks—plus luxuries like down-filled bedding and Missoni toiletries. The rooftop bar and restaurant enhance Playa's growing prominence as a dining destination. A Thompson Hotel is in the works for the same neighborhood, as are celeb chef restaurants. Playa has matured into a sophisticated destination, albeit one that hangs on to its hippie-chic vibe.

of the day. Besides its location and outgoing, helpful staff, small things—multiple intimate lounging areas, a coffee and tea corner, a never-ending supply of cookies and other snacks—make it quite homey, while the dense "jungle" surrounding the two outdoor pools feel exotic and remote. The mid-size rooms are Mexican contemporary style: white walls, wood-beam ceilings, solid wooden furniture, and red accents. All have balconies. Rooms facing the garden and pool are worth the higher price; less expensive rooms face the square, which is subject to unpredictable bursts of noise.

Calle 10 Norte (btw. Avs. 15 and 20). www.hotellapasion.com. ✆ **984/879-3005.** 30 units. High season 2,290–2,800 pesos double; low season 1,165–1,870 pesos double. Underground garage 126 pesos per night. Rates include two-course breakfast. No children 14 and under. **Amenities:** Restaurant; free Wi-Fi.

**La Tortuga ★★** There's a lot to love about this small hotel, which is more than ever a tropical oasis as a growing number of Cancún-sized buildings rise in the neighborhood. Just a block from Quinta Avenida, its meandering pool set in a lush garden is a major drawing card. Bright, contemporary rooms, refreshed in 2014, come in various sizes and configurations; five ground-floor swim-up rooms are just 2 feet from the water. Junior suites have balconies, private rooftop Jacuzzis, robes, and slippers. The staff is friendly and helpful, and the spa and Current restaurant are very good. Know going in that the boisterous CoCo Bongo nightclub, at the other end of the block, pounds out music all night; it doesn't bother most guests, but if you're a light sleeper, consider earplugs.

Av. 10 (at Calle 14 Norte). www.hotellatortuga.com. ✆ **866/550-6878,** U.S. and Canada 984/873-1484. 51 units. High season $131–$259 double; low season $78–$171 double. Discounted parking $10 in public lot. Rates include breakfast and beach passes. No children under 16. **Amenities:** Restaurant; bar; spa; outdoor pool; free Wi-Fi.

## CHOOSING AN all-inclusive IN THE RIVIERA MAYA

All-inclusive resorts far outnumber regular hotels in the Riviera Maya, and the trend continues to dominate new construction. Most folks are familiar with the AI (short for all-inclusive) concept—large hotels that work with economies of scale to offer lodging, food, and drink all for a single rate. Some AIs offer convenience and low rates good for families with many mouths to feed. Because they are enclosed areas, they make it easy for parents to watch their children. The system works well for multiple-generation family reunions and group meetings, and seasonal deals offer amazingly cheap getaways.

This type of all-inclusive is best booked through a vacation packager or travel agent. Their air and AI packages usually beat anything you can get by booking your own flight and room, even if you have frequent-flier miles to burn. In a recent comparison of package prices with the cost of separate direct air and hotel bookings, for example, a couple could save an average of more than $100 a night through BookIt.com, which offers a particularly good range of all-inclusive resorts among its deals.

I came to understand and appreciate this type of vacation while staying at the **Iberostar** (www.iberostar.com) complex on Paraíso Beach north of Playa del Carmen. The enormous compound includes five hotels in all price ranges, a golf course, shopping center, nightclubs, spacious beach, and terrific spa. A tram travels between the resorts. (Guests at the higher-end hotels can use the amenities at all hotels.) Despite the size, I never felt overwhelmed and enjoyed watching families play together and apart.

With several resorts of varying quality and style, **Karisma Hotels + Resorts** (www.karismahotels.com) merits attention. Their Azul resorts have a partnership with Fisher-Price, and their kids' clubs are amazing. Their adults-only Dorado resorts pamper grownups with spas and gourmet restaurants. Some of the hotels have Gourmet Inclusive plans offering all the amenities you expect in upscale resorts, all included in the rate.

Another all-inclusive concept offers beyond-luxurious resorts with fabulous suites, spas, pools, and beaches along with exceptional gourmet dining. Daily rates can soar beyond $1,000 per person per day. But more and more resort companies are moving in this direction, and big spenders have outstanding options. The **Grand Velas** (p. 168) excels in this category. The pricey **Royal Hideaway Playacar** (www.royalhideaway.com) is acclaimed as an idyllic wedding and honeymoon setting. The exclusive resorts sometimes have some odd rules, though. For example, my husband and I weren't able to enjoy the specialty restaurants at one resort because men were required to wear closed-toe dress shoes—even dressy leather sandals were verboten. Be sure you know such things before you go.

**Playa Maya ★** Distinguished from other beach hotels by its entrance right on the sand, Playa Maya offers clean, comfortable rooms, personal service, and a quiet location 1 block from Quinta Avenida that removes it from the street activity. Fresh off a 2014 remodel, guest rooms come in many configurations. They are not luxurious, but they are bright and spacious, with mini-fridges and cable TV. Many have balconies with glorious ocean views, and some have kitchenettes. The included breakfast is fresh and more generous than most. Depending on weather and current conditions (which change constantly), the beach directly in front of the hotel can be rocky; better swimming conditions are a short walk away. Minimum stays are required, but the hotel maintains a list of shorter stays available between other bookings.

On the beach (btw. calles 6 and 8 Norte). www.playa-maya.com. ✆ **984/803-2022.** 20 units. High season from $225 double; low season from $160 double. Rates include full breakfast. Limited street parking. **Amenities:** Restaurant; bar; Jacuzzi; outdoor pool; room service; free Wi-Fi.

### INEXPENSIVE

**Hotel Lab Nah ★** The entrance is a faux-Mayan arch, and the building's twists, turns, and bridges add a sense of adventure to this economy hotel just off Quinta Avenida. The spotless rooms have good beds and basic furnishings with no frills, although the free continental breakfast sometimes includes waffles, ham-and-cheese bagels, or other extras. One quirk to be aware of: The standard rooms, which have garden terraces, come with one or two full-size beds; it's actually less expensive to get a queen room, because they face Quinta and get some late-night noise during the busy season. It's worth the modest price hike to get a second-floor gardenview room or a partial-oceanview room with balcony on the third floor. The rooftop *palapa* unit can sleep up to four people and has a kitchenette (no air-conditioning, but sea breezes make that moot in all but the hottest weather).

Calle 6 Norte (btw. Av. 5 & the beach). www.labnah.com. ✆ **984/873-2099.** 33 units. High season $75–$95 double, from $130 *palapa;* low season $49–$69 double, from $79 *palapa*. Rates include continental breakfast. Limited street parking. **Amenities:** Small pool; free Wi-Fi.

**Hotel Plaza Playa ★** This amazing bargain was one of the best finds on a recent Playa visit. I approached the place with trepidation, hardly believing the low room rate, and was pleased to be greeted by two friendly ladies, one speaking perfect English. Once the air-conditioning kicked in, my room was perfectly comfortable, with a long counter for accumulated stuff; big windows; a large, immaculate bathroom with plenty of hot water; and a fridge, microwave, and several bottles of water. Yes, the mattress and pillows are thin, the Wi-Fi is erratic in the rooms (but fine in the lobby), and there's no elevator, but a full breakfast at the adjacent restaurant is included in the price. A nearby large grocery store and several small taco spots help keep expenses down, and some guests tend to linger a week or more.

Calle 20 (btw. calles 25 and 30). www.hotelplazaplaya.com. ✆ **984/803-0739.** 34 units. High season $77 double; low season $62 double. Street parking. **Amenities:** Restaurant; Wi-Fi.

## Where to Eat

Tiny cafes and fancy restaurants line Fifth Avenue and surrounding streets, and everybody's got an opinion on what's best. You can sample Argentinean beef, sushi, fancy pastas, and basic tacos al pastor, but be prepared—dining in Playa isn't cheap. The least expensive places are several blocks away from Quinta Avenida and close to Highway 307. For fish tacos and inexpensive seafood, try **El Oasis,** on Highway 307 at Calle 22 (✆ **984/803-2676**). For *arrachera* (marinated beef) tacos, the place to go is **Super Carnes H C de Monterrey,** Calle 1 Sur between avenidas 20 and 25 (✆ **984/803-0488**).

### EXPENSIVE

**Aldea Corazón ★★★** MEXICAN Built around a remnant of the ancient Maya jungle containing a *cenote* and stones left from a long-gone temple, this restaurant's verdant setting would be worth a visit even if the food weren't so good—but the fusion of Mexican and Maya cuisine is fresh, creative, and delicious. Try the Pastel Azteca

(Mexican lasagna) with blue-corn tortillas, or the poblano chile stuffed with vegetables and banana. The fresh catch with amaranth and *jamaica* (hibiscus) sauce is exceptional, as is the service. In the morning, you can get the usual *licuados,* egg dishes, and breakfast sandwiches, but I recommend the specialties, such as the classic Spanish tortilla, *huitlacoche* (a mushroom-like corn fungus) crepes, or *nopal* cactus *huaraches* (thick, oblong, slightly crispy stuffed tortillas).

Av. 5 (at Calle 14 Norte). www.grupoazotea.com/aldea-corazon. **984/803-1942.** Main courses 160–570 pesos. Daily 8am–midnight.

**Casa Mediterránea ★★** ITALIAN Whether it's as simple as light, buttery spinach and cheese ravioli or a feast such as Spaghetti ai Frutti di Mare (spaghetti with squid, octopus, shrimp, and lobster) this intimate restaurant, entered through a courtyard with lanterns hanging from the trees, nails it. The secret is the homemade pasta, made fresh every day, and it has been so successful for 15 years that Maria Michelon and Maurizio Gabrielli, the Italian owners, haven't found a reason to change much beyond tweaking a dish every year or so. The couple is very hands-on, with Maria making the pasta and the two of them greeting diners every day. The menu leans toward northern Italian but provides a few surprises, such as ravioli stuffed with fish and shrimp; lasagna may appear in daily specials with duck or rabbit sauce or spiked with sausage (go early; lasagna can sell out). They also do excellent, if somewhat pricey, straight-on meat and fish dishes, including a mixed grill (lobster, fish, squid, and shrimp) for two. Good news for travelers with special diet needs: They now offer gluten-free pasta and will gladly adjust recipes to accommodate allergies or prepare half-servings.

Av. 5 (btw. calles 6 and 8; look for the Jardín de Marieta hotel sign and enter the courtyard). ✆**984/876-4679.** Reservations recommended in high season. Main courses 175–330 pesos. Daily 2–11pm high season; Wed–Mon 2–11pm low season.

**La Casa del Agua ★★** EUROPEAN/MEXICAN European and Mexican tastes meet with excellent results in one of Quinta Avenida's most elegant restaurants. Its water theme extends from the musical waterfall on the terrace, to the flowing traffic pattern of the airy second-floor dining room, to the menu. Seafood, the German-Mexican owners' specialty, is at its purest in the excellent grilled seafood dish for two, but inventive combinations such as shrimp strudel, pollo Zurich with spaetzle, or duck and *jamaica*-strawberry sauce and sweet potatoes offer stiff competition. In the menu's "Mexican Corner," try spicy shrimp "a la Diablo," a straightforward poblano chicken with Oaxaca cheese, or the curious but delicious homemade *cochinita pibil* ravioli. Diners may also sit in the oceanview rooftop garden or downstairs in the more casual bistro, where the restaurant's La Malagueña wine bar holds Friday night tastings.

Av. 5 (at Calle 2). www.lacasadelagua.com. ✆**984/803-0232.** Reservations recommended in high season. Main courses 195–620 pesos. Daily 4pm–midnight.

## MODERATE

**La Cueva del Chango ★★** NATURAL FOOD/MEXICAN The location at the northern reaches of Quinta Avenida's tourist zone may be the only reason there's ever an empty seat at the Swiss-owned "Monkey's Cave"—which is indeed designed as a cave and has monkeys, mostly of fabric and wicker, in unlikely places. The relaxed, retro-hippie vibe and natural foods have earned a loyal following for more than 10 years and is especially popular for breakfast—a mix of *huevos motuleños, chilaquiles,* and other Mexican standards; international favorites such as crepes and French toast; and an enticing array of fresh juices and blended drinks. Lunch and dinner menus include delicious fish, seafood, and chicken prepared with *achiote* sauce, *xcatic* chiles, hibiscus flowers, mole, and other Mexican ingredients.

Calle 38 (btw. Av. 5 and the beach). www.lacuevadelchango.com. ✆ **984/147-0271.** Breakfast 46–88 pesos; main lunch and dinner courses 88–178 pesos. No credit cards. Mon–Sat 8am–11pm; Sun 8am–2pm.

**La Mission** ★★ MEXICAN An offshoot of the popular Cozumel restaurant, this open-air place serves Mexican favorites with an emphasis on seafood. The lobster, one of their specialties, is very good, and well priced. They have an especially flavorful version of the traditional Yucatecan *sopa de limón,* which comes with all entrees. Together with garlic bread, excellent guacamole and chips, and flan for dessert, all included for no extra charge, it makes for a less expensive meal than the prices would suggest. In the evening, go for a seat on the patio, which gets more air and is quite lovely; during the day, you'll want the shade of the *palapa.*

Av. 10 (at Calle 2 Norte). www.restaurantlamissionplaya.com. ✆ **984/873-3922.** Main courses 143–325 pesos. Daily 2pm until whenever the last guest leaves.

**La Vagabunda** ★★ MEXICAN/INTERNATIONAL One of the Quinta's most inviting sidewalk restaurants, the former Las Mañanitas (same owner) wins people over with its delicious breakfasts and brings them back for lunch and dinner. In addition to more than a dozen well-priced combination plates, breakfast dishes run the gamut from crepes, waffles, and muffins to omelets to Mexican favorites—the *chilaquiles* are terrific. Try to go on Sunday, when Mexican spiced *cafe de olla* is available. For lunch and dinner, you can have a simple, inexpensive meal or go all out with an Argentinean *churrasco* (a variety of grilled meats) or a grilled seafood plate. Standouts on the novella-sized menu include addictive jalapeño poppers, savory chimichangas, chicken enchilada mole, and super-fresh fish and shrimp tacos.

Av. 5 (btw. calles 4 and 6). www.vagabundaplaya.com. ✆ **984873-01114.** Main courses 119–240 pesos; breakfast 89–159 pesos. Daily 7am–midnight.

**Los Carboncitos** ★ MEXICAN/INTERNATIONAL This simple sidewalk restaurant mixes Mexican fusion dishes with Italian and other international recipes. It excels at *arrachera* (beef) or *al pastor* (pork) tacos, but the extensive menu ranges from filet mignon to enchiladas to lobster. The traditional Maya dishes are especially good; try the chicken *relleno negro,* which isn't found on many menus (the *negro* comes from burnt chiles). Also unusual for this area is a full page of vegetarian options, including brochettes, fajitas, and chile relleno.

Calle 4 (btw. avs. 5 and 10, in Hotel Cielo). www.hotelcielo.com/restaurant. ✆ **984/873-1382.** Main courses 105–470 pesos; order of tacos 99–160 pesos. No credit cards. Daily 7am–1am.

**Yaxche** ★★★ YUCATECAN This ode to native food is Playa's most intriguing restaurant, with a menu full of unpronounceable Maya dishes redolent with *achiote,* pumpkin seeds, sour orange, and *xcatic* peppers. Some hew to ancient cooking techniques handed down through the owner's family, while others have been updated: *Euxiquia,* a creamy soup of red peppers and stir-fried potatoes; *Xochitl-Nicte*, a salad with edible flowers and grilled papaya; *Pibxcatic,* a Maya version of the chile relleno stuffed with your choice of *cochinita pibil*, cheese and herbs, or cheese with tropical fruit and mint. Fresh seafood is one of Yaxche's strengths, and there's even a Maya version of fajitas. The restaurant added breakfast service in 2014.

Av. 5 (at Calle 22). www.mayacuisine.com. ✆ **984/873-3011.** Reservations recommended in high season. Main courses 110–360 pesos. Daily 8am–2pm and 5pm–11pm.

### INEXPENSIVE

**Aguachiles ★★★** MEXICAN/SEAFOOD Tourists who find their way to this locals' taqueria will be treated to traditional Mexican comfort food with a contemporary twist. Tostadas are made with corn tortillas lightly sautéed in olive oil, loaded with shrimp, tuna, or other fish, and crowned with red cabbage, cucumber, strawberry-habanero salsa, or any number of intriguing toppings; it's your choice. The place is also known for its ceviche and fish and seafood tacos served with a wide array of sauces. Because it closes at 7pm, it's busiest at lunchtime, but if you're willing to have an early dinner you'll have your pick of excellent seafood platters. Aguachiles opened a second location in mid-2012 on Av. Constituyentes, between avenidas 5 and 1, ✆ **984/803-1583.** (Same hours, though.)

Calle 34 (at Av. 25). ✆ **984/142-7380**. Main courses 93–221 pesos; tacos 26 pesos; tostadas 40–43 pesos. No credit cards. Daily noon–7pm.

**Fonda Regina ★★** MEXICAN Don't overlook this sweet little spot around the corner from Quinta Avenida. There's usually a bright pink sign outside showing daily specials. Duck through the vine-covered entryway and claim one of the seven yellow, pink, or blue wooden tables covered with purple lace, a floral cloth, or various other textiles. You'll soon receive a stone *molcajete* (normally used for grinding spices) with salsa and extra ingredients including chopped tomatoes, onions, and chiles for DIY flavor. The menu changes daily but you can count on getting black beans, rice, and veggies—all in separate clay bowls—with your entree. I adore the *aguachile* appetizer with its tangy lime marinade mixed with shrimp, and the hearty *pozole,* a hominy stew. You can't miss the aroma of *cochinita pibil* on Sundays, as the cooks roast marinated pork in banana leaves in an earthen pit with hot volcanic rocks—be prepared to wait for a table. Delightful.

Calle 38 (btw. Av. 5 and the beach). ✆ **984/147-2239.** Main courses 80–138 pesos. No credit cards. Daily 8:30am–10:30pm.

**Karma Bagels ★** SANDWICH SHOP This is the place to satisfy a bagel craving or just grab a light lunch or dinner on the breezy terrace. Surprisingly for a region where bagels are scarce, these are fresh, hot, and toasty. All come with cream cheese, but their highest and best use here is as a vehicle for a variety of tasty sandwiches, such as the Pakita (chicken breast, melted cheese, bean sprouts, and avocado) and El Mediterráneo (cream cheese, herbs, goat cheese, tomatoes, fresh basil, and olives on a dried-tomato bagel).

Av. 5 (at Constituyentes, second floor above Ah Cacao). www.karmabagels.com. ✆ **984/803-2192.** Bagels 60–80 pesos; salads 50–84 pesos. Daily 8am–midnight.

## Exploring Playa del Carmen

### BEACHES

Playa's most active pursuits revolve around simply enjoying the good life. The hippest sandy beaches for swimming, sunning, and people-watching are north of Avenida Constituyentes; central Playa's beach is more popular with local families and fishermen, and is home to a few inexpensive hotels and restaurants. Several beach clubs and bars line the sand, and vendors wander about offering to put your hair in braids *(trenzas)* or sell you jewelry, blankets, hats, and trinkets. The most beautiful beach—and unfortunately the most crowded—extends from Constituyentes north for 5 blocks to Las Mamitas and Kool beach clubs, between calles 28 and 30. Its gradually deepening

### Please Don't Touch

Monkeys, iguanas, macaws, and even baby tigers are showing up on Avenida Quinta with alarming frequency despite protests from local animal activists. These creatures taken from the wild for human amusement serve as props for businesses and roaming vendors who encourage tourists to pose while holding these frightened, abused animals, reptiles, and birds. Unfortunately, plenty of folks happily oblige, hamming it up while perching baby spider monkeys or iguanas on their shoulders. More and more animals are being abused in this manner as the creatures that have disappeared in the wild become commercialized mascots. Responsible visitors refrain from encouraging this practice and speak up when they witness others witlessly abusing helpless creatures.



waters and breaking waves farther out provide ample fodder for water play. The sublime sands farther north are increasingly being squeezed by condo developments.

### DIVING & SNORKELING

Playa's offshore reef offers decent diving, though it doesn't compare to Cozumel (p. 153) or Puerto Morelos (p. 165). Its primary virtue, which has earned it scores of dive shops, is access to Cozumel and a chain of inland *cenotes.* Reef dives generally cost $45 to $50 for one tank and $70 to $75 for two; two-tank *cenote* trips are around $110 to $120. Prices for Cozumel trips vary more and are noted below. (Cozumel dives almost always require you to take the ferry on your own and board the dive boat on the island.) Playa's dive shops also offer full-day trips (May–Oct) to snorkel with whale sharks off Isla Mujeres and Isla Holbox north of Cancún. Dedicated divers should look for the discounted multi-dive deals and dive/hotel packages offered by many shops. **Cyan Ha Dive Center** (www.cyanha.com; ✆ **984/803-2517**) was one of the first shops in Playa and still one of the most respected. **Tank-Ha Dive Center** (www.tankha.com; ✆ **984/873-0302**) takes divers to Cozumel directly on their own boat to Cozumel's reefs. The two-tank trip costs $135. **Yucatek Divers** (www.yucatek-divers.com; ✆ **984/803-2836**) specializes in *cenote* diving and in dives for people with disabilities. **Abyss Dive Center** (www.abyssdiveshop.com; ✆ **984/873-2164**) has a second shop in Tulum. Snorkeling isn't good in Playa since you can't reach the reefs by swimming from the beach. If you really want to snorkel, you're better off in the waters around Akumal and Xel-Ha.

### WATERSPORTS

Countless outfitters line the beach and have stands on La Quinta, offering excursions inland to *cenotes,* ruins, and adventure parks. Banana boating, tubing, and jet skiing are just a few of the (pricey) watersports you can enjoy in Playa's calm waters.

## Shopping

Playa is the Caribbean coast's retail heart, with huge box stores and shopping malls on the highway serving as supply houses for much of the coast. In the tourist zone, you'll find shops and boutiques along Quinta Avenida, where everyone seems to gather for leisurely strolls in the early evening. Once you get past the ferry terminal area, low-key, locally owned shops vie for your vacation dollar with high-end clothing, Cuban cigars, specialty tequila, handicrafts, jewelry, and beach wear. Sadly, chain jewelry, sportswear, and junky souvenir shops catering to cruise passengers, along with large department stores and fancy mini-malls, are claiming prime strolling areas—there's even a Victoria's Secret where a charming folk art shop once stood, forcing out the smaller businesses and sending rent rates sky-high. North of Calle Constituyentes, artists and artisans display their creations on the sidewalks on Saturday evenings. Credit cards are widely accepted in shops, most with fixed prices.

Some favorite shops along La Quinta, south to north: **De Beatriz Boutique,** Calle 2, west of Quinta Avenida (✆ **984/879-3272**), an unsung little side-street shop selling locally designed *manta* (Mexican cotton) clothing; **Rosalia,** between calles 12 and 14 (✆ **984/803-4904**), for fabulous textiles from Chiapas, including embroidered *huipiles* and inexpensive shawls, scarves, and bags; and **Corazon de Mexico** between calles 14 and 14 (✆ **984/803-3355**) for high-quality folk art. **Casa Tequila,** at Calle 16 (✆ **984/873-0195**), is the most popular place to sample tequilas from their stock of more than 100 brands. **Ah Cacao,** at Constituyentes (www.ahcacao.com; ✆ **984/803-5748**), is one of the area's most successful local businesses, expanding from its original Playa shop to several outlets in Cancún. Its specialty is intense and rare *criollo* chocolate, the Maya's "food of the gods," in bars, cocoa, or roasted beans—the cafe's fudgy mochas, frappes, and chocolate shots will ruin you for Starbucks, and the brownies cure any blues.

North of Constituyentes, artists display their works along Quinta Avenida, wine bars abound, and shops offer high-quality clothing, folk art, shoes, and trendy objets de art. This section is often used for art shows and festivals. **La Sirena,** at Calle 26 (✆ **984/803-3422**), offers trendy folk art with *calaca* (skull), *lucha libre,* and Frida Kahlo themes. Gorgeous woven hammocks swing outside **Hamacamarte** on Calle 38 between Av. 5 and the beach (✆ **984/873-1338**), where shelves are stocked with high-quality hammocks from the Yucatán, as well as from El Salvador and other countries. The silk, matrimonial-sized hammocks woven with thousands of colored strings cost $100 or more but last forever—mine's been hanging in my backyard for years.

## Entertainment & Nightlife

It seems as if everyone in town is out strolling La Quinta until midnight; there's pleasant browsing, dining, and drinking available at any number of establishments. One easy way to check out the scene is to book an evening out with **Playacrawl** (www. rockstarcrawls.com; ✆ **800/975-4341** in the U.S. and Canada or 984/ 165-0699). For $95 per person you are guided to three happening clubs, skip all lines, get VIP tables and treatment, and the price covers all you can drink, including bottle service, from 10pm to 3am. Clubs vary by night. Wild and crazy **CoCo Bongo** (✆ **984/803-5939**) presents a dazzling (and deafening) show with flying acrobats, strutting rock star impersonators ranging from Madonna to Queen, and costumed characters wandering about on stilts, followed by long nights of impassioned dancing among the guests. It's at Avenida 10 and Calle 12. On the beach, the **Blue Parrot** (✆ **984/873-0083**) at Calle 12 attracts a mixed crowd with its live rock acts and nightly fire show on the beach. **Kool Beach Club** (✆ **984/803-1961**) at Mamitas beach at the foot of Calle 28 manages to be both classy and casual, extending the daytime beach party far into the night with DJs and dancing. **Fusion** (✆ **984/873-0374**), on the beach at Calle 6, hosts live bands Monday through Saturday nights, alternating between jazz, reggae, and rock. **La Santanera,** on Calle 12 between avenidas 5 and 10, has long been the best late-night club.

Mexico knows how to do discos and dance clubs right. **Palazzo** (✆ **984/106-2269**) on Calle 12 between avenidas 5 and 10 makes all the right moves, with disco balls, light shows, fog machines, and driving beats that keep the mixed crowd of locals and tourists on their feet until dawn.

Though they technically close around sunset, several beach clubs north of Avenida Constituyentes occasionally book live acts. Look for action at the foot of calles 30 to 38.



## Organized Tours

**Alltournative,** Highway 307 Km 287 (www.alltournative.com; ✆ **877/437-4990** in the U.S., or 984/803-9999) is the largest culture and nature tour operator in the area. Their most popular full-day excursion begins with a visit to a village and adventure area for rappelling, swimming, canoeing, and a lunch of traditional Yucatecan food, followed by a tour of the archaeological site of Cobá. Prices start at $139 for adults and $109 for children. Other tours include Tulum, several Maya villages, and various adventures.

# SOUTH OF PLAYA DEL CARMEN

## Punta Venado: Horseback Riding

A few places along the highway offer horseback rides. The best of these, **Rancho Punta Venado ★** (www.puntavenado.com; ✆ **984/158-8912**), is just south of Playa, past the Calica Pier. This ranch is the least touristy—though it does cater to groups—and the owners take good care of the horses. It has a nice stretch of coast with a sheltered bay and offers horseback riding ($85 for 75 min.), ATV expeditions to caves and *cenotes,* and other activities. Transportation from Cancún, Playa del Carmen, and Tulum is available for an extra fee. Use of the beach club is included in tour prices. Make arrangements in advance so that they can schedule you on a day when they have fewer customers. The turnoff for the ranch is 2km (1¼ miles) south of the Calica overpass near Km 279.

## Río Secreto: Wondrous Cavern

**Río Secreto ★★★** NATURE RESERVE There are plenty of cave tours in the area. This community-based eco park stands above the rest for its commitment to the local community and its in-depth, enjoyable tours. Visitors learn about Maya beliefs regarding the "underworld" as they explore a 600m-long (less than ½-mile) cavern, which was hidden for centuries. As the story goes, a local *campesino* (country person) was chasing a meaty lizard into the brush and under a rock pile. The *campesino* followed, digging through rocks, until he heard a splash. The lizard, it seemed, had discovered a hiding place. The man found the entrance to a cave filled with stalactites and stalagmites. Local naturalists discovered a dazzling series of chambers with rock formations dating back 2.5 million years. The area was declared a nature reserve and opened to the public in April 2008.

Visitors must be accompanied by guides and wear short wetsuits and helmets as they walk and swim through the cavern. At times, it is so dark you feel like you're totally blind. Other times, sunshine streams through holes in the roof, illuminating the blue and pink striations caused by mineral-rich water dripping over earth-toned stone. An occasional swim through an emerald green pool adds to the fun, as does the guide's banter and knowledge. From donning your wetsuit to downing a filling lunch after the

## UNDERGROUND adventures

The Yucatán Peninsula's land surface is a thin limestone shelf jutting out like a footprint between the Gulf of Mexico and the Caribbean Sea. Rainwater seeps through the surface into *cenotes*, freshwater sinkholes that dot the underground world. Some *cenotes* are like small wells. Others are like giant green ponds with high rock walls—tempting sights to would-be Tarzans. *Cenotes* often provide access to magical caves where sunlight from holes in the land's surface glimmers on icicle-like stalactites and stalagmites. Riviera Maya is filled with these formations, and it seems every farmer and landowner has posted a sign offering access to their pools and caverns for a few pesos. Some are actually blasting the ground in search of *cenotes*, unfortunately. Many of the local *cenotes* are part of the Sac Aktun cave system, said to be the second largest in the world. Several elaborate parks with *cenotes* and underground rivers, including Xcaret, Hidden Worlds, Río Secreto, and Aktun Chen, are described in this chapter. Dozens of smaller *cenotes* and caves deserve your attention as well, and entry costs much less than at the big parks. Adventuresome types should seek out newly opened sites marked with rustic wooden signs. Below are a few *cenotes* accessible from Highway 307. Most have bathrooms, are open daily from about 8 or 9am until 5 or 6pm, and charge about 30 to 50 pesos.

**Cenote Azul** (approximately 2km/1¼ miles south of Puerto Aventuras, just south of Ecopark Kantun Chi): Situated close to the highway, with several large pools, Cenote Azul has a fun jump-off point on a section of overhanging rock, and a wooden lounging deck jutting over the water. Walkways along the edge make it easier to get in and swim with the abundant catfish. Families and timid visitors unhappy walking on slippery rocks find easy access here.

**Gran Cenote** (about 3km/1¾ miles west of Tulum on the road to Cobá): Divers are especially fond of this aptly named bottomless, crystal-clear *cenote* leading to caverns that seem to have no end. Snorkelers can follow the dive lights into caves close to the surface and see fantastic stalactites and stalagmites. Since it's off the main highway, this fabulous *cenote* is less popular with groups and feels like it's buried in jungle. The nearby **Temple of Doom,** also called **Calavera,** or Skull Cave, is marked by a small sign in front of a ramshackle house. The *cenote* is located in the backyard and is accessible only by an eight-foot jump into the water or a rusty ladder that also comes in handy for the return climb.

**Jardín del Edén** (1.6km/1 mile north of Xpu-Há, just south of Cenote Azul):

90-minute underground tour, it will take about 3½ hours. Hot showers and lockers are available; transportation from Cancún and Riviera Maya hotels is available for an extra fee.

Off Hwy. 307, 5 minutes south of Playa del Carmen. www.riosecreto.com. ✆ **888/844-5010** in the U.S. or 984/877-2377. Basic tour without transportation $79 adults, $40 children ages 4–11.

## Xcaret: Tribute to the Yucatán

You can't miss the billboards, tricked out buses, and ads plastered everywhere for this something-for-everyone attraction. **Xcaret ★★★** (Eesh-ca-*ret*) is the biggest deal in these parts and even has its own resort. Thousands visit every week; stay away if you

"El Edén" is one of my favorite *cenotes* because it's run by an accommodating family and has lots of rocky outcroppings where you can lounge in the warm sun after the freezing water leaves you covered in goose bumps. There's plenty of room along the edges of the *cenote,* which looks like a huge swimming pool. Shrieks fill the air as daredevils attempt swan dives from a high jump-off point. Snorkelers and divers find plenty of tropical fish and eels.

**Manatí** (Tankhah, east of the highway 10km/6¼ miles north of Tulum): The large, open lagoon near Casa Cenote restaurant is part of a long underwater cave system that ends at the sea. Freshwater bubbling up into ocean waters creates significant but not dangerous currents that attract a great variety of saltwater and freshwater fish. The *cenote* was named for the manatees that used to show up occasionally; the shy creatures have disappeared as the region has gained popularity.

**Sac Aktun** (1 km/⅔ mile north of Xel-Ha): Named for the larger cave system, this small park is located down a rutted dirt road but worth the effort. You can float and snorkel through two caves and *cenotes* here with a guide. The first requires a somewhat scary climb down into the cavern; the second has an above ground entrance. The fee is higher here than at most parks, at $30. But the isolation and excellent guides make it a worthwhile adventure.

**Xunaan Ha** (outside of Chemuyil, 12km/7½ miles south of Akumal): Gaining popularity because of its sense of authenticity, this one is reached by winding through a Maya village and growing town that is home to locals who work in and around Akumal. Signs point to the small *cenote* nearly hidden in the jungle, where you can swim, float, or snorkel with schools of fish and the occasional freshwater turtle. There's also a zip line here and a small spider monkey sanctuary.

Several dive shops along the Riviera Maya offer *cenote* and reef diving and snorkeling. Recommended outfitters that specialize in *cenotes* include **Yukatek Divers** (www.yucatek-divers.com; ✆ **984/803-2836**) and **Go Cenotes** (✆ **984/803-3924**), both in Playa del Carmen; and **Cenote Dive Center** (www.cenotedive.com; ✆ **984/876-3285**) and **Xibalba Dive Center** (www.xibalbadivecenter.com/diving.asp; ✆ **984/871-2953**) in Tulum. Rates start at $55 for a snorkel tour and $120 for two-tank cavern dives, which take place in open *cenotes* where you are always within reach of air and natural light; cave diving requires advanced technical training and specialized gear and is more expensive.

like solitude, but give it a shot if you want to combine nature, culture, gastronomy, art, and fun in one busy day. Xcaret samples everything the Yucatán—and the rest of Mexico—has to offer, and action junkies take full advantage of the pricey admission.

The myriad activities include scuba and snorkeling; cavern diving; hiking through tropical forest; horseback riding; an underwater river ride; swinging in a hammock under palms; and meeting indigenous Maya locals. Exhibits include a bat cave; a butterfly pavilion; mushroom and orchid nurseries; and a petting aquarium. Native jaguars, manatees, sea turtles, monkeys, macaws, and flamingos are also on display. The best folk art museum in Mexico is housed in the Hacienda Henequenera, a traditional Yucatecan hacienda with rooms decorated as if a family lived there. The wonderful folk art collection from throughout Mexico decorates the rooms, and the displays are always changing. The Cava, an amazing underground wine cellar, displays bottles from Mexico's many excellent wineries and offers wine tastings with advance reservations; the dining rooms looks like somewhere major global negotiations would take place. The Hacienda and Cava both offer guided tours; book them when purchasing your entrance tickets. The evening show celebrates Mexico in music and dance, and the costumes and choreography are unequaled anywhere in Mexico. This show is a genuinely mesmerizing spectacle, presenting so many aspects of the Mexican nation that you feel like you've toured the whole country by the time the performers take their last bow. Various packages include transportation, food and beverages, and admission to XPLOR (below) and Xel-Ha see p 190.

Xcaret is 10km (6¼ miles) south of Playa del Carmen. www.xcaret.com. ✆ **855/326-0682** in the U.S. and Canada, or 998/883-3143. Basic admission prices are $89 for adults, $45 for children 5 to 12. Xcaret at Night, with admission after 3pm, is $71 for adults and $35 for children. Daily 8:30am to 9:30pm.

The people who created Xcaret have another park called **Xplor ★** (www.xplor.travel; ✆ **855/326-0682** in the U.S. and Canada, or 998/883-3143) next door. The adventure park has a zip line, a four-wheel-drive track, and an underground river ride. There are two versions of the park, one for the daytime hours and one at night. XPLOR Fuego includes all the activities above taking place in the dark, illuminated by torches and spooky lights.

Xplor is open Monday to Saturday. Admission in daytime (9am–5pm) is $119 for adults, $60 for children (7 or older); XPLOR Fuego (5:30–10:30pm) costs $99 for adults and $50 for children.

## Paamul: Seaside Getaway ★

About 15km (9⅓ miles) beyond Xcaret and 25km (16 miles) from Playa del Carmen is Paamul (also written Pamul). The exit is clearly marked. You can enjoy the Caribbean in relative quiet here. The water at the out-of-the-way beach is wonderful, but the shoreline is rocky.

**Scuba-Mex** (www.scubamex.com; ✆ **888/871-6255** in the U.S., or 984/875-1066) is a fully equipped PADI- and SSI-certified dive shop next to the cabañas. Using two boats, the staff takes guests on dives 8km (5 miles) in either direction. If it's too choppy, the reefs in front of the hotel are also good. The cost for a one-tank dive with rental gear is $39. They also have multi-dive packages and certification instruction, and offer accommodations in four bedrooms in a beach house for $80 per night.

**Cabañas Paamul ★** Paamul works mostly with the trailer crowd, but there are also 13 modern "junior suites" near the water's edge. They are spacious and comfortable, and come with a kitchenette and two queen beds. Trailer guests have access to 200 RV spaces, 12 shared showers, and separate bathrooms for men and women. Laundry service is available nearby. The large *palapa* restaurant is open to the public and customers are welcome to use the beach, which is rocky along this stretch of the coast. Prices vary according to season.

Carretera Cancún–Tulum Km 85. www.paamul.com. ✆ **984/875-1050** or 612/597-0888. 33 units; 200 trailer spaces (all with full hookups). $100–$150 junior suite. RV space with hookups $30 per day, $600 per month. Ask about discounts for stays longer than 1 week. No credit cards. Free parking. **Amenities:** Restaurant; bar; dive shop; pool.

## Puerto Aventuras: Dolphins & Shipwrecks

Five kilometers (3 miles) south of Paamul and 104km (65 miles) from Cancún, Puerto Aventuras is a condo/marina development with a 9-hole golf course on Chakalal Bay. There's a large expat community, including many families, but it's not the best location for tourists wanting to explore the coast since there are few interesting businesses and activities within the compound. A small cluster of restaurants offering Italian, American, and Mexican food border the marina. The major attraction is swimming with the dolphins in a highly interactive program; make reservations well in advance with **Dolphin Discovery** (www.dolphindiscovery.com; ✆ **998/849-4757**). The surest way is through the website.

Puerto Aventuras is also popular for boating and deep-sea fishing. **Capt. Rick's Sportfishing Center** (www.fishyucatan.com; ✆ **888/449-3562** in the U.S., or 984/873-5195) will combine a fishing trip with some snorkeling, which makes for a leisurely day. The best fishing on this coast is from March to August. Puerto Aventuras has a few hotels, but most residential development is condos and homes. The most prominent hotel by the marina, the **Omni Puerto Aventuras ★** (✆ **888/444-6665** in the U.S., or 984/875-1950), has a clean, small beach and many return guests. Rates start at $179 per night. A few all-inclusive hotels are located just north of the marina.

## Xpu-Ha: Sublime Beach

Three kilometers (1¾ miles) beyond Puerto Aventuras is **Xpu-Ha ★★★** (Eesh-poo-*hah*), a wide bay lined by a broad, beautiful sandy beach. Much of the shore is filled with private houses and condos, along with a few all-inclusive resorts. The beach is one of the best on the coast and is long enough to accommodate hotel guests, residents, and day-trippers without feeling crowded.

**Al Cielo ★★** Far more modest than neighboring Esencia (below), this small property stands out for its flowing blue-and-white draped shade awnings on the beach and the fact that it's just about the only property on the coast where smoking is allowed in the rooms. The rooms have air-conditioning but lack TVs, clocks, phones, and techno distractions. Decor is rustic, with rooms located in a thatched-roof building. Four villas and a master suite are fancier—one even has an indoor sunken pool. The restaurant is popular with guests and outsiders enjoying Xpu-Ha's gorgeous beach. ***Note:*** Smoking is permitted in rooms and on property.

Carretera Cancún–Tulum Km 118. www.alcielohotel.com. ✆ **800/676-8590;** 984/840-9181. 9 units. Rooms from $298 double; villas from $333. Rates include full breakfast. Free secure parking. No children. **Amenities:** Restaurant; bar; free Wi-Fi.

**Esencia ★★★** I've stayed at this sublime escape three times over the past decade and am always delighted to find it has retained its standards for refined luxury and simplicity. Built as a vacation hideaway for an Italian duchess in 1988, the Mediterranean-style white guesthouse and villa opened as a hotel in 2006. The original rooms were designed in an elegantly simple style, with niches and arches in white stucco walls, large bathrooms with slatted wood floors in the showers (and divine Moulton Brown toiletries), remote-controlled shades, recessed lighting, and a few pieces of driftwood and fruit for decoration. Over the years, the property has been enlarged to include thatch-roofed two-story villas edging gardens and a broad lawn. The new rooms are nearly identical to the old, though all rooms now have modern touches including TVs and loaded iPods. Some villas have private plunge pools; the best are on the second floor, with balconies buried in trees where tropical birds flit about in early morning. The food, echoing regional Yucatecan recipes and ingredients along with classic Continental fare, is superb. The small spa is deceptively rustic, with slated wood walls and small dressing and relaxation areas. What it lacks in fancy accoutrements it more than makes up for with exceptionally skilled therapists. Yoga classes are held in an outdoor pavilion close to the beach, where comfy beach beds await sunbathers. Two pools have ample sun decks; one is designated for adults only. Some large two-story villas have private pools and full kitchens, perfect for families. There's an 8-day minimum stay during holidays and an optional meal plan.

Predio Rústico Xpu-Ha. www.hotelesencia.com. ✆ **877/528-3490** in the U.S. or Canada, or 984/873-4830. 29 units. High season $695 and up double or suite; low season $565 and up double or suite. Free valet parking. **Amenities:** Restaurant; 2 bars; Jacuzzi; 2 outdoor pools; room service; spa; free Wi-Fi.

## Akumal: Beautiful Bays & Cavern Diving

Continuing south on Highway 307 for 2km (1¼ miles), the turnoffs for Akumal ("Place of the Turtles") are marked by a traffic light; skip the overpass if you're planning to visit here. The ecologically oriented tourism community is spread among four bays, with two entrances off the frontage road parallel to the highway. The main entrance, labeled Akumal, leads to hotels, rental condos, and vacation homes. Take the Akumal Aventuras entrance to the Grand Oasis all-inclusive hotel and more condos and homes. No waterside road connects the two, so you'll need to know which exit to take. A white arch delineates the main entrance to the tourism community (years ago, the original residents were moved across the highway to a fast-growing town where many workers and business owners reside) and longstanding resort. Just before the arch are a couple of grocery stores and a laundry service. Just inside the arch, to the right, is the **Hotel Akumal Caribe** (see p. 189). If you follow the road to the left and keep to the left, you'll reach Half Moon Bay, lined with two- and three-story condos, and eventually Yal-ku Lagoon, a snorkeling park. To rent a local condo, contact **Akumal Vacations** (www.akumalvacations.com; ✆ **800/448-7137** in the U.S.) or **Loco Gringo** (www.locogringo.com). The beach nearest the arch is often packed with day visitors and outside snorkel tours, an unfortunate situation for hotel guests and the many turtles making their home here. Please, please, please don't touch these magnificent creatures. Way too many humans think it's a great idea to hold a turtle's shell for photos and otherwise create annoying disturbances.

Both bays have sandy beaches with rocky or silt bottoms. This is a popular diving area and home to Mexico's original diving club. Three dive shops are in the community, and at least 30 dive sites are offshore. The **Akumal Dive Shop** (www.akumal.com; ✆ **984/875-9032**), one of the oldest and best dive shops on the coast, offers cavern-diving trips and courses in technical diving along with reef dives. Modern sculptures punctuate gardens

### In Case of Emergency

The Riviera Maya is susceptible to power failures that can last for hours during and after heavy storms. Gas pumps and cash machines shut down when this happens, and once the power returns, they attract long lines. It's always a good idea to keep a reserve of gas and cash in small denominations.

beside the clear **Yal-ku Lagoon,** which is about 700m (2,297 feet) long and 200m (656 feet) at its widest. You can paddle around comfortably in sheltered water and see fish and turtles. It's a perfect place to learn how to snorkel and let kids swim about safely. Of course, there are many spots along the bays where you can snorkel for free, but this little park is an easy, relaxing outing. It's open daily from 8am to 5:30pm. Admission is 100 pesos for adults, 50 pesos for children 3 to 14.

**Centro Ecológico Akumal** ★★★ MUSEUM The gentle crescent of **Akumal Bay,** washing a wide, soft beach shaded by coconut palms, is one of the few places where you'll often be surprised by a sea turtle swimming along with you. This non-profit center works to protect the turtles and Akumal's coastal and marine ecosystems, and encourage sustainable development. Small exhibits provide information about turtle migration and nesting. During nesting season (May–July), visit the center in the morning to sign up for that evening's 9pm turtle walk (Mon–Fri). You'll help staff search for new nests, protect exhausted mothers making their way back to sea, and remove eggs to hatcheries where they can incubate safely.

East side of road at town entrance. www.ceakumal.org. ✆ **984/875-9005.**

## WHERE TO EAT

Akumal has about 10 places to eat and a convenient grocery store, **Super Chomak** (with an ATM), by the arch. A collection of businesses just inside the arch includes a bakery and coffeehouse. At the Hotel Akumal Caribe, **Lol-Ha** serves good breakfasts and dinners and has free Wi-Fi, and the **Palapa Snack** bar dishes out everything from ice cream cones to burgers with poblano chiles and avocado. Tell the guards at the hotel's entrance that you're there for a meal, and they'll direct you to special parking areas—and they don't notice if you take some time to wander along the hotel's beautiful beach.

**La Buena Vida** ★ SEAFOOD/REGIONAL A mirador lookout tower is the favorite sunset margarita spot at this funky, fun restaurant/bar in the condo section of Half Moon Bay. Regional dishes including *pescado tikin-xic* (fresh fish with a spicy marinade) and *pollo pibil* (saucy chicken in spices). This is one of precious few places in Akumal where you can join locals over cocktails and high-quality tequilas.

Half Moon Bay beach (btw. Akumal and Yal-ku Lagoon). www.labuenavidarestaurant.com. ✆ **984/875-9061.** Main courses 80–285 pesos. Daily noon–10pm.

**Turtle Bay Cafe & Bakery** ★★ AMERICAN Locals and guests gather at this classic favorite beside the main hotel for huge pancake or omelet breakfasts with American-style accompaniments including crispy hash browns and thick wheat toast. Lunch and dinner menus combine comfort favorites—burgers, chicken sandwiches, and French fries, with healthier options including lentil burgers and several salads. The dinner menu is more limited and expensive than breakfast and lunch, but the beer-battered shrimp and crab cakes over mashed potatoes are worth the splurge There's free Wi-Fi; coffee, smoothies, and pastries served all day; and plenty of friendly folks conversing with travelers in the *palapa*-shaded garden.

Plaza Ukana. www.turtlebaycafe.com. ✆ **984/875-9138.** Main courses 160–290 pesos.

## WHERE TO STAY

**Hotel Akumal Caribe** ★★ This old-timer with a fiercely loyal clientele was long the fanciest (if extremely rustic) place to stay along the coast. The first rooms resembled Maya *nas* (huts) with thatched roofs, concrete floors, and thin mattresses.

Conditions have grown more comfortable over the years, and red-tile-roofed bungalows with kitchenettes are spread about dense gardens. All rooms have purified water jugs, negating the need for piles of disposable plastic bottles. A small beachside hotel also has kitchenette facilities and somewhat fancier furnishings, but there's nothing elegant or luxurious here. The decor is more about beachside practicality, providing a comfortable space where sandy feet and wet bodies won't cause any harm. The Internet can be spotty, but works fine in the Lol-Ha restaurant. The hotel also books condos and villas with multiple bedrooms and a shared pool on Half Moon Bay. The two gift shops display some of the finest folk art and jewelry you'll find in the Riviera Maya. Visiting the restaurants and shops will get you past the guards into free parking lots. Return guests tend to spend weeks in their favorite cottages. Book early for a spot close to the beach.

Hwy. 307 Km 104. www.hotelakumalcaribe.com. ✆ **800/351-1622** in the U.S., 800/343-1440 in Canada, or 915/584-3552. 70 units. High season $149 bungalow, $179 hotel double; low season $130 bungalow, $149 hotel double. Low season packages and reduced Web rates available. Rates include continental breakfast. Free parking. **Amenities:** 2 restaurants; bar; dive shop; outdoor pool; free Wi-Fi.

**Vista del Mar Hotel and Condos ★** Set amid small condo buildings and private homes on Half Moon Bay, this small property on the sand rents hotel rooms and condos by the day or week. Rooms are basic and inexpensive; condos range in size and amenities and can include several bedrooms and bathrooms, full kitchens and living areas, and terraces on the beach. The on-site dive shop offers dive and snorkeling trips and watersports gear. Several rooms come with whirlpool tubs, and all have hammocks hanging in the sea breezes.

Half Moon Bay. www.akumalinfo.com. ✆ **888/425-8625** in the U.S. or 984/875-9060. 27 units. High season $110 double, $170 condo; low season $95 double, $135 condo. Limited free parking. **Amenities:** Restaurant; bar; dive shop; small pool; free Wi-Fi.

## Xel-Ha: Snorkeling, Swimming, and Caverns ★★

**Aktun Chen ★★** NATURE RESERVE This is one of the Yucatán's best caverns, with lots of geological features, good lighting, several underground pools, and large chambers, all carefully preserved. It has thrived under management by the local community rather than outside tour companies. The cavern tour takes about 90 minutes and requires a lot of walking, but the footing is good. Other choices are snorkeling in a *cenote* or soaring above the jungle on zip lines. There is also a zoo with spider monkeys and other local fauna; some critters are allowed to run about freely and will happily grab anything you're not holding tightly. The turnoff is to the right, and the cave is about 4km (2½ miles) from the road.

3km/2 miles S of Akumal. www.aktun-chen.com. ✆ **984/809-4962.** Cave tour $33 adults, $17 children. Mon–Sat 9am–5pm (closed Sundays, Christmas, and New Year's Day).

**Xel-Ha ★** NATURE RESERVE Prices to visit this water park are high, similar to other parks affiliated with Xcaret. Unless you're willing to splurge on more than one park, skip this one in favor of the more extensive offerings at Xcaret. But, if nature is your main interest, choose Xel-Ha. The centerpiece is a large, beautiful lagoon where freshwater and saltwater meet. You can swim, float, and snorkel in beautifully clear water surrounded by jungle. A small train takes you to a drop-off point upriver, and you float back down on water moving calmly toward the sea. With no waves or currents to pull you around, snorkeling here is more comfortable than in the open sea, and the water has several species of fish, including rays.

The park rents snorkeling equipment and underwater cameras. Platforms allow non-snorkelers to view the fish. Even better, use the park's Snuba gear, a contraption that allows you to breathe through 6m (20-foot) tubes connected to scuba tanks floating on the surface. Like Snuba but more involved is sea-trek, an elaborate plastic helmet with air hoses that allows you to walk around on the bottom, breathing normally, and perhaps help to feed the stingrays. These and other activities, including manatee and dolphin encounters, cost an additional fee.

Other attractions include a plant nursery and an apiary for the local stinger-less bees. All-inclusive admission includes meals, drinks including an open bar serving national beverages, use of snorkeling gear, inner tubes, life vest, shuttle train to the river, and changing rooms and showers. Web deals are often available.

13km/8 miles S of Akumal. www.xelha.com. ✆ **984/875-6000**. All-inclusive $89 adults, $44 children. Daily 8:30am–7pm.

**Hidden Worlds Cenotes ★★★** NATURE RESERVE Hidden Worlds Cenotes offers an excellent opportunity to snorkel or dive in a couple of nearby caverns. The caverns are part of a vast network that makes up a single underground river system. The water is crystalline (and cold), and the rock formations impressive. These caverns were filmed for the IMAX production *Journey Into Amazing Caves.* The main form of transportation is "jungle mobile," with a guide tossing out information and lore about the jungle plant life you see. You'll be walking some, so take shoes or sandals. If you've toured caverns before, floating through gives you an entirely different perspective. The owners have also installed a 180m (590-foot) zip line on the property, a zip line roller-coaster-style ride called Avatar, and a Skycycle that has you riding a recumbent bike over the treetops. They now offer full-day packages that include several activities. Transportation from Tulum, Akumal, and Puerto Aventuras is included in admission fees.

About 2km (1¼ miles) south of Xel-Ha. ✆ **888/339-8001** U.S. and Canada, or 984/877-8535. Admission including all land activities and snorkeling $80 adults, $40 children. Cenote diving $130. Daily 9am–5pm.

**LabnaHa Ecopark ★★★** NATURE RESERVE Less crowded than other parks in the area, LabnaHa restricts entrance to small guided groups. The 200-hectare (492-acre) complex includes three *cenotes* linked by eco paths through dense foliage. Two zip lines soar above the *cenotes,* and paths and boardwalks lead through underground caves with stalactites and stalagmites glowing in brief streams of sunlight. Claustrophobes beware: The enclosed caves may be more than you can handle. Swimming, snorkeling, kayaking, and canoeing are available in two caves; diving is also available for an extra fee. The LabnaHa team helps support small Maya communities in the area and includes the residents in park activities. Guides explain the Maya philosophy concerning the underworld and the deities during the tour. The whole experience lasts about five hours; at times, there are few people there and you actually feel like you're exploring the unknown jungle beyond the tourism areas. Advance reservations are required.

Hwy 307 Km 240. www.labnaha.com. ✆ **984/806-6040.** Admission including all land activities and snorkeling $105. Daily 9am–5pm.

## Soliman Bay: Secluded Beauty

**Jashita ★★** Seclusion and pampering are ensured at this small inn hidden along a side road on Bahía de Soliman. You may want to hide away in one of the elegant suites with private terraces and plunge pools, sipping the complimentary wine and nibbling on chocolates while gazing at the sea from your puffy white-draped bed. Even the suites that don't face the sea are blissful, and the relatively inexpensive small double rooms buried beneath the palms are fine if you're happy outdoors most of the time. And why wouldn't you be? The hotel stands beside one of the coast's most beautiful bays, so clear you can watch sea creatures floating about without even stepping into the shallow water. A reef protects the bay from the winds and is so close you can kayak there to snorkel. One private five-bedroom villa is also available for rent. The Sahara restaurant blends Indonesian and other Asian touches with fine Italian cuisine, along with seafood and a few Mexican dishes. It's open to non-guests and is a lovely spot for lunch overlooking the bay.

Bahía Punta Soliman. www.jashitahotel.com. ✆ **984/139-5131.** 13 suites, 4 double rooms, 1 villa. High and low season $44 and up double, $120 for double room. Free parking. **Amenities:** Restaurant; bar; outdoor pool; free Wi-Fi.

## Tankah Bay: Bubbling Cenote

Tankah Bay (about 3km/1¾ miles from Hidden World Cenotes) is best known for its **Casa Cenote ★★★,** named for the restaurant and hotel that sits beside the bay. On the other side of the sandy road, a freshwater underground river surfaces at a *cenote,* then goes underground and bubbles up into the sea just a few feet offshore. It's become a popular spot for group tours; fortunately, it's large enough to accommodate dozens of snorkelers and kayakers. You'll be happiest, however, if you arrive early or late in the day and have the place to yourself. Thick vines and trees border the gorgeous clear green water, refreshingly cool under the brilliant sun. Some dive shops bring groups here and hold classes as well. ***Tip:*** Start your excursion in the sea, swimming and snorkeling above tropical fish. When the sun starts cooking your skin, cross over to the *cenote* for a refreshing dip.

### KITEBOARDING

Kiteboarding (also called kite-surfing) is hugely popular along the coast, but many beaches have become too crowded for safe sailing. **Extreme Control** (www.extremecontrol.net; ✆ **984/745-4555**), one of the first operators in the area, has scaled down their operations in Tulum and moved a few minutes north to Tankah, where conditions are far less crowded (for now). Their basic introductory kiteboarding lesson costs $60, and there are several levels of classes to increase your skills. They also have Stand Up Paddleboarding (SUP) classes and rentals.

The area has a handful of rental houses and condos. **Casa Cenote** (www.casacenote.com; ✆ **998/874-5170**) hotel and restaurant were here long before large groups of travelers discovered the bay, and it has a pleasant Robinson Crusoe feel when the crowds are gone. There are seven beach bungalows with rates running from $125 to $175, depending on the season (excluding holidays). Budget travelers staying in a few simple, rustic cabins share baths and a kitchen space and get off relatively cheaply (considering the competition) for $125 in high season and $75 low season. The American owner provides kayaks and snorkeling gear and can arrange dives, fishing trips, and sailing charters. Local expats have been gathering at the restaurant of the same name for decades, especially for the Sunday afternoon barbecue. It's one of the few places on the coast that harkens back to simpler times.

# TULUM ★★★

Tulum (130km/80 miles from Cancún) is best known for its archaeological site, a walled Maya city of the Postclassic age perched dramatically on a rocky cliff overlooking the Caribbean. The coastline south of the site is packed with *palapa* hotels and upscale retreats for a well-heeled crowd seeking a "rustic" hideaway. This stretch of incredible white beaches has become the unofficial center of the Tulum Hotel Zone—a collection of more than 30 small hotels stretching from the Tulum ruins south to the entrance of the Sian Ka'an Biosphere Reserve. The official town of Tulum is bisected by Highway 307 where it intersects the road to Cobá. The commercial center sprawls along both sides of Highway 307 for about 20 blocks jam-packed with gas stations, auto repair shops, *farmacias,* banks, markets, tour offices, and eateries. Two *glorietas* (traffic circles) slow the traffic through town; frontage roads allow access to parking spaces and driveways. Restaurants and hotels pop up alongside streets around the plaza. Anyone who thinks of Tulum as a charming pueblo hasn't been here for a few years. The growth is astounding and shows no sign of slowing.

## Essentials

### GETTING THERE

**BY CAR** Highway 307 runs straight from Cancún through the town of Tulum.

**BY BUS** Several buses a day leave Playa del Carmen for Tulum.

**VISITOR INFORMATION** A particularly handy resource is the travel agency/communications/package center called **Savana** (http://www.tulumtravelandtours.com; ✆ **984/871-2081**), on the east side of Avenida Tulum between calles Orion and Beta. Most of the staff speaks English and can answer questions about tours and calling home. The website www.todotulum.com is packed with local tips and info.

### GETTING AROUND

A rental car makes everything easier in Tulum, especially if you're staying in town and want to spend considerable time at the beach. Bicycles are readily available at hotels, and an excellent bike path runs from the intersection at Highway 307 and the road to the coast to several beach hotels. Taxis are abundant.

#### CITY LAYOUT

From the north, Highway 307 passes the entrance to the ruins before you enter town. When you come to an intersection with a traffic light, the highway to the right leads to the ruins of Cobá (p. 202). Turn left to reach Tulum's beach Hotel Zone, beginning about 2km (1¼ miles) away; the road sign reads BOCA PAILA. When you come to a T-junction, there will be hotels in both directions. If you turn left (north), you'll be heading toward the back entrance of the ruins. If you take a right, you'll pass a long line of small hotels until you reach the entrance to Sian Ka'an. In the town of Tulum, Highway 307 widens and is called Avenida Tulum.

## Where to Stay

At least 30 small hotels claim any available space on Tulum's soft white-sand beaches, and a confounding collection of signs point in various directions beside the narrow road along the coast. The drive can be confusing for first-timers trying to dodge bicyclists, pedestrians, and delivery trucks. The beach's popularity has driven prices into the stratosphere, and you'll have a hard time finding a room for less than $120 per night in high season. Several hotels now have air-conditioning, 24-hour electricity,

## On the Cheap

Once the cheapest place to stay on the coast, with campgrounds aplenty for budget travelers who hung around for months, Tulum has become nearly as pricey as the rest of the Riviera Maya. These days, the least expensive hotels are now located in town and most beach hotels charge typical Riviera Maya prices. There are a few places with rustic cabañas on the sand along the beach road. **Cabañas Zazil-Kin** charges about $17 for an extremely basic shack, and **Cabañas Santa Fe** has a camping area for about $5, cabañas without bed for about $10, and cabañas with bed for $25. Some beach hotels offer a few cabins or camping spaces; look for signs along the road. Improve your comfort level with these tips: Bring several gallons of fresh water, as most cheap places have saltwater showers; load up on bug repellant and consider bringing a mosquito net; bring bags and ropes to hang your food items away from the ground; and invest in a hammock and sturdy ropes, as it's often far more comfortable to sleep in the open than in a rickety hot cabin. If you don't mind staying in town, go for the **Weary Traveler Hostel** on Polar Poniente in town (www.wearytravelerhostel.com; ✆ **984/142-9283**). The hostel moved to a new building and location in winter 2015 and rates and accommodations were still being sorted out at press time. Count on paying $10 to $15 per night for a dorm room. Amenities include Internet (paid), communal kitchen, and beach transport.

Wi-Fi, and freshwater pools, and cell service is usually good. Some beach hotels don't accept credit cards (though there's now an ATM on the beach road).

## ON THE BEACH

### Expensive

**Cabañas Tulum ★★** This long-time favorite manages to combine Tulum's old-fashioned rustic feel with modern conveniences like air-conditioning (from 7pm to 7am) and 24-hour electricity. Beachfront bungalows and rooms in a two-story building with only partial views are similarly designed in a sparse fashion with white walls, light wood furnishings, and large bathrooms. The best part is the front porch, with hammocks swaying in sea breezes. Rooms on the second floor get the most cooling air, a delight on sweltering days. Ceiling fans and screened windows do help beat the heat in all rooms, though. Rates are high, but not outrageous when compared with the competition, and you can get significant breaks by booking early or for several nights. The beach is one of Tulum's finest, with a broad stretch of white sand and the ever-popular Ziggy's Beach Club and restaurant. A small pool and shady sundeck provide a break from the sand. The owners have opened a more luxurious adults-only boutique hotel called The Beach Tulum (www.thebeach-tulum.com) beside the cabañas.

Carretera Punta Allen Km 7. www.hotelcabanastulum.com. ✆ **866/550-6878** in the U.S. and Canada, or 984/157-9645. 16 units. High season $219-$299 double; low season $199-$229 double. Rates include breakfast. Free parking. **Amenities:** Restaurant; bar; free erratic Wi-Fi in restaurant.

### Moderate

**El Paraíso Hotel ★★** The name (The Paradise Hotel) suits this pocket of serenity on the sand far from the beachfront hotel zone and close to the back entrance to the Tulum ruins. The property is enormous by Tulum standards, with a long, broad beach and a one-story building set back from the action but close enough for sea views from the terrace. The rooms are among the best equipped in the area, with reliable, quiet

## Tulum Pueblo & Hotel Zone

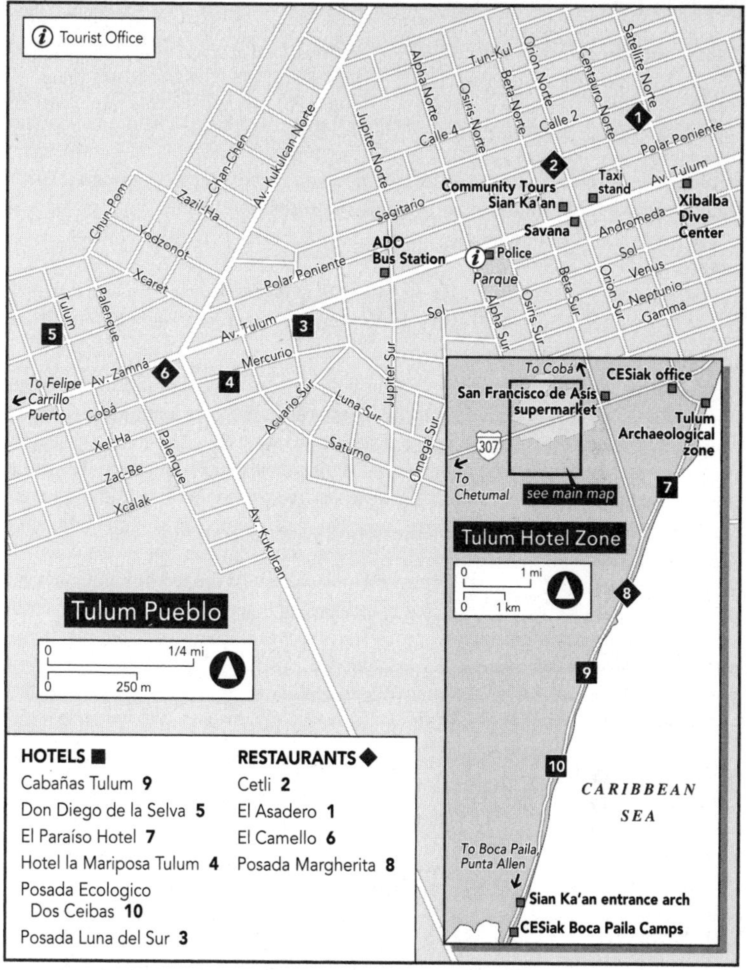


air-conditioning, satellite plasma TV, dependable hot showers, and safe-deposit boxes (a rarity here). They're on the small side but have all you need, including decent beds, ceiling fans, and low-slung chairs on the terrace outside the front door. The rooms are set far enough away to be free from any disturbance from the very popular beach club and restaurant, which closes at 6pm. Bus tour groups sometimes stop here after visiting the ruins, but there's plenty of space for all. To reach the hotel, turn left at the T-intersection by the beach; most hotels and restaurants are located to the right. There's also a gorgeous adjacent hacienda for rent.

Carretera Tulum–Boca Paila 500 meters south of Tulum ruins. www.elparaisohoteltulum.com. ✆ **310/295-9491** in the U.S., or 984/113-7089. 11 units. High season $188 double; low season $110 double. No credit cards. Sand parking lot. **Amenities:** Free Wi-Fi.

**Posada Ecologico Dos Ceibas ★** Solar and wind power, dense native plant gardens, minimal electricity, and other green practices make this small spot worthy of the eco designation (unlike many others that are eco in name only). Of course, those benefits are also drawbacks depending on your tolerance for heat. The rooms do have electricity, but it's very unreliable and fans tend to stop unexpectedly. There are no in-room outlets, but you can charge your toys in the restaurants. That said, this place harkens back to the old camping-on-the-beach days. Blue, yellow, and pink bungalows are rustic but have private bathrooms and hammocks on porches or terraces. Ocean-facing rooms are best for views and breezes; rooms toward the back of the property in the gardens can be sweltering in summer. Rates are high for what you get, though rustic simplicity away from the busier parts of the beach has its benefits.

Carretera Tulum–Boca Paila Km 10. www.dosceibas.com. ✆ **984/877-6024.** 13 units. High season $135 and up double; low season $95 and up double. **Amenities:** Restaurant; free Wi-Fi (in restaurant).

### Inexpensive

**Don Diego de la Selva ★★** The lush gardens at this small hideaway provide privacy for the rooms, all with hammocks on terraces, orthopedic mattresses, skylights, and toiletries made by a local collective. The French owners pay close attention to their guests, wandering through the dining rooms during meals, including the full breakfast included in the rate. The pool wasn't clear when I was there, but I'm told it normally is. The beach is about a 5-minute drive away, but the comforts here—air-conditioning, 24-hour electricity, powerful showers, hairdryers—outweigh the lack of sea view. The owners raise *meliponia* (stingless) bees at the far end of the property to provide honey for local collectives. The honey is used in bath products and bottled for use in its natural state—the shampoo is fabulous.

Av. Tulum, Mza. 24 Lote 3 (1km/⅔ mile south of ADO bus station). www.dondiegodelaselva.com. ✆ **984/114-9744.** 13 units. High and low season $105 double with A/C; $85 double with fan. Rates include breakfast. Small parking lot. **Amenities:** Restaurant; bar; shared fridge; pool; free Wi-Fi.

**Hotel La Mariposa Tulum ★** I discovered this back street hotel when I'd neglected to book a room in advance in Tulum, and hit upon the best bargain I've found in this area. A tall beige tower with a blue butterfly *(mariposa)* serves as a landmark as you wind through a couple of back streets off Avenida Tulum at the south end of town; the cheery restaurant in front implies you've found a hidden treasure. The seven "apartment" rooms have full kitchens, dining areas, and a backyard patio or balcony; regular rooms have small fridges, and all have somewhat noisy air-conditioning. You can't call the decor boring; my room had bright fuchsia walls and a bright flora shower curtain straight out of the '60s. Others have pretty stenciled flowers and butterflies over the bed, and bright Mexican textiles prevail. Best of all, the family owners are absolutely delightful. Rates are typically less than those listed below and there's usually a website discount. I paid $50 for a double room and decided to skip the pricey beach hotels for the rest of my stay.

Calle Mercurio Poniente. www.hotellamariposatulum.com. ✆ **984/802-5304.** 11 units. High season $75 double; low season $62 double. Rates include hot breakfast. No credit cards. Limited covered parking. **Amenities:** Free Wi-Fi.

**Posada Luna del Sur ★★** You may decide to come back for a week or more after realizing why so many guests return to this comfortable, efficient, and inexpensive little gem. I stayed there a few years back when the owners were still in the building stage, and was pleased to see they'd considered all the important details. All rooms

## cultural **IMMERSION**

Cultural tours in the Riviera Maya have long concentrated on established archeological sites and visits to Maya communities that have been groomed and amplified to provide education and entertainment for groups. An organization formed in 2014 aims to expand that focus. Several Maya communities of the area, with help from government and private investment, have created a program called **Maya Ka'an.** Emphasizing culture, eco-tourism, and sustainable projects in Maya communities, Maya Ka'an encompasses tours to small villages, colonial towns, and untrammeled archaeological sites where local guides provide insight into daily life. Punta Allen and Sian Ka'an are included in project, and tours include bird watching, kayaking, traditional medicine, history, and a creepy cave where snakes hang from crevices to hunt bats. The companies running Maya Ka'an's tours include small *cooperativas* where some members are trained as licensed guides while others are learning how to interact with foreign visitors and share their knowledge about everything from the use of indigenous plants to cooking in *pibs* (wood-burning ovens) and raising stingless bees to produce honey. Natural products are sometimes sold to guests—the honey shampoo is amazing. For more information go to www.mayakaan.travel.



have a five-gallon jug of purified water, small fridges, coffeemakers with Mexican coffee, kitchen sink, silverware, and dishes. What more could you need? How about one or two comfy beds, a balcony or patio, your own water heater for dependable showers, and quiet air-conditioning? Breakfast is served on the spacious rooftop patio during high season, and guests gather here throughout the day to lounge, exchange books, and use the unreliable Wi-Fi (there's none in the rooms). The beach is a 10-minute drive away and there are plenty of markets, restaurants, and shops in easy walking distance. Book far in advance here. There's a 3-night minimum year-round and a 5-night minimum on holidays. Exceptions are made if rooms are available. Reservations are guaranteed with full payment via PayPal.

Calle Luna Sur 5. www.posadalunadelsur.com. ✆ **984/871-2984.** 12 units. High season $120–$150 double; low season $80 double. High-season rates include hot breakfast. Limited covered parking. No children 15 and under. **Amenities:** Rooftop dining area; free Wi-Fi in common areas.

## Where to Eat

Tulum's dining scene is surprisingly sophisticated, given its laid-back beach vibe. The variety is best in town, where classy restaurants, rowdy bars, and bare-bones taco stands crowd together along Avenida Tulum and side streets. Many beach hotels have great food as well, though the prices are sometimes appallingly high. Several markets and grocery stores provide do-it-yourself supplies.

**Cetli** ★★★ MEXICAN Some of the finest gourmet Mexican cuisine on the coast is served in this beautiful house on a back street in town that feels like a lovingly decorated family gathering spot. Chef Claudia Pérez Rívas has devoted her considerable talents to preparing *alta cocina mexicana* (gourmet Mexican cuisine) completely from scratch, down to grinding spices and herbs in stone *metates.* She enjoys educating diners, explaining traditional Mexican cuisine and presenting a sampling of the night's moles and other sauces. Waiters begin your meal by bringing a complimentary plate of appetizers, including empanadas and Mexican cheeses, as you study the menu. Traditional dishes include *chiles en nogada* (a chile stuffed with meats, raisins, and spices and topped with a white sauce and pomegranate seeds), considered Mexico's national dish and traditionally served during August and September, around Independence Day. Pérez specializes in moles (sauces with multitudinous ingredients) and it would be a shame to not share at least one such dish. Her grilled shrimp atop a bed of *huitlacoche* (a savory corn mushroom) is also outstanding.

Calle Polar Poniente at Calle Orion Norte. ✆ **984/108-0681.** Main courses 260–300 pesos. No credit cards. Thurs–Tues 5–10pm.

**El Asadero ★★** STEAKHOUSE When all that exercise and partying leave you craving serious protein, wander down a side street to this casual carnivore's delight. It's not fancy or trendy, but the decor is consistently improving as the restaurant's fame grows. Simple wooden tables line the sidewalk and inside the warm dining area. But the food—oh my. I've been known to eagerly consume a large *arrachera,* or marinated flank steak, covered with grilled onions and chiles, plus a baked potato and salad with little conversation between bites. Rib-eye, T-bone, and New York steaks are grilled beside the front door, along with a yummy, spicy chorizo. Those with smaller appetites can order several tacos stuffed with various meats, cheeses, or *nopales* (cactus). Try to restrain yourself from nibbling too many fresh chips with the four complimentary salsas before your meal arrives. Not a meat eater? No problem. There are baked potatoes stuffed with just about anything on the menu, a yummy *queso fundido* (melted cheese with warm tortillas), and fish selections.

Av. Satelite Norte btw. Sagitario and 2 Poniente. ✆ **984/128-6258.** Main courses 120–245 pesos. No credit cards. Mon–Sat 5–11pm.

**El Camello ★★** SEAFOOD Long lines are a common sight outside this busy *marisquería* serving the freshest possible seafood prepared by the best cooks in town. Fishermen deliver their catch to the fish market next door to supply the busy kitchen as diners hover over tables about to be vacated and fans stand in line for takeout orders. Once you're settled at a plastic table, study the menu carefully and be ready to order when the server appears—there's no time for dilly-dallying here. The simple tomato, onion, cilantro, chile, and lime ceviche is just about the best I've ever had and the smallest order is large enough to feed at least two hungry eaters. You also need at least two people to eat the whole fried fish with beans and rice; order the fish filet with garlic for a lighter meal. The cooks know their way around *pulpo* (octopus). I've tried just about every preparation and have loved them all. Try not to gorge on the

### Getting to the Beach

If you're staying elsewhere but want excellent, uncrowded beach time in Tulum, the easiest way is to drive to Playa Paraíso, fronting the small hotel fittingly named El Paraíso (see p. 194; www.elparaisohoteltulum.com; ✆ **984/113-7089**), about 1km (⅔ miles) south of the ruins (take a left at the T-junction). This is a great place with a long, broad beach that is pure sand, and access is free. The owners of the small hotel El Paraíso have a restaurant on the sand and make money by selling food and drinks, so they ask you not to bring your own. For true isolation, check out the small hotels in Sian Ka'an and Punta Allen.

### FINDING solitude AMID MAYA HISTORY

I'm always grateful for my early adventures in Tulum, when I climbed the overgrown Castillo and explored crumbling temples nearly alone. But that was in the 1980s, before the region became a wildly popular tourism destination and crowds descended on natural and cultural treasures. These days, when I want to feel the spirit of the ancient Maya, I drive about 15km (9 miles) south of Tulum on Highway 307 to a sign pointing the way to **Muyil.** I've yet to see a tour bus in the dirt parking lot here, though I suppose that could change soon. Meanwhile, the thrill of wandering dirt trails through thick undergrowth to groups of structures as butterflies flutter about is unbeatable. Muyil, also called Chunyaxche, was settled around 300 B.C. and partially excavated in the 1990s and is the largest archaeological site in Sian Ka'an; at 57 feet high, its Castillo is the tallest structure on the east coast. Some original blue and red paint remains on the wood lintel atop the Castillo, which visitors are still allowed to climb. A broad white *sacbé* (rock road) leads to a huge freshwater lagoon, suggesting the site was both a ceremonial and commercial center on the route to the coast. Though wandering alone here is delightful, you'll get a better understanding of the site on a tour with Community Tours Sian Ka'an (p. 206).

fresh chips and pico de gallo even though they're amazing. Prices for food and beers are impressively low. Though you might be tempted to linger, have pity on the folks in line.

Av. Zamná. btw. Kukulcán and Palenque. No phone. Main courses 80–120 pesos. No credit cards. Thurs–Tues 11am–9pm (6pm on Sun).

**Posada Margherita ★★** ITALIAN It might seem like Italian restaurants outnumber Mexican in Tulum; there's no shortage of fair to good pizza and pasta parlors. This beachside favorite is the real thing, however. The pasta is prepared fresh daily, as are the sauces, and the chef manages to get the absolute finest ingredients. Your taste buds will tingle the minute you start nibbling from the antipasto platter and remain happy though platters of lobster or shrimp pasta, snapper poached in saltwater, even the simplest primavera with fresh tomatoes and basil. The mojitos are darn good as well, and there's a fine wine list. The setting couldn't be better, beside Tulum's famed powdery white sand and crystal blue water. Go for dinner before sunset, as the lighting is low.

Carretera Punta Allen Km 4.5 on the beach. ✆ **984/801-8493.** Main courses $10–$15. No credit cards. Daily 7am–10pm.

## Shopping

Unlike the other major Riviera Maya destinations, Tulum has yet to be overrun by big box chains. Instead, Avenida Tulum (also known as Highway 307) running through the center of town is lined with small *tiendas* (stores) and open-air markets selling fresh fruits, vegetables, and herbs along with canned goods, juices, and whatever the proprietor feels is important. Shopping at these small family-owned spots is a great way to support the local community. Most places, even the more established shops, lack exact addresses or phone numbers, but Tulum is small enough that you'll easily find those recommended here. Small shops specialize in hardware, plastic goods, or shoes, and alcohol outlets abound. The long-time grocery store **San Francisco de Asís** at the intersection of Avenida Tulum and the road to Cobá stocks the staple food and household items, along with insect repellant, coolers, a few beachwear items, and beach towels. You never know what you'll find here—I even came across a tiny electric one-cup coffeemaker when I was desperately seeking a way to prepare instant coffee in my room. A large **Chedraui** supermarket opened on the road to Tulum beach in 2014 and carries just about anything you might need, but it lacks that local touch.

Several crafts markets display endless arrays of *pareos* (sarongs), T-shirts, Maya-themed statues, blankets, seashell trinkets, and all sorts of cheap souvenirs; I've found a better selection at the ones along Avenida Tulum than those at the beach and ruins. The finest folk art shop I've found is **Mixik,** with branches across from the Zamas hotel at the beach and on Avenida Tulum near Calle Jupiter. I always find something irresistible here, from whimsical coconut masks to organic lotions and original silver jewelry. **MexicArte** on Avenida Tulum at Calle Osiris also carries a good selection of handcrafted folk art along with manufactured items. **Art Gallery Miniature** on Calle Polar Oriente displays gorgeous ceramic bowls, plates, and other wares created by artists in San Miguel de Allende and Guanajuato. Many hotels allow vendors to sell their wares on property—I've collected sweet embroidered woolen animals from Chiapas and honey-based shampoos from local Maya communities during hotel stays.

## Exploring In & Around Tulum

The main attractions in this area are Tulum's archaeological site and the biosphere reserve at Sian Ka'an, but there are enough other diversions to keep you busy for a week or more.

### EXPLORING THE TULUM RUINS

Thirteen kilometers (8 miles) south of Xel-Ha are the ruins of Tulum, a Maya fortress-city on a cliff above the sea. By A.D. 900, the end of the Classic period, Maya civilization had begun its decline and the large cities to the south were abandoned. Tulum is one of the small city-states that rose to fill the void. It came to prominence in the 13th century as a seaport, controlling maritime commerce along this section of the coast, and remained inhabited well after the arrival of the Spanish. The primary god here was the diving god, depicted on several buildings as an upside-down figure above doorways. Seen at the Palace at Sayil and Cobá, this curious, almost comical figure is also known as the bee god.

The most imposing building in Tulum is a large stone structure above the cliff called **El Castillo** (the castle). A temple as well as a fortress, it was once covered with stucco and paint. In front of the Castillo are several unrestored palace-like buildings partially covered with stucco. Tourists swim and sunbathe on the **beach** below, where the Maya once came ashore.

The **Temple of the Frescoes,** directly in front of the Castillo, contains interesting 13th-century wall paintings, though entrance is no longer permitted. Distinctly Maya, they represent Chaac, the rain god; and Ixchel, goddess of weaving, women, the moon, and medicine. The cornice of this temple has a relief of Chaac's head; from a slight distance, you can make out the eyes, nose, mouth, and chin. Notice the remains of the red-painted stucco—at one time all of Tulum's buildings were painted bright red.

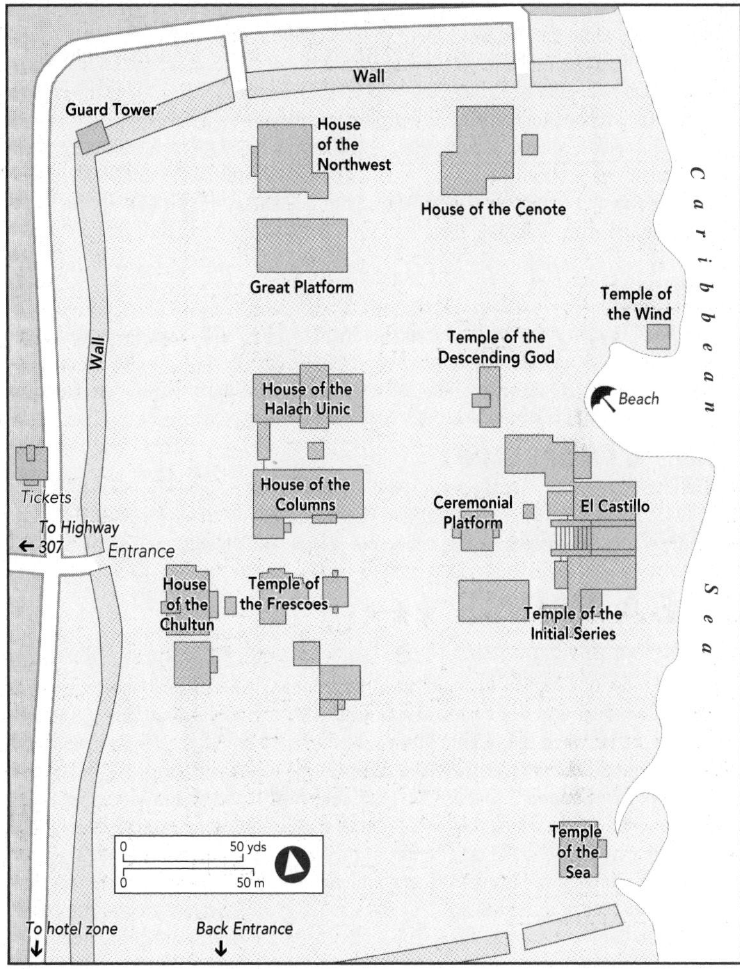


Much of what we know of Tulum at the time of the Spanish Conquest comes from the writings of Diego de Landa, third bishop of the Yucatán. He wrote that Tulum was a small city inhabited by about 600 people who lived in platform dwellings along a street and supervised the trade traffic from Honduras to the Yucatán. Though it was a walled city, most inhabitants probably lived outside the walls, leaving the interior for the ceremonial structures and residences of governors and priests. Tulum survived for about 70 years after the conquest before finally being abandoned.

Because of the great number of visitors this site receives, it is no longer possible to climb many of the ruins (and you should aim to beat the crowds, which arrive around 10am). In some cases, visitors are asked to remain behind roped-off areas. Licensed guides at the stand next to the path to the ruins charge 200 pesos for a 45-minute tour in English, French, or Spanish for up to four people. In some ways, they are performers who will tailor their presentation to the responses they get from you. There's a beautiful small cove below the Castillo, where visitors cool off after trekking in the hot sun. There are no facilities at the beach, however; restrooms are located by the entrance to the ruins. The main entrance compound and parking lots are located about a 5-minute walk from the archaeological site. An open-air tram shuttles visitors between the two. You'll find artisans' stands, a bookstore, a museum, a restaurant, several large bathrooms, and a ticket booth here, and there are often performances by Voladores de Papantla, elaborately costumed men who climb a 900-foot-high pole, attach themselves to the top with a binding, then twirl upside down to the ground.

Admission 59 pesos; shuttle 15 pesos; parking 50 pesos. Winter daily 8am–5pm, summer 8am–6pm.

### ECO-TOURS

**Mexico Kan Tours** (www.mexicokantours.com; ✆ **984/140-7870**), at Avenida Tulum between Orion Sur and Centauro Sur, uses local guides for tours to the Maya community of Punta Laguna near Cobá, inland *cenotes,* and the archaeological site of Muyil. They also run boat tours through Sian Ka'an's Maya canals.

### DIVING & SNORKELING

**MexiDivers** (www.mexidivers.com; ✆ **984/807-8805**) at the Zamas Hotel on the beach offers two-tank ocean dives for $100 and ocean snorkeling tours for $40. Two-tank cenote dives start at $90. Dive certification classes are available, as are fishing trips.

# COBÁ RUINS ★★★

168km (104 miles) SW of Cancún

Older than most of Chichén Itzá and much larger than Tulum, Cobá was the eastern Yucatán's dominant city before A.D. 1000. The site is widely spread out, with thick forest growing between the temple groups. Rising high above the forest canopy are tall, steep pyramids of the Classic Maya style. Of the major sites, this one is the least reconstructed, with mounds that are likely structures still covered in vines and roots. Left in the condition in which they were found, most of the stone sculptures are worn down and impossible to make out, but the structures themselves, the surrounding jungle, and the twin lakes are impressive and enjoyable. The forest canopy is higher than in the northern part of the peninsula, and the town of Cobá is much like those in Yucatán's interior.

Cobá is my favorite easy escape from the action on the coast. Spending a night here gives you a chance to roam through the archaeological site in early morning when birds chatter, butterflies hover over flowers, and trees shade solitary trails. In the evening, you can easily spot turtles and crocodiles in the lake and graceful white egrets fishing for their dinners. Locals walk along the lakeside and gather outside their simple homes, chatting and watching children run about. I often wish I could spend several nights in this peaceful enclave.

## Essentials

### GETTING THERE & DEPARTING

**BY CAR** The road to Cobá begins in Tulum and continues for 65km (40 miles). Watch out for *topes* (speed bumps) and potholes. The road is wide and well paved and should be in good condition. More restaurants and artisan stands pop up each year;

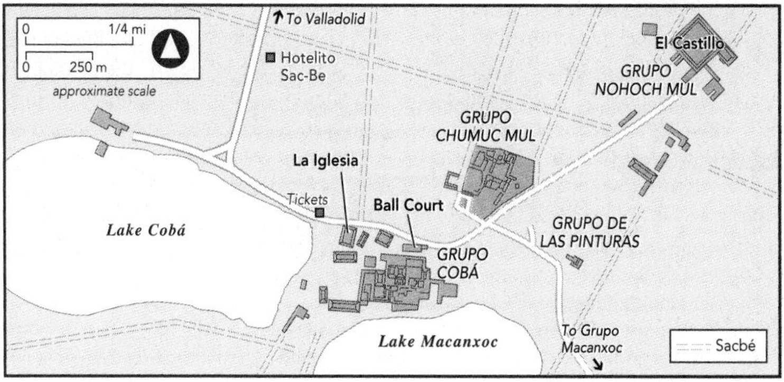

0 1/4 mi
0 250 m
approximate scale
To Valladolid
Hotelito Sac-Be
El Castillo
GRUPO NOHOCH MUL
GRUPO CHUMUC MUL
La Iglesia
Tickets
Ball Court
Lake Cobá
GRUPO DE LAS PINTURAS
GRUPO COBÁ
Lake Macanxoc
To Grupo Macanxoc
Sacbé

most have a sweet, local feel and you can tell you're supporting the communities—just stay away from any with large buses parked in front. There are also several popular *cenotes* (Gran Cenote and Carwash have facilities) along this road, and small villages where locals ride *triciclos* (three-wheeled bikes) and hack away at roadside vegetation with machetes. Close to the village of Cobá, you will come to a triangle; be sure to follow the road to Cobá and not Nuevo Xcan or Valladolid. The entrance to the ruins is a short distance down the road past some small restaurants and the large lake.

**BY BUS** Several buses a day leave Tulum and Playa del Carmen for Cobá. Several companies offer bus tours.

## Exploring the Cobá Ruins

The Maya built many intriguing cities in the Yucatán, but few as grand as Cobá ("water stirred by wind"). Much of the 67-sq.-km (26-sq.-mile) site remains unexcavated. Scholars believe Cobá was an important trade link between the Caribbean coast and inland cities. A 100km (62-mile) *sacbé* (raised road) through the jungle linked it to Yaxuná, once an important Maya center 50km (31 miles) south of Chichén Itzá. This is the Maya's longest-known *sacbé,* and at least 50 shorter ones lead from here. An important city-state, Cobá flourished from A.D. 632 (the oldest carved date found here) until after the rise of Chichén Itzá, around 800. Then Cobá faded in importance and population until it was finally abandoned.

Once at the site, keep your bearings—you can get turned around in the maze of dirt roads in the jungle. Branching off from every labeled path, you'll see unofficial narrow paths into the jungle, used as shortcuts by locals. These are good for birding, but be careful to remember the way back.

The **Grupo Cobá** holds an impressive pyramid, **La Iglesia (the Church).** Take the path bearing right after the entrance. Resist the urge to climb the temple; the view is better from El Castillo in the Nohoch Mul group farther back.

Return to the main path and turn right, passing a sign pointing to the restored **juego de pelota (ball court).** Continuing for 5 to 10 minutes, you'll come to a fork in the road, where you'll notice jungle-covered, unexcavated pyramids to the left and right. At one point, a raised portion of the *sacbé* to Yaxuná is visible as it crosses the

## A day in the life OF A MAYA VILLAGE

In the tropical forest near Cobá, a village of 27 families exists much as their long-ago ancestors did, living in round thatch huts with no electricity, indoor plumbing, or paved roads, gathering plants in the jungle for medicinal and other uses on their way to dip into a hidden *cenote,* appealing to the gods for successful crops. And every day, the people of Pac Chen open their homes to as many as 80 tourists who want to know what Maya village life is in the 21st century.

The only way to visit Pac Chen is on trips with **Alltournative** (www.alltournative.com; ✆ **877/437-4990** in the U.S., or 984/803-9999), an eco-tour company that works with villagers to help them become self-sustaining. Farming continues, but tourism income allows them to survive without burning their land to squeeze out the last remaining nutrients.

The arrangement is a boon to tourists, too. On your own, it would be pretty well impossible to walk into a Maya village and be ushered through the jungle and lowered into a *cenote* or to glide through the forest canopy on a zip line, kayak a lagoon full of birds, eat lunch cooked by village women, and receive a copal-incense blessing from a village elder for a safe trip home. The Maya Encounter tour costs $139 for adults and $109 for children.

pathway. Throughout the area, carved stelae stand by pathways or lie forlornly in the underbrush. Although protected by crude thatched roofs, most are weatherworn enough to be indiscernible.

The left fork leads to the **Grupo Nohoch Mul,** which contains **El Castillo.** Except for Structure 2 in Calakmul, this is the tallest pyramid in the Yucatán, outreaching El Castillo at Chichén Itzá and the Pyramid of the Magician at Uxmal. From the top, you can see unexcavated, jungle-cloaked pyramids poking through the forest canopy all around.

The right fork (more or less straight on) goes to the **Conjunto Las Pinturas,** whose main attraction is the **Pyramid of the Painted Lintel,** a small structure with traces of its original bright colors above the door. You can climb up for a close look. Visit Cobá in the morning or after the heat of the day has passed. Mosquito repellent, drinking water, and comfortable shoes are imperative. Distances between sites are significant and it seems like it's always steamy and sweltering. It's far easier to explore with wheels. Bicycles are available for rent for 40 pesos per hour at a stand just past the entrance. You can also hire a *triciclo* with driver to carry you around the site; rates start at 120 pesos. It's a great way to get around, and you're helping support locals in an area with few employment opportunities. Clever *triciclo* drivers also park at Nohuch Mul to carry hot, tired passengers back to the entrance.

Admission is 59 pesos, free for children younger than 12. Parking is 50 pesos. Open daily 8am to 5pm.

## Where to Stay & Eat

Cobá offers a few hotels, restaurants, and markets, and food choices at stands near the entrance when the archaeological site is open are limited. Prices are refreshingly realistic, and you'll find lots of places with cold drinks along with a newish, clean building with toilets. Unfortunately, my absolute favorite place to stay—the enchanting Villas Arqueológicas—has closed, but I'm hoping someone has the good sense to reopen it.

A few truly rustic hostelries offer hard mattresses and cold-water showers for budget travelers, and a couple of hotels are on the road to Tulum. Making reservations is difficult, as phone and Internet service is spotty, but it's a good idea to give it a shot during high season.

**Hotelito Sac-Be ★** This small, simple hotel on the main road in the small town by the ruins is your best choice for comfortable accommodations. Rooms are blessedly air-conditioned—a major plus right there—and are immaculately clean, with tiled floors, thin mattresses, and good screens on the windows. The second-story restaurant is the best in town and fills up with day-trippers at lunch. A small shop carries basic toiletries, sunscreen, and bug repellant. It's hard to find places where you feel like you're staying in an authentic small village in the Riviera Maya. If you prefer that sort of experience, consider using this as your base for exploring the coast and Chichén Itzá.
On the road through town. www.hotelsacbe.com. ✆ **984/144-3006.** 9 units. $23–$50 double. No credit cards. Parking lot. **Amenities:** Restaurant; free Wi-Fi in restaurant.

# SIAN KA'AN & THE PUNTA ALLEN PENINSULA ★★★

Just past Tulum's last cabaña hotel is the entrance arch to the vast (526,000-hectare/1.3-million-acre) **Sian Ka'an Biosphere Reserve.** This inexpressibly beautiful tract of wild land is the domain of howler monkeys, ocelots, crocodiles, jaguars, tapirs, sea turtles, and thousands of species of plants. The Mexican government created this reserve in 1986; the following year, the United Nations declared it a World Heritage Site. Sian Ka'an protects 10% of Quintana Roo's landmass, including almost one-third of the Caribbean coastline, from development. Another 319,000 hectares (788,300 acres) of land was added to the reserve in 2010.

The entrance to the Punta Allen Peninsula, a small portion of the reserve, is one of two main entrances to the reserve; the other is from the community of Muyil off Highway 307 south of Tulum, where you take a boat down canals built by the Maya to the Boca Paila lagoon.

Legends still swirl about the 4 hours it takes to drive the 50km (31 miles) over potholes, ruts, and rivulets to the town of Punta Allen at road's end. In fact, the road has been much improved, though it is still dirt, still pockmarked to varying degrees, and subject to weather-related conditions. During the spring of 2014, I made it all the way in 1½ hours, including a few photo stops. Earlier that year, however, heavy rains closed the road completely. Ask several locals about the road conditions, and give yourself plenty of time no matter what they say. It can be tempting to drive as fast as the locals in the four-wheel drive vehicles that leave you in a cloud of dust, but they know where the next patch of deep ruts is located. Take your time and enjoy the scenery. If you plan on reaching Punta Allen on a day trip, head out early and return way before dark—it's nearly impossible to see once the sun sets. Bring more water than you think you could possibly need and pesos in small denominations, and make sure you have plenty of gas and oil. If you don't fancy yourself a road warrior, you can drive through the entrance arch in Tulum (entry 25 pesos per person) and continue south about 4km (2½ miles) to where a beach comes into view, pull over, and spread out your beach towel.

The entry fee at the guard station is 56 pesos.

## The Punta Allen Peninsula

As you drive the skinny peninsula that separates the Boca Paila Lagoon from the sea, you'll find no trails leading into the jungle, and much of the coastal side of the road is fenced off. But you can swim or snorkel off the beaches that come into view. Guided tours are the only way to see most of the reserve. Otherwise, there is no practical way to visit Sian Ka'an except by car.

### THE SIAN KA'AN BIOSPHERE RESERVE ★★★

Maya life in ancient times remains essentially a mystery, but there's no wondering why they named this land Sian Ka'an (See-*an* Caan), Maya for "where the sky is born." Sunrise here truly is like witnessing the birth of a day.

The reserve encompasses most of the ecosystems that exist on the entire Yucatán Peninsula: medium- and low-growth jungles, beaches, savannas, marshes, freshwater and brackish lagoons, *cenotes,* underground rivers, and untouched coral reef. Numerous archaeological sites have also been found within its borders.

More than 2,000 people, most of them Maya, live in Sian Ka'an. Most are original residents of the area, or their descendants. Tours to the reserve are often led by locals who grew up nearby in homes occupied for countless generations. They'll almost never consult a field guide; their knowledge about the birds, the plants, the water, and the ruins is simply a part of their lives.

To access the reserve beyond the road, arrange for a tour in Tulum. Two organizations in particular keep their groups small and work only through the local people.

The **Centro Ecológico Sian Ka'an,** or CESiaK, with an office on Highway 307 just south of Tulum ruins turnoff (www.cesiak.org; ✆ **984/871-2499**), is a nonprofit group supporting the reserve with education and community development programs. Its popular all-day canal tour ($78 per person, including lunch and tax) includes a guided walk through coastal dunes and jungle and a boat trip across two brackish lagoons where freshwater *cenotes* well up from under the ground. Boats follow a narrow channel through mangroves to a small temple where Maya traders stopped to make offerings and ask for successful negotiations. You'll don life jackets and float part of the way in the currents of a freshwater lagoon and snorkel in a *cenote* before the day is over. Other tours include a sunset bird-watching trip and single- and multiday fly-fishing packages. Tours depart from the CESiaK center at the Boca Paila Camps, 4km (2½ miles) south of the reserve entrance.

**Community Tours Sian Ka'an,** Avenida Tulum between calles Centauro and Orión (www.siankaantours.org; ✆ **984/871-2202**), is a local cooperative that runs snorkeling, birding, and adventure tours into the biosphere. The guides run their tours out of the downtown office and an eco-oriented visitor center near Muyil. Their "Forest and Float" canal tour ($99 per adult, $70 child) begins with an in-depth tour of the Muyil archaeological site, followed by a jungle walk to the edge of a lagoon where snacks are served while guests visit rustic restrooms. Guests then board small boats for an amazing ride through a crystalline lagoon toward canals carved from the landscape by the Maya. After visiting the small ruin, guests don life jackets and float with the current along the canals to a platform where they reboard the boats and head back. The tour ends with lunch at the visitor center, where members of the community are available to chat about their way of life and traditions. Transportation is available from Riviera Maya hotels for an extra charge.

## ANATOMY OF A biosphere RESERVE

Unlike its national parks, which focus on historical and aesthetic features, Mexico's biosphere reserves were created purely to protect its last natural ecosystems. Recognition by UNESCO (United Nations Educational, Scientific, and Cultural Organization) requires that the biosphere contain at least 10,000 hectares (about 39 sq. miles), at least one pristine area of biological diversity, and threatened or endangered endemic species.

Mexico pioneered the zoning system that allows some carefully managed tourism. The core area—the heart of the reserve—is limited to scientific research and is surrounded by a buffer zone that allows only conservation-related activity. On the periphery, a transition zone permits sustainable use of natural resources to benefit local communities, as **CESiaK's tours** (p. 206) do. Biosphere reserves allow original residents to remain; local people, in fact, are recruited to research, monitor, and manage the ecosystem while developing sustainable activities such as eco-tourism. As time has gone by, however, some locals are selling their property to outsiders intent on building fancy homes. Environmentalists are concerned that construction alone, never mind increasing population, will drive away the creatures that rely on these protection regions. The non-profit organization Amigos de Sian Ka'an (www.amigosdesiankaan.org) was founded in 1986 to monitor and protect the reserve and relies on corporate and private donations for their work.

### THE ROAD TO PUNTA ALLEN

About 11km (6¾ miles) past the arch, you'll come to the **Boca Paila Fishing Lodge** (www.bocapaila.com; ✆ **998/185-3570**). Not for the general traveler, it specializes in weeklong, all-inclusive packages for fly-fishers. The peninsula is so narrow here that you see the Boca Paila lagoon on one side and the sea on the other. In another 3km (1¾ miles), you will be flooded by false hope when you reach a smooth, concrete roadway—this is the foot of the Boca Paila Bridge, which spans the inlet between the ocean and the lagoon, and the pavement disappears as quickly as it appeared. You'll often see people fishing off the sides. This is a good place to stop and stretch your legs while taking in ethereal water views from either side.

After the bridge, it's mostly deserted coastline until you get to Punta Allen. Your only companions will be enormous lizards sunning in the road and the occasional bored mutt.

## Punta Allen

Punta Allen, the peninsula's only town, is a lobster fishing village on a palm-studded beach perched between Ascension Bay and the Caribbean Sea. About 100 families survive by lobster fishing and, increasingly, tourism; many of the young men now are expert fly-fishing guides.

Isolated and rustic, this is very much the end of the road. The town has a lobster cooperative, a few sand streets with modest homes, and a lighthouse. The generator, when it's working, comes on for a few hours in the morning and a few more at night. Your cellphone might work here, and there is Wi-Fi for a few hours each day. Without the help of a friendly local, it's a challenge to figure out when any of the businesses are open.

## SLEEPING WHERE THE sky IS BORN

To see the sun rise in Sian Ka'an as the Maya did, you can stay in CESiaK's **Boca Paila Camps ★★,** 4km (2½ miles) past the entrance arch. The eco-lodge's tent cabins are tucked into the edge of the jungle on a clean, white beach, raised on platforms to avoid interfering with the sand's natural processes. The sheets, towels, and solid wood furniture make it feel less like camping, but when night falls and you're stumbling around by flashlight, it feels plenty rustic. Guests share showers and scrupulously clean bathrooms, which have composting toilets. Tent cabins with one queen and ocean or lagoon views are $80 to $100. Meals are extra. The camp has no electricity—guests get battery-powered lamps—but wind and solar power provide hot water. Things do not always run perfectly smoothly: The restaurant, which is reasonably priced and turns out better meals than it has any right to in this remote location, sometimes runs out of ingredients for a popular menu item. The cabins need refurbishment; those in the jungle have rickety stairs to the tent platform. A few face the ocean and have fabulous views, but they can be uncomfortable if sand is blowing around. The rooftop lookout is the most popular spot at sunset, and the panorama of sea, sky, and endless wilderness is amazing. Bring along sunscreen, bug repellant, and a flashlight. The staff knows the reserve's plants, animals, and local culture backward and forward and leads fascinating tours through the canals.

Still, it's a great getaway for a night or two. On my last stay, I thoroughly enjoyed wandering along the beach under the stars for fresh ceviche, lobster, and cold beer at El Muelle Viejo, the best restaurant around, and heading down the for coffee and breakfast at Casa Ana—just about the only place with strong java in early morning. The sea here is languid and warm, and fishermen will take you out to the reef for snorkeling. During the winter season, you'll find kayaks for rent and guides who'll take you on hiking and bird-watching trips in the jungle. Fly-fishing enthusiasts flock here in winter, when permit, snook, and other fish gravitate to Ascension Bay just offshore. It's the kind of slow-paced, tight community that's hard to find these days, a place where families gather at the plaza near the sea in evenings after kids get home from school. Bring small denominations of pesos—credit cards are useless here, plus plenty of sunscreen, a flashlight, strong bug repellant (tiny sand fleas are brutal at sunset), and plenty of drinking water.

**Cuzan Guesthouse ★** Kind of worn-down and certainly rustic, this small place is one of the town's original fishing lodges. A few beach huts with palm thatch roofs sit right on the sand and have toilets and cold-water showers, and okay beds with mosquito netting. Hammocks swing beneath *palapas* on the beach—in warm weather, guests gravitate there through the night hoping for a breeze. There's a restaurant, full bar, and all-inclusive fishing packages.

Apdo. Postal 24, Felipe Carrillo Puerto. www.flyfishmx.com. ✆ **983/834-0358.** 12 units. $50–$110 cabañas. No credit cards.

**Rancho Sol Caribe ★★** It's hard to believe anyone could create such an idyllic setting so far from modern conveniences. But this gorgeous small hotel and gourmet restaurant is equal to, if not better than, any hotel in Tulum. The property's been around for more than 20 years but got a complete overhaul in 2011. It now has two cabañas on the sand and a small main building with three beachfront suites and two loft suites. Though I always enjoy sleeping right by the sea, I prefer the spacious loft suites with simple rattan and dark wood furnishings, wood-shuttered windows, double sinks in the bath, and a good overview from the balcony chairs. The restaurant is immensely popular with local business owners and foreigners; no place else serves lobster mousse with fresh pasta or Thai, Italian, and Argentinian specialties. Weddings are held in a thatch-roofed gazebo beside the sea, and the hotel sometimes hosts yoga retreats. The hotel is about a five-minute drive north of Punta Allen.

Careterra Tulum-Punta Allen Km 35. www.solcaribe-mexico.com. ✆ **984/139-3839.** 7 units. High season $145 and up double; low season $185 and up double. **Amenities:** Restaurant; bar; free Wi-Fi.

**Serenidad Shardon ★★** You can park your car for the length of your stay at this modest hideaway a 5-minute walk from town. If you're traveling with a group, the two-story, three-bedroom beach house is ideal. The lower level has a kitchen and private bath; the upper consists of a large dorm-style room for four with a separate entrance and bathroom outside the building. You can rent it all or just one floor. The cabaña on the sand with refrigerator and private bath is perfect for two, and the two-story cabaña across the sandy road sleeps four. There's also camping available on the jungle-like grounds. Electricity is available during certain hours, as is Wi-Fi at the main house, but there's no air-conditioning. Restaurants and stores are a quick walk away, and Serenidad's cheerful owner can set up tours and offer suggestions for wandering about.

Beach road south of town square. www.shardon.com. ✆ **616/827-0204** in the U.S., or 984/107-4155. 3 units. $150 cabaña; $250 house; $500 beach house ($375 lower floor only). No credit cards. No phone in room. **Amenities:** Free Wi-Fi for a few hours daily.

# THE COSTA MAYA

7

by Christine Delsol

Tourism has trickled to the quiet southern half of the Caribbean coast, known as the Costa Maya, or Gran Costa Maya when including Bacalar and the state capital of Chetumal. This peninsula, jutting out from the mainland, is tucked under the Sian Ka'an Biosphere Reserve. The idyllic landscape of low jungle, virgin mangrove wetlands, and long stretches of white-sand beach remained largely unnoticed—except by fly-fishers—while resorts gobbled up the beaches of Cancún and the Riviera Maya over the past few decades.

Lying 354km (220 miles) from Cancún's airport and more than 48km (30 miles) from the highway, the Costa Maya's beaches probably will never see Riviera Maya-scale development. But since Carnival Cruise Line built a port in Mahahual (originally but less frequently spelled Majahual) and began port calls there in 2002, increasing tourism has brought some changes to the area. Except for the nuisance factor Mahahual residents put up with on port days, most of those changes have been beneficial so far, including better, safer roads and more businesses where English is spoken.

## MAHAHUAL, XCALAK & THE CHINCHORRO REEF ★★★

Once a tiny fishing village—and still a fishing village even if not as tiny—Mahahual has grown into the unofficial capital of Costa Maya.

### Essentials

#### GETTING THERE

**BY CAR** The easiest and most flexible way to visit is by car. About 45 minutes' drive south of Felipe Carrillo Puerto, a few kilometers past the town of Limones at El Cafetal, is the clearly marked **Mahahual** turnoff. It's 56km (35 miles) on a good paved road to the coast. The turnoff for **Xcalak** to the south comes 2km (1¼ miles) before Mahahual; if you come to the Pemex station, you've passed it; turn around and take the first turn to the left. Xcalak is 55km (34 miles) to the south, less than an hour's drive. The **cruise port** turnoff is at a little traffic circle 3.8km (2⅓ miles) east of the Xcalak turnoff. Avenida Paseo del Puerto leads through new residential

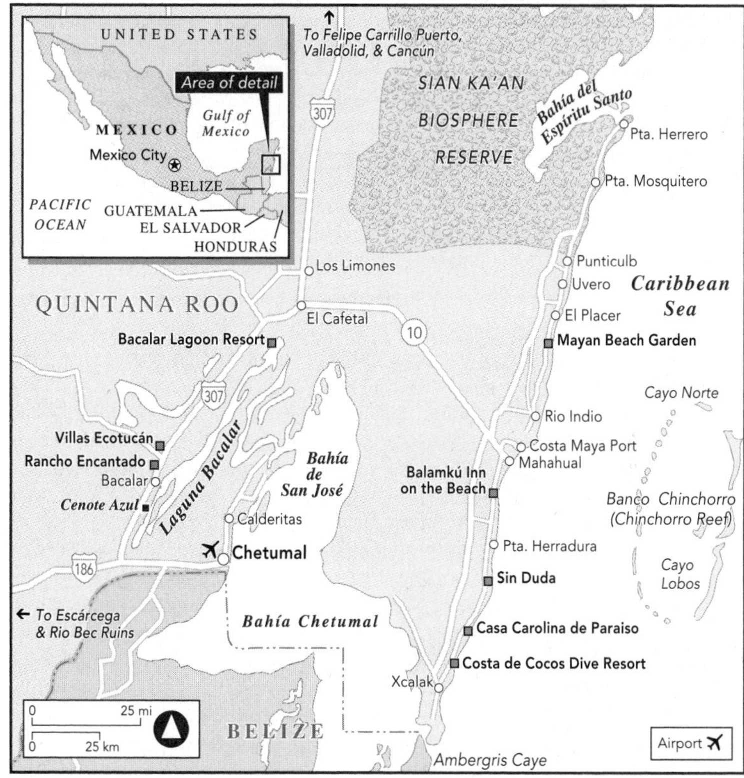


streets and jungle to the port itself, which accommodates up to three ships. Stay on the highway for another 700m (about ½ mile) to reach town, turning right just before the lighthouse.

**BY BUS** Bus service to Costa Maya is limited. **ADO** (www.ado.com.mx) has one bus from Cancún to Mahahual at 6:45am (370 pesos); from the airport, you need to take a bus to Playa del Carmen and transfer to Mahahual. **Sandals & Skis** (www.sandalsandskis.com) offers a shuttle from Cancún's airport on weekends for $70. **Caribe** buses run between Mahahual (at the cruise pier entrance, or flag it on its way through town) and Chetumal (across from the Maya museum) approximately every two hours from early morning to late afternoon, for 100 pesos.

## Mahahual

Since the cruise ship pier arrived, the port area has become a tourist zone unto itself, nicknamed *Nuevo Mahahual,* with a beach club, a shopping compound, tour companies offering dozens of excursions, and, yes, Señor Frog's and Hard Rock Cafe. A mini-city of markets, homes, and apartments has sprung up. Only a few years ago, the town wasn't much of a tourist draw. Though some cruise passengers who opted to

### Information, Please

Good, up-to-date information about the Costa Maya is still hard to come by. The official tourist site, **www.grandcostamaya.com**, is in Spanish, but downloadable brochures include English translations. The maps are useful, and destination overviews include interesting, little-known areas. Run by local businesses, **www.bacalarmosaico.com** isn't very well organized, but it has some good information about Bacalar and Chetumal for those willing to spend some time looking; it also has the only usable (if cluttered with business logos) street map of Bacalar I've found. For the latest goings-on, sign up for the detailed and gossipy newsletter from Mayan Beach Garden in Mahahual (p. 213); the inn's website also has lots of advice about exploring the region.

explore locally rather than take a packaged shore excursion might briefly swarm the town, it always returned to somnolence at night.

These days, it's a different story. Rising tourism income has led to numerous improvements and made a more cohesive community. Mahahual is coming into its own as a destination distinct from the cruise business; Mexican tourists come every weekend from as far away as Mérida, Veracruz, and Tabasco. Newer and better hotels and restaurants have arrived, and the **Yaya Beach** area south of the football field is developing into a trendy complex of small businesses with a New Age edge; you'll find restaurants with tables on the sand within steps of the water, an Italian gelateria, yoga classes, stand-up paddling, and massages on the beach. The best dive shop in town is also here: **Doctor Dive** (Av. Mahahual at Calle Coronado; www.doctordive.com; ✆ **983/834-5619** or 103-6013) offers the Costa Maya's only lionfish hunting tour ($75) and is always open, rain or shine, high season and low. One-tank dives are $55, two tanks $85, and snorkeling $25.

My favorite addition is the beautiful new *malecón* (seafront promenade) along the fine white beach, at its best around sunset. When a ship is in port, the walk is lined with watersports and tour vendors; otherwise it's mostly locals out to meet and greet and enjoy the beach. A 2-km (1¼-mile) extension south of the fishing pier was started in late 2014.

## ORIENTATION

The telephone area code is **983.**

Mahahual proper consists of three long, roughly parallel north-south streets linked by short side streets. Most hotels and services line the sand road running through town and south along the beach. You enter on Calle Huachinango (the middle road), which ends at Calle Mojarra near the south end of town. You can turn left to the beach road (called Calle Mahahual in addresses, but rarely in conversation) and continue south, or turn right to Calle Sardina, the westernmost road. Calle Sardina is one way leading back out of town, but at this point you can also take it south for a few blocks before it funnels you onto the beach road. You won't see many signs telling you what street you're on, but knowing the names will help when asking directions.

## WHERE TO STAY

Besides the hotels reviewed below, **Posada de los 40 Canones** (www.40canones.com; ✆ **983/834 5730;** high season $120–$140 double; low season $95–$110 double) is a longtime fixture on the beach that has held up well, while **El Hotelito** (www.elhotelitomahahual.com; ✆ **983/834-5702;** high season 900–1200 pesos; low season 750–1000 pesos), a block from the beach, is a clean, modern budget option with good beds and an extraordinarily friendly manager. Both are in town; if you want a secluded beach hideaway, opt for an inn on the beach road north or south of town.

**Balamkú Inn on the Beach ★★★** Owned by friendly Canadians with a commitment to environmentally sensitive use of resources, this collection of one- and two-story *palapa*-roof bungalows on the coast road south of town offers large, breezy, oceanview rooms with private terraces, on a sparkling white-sand beach. Louvered windows let you control the breeze coming in, mattresses are just right, and bathrooms are large. Sun and wind energy provide 24-hour power, eliminating the need for a generator, and rain meets the inn's water needs before being rerouted to nourish the wetlands—but the most impressive feat is a non-polluting composting waste system that allows guests to actually flush their toilet paper; in fact, the owners encourage it.

Carretera Costera Km 5.7. www.balamku.com. ✆ **045-983/732-1004** or 011-521/983-732-1004 (from North America). 10 units. High season $95 double; midseason $85; low season $80. Rates include full breakfast. No credit cards (except for deposits). **Amenities:** Restaurant (breakfast and lunch); bar (afternoons); kayaks and snorkeling gear; free Wi-Fi.

**El Caballo Blanco ★★** The only way to get to this hotel is to walk—it's that close to the water. All rooms are air-conditioned and have two comfy queen-size beds clad in luxury linens; one has an extra futon to sleep up to six. Showers have admirable water pressure. Each has a balcony overlooking the *malecón* and the Caribbean or, in ground rooms, a private terrace. Definitely get the balcony; you'll have a hard time pulling yourself away from the scene at your feet. The owner, a nurse, lives on-site and also owns the *farmacia* in the same building. The small but adequate rooftop pool has terrific views from the upper atmosphere of one of Mahahual's tallest buildings.

Calle Mahahual/beach road (btw. calles Martillo and Coronado). www.hotelelcaballoblanco.com. ✆ **983/834-5830** or 983/126-0319. 7 units. 1100–1300 pesos double. **Amenities:** Outdoor pool; bar; pharmacy; watersports gear; free Wi-Fi.

**Matan Ka'an ★** A block off the beach, this well-managed boutique hotel was designed by its former Italian owners but now belongs to the Ko'ox hotel group. At least in part because of the founders' whimsical design, room space and configuration are inconsistent; some are more spacious than you'd expect, others much less. Decor also varies, but all rooms feature Mexican crafts and artwork and are quite attractive. Beds may be too hard for some travelers, but they are scheduled to be replaced in 2015. Bottom line: It's clean and comfortable, and things just work.

Calle Huachinango at Calle Coronado. www.kooxhotels.com. ✆ **983/834-5679.** 25 units. High season 1022–1238 pesos; low season 937–1498 pesos. **Amenities:** Restaurant; cafeteria-bar; outdoor pool; beach club privileges; free Wi-Fi.

**Mayan Beach Garden Inn ★★★** To *really* get away from it all, without giving up a thing, head north to this off-the-grid B&B a 30-minute drive from town on a lovely stretch of soft beach. Large, well-furnished rooms have king-size pillow-top beds—two with splendid mosaic headboards—placed to take in the views. The friendly staff works hard to please, and the owners will show you every prime snorkeling spot and undiscovered Maya site in the area. The restaurant is terrific; try to catch the weekly tequila night (in high season). Four oceanview rooms and three beachfront cabañas (one suite sleeps four) have large covered decks with hammocks and lounges. Solar power runs lights, ceiling fans, and hot water around the clock, but most appliances work only when the backup generator runs, so ask for the schedule. Marcia, one of the owners, can direct you to the little-known southern entrance to the Sian Ka'an Biosphere reserve for an entirely different experience from Riviera Maya entry points.

Camino Costera Km 20.5. www.mayanbeachgarden.com. ✆ **983/132-2603.** 7 units. High season $96–$115 double, $125 suite; low season $76–$85 double, $92 suite. Rates include full breakfast; all-inclusive packages available. **Amenities:** Restaurant/bar; kayaks; snorkel and stand-up paddle gear rentals; kitchenettes (in some units); free Wi-Fi.



### WHERE TO EAT

Mahahual is well stocked with restaurants; most are okay but not memorable, and many keep erratic hours. Among the most reliable are friendly **Ibiza Sunset** (✆ **983/154-2293**) on the *malecón's* southern extension, with its eclectic menu of fresh local food (including good vegetarian options), good music, and great, reasonably priced drinks; and nearby **Luna de Plata** (www.lunadeplata.info; ✆ **983/125-3999**), in the hotel of the same name, with fresh pasta dishes. **Travel In'** (www.travel-in.com.mx; ✆ **983/110-9496**), a guest house at Km 5.8 (convenient to Balamkú) on the beach road south of town, makes fresh pita bread and daily appetizers, and also serves pizza, fish, meat, and vegetarian specialties. Another good choice is **Pizza Papi** (✆ **983/834-5642**), 4 blocks in from the highway's port entrance on Avenida Paseo del Puerto. Do stop in for a drink at **Fernando's 100% Agave** (✆ **983/134-1094**) on the *malecón*—not for the food, which is average, but for Fernando's masterful drinks; he's the tequila wizard who educates and entertains during Mayan Beach Garden's tequila nights.

## Xcalak

This tiny village is Quintana Roo's last stand, at the channel separating Mexico from Belize's Ambergris Caye; if you could see beyond the narrow spit and west across Chetumal Bay, you'd be looking at the Shipstern Nature Reserve on mainland Belize. **Xcalak** (Eesh-kah-*lahk*) is a former military outpost that had a population of about 1,200 before a hurricane washed most of the town away in 1958; only about 600 live there now. This idyllic settlement was virtually unknown outside of Mexico until fly-fishers discovered it in the 1980s; they still pull prizes out of the clear turquoise water. While Xcalak oozes shabby charm, the inns north of town are the stuff of dreams.

### WHERE TO STAY & EAT

You'll likely eat most of your meals wherever you stay, but don't miss the **Leaky Palapa ★★★** (www.leakypalaparestaurant.com; late Nov–May, Fri–Sun 5–10pm) in town. The two women who run the place do wonderful things with the best local ingredients available from day to day, taking their inspiration from Mexican, Caribbean coast, and a bit of Continental cuisine. The short but varied menu may change from day to day but generally ranges from 100 to 300 pesos, with most falling in the middle. Reservations recommended.

**Costa de Cocos** (below) also runs a full-service restaurant, open daily for breakfast, lunch, and dinner, serving traditional Mexican *botanas* (snacks), sandwiches and burgers, fresh seafood, and steaks. It's a great place for fish tacos or pizza. Breakfast ranges from $4 to $6, with most main courses $4.50 to $10; steak and lobster are $25 to $28. It opens at 7am daily and closes between 8:30 and 11pm, depending on the number of guests.

**Casa Carolina de Paraiso ★★★** Taken over by new owners in 2014, this sweet beachfront inn has lost none of its charm while gaining subtle updates, such as more

## DIVING THE chinchorro REEF

The **Chinchorro Reef Underwater National Park,** about 30km (19 miles) off this coastline, is by most accounts the largest coral atoll in the Northern Hemisphere, at 38km (24 miles) long by 13km (8 miles) wide. Its coral formations, massive sponges, and abundant sea life are certainly among the most spectacular. The oval reef is as shallow as 1m (3⅓ ft.) at its interior and as deep as 900m (2,953 ft.) at its exterior. It's invisible from the ocean side and has doomed scores of ships. Most of the 30 or so **shipwrecks** are protected by the Banco Chinchorro Biosphere. However, the reef offers at least a dozen other stellar dive sites. And most wrecks, including the famous **40 Cannons** on the northwest side, are shallow enough to be explored by snorkeling. The west side of the reef is a wonderland of walls and coral gardens.

Because of fickle sea conditions and the strict limit on diving permits, it can be a challenge to get to Banco Chinchorro. **XTC Dive Center** (www.xtcdivecenter.com; ✆ **983/839-8865**) in Xcalak specializes in Chinchorro trips—the company's name stands for "Xcalak to Chinchorro"—including expeditions to the largest known population of American crocodiles. XTC also offers other reef and *cenote* dives. **Costa de Cocos** (below) also has a dive center on site. Expect to pay about $60 for a one-tank dive, $70 to $90 for two; $28 to $40 for two to three hours of snorkeling, and $375 to $387 for PADI certification. This is one of the best places in Mexico to see **manatees.** Whether you're diving, snorkeling, or boating, one of the shy creatures often shows itself when you least expect it. Various species of **rays** are also abundant, sometimes feeding close to shore at dusk right below the balcony of your hotel.

flowers, stronger Wi-Fi in every room, and new paint in the *palapa* that serves as the inn's command center. A massage area and yoga sessions on the beach were in the planning stages at the end of 2014. Each unit has a fully equipped kitchen and beautifully tiled bathroom. Upstairs rooms have sliding glass doors opening onto balconies with expansive sea views.

Camino de la Costera (2.4km/1½ miles from bridge at north end of town). www.casacarolina.net. ✆ **678/630-7080.** 4 units. Rates include expanded Continental breakfast. High season $120; low season $110. **Amenities:** Complimentary snorkeling gear and bicycles; kitchens; free Wi-Fi.

**Costa de Cocos Dive & Fly-Fishing Resort ★★** This diver and fly-fisher favorite is also a great choice for get-away-from-it-all vacationers. Most of the wooden, *palapa*-roofed cabañas, surrounding a wide beach shaded by coconut palms, have one king- or queen-size bed or two doubles; one is a two-bedroom unit with two bathrooms. With plenty of cross-ventilation, ceiling fans suffice to keep the rooms comfortable; 24-hour electricity comes primarily from wind and solar power. Activities include kayaking, snorkeling, scuba diving, and fly-fishing. The PADI-certified dive center offers English-speaking fishing guides and a dive instructor. The casual restaurant/bar (above) offers good home-style cooking and serves craft beer and whiskey made by the owners.

Camino de la Costera (½ mile north of town). www.costadecocos.com. ✆ **983/839-8537.** 16 units. High season $90 double; low season $84 double. Dive and fly-fishing packages available by e-mail request. Rates include breakfast buffet. Free parking. **Amenities:** Restaurant; bar; dive shop; watersports; free Wi-Fi.

## LIONFISH: devastating BEAUTY

Mexico normally preaches conservation, but there is one species it is actively trying to stamp out. *Pterois volitans,* the colorful and spectacularly finned lionfish, is armed with poisonous spines and has no natural predators outside of its native South Pacific and Indian oceans. Thriving at any ocean depth, it gobbles everything in sight. Lionfish have robbed Caribbean and Atlantic waters of so much native sea life in a few years that marine biologists predict they could denude those oceans in our lifetime. Coastal communities now hold lionfish tournaments and encourage recreational divers to kill as many as they can. Local artisans turn lionfish fins into jewelry and other items, and chefs create ceviche and filet recipes. The good news is that travelers can help by doing what they always do on vacation: Go diving, buy some pretty souvenirs, and chow down on that delicious local seafood.

**Sin Duda Villas ★★★** Even by Xcalak standards, this inn is remote, quiet, and private. The beautiful beach, homey accommodations, and sociable owners—who bought the place in 2013 and serve nightly "Margo-ritas" in honor of their predecessors—are worth the trek over a rough beach road. Colorful guest rooms all have great ocean views and patios or balconies, with ceiling fans to augment ocean breezes. Three double rooms, a "treehouse" studio, and two two-bedroom apartments are available. In the main house, a bright kitchen, which doubles as a library, is stocked with granola, yogurt, and Chiapas coffee and is available for cooking other meals (bring groceries). Two rooftop decks offer dazzling views of jungle, lagoon, and sea.

Camino de la Costera (8km/5 miles north of town). www.sindudavillas.com. ✆ **306/500-3240** (Canadian number; messages only). 6 units. High season $90–$110 doubles, $120 apartments; low season $75–$100 doubles, $114 apartments. Children 8 and older accepted. Rates include light breakfast. **Amenities:** Communal kitchen/library; snorkeling gear, bikes, and kayaks; free Wi-Fi.

# LAGUNA BACALAR ★★

104km (65 miles) SW of Felipe Carrillo Puerto; 37km (23 miles) NW of Chetumal

On a sunny day, you'll see why Laguna Bacalar is called *Lago de los Siete Colores* (Lake of the Seven Colors): The white sandy bottom turns the crystalline water pale turquoise in shallow areas, morphing to vivid turquoise and through a spectrum to deep indigo in the deeper center. Colors shift further with the passing of the day, making a mesmerizing, living backdrop.

In truth, Bacalar is a lagoon, with a series of waterways making their way to the ocean. Fed by underground *cenotes,* it is almost 50km (31 miles) long. You'll glimpse the jewel-toned water long before you reach the town of Bacalar, about two-thirds of the way down. It's a quiet, traditional town, though it seems every year brings a new cadre of expats looking for a new start. One of the few things you really should bestir yourself to do is visit the **Fuerte San Felipe Bacalar,** built in 1733 to ward off pirates and Maya rebels. Just east of the central plaza, overlooking the lagoon, the fort's excellent museum is devoted to regional history, with a focus on the pirates who repeatedly descended upon these shores. Admission is 64 pesos.

Bacalar also boasts Mexico's biggest and deepest *cenote,* less than 2km (about a mile) south of town at Km 15. Measuring 185m (607-feet) across, **Cenote Azul** is surrounded by lush flowers and trees, and filled with water so clear that you can see 60m (200 feet) down into its nearly 91m (300-foot) depth. You can swim in the *cenote* (as long as you aren't wearing lotions or deodorant) or just watch others take the plunge.

Some lovely inns dot the lagoon's western shore, which makes Bacalar an appealing alternative base to Chetumal for exploring the Maya ruins of the nearby Río Bec area.



### GETTING THERE

Driving south on Hwy. 307, the town of Bacalar is 1½ hours beyond Felipe Carrillo Puerto, clearly marked by signs. If you're driving north from Chetumal, it takes about a half-hour. **ADO** and **Mayab** run frequent buses from Cancún and Playa del Carmen (208–294 pesos) that stop here, and there are even more frequent buses from Chetumal.

## Where to Stay

It doesn't cost much to stay quite comfortably in Bacalar. My favorite inn is **Amigos Hotel Bacalar** ★ (www.bacalar.net; ✆ **987/872-3868** or 983/834-2093), with five rooms of various sizes and configurations overlooking the water on Avenida Costera, about 1.6km (a mile) south of the plaza. Doubles are 700 pesos. Closer to the plaza on the same road, quirky **Casita Carolina** (www.casitacarolina.com; ✆ **983/834-2334**) offers three units in a converted family home that share a common living room and kitchen, plus a private *palapa,* a casita, and two small camping trailers in a large, grassy garden on the shore. Rates are 350 to 800 pesos a night for two. The modern, all-suite **Villas Bacalar** (www.villasbakalar.com; ✆ **983/834-2049**) has lovely lagoon views but no direct access to the water, a block away. Rates range from $109 to $219.

If you want to go wild, try **Bacalar Lagoon Resort** (www.bacalarlagoonresort.com; ✆ **983/132-2896**), at the top of the lagoon—about a 40-minute drive north of Bacalar at the end of a long, bumpy jungle road. It offers seven immaculate cabañas with small, simple bedrooms and large, contemporary bathrooms on a beautifully landscaped shoreline property. Doubles go for $115. **Villas Ecotucán** (www.villasecotucan.info; ✆ **983/120-5743**), about 5km (3 miles) north of town, sits on about 99 acres of largely undeveloped land and offers all kinds of jungle walks, kayak tours, and other outdoor activities. Five spacious *palapa*-roofed cabañas and two suites rent for 850 to 985 pesos. And the well-known **Rancho Encantado** ★ (www.encantado.com; ✆ **877/229-2046** in the U.S., or 998/884-2071) near Highway 307 north of town, rents 12 large white stucco cottages scattered over a shady lawn beside the lake, surrounded by native trees, orchids, and bromeliads. Rates start at 2,056 pesos double in high season, 1,558 in low season.

## Where to Eat

I've had good, simple meals at **Laguna de Bacalar** on the north side of the town plaza, and great dinners at the more upscale **Los Aluxes** (✆ **983/834-2817**) on Avenida Costera, south of Amigos B&B. A vantage point overlooking the *cenote* is the big prize at **Restaurante Cenote Azul** (✆ **983/834-2460**), which offers a varied menu of decent food. You can join the locals for an authentic Mexican *comida corrida* (lunch special) at **Cocina Orizaba** (Av. 7 btw. calles 24 and 26; ✆ **983/834-2069**) and great pizza at **Pizzeria Bertilla** next to the plaza (Av. 5 btw. calles 18 and 20; ✆ **983/123-5467**), run by an Italian family. The new **El Barril Grill** (Av. 7 btw. calles 20 and 22; ✆ **983/130-1474**) is a brewpub with very good barbecue, hamburgers, and steaks.

# CHETUMAL

251km (156 miles) S of Tulum; 37km (23 miles) S of Lago Bacalar

Quintana Roo's capital and third-largest city (after Cancún and Playa del Carmen), Chetumal is of interest to tourists primarily as the gateway to Belize, Tikal (Guatemala), and Río Bec ruins (p. 220). But it also boasts the best museum of Maya culture outside of Mexico City. Also worth a visit: The federal government has been rebuilding the rundown **Payo Obispo Zoo** (Av. Insurgentes at Andrés Quintana Roo), briefly called Biouniverzoo, into a modern, interactive facility devoted to native species. It has created some terrific doppelgangers of the animals' natural habitats, such as a *cenote* populated by bats that people descend into and view through glass walls, and a lush jungle filled with jaguars—including a rare black jaguar. It's designed so that visitors feel they are part of the exhibitions with the animals—more than 200 species including monkeys, tapirs, parrots, crocodiles, and snakes.

## Essentials

### GETTING THERE & DEPARTING

**BY PLANE** Chetumal (airport code CTM) currently has no direct service from foreign destinations. The Mexican airline **Interjet** (www.interjet.com.mx; ✆ **866/285-9525** in the U.S.), which serves New York, Miami, Houston, San Antonio, and Las Vegas, flies to Chetumal through its Mexico City hub; the two legs must be booked separately. The airport is west of town, just north of where you enter from the highway.

**BY CAR** Chetumal is about four-and-a-half hours' drive from Cancún. If you're continuing to Belize, be aware that rental companies don't allow you to take their cars across the border. To get to the ruins of Tikal in Guatemala, you must go through Belize and cross the border at Ciudad Melchor de Mencos.

**BY BUS** The main bus station (✆ **983/832-5110**) is just off Av. Insurgentes at Javier Barros Sierra. Buses go to Cancún, Tulum, Playa del Carmen, Puerto Morelos, Mérida, Campeche, Villahermosa, and Tikal, Guatemala.

**To Belize:** Buses run by Belizean companies depart from the Mercado Nuevo (also called Mercado Lázaro Cárdenas) at Calzada Veracruz and Av. Confederación Nacional Campesina. First-class buses go to the main bus terminal and depart for Belize from there, while the clunky older buses head directly for the border. Premiere, with three departures a day, is one of the better lines.

### VISITOR INFORMATION

The **State Tourism Office** (✆ **983/835-0860**) is at Centro de Convenciones Anexo A, at Ignacio Comonfort. It's open Monday to Friday from 9am to 6pm.

### ORIENTATION

Traffic enters the city from the west on Hwy. 186 and feeds onto Avenida Obregón into town. Stay on Obregón and don't take the exit veering left for Avenida Insurgentes (unless you're looking for the zoo or the huge Plaza Las Americas mall). Turn left on Avenida Héroes, the main north–south street through downtown, to reach the museum, market, and hotels.

## A Museum Not to Miss

**Museo de la Cultura Maya ★★★** This sophisticated museum unlocks the complex world of the Maya through interactive exhibits and genuine artifacts. A slide show explains medicinal and domestic uses of plants with their Maya and scientific names; a video station shows you how to write your birth date in Maya glyphs. A fascinating exhibit describes the Maya's ideal of personal beauty, which prompted them to deform craniums, scar the face and body, and induce *estrabismo,* or cross-eyed vision.

An enormous screen flashes aerial images of more than a dozen Maya sites from Mexico to Honduras. Another large television shows the architectural variety of Maya pyramids and how they were probably built. You can walk on a glass floor over models of various Maya ruins. The museum is built around a stylized three-story ceiba tree, which the Maya believed connected Xibalba (the underworld), Earth, and the heavens, and each museum floor corresponds to those levels of the Maya cosmos. Try to see the museum before you tour the Río Bec ruins; signs are in Spanish and English.

Av. Héroes s/n (at Mahatma Gandhi, just past Capital Plaza Hotel). ✆ **983/129-2832.** Admission 57 pesos. Tues–Sat 9am–7pm; Sun 9am–2pm.



## Where to Stay

Chetumal is not nearly as appealing a base for exploring as Bacalar, about 30 minutes away, but it does have some serviceable hotels near the museum.

**Capital Plaza Hotel ★** This modern hotel—formerly a longtime Holiday Inn that closed in 2014—has been mildly updated by the new ownership and remains a reliable, if not inspiring, option. It has comfortable beds and the best air-conditioning in town, and is only a block from the museum. Most rooms are midsize and come with one king or two double beds. Bathrooms are roomy and well lit. And you couldn't ask for a better location,

Av. Héroes 171-A (btw. Aguilar & Mahatma Gandhi, half a block south and across the street from Maya museum). www.capitalplaza.mx. ✆ **983/835-0400.** 85 units. High season $72–$83 double. Free secure parking. **Amenities:** Restaurant; bar; fitness room; outdoor pool; room service; free Wi-Fi.

**Hotel Los Cocos ★** The bedspreads in this low-slung, modern hotel are a bit garish for my taste, but rooms are otherwise pleasant, bathrooms are scrupulously clean, and the grounds are nicely landscaped—all for a bargain price. The nicest rooms face the courtyard, where there is a small but inviting pool and Jacuzzi. The restaurant, which does brisk business from visitors to the museum 2 blocks away, does a good job with Mexican favorites.

Av. Héroes 134 (corner of Chapultepec, 2 blocks south of Maya museum). www.hotelloscocos.com.mx. ✆ **983/835-0430.** 176 units. $52–$59 double. Off-street parking. **Amenities:** Restaurant; bar; pool; Jacuzzi; room service; free Wi-Fi.

## Where to Eat

The closest decent restaurant to the Maya museum is in **Hotel Los Cocos** (above). About seven blocks south and west, **Marisqueria El Taco Loco** (www.tacolocochetumal.com; ✆ **983/832-1213;** on Jose Maria Morelos between Plutarco and Zaragoza) serves very good, moderately priced seafood tacos and fish. In the same neighborhood, try **Sergio's Pizza** (✆ **983/832-2991;** on Alvaro Obregon between Jose Maria Morelos and Francisco I. Madero) for upscale—but still reasonable, because this *is* Chetumal—pizza as well as steak, seafood, and pasta with Italian and Mexican influences. Nearby **Pasion Turca** (www.pasionturca.com.mx; ✆ **983/832-7869**) offers a change of pace with hummus, kibis, stuffed grape leaves, and kebabs, on Avenida Heroes at Ignacio Zaragoza. For fine dining from a menu of Italian, Mexican, and international dishes, head east to Chetumal Bay, where **Spezias** (✆ **983/129-2774**) is set in a lovely square full of historic architecture on Prov. Bahia between Rafael E. Melgar and Emiliano Zapata.

## Onward from Chetumal



The Maya ruins of Lamanai, in Belize, are an easy day trip if you have transportation (not a rental car). To explore the Río Bec route (below), take Highway 186 west.



# SIDE TRIPS TO MAYA RUINS FROM CHETUMAL ★★

The area of Maya settlement known as the Río Bec region begins a few miles west of Bacalar and Chetumal. Numerous ruins stretching well into the state of Campeche are intriguing for their stylized, lavishly decorated architecture. Excavation has brought some restoration, but these cities have not been rebuilt to the degree found at Tulum and Chichén Itzá. Many buildings were so intact that reconstruction was unnecessary.

Unlike like the Yucatán's marquee sites, Río Bec ruins are swathed in a profusion of trees and vines, creating an atmosphere of storybook lost cities. You can easily imagine what John Lloyd Stephens and Frederick Catherwood must have felt when they traipsed through the Yucatán in the mid-19th century. (Their well-written and meticulously illustrated account, *Incidents of Travel in Yucatán,* remains compelling today and is still in print; be sure to get the two-volume version.)

Along this wildlife-rich route, you might see a toucan, a grand curassow, or a macaw flitting about or scolding you from the treetops. Orioles, egrets, and several birds of prey are also common. Gray fox, wild turkey, *tesquintle* (a bushy-tailed, plant-eating rodent), and coatimundi (playful raccoon kin) are abundant. Several bands of spider and howler monkeys circulate Calakmul and the surrounding jungle.

**THE ROUTE** Halfway between Bacalar and Chetumal, about 20km (12 miles) from either, is the well-marked turnoff for Highway 186 to Escárcega. This same road leads to Campeche, Palenque, and Villahermosa. A couple of gas stations are en route, including one in the town of Xpujil. Carry plenty of cash, as credit cards are rarely accepted in the area.

The Río Bec sites lie varying distances off the highway. You pass through a checkpoint at the Campeche state border; guards might ask for your travel papers or simply inquire where you've been and where you are going before waving you on. Rarely, they will want to inspect your luggage. With an early start, you can easily visit several of these sites in a day from Bacalar or Chetumal. You can make several day trips, or spend the night in the area.

Evidence, especially from Becán, shows that these ruins were part of the **trade route** linking the Caribbean coast at Cobá to Edzná (Campeche State) and the Gulf Coast, and to Lamanai in Belize and beyond. A great number of cities once thrived here, and much of the land was dedicated to cultivating maize. All has been swallowed by the dense jungle blanketing the land from horizon to horizon.

The sites that follow are listed east to west, as you would encounter them driving from the Caribbean coast—ideally after visiting the Museo de la Cultura Maya (p. 218) in Chetumal to gain some context. If you would like a knowledgeable guide, **Dan Griffin** (www.mayako-ox.com) is a Mérida-based archaeologist who has worked with Harvard, *National Geographic,* and other institutions throughout the Yucatán. He tailors his tours to clients' interests anywhere in the region, but his strength is a deep knowledge of the local population and the archaeologists at work in the area. His independent tours of lesser-known archaeological sites and abandoned haciendas not yet snapped up by Starwood are terrific; he also knows the best bird-watching sites.

Informational signs are in Maya, Spanish, and English. Few if any refreshments are available—bring your own water and food—but all the principal sites have toilets.



**FOOD & LODGING** The only town in the region with basic tourist services is Xpujil, which has little else going for it. Of the basic affordable hotels in town, the best food and lodging is at **Restaurant y Hotel Calakmul ★** (**✆ 983/871-6029**), which rents air-conditioned doubles with TV for 590 pesos. They have tile floors, private bathrooms with hot water, and good beds. There's a nice pool in the courtyard, and the restaurant does a good job (daily from 6am to midnight).

A rental car opens up some better options. Just beyond Xpujil, across from the ruins of the same name, is **Chicanná Eco Village ★** at Carretera Escárcega–Chetumal Km. 144 (www.chicannaecovillageresort.com; **✆ 981/811-9192**). Its 42 comfortable, nicely furnished rooms are distributed among several two-story thatched bungalows. They offer doubles or a king-size bed (quite firm), ceiling fans, a large bathroom, and screened windows. Paths through manicured lawns and flower beds link the bungalows to one another and to the restaurant and swimming pool. Doubles go for 1,350 pesos.

**Río Bec Dreams ★★,** Carretera 186, Escárcega–Chetumal Km. 142 (11km/6¾ miles west of Xpujil; www.riobecdreams.com; **✆ 983/126-3526**) rents "jungalows"—small, wooden cabins on stilts—scattered through a tropical forest. They have good screens and such niceties as curtains, tile counters, hand-painted sinks, porches, and comfortable beds with mosquito netting. Guests in some jungalows share spotless bathrooms, while others have their own. Roomy cabañas have screened-in porches and private bathrooms. The British/Canadian owners are devoted students of Río Bec architecture who guide tours of the ruins, from short excursions to smaller ruins to all-day treks through Calakmul. They are a wonderful resource and good companions around the open-air bar. The restaurant is the best in the area, though service can get bogged down when they are busy. Jungalows cost 595 to 865 pesos, cabañas 1080 to 1,240 pesos; extra 50 pesos for 1-night reservations.

### Opening Hours & Fees

Archaeological sites along the Río Bec route are open daily 8am to 5pm, with entry fees ranging from 39 to 62 pesos—except for Calakmul, which has its own fee structure (p. 224).

## Dzibanché & Kinichná

Dzibanché (or Tzibanché) means "place where they write on wood"—obviously not the original name, which remains unknown. This ancient city dates from the Classic period (A.D. 300–900) and was occupied for about 700 years. Scattered over 42 sq. km (16 sq. miles) are several groupings of buildings and plazas; only a small portion is excavated. The turnoff, 37km (23 miles) from the highway intersection, is well marked; another 23km (14 miles) brings you to the ruins. Ask about the condition of the road before setting out. These unpaved roads can go from good to bad pretty quickly, but this is an important enough site that road repair is generally kept up.

## recommended READING

A little background reading will greatly enhance your visit. The Stephens & Catherwood book (p. 220) is unparalleled for capturing the wonder of discovery. Other books that will help you make the most of your visit include *A Forest of Kings: The Untold Story of the Ancient Maya,* by Linda Schele and David Freidel; *The Blood of Kings: Dynasty and Ritual in Maya Art,* by Linda Schele and Mary Ellen Miller; and *Maya Cosmos,* by David Freidel, Linda Schele, and Joy Parker. A good companion is Joyce Kelly's *An Archaeological Guide to Mexico's Yucatán Peninsula,* even though many sites have expanded since it was written.

**TEMPLES & PLAZAS** Two large adjoining plazas have been cleared. The most important structure yet excavated is the **Temple of the Owl** in the main plaza, Plaza Xibalba. Archaeologists found a stairway descending from the top of the structure to a burial chamber deep inside the pyramid (not open to visitors). The chamber yielded beautiful polychromatic lidded vessels, one of which has an owl painted on the top handle with its wings spreading onto the lid. White owls were messengers of the underworld (Xibalba) gods of Maya religion. Other finds include the remains of a sacrificial victim and what appear to be the remains of a Maya queen, which is unique in Maya archaeology.

Opposite the Temple of the Owl is the **Temple of the Cormorant,** named after the bird depicted on a polychrome drinking vessel found here. Archaeologists also found evidence of an interior tomb, yet to be excavated, similar to the one in the Temple of the Owl. Other magnificently preserved pottery pieces uncovered include an incense burner bearing an almost three-dimensional figure of the diving god, and another incense burner with an elaborately dressed representation of the god Itzamná.

Standing alone, **Structure VI** is a miniature rendition of Teotihuacán-style architecture: Each step of the pyramid is made of a *talud* (sloping surface) crowned by a *tablero* (vertical stone facing). Though located near present-day Mexico City, Teotihuacán's influence reached as far as Guatemala. At the top of the pyramid is a doorway whose wooden lintel is carved with glyphs for the year A.D. 733, which survived centuries of weathering and gave the site its name.

Another nearby city, **Kinichná** (Kee-neech-*nah*), is about 2.5km (1½ miles) north. Best-known for an Olmec-style jade figure discovered there, it has a large acropolis with five buildings on three levels, which have been restored. They are in good condition, with fragments of the original stucco still visible. The road leading to Kinichná becomes questionable during the rainy season.

## Kohunlich ★

Kohunlich (Koh-*hoon*-leech), 42km (26 miles) from the turnoff for Highway 186, dates from around A.D. 100 to 900. Turn left off the road, and the entrance is 9km (5⅔ miles) farther. Enter the grand, parklike site, cross a large, shady ceremonial area flanked by four large pyramids, and continue walking straight ahead to Kohunlich's famous **Pyramid of the Masks.** Beneath a *palapa* shelter, six stucco heads more than 2.4m (8 feet) tall flank the giant staircase. Dating from around A.D. 500, each is slightly different but all are elongated and wear headdresses with masks on both the crest and the chin piece—essentially masks within masks. Masks are believed to have decorated the facade of this Río Bec–style building, built with rounded corners, a false stairway, and a false temple on top. More than one theory holds that the masks are a composite of several rulers at Kohunlich.

Excavations in the buildings immediately to the left after you enter the site uncovered two intact pre-Hispanic skeletons and five decapitated heads that may have been used in a ceremonial ritual. To the right, follow the shady path through the jungle to another recently excavated high plaza with sublime views that show why the city's founders chose this site: Any invaders would be spotted from miles away. The fine architecture and the high quality of pottery found there suggest this complex housed priests or rulers. Scholars believe overpopulation led to Kohunlich's decline.

## Xpujil

Xpujil (Eesh-poo-*heel;* also spelled Xpuhil), meaning either "cattail" or "forest of kapok trees," flourished between A.D. 400 and 900. The small, well-preserved site is easy to get to; look for a highway sign pointing right (north). The entrance is just off the highway; the main structure is a 180m (590-foot) walk farther. Along the path are some *chechén* trees, recognizable by their blotchy bark. Don't touch; their toxins can cause blisters. A platform to the right supports a restored two-story building with a central staircase; remnants of a decorative molding and two galleries are connected by a doorway. About 90m (295 feet) farther you come to **Structure I,** the site's main structure. This rectangular ceremonial platform, 2m (6½ feet) high and 50m (164 feet) long, supports the palace and is decorated with three tall towers shaped like miniature versions of the pyramids in Tikal, Guatemala. These towers are purely decorative, with false stairways and temples too small to serve as such. The effect is beautiful. The building's 12 rooms are now in ruins.

## Becán ★★★

Becán (Beh-*kahn*), about 7km (4⅓ miles) beyond Xpujil, is visible on the right side of the highway. The name means "moat filled by water," and the city was in fact protected by a moat spanned by seven bridges. This is a stellar (and rare) example of Maya fortification; dirt from digging the moat was piled up to create a wall around the city. The extensive site dates from the early Classic to the late Postclassic (600 B.C.–A.D. 1200) period. Although it was abandoned by A.D. 850, it was still a ceremonial site as late as 1200. Becán was an administrative and ceremonial center with political sway over at least seven other cities, including Chicanná, Hormiguero, and Payán.

The first plaza group you see upon entering was a grand ceremonial center. From the highway, you can see the back of **Structure I,** a pyramid with two temples on top. Beyond and in between the two temples you can see the temple atop **Structure IV,** opposite Structure I. When the high priest exited the mouth of the earth monster in the center of this temple (reached by a hidden side stairway that's now partially exposed), he would have been visible from well beyond the immediate plaza, where it's thought the commoners stood. The back of Structure IV is believed to have been a civic plaza where rulers sat on stone benches. The second plaza group dates from around A.D. 850 and is crowned by two perfect twin towers. Under the platform supporting the towers are 10 rooms that are thought to be related to Xibalba (Shee-*bahl*-bah), the underworld. Earth-monster faces probably covered this building (and appeared on other buildings as well). Remains of at least one ball court have been unearthed. Next to the ball court is a well-preserved figure in an elaborate headdress behind glass, excavated not far from where he is now displayed. The markings are still well defined.

## Chicanná

Slightly more than 1.5km (1 mile) beyond Becán, left of the highway, is Chicanná, which means "house of the serpent's mouth." The central square is surrounded by five buildings. **Structure II,** the site's outstanding building, features a monster-mouth doorway and an ornate stone facade with more superimposed masks. As you enter the mouth of the earth monster, you are on a platform configured as the monster's open jaw, with stone teeth on both sides. This is another lovely example of an elongated building with the typical Río Bec ornamental miniature pyramids on each end.

## Calakmul ★★★

This area is both a massive Maya archaeological zone, with at least 60 sites, and a 70,000-hectare (172,900-acre) rainforest, designated in 1989 as the Calakmul Biosphere Reserve with territory in both Mexico and Guatemala. The best way to see Calakmul is to spend the night nearby (p. 221) and leave early in the morning for the reserve. If you're the first to drive down the narrow access road to the ruins (1½ hours from the highway), you should see plenty of wildlife. On my last trip, I saw two groups of spider monkeys swinging through the trees on the outskirts of the city and a group of howler monkeys sleeping in the trees in front of Structure II.

To get there, you'll first need to pay a 56-peso fee at the gate for the car and driver, plus 28 pesos per passenger. There is an additional biosphere fee of 56 pesos per person, and another 52 pesos per person INAH (National Institute of Anthropology and History) fee to enter the archaeological site. The rainy season, when the place is soaked, is from June to October.

**CALAKMUL BIOSPHERE RESERVE** Set aside in 1989, this is the Yucatán's only high forest, a rainforest that annually records as much as 5m (16 feet) of rain. The tree canopy is higher here than in the forest of Quintana Roo, and plant life includes cacti, epiphytes, and orchids. Endangered animals include the white-lipped peccary, jaguar, and puma. So far, more than 250 species of birds have been recorded. At present, no overnight stay or camping is permitted. If you want a tour of a small part of the forest and you speak Spanish, you can inquire for a guide at one of the two nearby *ejidos* (cooperatives). Some old local *chicleros* (the men who tap sapodilla trees for their gum) have expert knowledge of flora and fauna and can take you on a couple of trails.

The turnoff on the left for Calakmul is 53km (33 miles) from Xpujil, just before the village of Conhuas. Then it's an hour's drive on a paved one-lane-road to the ruins. Bring food and drink for the day, and bug spray.

**THE ARCHAEOLOGICAL ZONE** Archaeologists have been excavating the ruins of Calakmul, which date from 100 B.C. to A.D. 900, since 1982. It's the largest of the known Río Bec sites. Approximately 7,000 buildings have been discovered and mapped. At its zenith, at least 60,000 people may have lived around the site, but by the time of the Spanish Conquest in 1519 fewer than 1,000 remained. Arriving at a large plaza filled with trees, you immediately see several stelae; Calakmul contains more than 100—more than any other site—but they are much more weathered and indistinguishable than those at Palenque or Copán in Honduras. Looters have cut the faces off some. By Structure XIII is a stela of a woman thought to have been a ruler that dates from A.D. 652.

Some structures here are built in the Petén style characteristic of Guatemala, with extraordinarily high crested structures, steep staircases, and false facades. Others are typical Río Bec style. **Structure III** must have been the residence of a noble family.

Its lovely design is unique; it retains its original form, never having been remodeled. Offerings of shells, beads, and pottery were found inside. **Structure II** is the tallest pyramid in the Yucatán, at 54m (177 feet). From the top, you can see the outline of the ruins of El Mirador (whose El Tigre pyramid is quite similar) 50km (31 miles) across the forest in Guatemala. Two stairways along the sides of the pyramid's principal face in the upper levels are broken up by masks.

**Structure IV** charts the sun's path from June 21, when it falls on the left (north) corner; to September 21 and March 21, when it lines up in the east behind the middle temple on the top of the building; to December 21, when it falls on the right (south) corner. Numerous jade pieces, including spectacular masks, were uncovered here and are displayed in the Museum of Mayan Culture in Chetumal (p. 218). **Structure VII** is largely unexcavated except for the top, where, in 1984, the most outstanding jade mask yet found at Calakmul was uncovered. In their book *A Forest of Kings,* Linda Schele and David Freidel tell of wars among the Calakmul, Tikal, and Naranjo (the latter two in Guatemala), and how Ah-Cacaw, king of Tikal (120km/75 miles south of Calakmul), captured King Jaguar-Paw in A.D. 695 and later Lord Ox-Ha-Te Ixil Ahau, both of Calakmul.

## Balamkú ★★

Balamkú (Bah-lahm-*koo*), just off Highway 186 about 5km (3 miles) west of Conhuas, is easy to reach and worth the visit. A couple of buildings in the complex were so well preserved that they required almost no reconstruction. Inside the **Temple of the Four Kings,** covered by a later pyramid built over it, is one of the largest stucco friezes in the Maya world. The three major figures—looters made off with a fourth before the frieze was discovered in 1990 and protected—are a rabbit, an alligator, and a crocodile, flanked by many carvings of animals, mythological beings, and kings. The concept behind this temple is life and death, and figures of men sit in the gaping maws of crocodiles and toads as they descend into the underworld. On each stucco figure's head are the eyes, nose, and mouth of a jaguar, followed by the full face of the human figure, then a neck formed by the eyes and nose of another jaguar, and an Olmec-like face on the stomach, with its neck ringed by a necklace. The frieze is under lock and key, and visitors must ask a caretaker to let them view the unique art. Much of the original painting remains, so flash photography is not allowed.

# PLANNING YOUR TRIP TO CANCÚN & THE CARIBBEAN COAST

8

by Maribeth Mellin

Any great vacation begins with pre-trip research. This chapter contains practical information to help with preparation; more specific details about navigating and finding local resources are in the "Essentials" section of the destination chapters.

## WHEN TO GO

High season in the Yucatán begins around December 20 and continues to Easter week. This is usually the best time for reduced humidity and calm, temperate weather, though chilly rainstorms do pop up occasionally. Locals accustomed to steamy heat don jackets and jeans during the winter months; travelers from cooler climes are happy in shorts in daytime and a light jacket some nights.

Low season begins after Easter and continues to mid-December, with bursts of high tourism in August (popular with Europeans) and national and international holidays. During low season, prices may drop 20% to 30%. Many hotels in Cancún and the Riviera Maya subdivide these into as many as eight different mini-seasons; some hotels now charge high-season rates during June and July, when Mexican, European, and school-holiday visitors often travel, although rates may still be lower than in winter months.

Generally speaking, Mexico's dry season runs from November to April, with the rainy season stretching from May to October. Temperatures and humidity from May through August can be downright miserable for those who abhor heat. Later in the rainy season, the frequency of unpredictable tropical storms and hurricanes increases. Destructive hurricanes are rare, but Hurricane Wilma in 2005 was particularly hard on Cancún. Storms typically lower temperatures and bring cool air and a slight wind, making climbing ruins and exploring the jungle more fun. Storms can decrease underwater visibility for divers, and conditions may prevent boats from even going out. For information on national holidays see chapter 2 (In Context), p. 38.

## Cancún's Average Temperatures

| | JAN | FEB | MAR | APR | MAY | JUNE | JULY | AUG | SEPT | OCT | NOV | DEC |
|---|---|---|---|---|---|---|---|---|---|---|---|---|
| AVG. HIGH (°C) | 27 | 28 | 29 | 29 | 31 | 32 | 32 | 32 | 32 | 31 | 29 | 28 |
| AVG. HIGH (°F) | 81 | 82 | 84 | 85 | 88 | 89 | 90 | 90 | 89 | 87 | 84 | 82 |
| AVG. LOW (°C) | 19 | 20 | 22 | 23 | 25 | 26 | 26 | 25 | 24 | 23 | 22 | 21 |
| AVG. LOW (°F) | 67 | 68 | 71 | 73 | 77 | 78 | 78 | 77 | 76 | 74 | 72 | 69 |

# GETTING THERE

## By Plane

Cancún (www.cancun-airport.com; ✆ **998/848-7200**), known by its airport code CUN, is one of Mexico's largest international airports and is the main arrival point for all the coastal destinations in Quintana Roo. It's about a 25-minute drive to the heart of the Hotel Zone and slightly less to downtown Cancún. Figure about 30 minutes to Puerto Morelos, an hour to Playa del Carmen, 2 hours (one on the road, one on the ferry) to Cozumel, 2 hours and 15 minutes to Tulum, 4 hours to Bacalar, and roughly 4½ hours to Mahahual or Chetumal.

Though Terminal 3 is designated the international terminal and Terminal 2 the domestic terminal, these distinctions don't always hold. Among international airlines serving the U.S. and Canada, **Aeroméxico** (www.aeromexico.com; ✆ **877/262-0455** in the U.S. or 800-021-4000 in Mexico), **Air Canada** (www.aircanada.com; ✆ **888/247-2262** in the U.S. and Canada), **Southwest** (www.southwest.com; ✆ **800/435-9792** in U.S.), **American** (www.aa.com; ✆ **800/433-7300** in the U.S.), **JetBlue** (www.jetblue.com; ✆ **800/538-2583** in U.S.), and **Spirit** (www.spirit.com; ✆ **800/772-7117** in the U.S.) use Terminal 2. Mexican airlines **InterJet** (www.interjet.com.mx; ✆ **866/285-9525** in the U.S. or 01-800/011-2345 in Mexico), **VivaAerobus** (www.vivaaerobus.com; ✆ **888/935-9848** in U.S. or 998/296-0000 in Mexico), and **Volaris** (www.volaris.com.mx; ✆ **866/988-3527** in U.S. or 01-800/122-8000 in Mexico), which also serve U.S. destinations, uses Terminal 2 as well.

U.S. airlines operating out of Terminal 3 are Alaska Airlines (www.alaskaair.com; ✆ **800/864-8331**), **Delta** (www.delta.com; ✆ **800/221-1212**), **Frontier** (www.frontierairlines.com; ✆ **800/432-1359**), **SunCountry** (www.suncountry.com; ✆ **800/359-6786**), **United** (www.united.com; ✆ **800/864-8331**), and **US Airways** (www.usairways.com; ✆ **800/428-4322**) use Terminal 3.

Terminal 1, the oldest, has been remodeled and is used for domestic, private, and charter airlines. Many **charter** companies—such as **Apple Vacations** (www.applevacations.com) and **Funjet** (www.funjet.com)—bring as many as half the city's U.S. visitors to Cancún on package tours. **Mayair** (www.mayair.com.mx; ✆ **998/881-9413** in Mexico) runs flights to and from Cozumel out of the FBO terminal next to Terminal 1.

Cozumel (CZM, http://cozumelairport.org, ✆ **987/ 872-2081**) receives a few international flights, with more added in high season.

**Tip**

Three-wheeled bicycles, called *triciclos*, with riding platforms behind the driver, serve as convenient and cheap taxis in Cozumel, Playa del Carmen, and most smaller towns. They're especially helpful for reaching the ferry pier in Playa del Carmen, since cars are banned from the final blocks to the pier.

## By Car

Driving is definitely not the easiest way to get to the Yucatán peninsula. The better option is to rent a car once you arrive and tour around a specific region. See Getting Around, below.

## By Ship

Numerous cruise lines serve Mexico. Some (such as Carnival and Royal Caribbean) cruise from Houston or Miami to the Caribbean (which often includes stops in Cozumel, Puerto Calica in the Riviera Maya, and Majahual in the Costa Maya). Several cruise-tour specialists sometimes offer last-minute discounts on unsold cabins. One such company is **CruisesOnly** (www.cruisesonly.com; ✆ **800/278-4737**).

## By Bus

We've listed bus arrival information in each applicable section of this book.

# GETTING AROUND

## By Plane

Most destinations in Quintana Roo and nearby Yucatán are accessible by car and bus only. MAYAir (www.mayair.com.mx) flies between Cozumel and Cancún.

## By Car

### CAR RENTALS

National and international car rental companies have offices in Cancún, Cozumel, and Playa del Carmen. You'll get the best price if you reserve a car on the Internet. Rentals are easiest if you are 25 or older and have a major credit card, valid driver's license, and passport with you. One-way rentals are usually simple to arrange, but they are more costly.

You will pay the least for a manual car without air-conditioning or a radio. Topless jeeps and cars are popular for day tripping but impractical if you need to store and hide luggage and personal possessions. Automatic transmission and air-conditioning cost a bit more.

**Insurance** can be complicated. Some credit cards cover rental insurance, with certain conditions. Check to make sure coverage includes Mexico. Most companies will require an additional liability insurance purchase regardless of your existing coverage; it typically costs around $12 to $15 per day. Insurance within Mexico is offered in two parts. Collision and damage insurance covers your car and others if the accident is your fault, and personal accident insurance covers you and anyone in your car. Note that insurance may be invalid if you have an accident while driving on an unpaved road.

### Point-to-Point Driving Directions

You can get point-to-point driving directions in English for anywhere in Mexico from the website of the Secretary of Communication and Transport. The site will also calculate tolls, distance, and travel time. Go to http://aplicaciones4.sct.gob.mx/sibuac_internet, and click on "Rutas punto a punto" in the left-hand column. Then select the English version.

### Bumps in the Road

If your car breaks down on the road, help might already be on the way. Radio-equipped green repair trucks, run by uniformed English-speaking officers, patrol major highways during daylight hours (usually 8am–6pm). These **Angeles Verdes/Green Angels** perform minor repairs and adjustments for free, but you pay for parts and materials. To contact them in Mexico, dial ✆ **078.** For more information, see www.sectur.gob.mx. Your best guide to repair shops is the Yellow Pages. For repairs, look under Automóviles y Camiones: Talleres de Reparación y Servicio; auto-parts stores are under Refacciones y Accesorios para Automóviles. To find a mechanic on the road, look for the sign reading *taller mecánico*. Places called *vulcanizadora* or *llantera* repair flat tires, and it is common to find them open 24 hours a day on the most-traveled highways.

Minor accidents are often settled informally between drivers to avoid involving the police. If the police arrive while the involved persons are still at the scene and the drivers are not insured, the cars could be confiscated and both parties might have to appear in court. Both parties may also be taken into custody until liability is determined. Foreigners who don't speak fluent Spanish are at a distinct disadvantage when trying to explain their version of the event. Three steps may help the foreigner who doesn't wish to do as the Mexicans do: If you are in your own car, notify your Mexican insurance company, whose job it is to intervene on your behalf. If you are in a rental car, notify the rental company immediately and ask how to contact the nearest adjuster. (You did buy insurance with the rental, right?) If you're in a well-trafficked area, chances are good an insurance company representative will appear at the crash site to help negotiate details. Rest assured the process will be lengthy and complicated, and impatience and anger will only exacerbate the situation.

I've only been in one accident in decades of driving in Mexico and learned a valuable tip from the car-rental representative. As we sat in the sun for hours with various police departments debating the situation, the representative suggested I dash to the market up the street and purchase as many cold sodas as I could carry. I then handed them out to the various officers and felt much of the tension dissolve immediately. In Mexico, as everywhere, a little courtesy goes a long way.

Deductibles come out of your pocket immediately in case of damage. Inspect your car carefully and note every damaged or missing item, no matter how minute, on your rental agreement, and make sure you have phone numbers for emergencies and various offices.

**Gasoline** and oil are sold by the liter, which is slightly more than a quart (1 gal. equals about 3.8L). Many stations have bathroom facilities and convenience stores. Gas stations accept cash and credit and debit cards for gas purchases, and a small tip—5 to 10 pesos—is appreciated for the standard full service.

## By Taxi

Taxis are the preferred way to get around almost all of Mexico's resort areas. Fares for short trips within towns are generally preset by zone. Fares in Cancún are relatively high, especially in the Hotel Zone and at night; fares in other areas are far less. Taxis awaiting passengers at hotels, restaurants, and bars charge more than those on the street. For longer trips or excursions to nearby cities, taxis can be hired for $25 and higher per hour, or for a negotiated daily rate. For anyone uncomfortable driving in Mexico, this is a convenient, comfortable alternative.

## By Bus

Mexican buses run frequently, are readily accessible, and can transport you almost anywhere you want to go. For bus travel within Yucatán, see the destination chapters. The following website provides reservations and bookings for numerous providers throughout Mexico: www.boletotal.mx.



# HEALTH

For the latest information on health risks when traveling to Mexico, and what to do if you get sick, consult the U.S. State Department's website at www.travel.state.gov, the CDC website at www.cdc.gov, or the website of the World Health Organization at www.who.int. Healthcare that meets basic U.S. standards is available in Cancún and other resort destinations. See destination chapters for local services. Prescription medicines are broadly available at Mexico pharmacies, and some that typically require a prescription can be obtained in Mexico simply by asking. However, you need a prescription from a doctor in Mexico for most heavy-duty painkillers and psychotropic drugs. Carry copies of your prescriptions and keep prescription drugs in their original containers.

Travelers' diarrhea, sometimes accompanied by fever, nausea, and vomiting, is possible when traveling anywhere foreign. Travelers and locals tend to rely on bottled drinking water for drinking, and restaurants catering to tourists use purified water and ice. If you do come down with this ailment, nothing beats Pepto Bismol, readily available in Mexico. Imodium is also available in Mexico and helps with diarrhea. Be careful to replace fluids and electrolytes by drinking Gatorade, Pedialyte, or other rehydration solution.

Mosquitoes and sand flies are prevalent along the coast and in the Yucatán lowlands. Pack a repellent that contains DEET. *Repelente contra insectos* (insect repellent) is available at pharmacies and gift shops. If you're sensitive to bites, pick up some antihistamine cream from a drugstore at home.

### Tropical Illnesses

You shouldn't be overly concerned about tropical diseases if you stay on the normal tourist routes and don't eat street food. However, both dengue fever and cholera have appeared in Mexico in recent years, usually after severe storms. Talk to your doctor or to a medical specialist in tropical diseases about precautions you should take. You can also protect yourself by watching what you eat and drink; not swimming in stagnant water (ponds, slow-moving rivers, or still wells); and avoiding mosquito bites by covering up, using repellent, and sleeping under netting. The most dangerous areas are away from the big resorts.

## Driving in Mexico

The spirited style of Mexican driving sometimes requires keen vision and reflexes. Be prepared for new customs, as when a truck driver flips on his left turn signal when there's not a crossroad for many kilometers. He's probably telling you the road's clear ahead for you to pass. Here are a few other customs that might take a bit of getting used to:

- Turning right on a red light is illegal, unless a sign indicates otherwise.
- In cities, many large avenues have laterals—separate lanes running on either side of the main roadway. You must take the mini off-ramps onto the laterals in order to stop or, often, to make turns.
- In the absence of a designated left-turn lane on a highway, it is customary to pull to the right, wait until the road is clear, then cross it straight on.
- Flashing headlights behind you means the car wants to pass. Newer roads in the region have shoulders wide enough (just barely) for a car to drive in, and you are expected to pull over.
- If a car in front of you turns on its emergency lights, or an oncoming car flashes its headlights at you, be prepared for some road trouble ahead.

# [Fast FACTS] CANCÚN & THE CARIBBEAN COAST

**ATMs/Banks** All major destinations and many small towns have banks where you can change currency at favorable rates. Except in the smallest towns, they tend to be open weekdays from 9am until 5pm, and often for at least a half-day on Saturday. ATMs are located in hotels, restaurants, and shopping areas in the tourism destinations. Most machines offer Spanish/English menus and dispense pesos, but some offer the option of withdrawing dollars. Most banks charge a fee when you use a foreign ATM, though some credit card companies will refund the fee. Visa, MasterCard, and American Express are the most accepted credit cards. Generally you receive the favorable bank rate when paying by credit card, though the card company may charge a fee based on the purchase price, negating any savings. Some establishments offer discounted prices if you pay with cash. *Casas de cambio* (exchange houses) are becoming less common as more tourists use ATMs, but you can usually find one on a major shopping street; most hotels also change currency. Large airports have currency-exchange counters that often stay open whenever flights are operating. Though convenient, they generally do not offer the most favorable rates. For help with currency conversions, tip calculations, and more, download Frommer's convenient Travel Tools app for your mobile device.

**Business Hours** Most businesses in larger cities are open between 9am and 7pm; in smaller towns they may close between 2 and 4pm. Many close on Sunday. In resort areas, stores are commonly open daily but may have limited Sunday hours. Some tourist-oriented shops stay open late, until 8 or even 10pm.

**Customs** At most points of entry, tourists are requested to press a button in front of what looks like a traffic signal, which alternates on touch between red and green. Get a green light and you go through without inspection; red light and your luggage may be inspected. If you have an unusual amount of luggage or an oversize piece, you may be subject to inspection anyway. Passengers who arrive by air will be required to put their bags through an X-ray machine, and then move to the kiosk and push a button to determine whether their luggage will be selected for any further inspection.

Visitors are allowed to carry electronics for personal use during their stay; items that could be sold are subject to duty. Those entering Mexico by air or sea can bring in gifts worth a value of up to $300 duty-free, except alcohol or tobacco products. The website for Mexican Customs (*Aduanas*) is **www.aduanas.gob.mx**.

## Disabled Travelers

Mexico presents a challenge for travelers with disabilities, though services in Cancún and the other major destinations are improving and the international chain hotels are almost on par with those in the U.S. Steep stairs are more common than elevators or escalators, but if you search long enough you'll find a way to get where you want to go. Porters are generally available to help with luggage at airports and large bus stations. Those traveling on a budget should stick with one-story hotels or hotels with elevators. Even so, there will probably still be obstacles. Generally speaking, no matter where you are, someone will lend a hand. Not all restrooms are equipped for travelers with disabilities; when one is available, access may be through a narrow passage that won't accommodate a wheelchair or a person on crutches. Many deluxe hotels (the most expensive) now have rooms with bathrooms designed for people with disabilities. The **Society for Accessible Travel & Hospitality** (www.sath.org; ✆ **212/447-7284**) and **Access-Able Travel Source** (www.access-able.com) offer a comprehensive database of destination-specific access information and links to resources.

**Doctors** See "Fast Facts" in destination chapters.

**Drinking Laws** The legal drinking age in Mexico is 18; however, asking for ID or denying purchase is extremely rare. Grocery stores sell everything from beer and wine to national and imported liquors. You can buy liquor 24 hours a day, but during major elections dry laws often are enacted by as much as 72 hours in advance of the election—and they apply to tourists as well as local residents. Enforcement of the law is up to each state, and is not enforced in most tourist areas. Mexico does not have laws that apply to transporting liquor in cars, but authorities are beginning to target drunk drivers more aggressively. It's a good idea to drive defensively. It's illegal to drink in the street and the police are enforcing the law more stringently with inebriated tourists.

**Electricity** The electrical system in Mexico is 110 volts AC (60 cycles), as in the United States and Canada.

**Embassies & Consulates** Most countries have an embassy in Mexico City, and many have consular offices or agencies around the country. U.S. consular agencies are in Cancún in the Torre La Europea, Bulevar Kukulcán Km 13 (http://merida.usconsulate.gov; ✆ **998/883-0272**), and in Playa del Carmen in "The Palapa," Calle 1 Sur btw. avs. 15 and 20 (✆ **984/873-0303**). Canadian consular agencies are in Cancún at the Centro Empresarial, Bulevar Kukulcán Km 12 (www.mexico.gc.ca; ✆ **998/883-3360**), and in Playa del Carmen at Plaza Paraíso Caribe, Av. 10 Sur btw. calles 3 and 5 (✆ **984/803-2411**). The United Kingdom also has a consular office in Cancún at the Royal Sands Hotel, Bulevar Kukulcán Km 13.5 (http://ukinmexico.fco.gov.uk/en; ✆ **998/881-0100**). Citizens of Ireland, Australia, and New Zealand should contact their embassies in Mexico City. Consular offices are generally open from 8 or 9am to 1 or 2pm.

It is a good idea to register with your embassy or consulate when visiting Mexico. The Smart Traveler Enrollment Program (STEP) is a free service provided by the U.S. government to U.S. citizens who are traveling to, or living in, a foreign country. STEP allows them to enter information about their upcoming trip abroad so that the Department of State can better assist them in an emergency, and also allows Americans residing abroad to obtain routine information from the nearest U.S. embassy or consulate. Visit https://step.state.gov/step.

**Emergencies** In case of emergency, dial ✆ **066.** Dial ✆ **065** for the Red Cross or ✆ **068** for the fire department. For police emergency numbers, turn to the "Fast Facts" sections in each of the individual chapters.

**Insurance** Before leaving home, find out what medical services your health insurance covers. For information on traveler's insurance, trip cancelation insurance, and medical insurance while traveling, please visit www.frommers.com/planning.

**Internet & Wi-Fi** Wi-Fi is common in resort areas. Most hotels offer Wi-Fi in the guest rooms for free or for a fee. Hotel lobbies often have Wi-Fi as well, as do many restaurants and bars.

**Language** Spanish is the official language in Mexico. English is spoken and understood in tourist areas. Mexicans are very accommodating with foreigners who try to speak Spanish, even in broken sentences.

**LGBT Travelers** Mexico is a conservative country, with deeply rooted Catholic religious traditions. Public displays of same-sex affection are rare and still considered surprising. Women in Mexico frequently walk hand in hand, but anything more would cross the boundary of acceptability. However, gay and lesbian travelers are generally treated with respect and should not experience harassment, assuming they give the appropriate regard to local customs. While much of Mexico is socially conservative, the coastal resorts offer gay-friendly accommodations, bars, and activities. For more information, visit **MexGay Vacations** at www.mexgay.com and **Gay Travel** at www.gaytravel.com.

**Mobile Phones** **Telcel** is Mexico's expensive, primary cellphone provider. It operates on GSM and offers good coverage in major cities and resorts. You can purchase prepaid disposable cellphones at convenience stores. Many North American and European cellphone companies offer roaming coverage in Mexico. Rates can be high, so check with your provider before committing to making calls this way. **Nextel** (www.nextel.com.mx) features a range of service options. **Cellular Abroad** (www.cellularabroad.com) offers cellphone rentals and purchases as well as SIM cards for travel abroad. Whether you rent or purchase the cellphone, you need to purchase a SIM card that is specific for Mexico. If you have Web access while traveling, consider a broadband-based telephone service (in technical terms, **Voice-over Internet Protocol,** or **VoIP**) such as **Skype** (www.skype.com) or **Vonage** (www.vonage.com), which allow you to make free international calls from your laptop. Neither service requires the people you're calling to also have that service (though there are fees if they do not). Check the websites for details. **WhatsApp** is an app for iPhone, BlackBerry, Android, Windows Phone, and Nokia, free for the first year then 99¢ per year, and **Viber** is a free app for iPhone and Android. You can use them to text people internationally for free (over Wi-Fi), and Viber allows international calls over Wi-Fi.

**Money & Costs** Frommer's lists exact prices in the local currency (unless rates are given in U.S. dollars). The currency conversions quoted below were correct at press time. Check a currency exchange website such as www.oanda.com/convert/classic for up-to-the-minute rates.

The most expensive destinations are those with the largest number of foreign visitors, such as Cancún and Playa del Carmen. The least expensive are those off the beaten path, including Punta Allen and Xcalak.

Mexico's currency is the peso. Paper currency comes in denominations of 20, 50, 100, 200, and 500 pesos.

## The Value of the Mexican Peso vs. Other Popular Currencies

| PESOS | US$ | CAN$ | UK£ | EURO (€) | AUS$ | NZ$ |
|---|---|---|---|---|---|---|
| 100 | US$6.73 | C$8.52 | £4.47 | €5.95 | A$8.67 | NZ$9.27 |

Coins come in denominations of 1, 2, 5, 10, and 20 pesos. Always keep a good supply of small denomination bills; it can be hard to change larger bills, especially in small towns.

Many establishments that deal with tourists, especially in resort areas, quote prices in U.S. dollars. To avoid confusion, they use the abbreviations "Dlls." for U.S. dollars and "M.N." (*moneda nacional*, or national currency) or "M.X.P." for Mexican Pesos.

The **universal currency sign ($)** is sometimes used to indicate pesos in Mexico. The use of this symbol in this book, however, denotes U.S. currency. ***Note:*** Establishments that quote their prices primarily in U.S. dollars are listed in this guide with U.S. dollars.

***Note:*** Payment in dollars is widely accepted in Cancún and the Riviera Maya, but federal law now limits cash transactions to $100, and foreign visitors may exchange no more than $1,500 per month. Some banks and businesses have stopped exchanging dollars; banks that do exchange dollars will require a copy of your passport. The limits do not apply to ATM withdrawals, so the best strategy is to rely on credit cards and ATMs.

**Newspapers & Magazines** Many hotels provide a printed compilation of daily news stories. You can find major U.S. newspapers and magazines in Cancún and Playa del Carmen. The *News* (www.thenews.com.mx) is an English-language daily with Mexico-specific news, published in Mexico City.

**Passports** See www.frommers.com/planning for information on how to obtain a passport. Citizens from most countries are required to present a valid passport for entry to Mexico. Citizens from some countries will need a Mexican visa. Visit the U.S. State Department's website, www.state.gov, for up-to-date information on travel to Mexico (U.S. citizens living or traveling in Mexico are encouraged to sign up on the same website for the Smart Traveler Enrollment Program to get updated information on local travel and security).

**Safety** Mexico is one of the world's great travel destinations, and millions of visitors travel safely here each year. Yet drug-related violence and widespread media coverage of Mexico's insecurity have impacted its tourism industry. The region covered by this guide, Cancún and the Yucatán, has generally not experienced the violence or insecurity affecting many other parts of the country. It's uncommon for foreign visitors to face anything worse than petty crimes such as pickpocketing and purse snatching. Always use common sense and exercise caution when in unfamiliar areas. Leave valuables and irreplaceable items in a safe place, or don't bring them at all. Use hotel safes when available. You can generally trust a person whom you approach for help or directions, but be wary of anyone who approaches you offering the same.

The U.S. State Department's **U.S. Department of State travel advisories for Mexico** (www.state.gov; ✆ **888/407-4747** toll-free in the U.S. and Canada) encourages its citizens to use main roads during daylight hours, stay in well-known tourist destinations and tourist areas with better security, cooperate fully with Mexican military and other law enforcement checkpoints, and provide an itinerary to a friend or family member not traveling with them. Some bars and nightclubs, especially in resort cities such as Cancún, can be havens for drug dealers and petty criminals.

**Bribes & Scams:** For years, Mexico was known as a place where bribes—called *mordidas* (bites)—were expected; however, the country is rapidly changing. Frequently, offering a bribe today, especially to a police officer, is considered an insult, and it can land you in deeper trouble. Many tourists have the impression that everything works better in Mexico if you "tip"; however, in reality, this only perpetuates the *mordida* tradition. You shouldn't tip simply to attempt to get away with something illegal or inappropriate—such as evading a traffic ticket that's deserved. Whatever you do, **avoid impoliteness;** you won't do yourself any favors if you insult a Mexican official. Extreme politeness, even in the face of adversity, rules Mexico. By adopting the local custom of excessive courtesy, you'll have greater success in negotiations of any kind. Stand your ground, but do it politely.

**Smoking** In early 2008, the Mexican president signed into law a nationwide smoking ban in workplaces and public buildings, and on public transportation. Private businesses are only permitted to allow public smoking in enclosed ventilated areas. Hotels in resort areas are usually smoke-free in rooms and public spaces. The law places Mexico—where a significant percentage of the population smokes—at the forefront of efforts to curb smoking and improve public health in Latin America.

**Taxes** Mexico has a value-added tax of 16% (*Impuesto de Valor Agregado*, or IVA; pronounced "ee-bah") on most everything, including restaurant meals, bus tickets, and souvenirs. Hotels charge the usual 16% IVA, plus a locally administered bed tax of 3% (in most areas), for a total of 19%. In Cancún, Los Cabos, and Cozumel, hotels charge the 11% IVA plus 3% room tax, for a total of 14%. The prices quoted by hotels and restaurants do not necessarily include the tax. You may find that upper-end properties (three or more stars) often quote prices without tax included, while lower-priced hotels include tax. Ask if the tax is included.

**Telephones** Phone numbers in Yucatán and Quintana Roo have three-digit area codes; local numbers have seven digits. To place a local call, you do not need to dial the area code. The country code for Mexico is 52.

To call Mexico:

1. Dial the international access code: 011 from the U.S. and Canada; 00 from the U.K., Ireland, or New Zealand; or 0011 from Australia.
2. Dial the country code: 52.
3. Dial the two- or three-digit area code, then the seven- or eight-digit number.

**To make international calls from Mexico:** To make international calls from Mexico, dial 00, then the country code (U.S. or Canada 1, U.K. 44, Ireland 353, Australia 61, New Zealand 64). Next, dial the area code and number.

**For directory assistance:** Dial ✆ **040** if you're looking for a number inside Mexico. ***Note:*** Listings usually appear under the owner's name, not the name of the business, and your chances of finding an English-speaking operator are slim.

**For operator assistance:** If you need operator assistance in making a call, dial ✆ **090** to make an international call, and ✆ **020** to call a number in Mexico.

**Toll-free numbers:** Numbers beginning with 800 within Mexico are toll-free, but calling a U.S. toll-free number from Mexico costs the same as an overseas call. To call an 800 number in the U.S., dial 001-880 and the last seven digits of the toll-free number. To call an 888 number in the U.S., dial 001-881 and the last seven digits of the toll-free number. For a number with an 887 prefix, dial 882; for 866, dial 883.

**Tipping** Most service employees in Mexico count on tips for the majority of their income. Bellboys should receive the equivalent of $1 per bag; waiters generally receive 10% to 15%, depending on the level of service. It is not customary to tip taxi drivers, unless they are hired by the hour or provide touring or other special services.

**Toilets** Public toilets are not common in Mexico, but an increasing number are available, especially at fast-food restaurants and Pemex gas stations.

**Visas** All travelers from Australia, Canada, New Zealand, the U.K., and the U.S., among others, can get their visas upon arrival in Mexico. For the latest requirements, check **www.inm.gob.mx/index.php/page/paises_visa/en.html**. Once in Mexico, all travelers must be in possession of a tourist card, also called Tourist Migration Form. This document is provided by airlines or by immigration authorities at the country's points of entry. You must fill out both the top and bottom sections of the card. You'll receive the bottom section as you go through immigration. Be careful not to lose this card, as you will be required to surrender it upon departure and you will be fined if you lose it.

**Visitor Information**

The **Mexico Tourism Board** (www.visitmexico.com) is an excellent source for general information.

# SPANISH & MAYAN TERMS & PHRASES

Most Mexicans are very patient with foreigners who try to speak their language; it helps a lot to know a few basic phrases. Included here are simple phrases for expressing basic needs, followed by some common menu items. We have also included a selection of Mayan words and phrases, since many Maya living on the Yucatán Peninsula today still speak their mother tongue.

9

## English-Spanish Phrases

| English | Spanish | Pronunciation |
|---|---|---|
| Good day | Buen día | **Bwehn *dee*-ah** |
| Good morning | Buenos días | ***Bweh*-nohs *dee*-ahs** |
| How are you? | ¿Cómo está? | ***Koh*-moh eh-*stah*** |
| Very well | Muy bien | **Mwee byehn** |
| Thank you | Gracias | ***Grah*-syahs** |
| You're welcome | De nada | **Deh *nah*-dah** |
| Goodbye | Adiós | **Ah-*dyohs*** |
| Please | Por favor | **Pohr fah-*bohr*** |
| Yes | Sí | **See** |
| No | No | **Noh** |
| Excuse me | Perdóneme | **Pehr-*doh*-neh-meh** |
| Give me | Déme | ***Deh*-meh** |
| Where is . . . ? | ¿Dónde está . . . ? | ***Dohn*-deh eh-*stah*** |
| the station | la estación | **lah eh-stah-*syohn*** |
| a hotel | un hotel | **oon oh-*tehl*** |
| a gas station | una gasolinera | ***oo*-nah gah-soh-lee-*neh*-rah** |
| a restaurant | un restaurante | **oon res-tow-*rahn*-teh** |
| the toilet | el baño | **el *bah*-nyoh** |
| a good doctor | un buen médico | **oon bwehn *meh*-dee-coh** |
| the road to . . . | el camino a/hacia | **el cah-*mee*-noh ah/*ah*-syah** |

| English | Spanish | Pronunciation |
|---|---|---|
| To the right | A la derecha | **Ah lah deh-*reh*-chah** |
| To the left | A la izquierda | **Ah lah ees-*kyehr*-dah** |
| Straight ahead | Derecho | **Deh-*reh*-choh** |
| I would like | Quisiera | **Key-*syeh*-rah** |
| I want . . . | Quiero . . . | ***Kyeh*-roh** |
| to eat | comer | **koh-*mehr*** |
| a room | una habitación | ***oo*-nah ah-bee-tah-*syohn*** |
| Do you have . . . ? | ¿Tiene usted . . . ? | **Tyeh-neh oo-*sted*** |
| a book | un libro | **oon *lee*-broh** |
| a dictionary | un diccionario | **oon deek-syoh-*nah*-ryoh** |
| How much is it? | ¿Cuánto cuesta? | ***Kwahn*-toh *kweh*-stah** |
| When? | ¿Cuándo? | ***Kwahn*-doh** |
| What? | ¿Qué? | **Keh** |
| Is there . . . ?) | (¿)Hay ( . . . ?) | **Eye** |
| What is there? | ¿Qué hay? | **Keh eye** |
| Yesterday | Ayer | **Ah-*yer*** |
| Today | Hoy | **Oy** |
| Tomorrow | Mañana | **Mah-*nyah*-nah** |
| Good | Bueno | ***Bweh*-noh** |
| Bad | Malo | ***Mah*-loh** |
| Better (best) | (Lo) Mejor | **(Loh) Meh-*hohr*** |
| More | Más | **Mahs** |
| Less | Menos | ***Meh*-nohs** |
| No smoking | Se prohibe fumar | **Seh proh-*ee*-beh foo-*mahr*** |
| Postcard | Tarjeta postal | **Tar-*heh*-tah poh-*stahl*** |
| Insect repellent | Repelente contra insectos | **Reh-peh-*lehn*-teh *cohn*-trah een-*sehk*-tohs** |
| Do you speak English? | ¿Habla usted inglés? | ***Ah*-blah oo-*sted* een-*glehs*** |
| Is there anyone here who speaks English? | ¿Hay alguien aquí que hable inglés? | **Eye *ahl*-gyehn ah-*kee* keh *ah*-bleh een-*glehs*** |
| I speak a little Spanish. | Hablo un poco de español. | ***Ah*-bloh oon *poh*-koh deh eh-spah-*nyohl*** |
| I don't understand Spanish very well. | No (lo) entiendo muy bien el español. | **Noh (loh) ehn-*tyehn*-doh mwee byehn el eh-spah-*nyohl*** |
| The meal is good. | Me gusta la comida. | **Meh *goo*-stah lah koh-*mee*-dah** |
| What time is it? | ¿Qué hora es? | **Keh *oh*-rah ehs** |
| May I see your menu? | ¿Puedo ver el menú (la carta)? | ***Pweh*-doh vehr el meh-*noo* (lah *car*-tah)** |
| The check, please. | La cuenta, por favor. | **Lah *kwehn*-tah pohr fa-*borh*** |
| What do I owe you? | ¿Cuánto le debo? | ***Kwahn*-toh leh *deh*-boh** |
| What did you say? | ¿Mande? (formal) | ***Mahn*-deh** |
|  | ¿Cómo? (informal) | ***Koh*-moh** |

| English | Spanish | Pronunciation |
|---|---|---|
| I want (to see) . . . | Quiero (ver) . . . | ***Kyeh*-roh (vehr)** |
| a room | un cuarto, una habitación | **oon *kwar*-toh, *oo*-nah ah-bee-tah-*syohn*** |
| for two persons | para dos personas | ***pah*-rah dohs pehr-*soh*-nahs** |
| with (without) bathroom | con (sin) baño | **kohn (seen) *bah*-nyoh** |
| We are staying here only . . . | Nos quedamos aquí solamente . . . | **Nohs keh-*dah*-mohs ah-*kee* soh-lah-*mehn*-teh** |
| one night | una noche | ***oo*-nah *noh*-cheh** |
| one week | una semana | ***oo*-nah seh-*mah*-nah** |
| We are leaving . . . | Partimos (Salimos) . . . | **Pahr-*tee*-mohs (Sah-*lee*-mohs)** |
| tomorrow | mañana | **mah-*nyah*-nah** |
| Do you accept . . . | ¿Acepta usted . . . ? | **Ah-*sehp*-tah oo-*sted*** |
| traveler's checks? | cheques de viajero | ***cheh*-kehs deh byah-*heh*-roh** |

## Numbers

| English | Spanish | Pronunciation |
|---|---|---|
| one | uno | ***ooh*-noh** |
| two | dos | **dohs** |
| three | tres | **trehs** |
| four | cuatro | ***kwah*-troh** |
| five | cinco | ***seen*-koh** |
| six | seis | **sayes** |
| seven | siete | ***syeh*-teh** |
| eight | ocho | ***oh*-choh** |
| nine | nueve | ***nweh*-beh** |
| ten | diez | **dyehs** |
| eleven | once | ***ohn*-seh** |
| twelve | doce | ***doh*-seh** |
| thirteen | trece | ***treh*-seh** |
| fourteen | catorce | **kah-*tohr*-seh** |
| fifteen | quince | ***keen*-seh** |
| sixteen | dieciséis | **dyeh-see-*sayes*** |
| seventeen | diecisiete | **dyeh-see-*syeh*-teh** |
| eighteen | dieciocho | **dyeh-see-*oh*-choh** |
| nineteen | diecinueve | **dyeh-see-*nweh*-beh** |
| twenty | veinte | ***bayn*-teh** |
| thirty | treinta | ***trayn*-tah** |
| forty | cuarenta | **kwah-*ren*-tah** |
| fifty | cincuenta | **seen-*kwen*-tah** |

| English | Spanish | Pronunciation |
|---|---|---|
| sixty | sesenta | **seh-*sehn*-tah** |
| seventy | setenta | **seh-*tehn*-tah** |
| eighty | ochenta | **oh-*chehn*-tah** |
| ninety | noventa | **noh-*behn*-tah** |
| one hundred | cien | **syehn** |
| two hundred | doscientos | **do-*syehn*-tohs** |
| five hundred | quinientos | **kee-*nyehn*-tohs** |
| one thousand | mil | **meel** |

## Transportation Terms

| English | Spanish | Pronunciation |
|---|---|---|
| Airport | Aeropuerto | **Ah-eh-roh-*pwehr*-toh** |
| Flight | Vuelo | ***Bweh*-loh** |
| Rental car | Renta de autos | **Ren-tah deh *ow*-tohs** |
| Bus | Autobús | **Ow-toh-*boos*** |
| Bus or truck | Camión | **Ka-*myohn*** |
| Lane | Carril | **Kah-*reel*** |
| Nonstop (bus) | Directo | **Dee-*rehk*-toh** |
| Baggage (claim area) | Equipajes | **Eh-kee-*pah*-hehss** |
| Intercity | Foraneo | **Foh-rah-*neh*-oh** |
| Luggage storage area | Guarda equipaje | ***Gwar*-dah eh-kee-*pah*-heh** |
| Arrival gates | Llegadas | **Yeh-*gah*-dahss** |
| Originates at this station | Local | **Loh-*kahl*** |
| Originates elsewhere | De paso | **Deh *pah*-soh** |
| Are seats available? | Hay lugares disponibles? | **Eye loo-*gah*-rehs dis-pohn-*ee*-blehss** |
| First class | Primera | **Pree-*meh*-rah** |
| Second class | Segunda | **Seh-*goon*-dah** |
| Nonstop (flight) | Sin escala | **Seen ess-*kah*-lah** |
| Baggage claim area | Recibo de equipajes | **Reh-*see*-boh deh eh-kee-*pah*-hehss** |
| Waiting room | Sala de espera | ***Sah*-lah deh ehss-*peh*-rah** |
| Toilets | Sanitarios | **Sah-nee-*tah*-ryohss** |
| Ticket window | Taquilla | **Tah-*kee*-yah** |

## Food Glossary

### MEALS

**Desayuno** Breakfast.

**Comida** Main meal of the day, taken in the afternoon.

**Cena** Supper.

### COURSES

**Botana** A small serving of food that accompanies a beer or drink, usually served free of charge.

**Entrada** Appetizer.
**Sopa** Soup course. (Not necessarily a soup—it can be a dish of rice or noodles, called *sopa seca* [dry soup].)
**Ensalada** Salad.
**Plato fuerte or plato principal** Main course.
**Postre** Dessert.
**Comida corrida** Inexpensive daily special usually consisting of three courses.
**Menú del día** Same as *comida corrida.*

## FOOD TEMPERATURES

**Término un cuarto** Rare, literally means one-fourth.
**Término medio** Medium rare, one-half.
**Término tres cuartos** Medium, three-fourths.
**Bien cocido** Well-done.

*Note:* Keep in mind, when ordering a steak, that *medio* does not mean "medium."

## MISCELLANEOUS RESTAURANT TERMINOLOGY

**Cucharra** Spoon.
**Cuchillo** Knife.
**La cuenta** The bill.
**Plato** Plate.
**Plato hondo** Bowl.
**Propina** Tip.
**Servilleta** Napkin.
**Tenedor** Fork.
**Vaso** Glass.
**Iva** Value-added tax.
**Fonda** Strictly speaking, a food stall in the market or street, but now used in a loose or nostalgic sense to designate an informal restaurant.

## POPULAR MEXICAN & YUCATECAN DISHES

**A la tampiqueña** (Usually *bistec a la tampiqueña* or *arrachera a la tampiqueña.*) A steak served with several sides, including but not limited to an enchilada, guacamole, rice, and beans.
**Achiote** Small red seed of the annatto tree, with mild flavor, used for both taste and color.
**Adobo** Marinade made with chiles and tomatoes, often seen in adjectival form *adobado/adobada.*
**Agua fresca** Any sweetened fruit-flavored water, including *limonada* (limeade), *horchata, tamarindo, sandía* (watermelon), and *melón* (cantaloupe).
**Alambre** Brochette.
**Antojito** Literally means "small temptation." It's a general term for tacos, tostadas, quesadillas, and the like, which are usually eaten for supper or as a snack.
**Arrachera** Skirt steak, fajitas.
**Arroz** Rice.
**Bistec** Steak.
**Calabaza** Zucchini squash.
**Camarones** Shrimp. For common cooking methods, see *pescado.*
**Carne** Meat.
**Carnitas** Slow-cooked pork dish from Michoacán and parts of central Mexico, served with tortillas, guacamole, and salsa or pickled jalapeños.

**Cebolla** Onion.

**Cecina** Thinly sliced pork or beef, dried or marinated, depending on the region.

**Ceviche** Fresh raw seafood marinated in fresh lime juice and garnished with chopped tomatoes, onions, chiles, and sometimes cilantro.

**Chalupas poblanas** Simple dish from Puebla consisting of handmade tortillas lightly fried but left soft, and topped with different chile sauces.

**Chayote** A type of spiny squash boiled and served as an accompaniment to meat dishes.

**Chilaquiles** Fried tortilla quarters softened in either a red or a green sauce and served with Mexican sour cream, onion, and sometimes chicken *(con pollo).*

**Chile** Any of the many hot peppers used in Mexican cooking, in fresh, dried, or smoked forms.

**Chile ancho** A dried *chile poblano,* which serves as the base for many varieties of sauces and *moles.*

**Chile chipotle** A smoked jalapeño sold dried or canned in an adobo sauce.

**Chile en nogada** *Chile poblano* stuffed with a complex filling of shredded meat, nuts, and dried, candied, and fresh fruit, topped with walnut cream sauce and a sprinkling of pomegranate seeds.

**Chile poblano** Fresh pepper that is usually dark green in color, large, and not usually spicy. Often stuffed with a variety of fillings (chile relleno).

**Chile relleno** Stuffed pepper.

**Chivo** Kid or goat.

**Churro** Fried pastry dusted with sugar and served plain or filled. The Spanish equivalent of a doughnut.

**Cochinita pibil** Yucatecan dish of pork, pit-baked in a *pibil* sauce of achiote, sour orange, and spices.

**Consomé** Clear broth, usually with rice.

**Cortes** Another way of saying steaks; in full, it is *cortes finas de carne* (fine cuts of meat).

**Cuitlacoche** Variant of *huitlacoche.*

**Elote** Fresh corn.

**Empanada** For most of Mexico, a turnover with a savory or sweet filling. In Oaxaca and southern Mexico, it is corn *masa* or a tortilla folded around a savory filling and roasted or fried.

**Empanizado** Breaded.

**Enchilada** A lightly fried tortilla, dipped in sauce and folded or rolled around a filling. It has many variations, such as *enchiladas suizas* (made with a cream sauce), *enchiladas del portal* or *enchiladas placeras* (made with a predominantly *chile ancho* sauce), and *enchiladas verdes* (in a green sauce of tomatillos, cilantro, and chiles).

**Enfrijoladas** Like an enchilada, but made with a bean sauce flavored with toasted avocado leaves.

**Enmoladas** Enchiladas made with a *mole* sauce.

**Ensalada** Salad.

**Entomatadas** Enchiladas made with a tomato sauce.

**Escabeche** Vegetables pickled in a vinegary liquid.

**Flan** Custard.

**Flautas** Tortillas that are rolled up around a filling (usually chicken or shredded beef) and deep-fried; often listed on a menu as *taquitos* or *tacos fritos.*

**Frijoles refritos** Beans mashed and cooked with lard.

**Gorditas** Thick, fried corn tortillas, slit open and stuffed with meat or cheese filling.

**Huevos mexicanos** Scrambled eggs with chopped onions, chiles serranos, and tomatoes.

**Huevos rancheros** Fried eggs, usually placed on tortillas and bathed in a light tomato sauce.

**Huitlacoche** Salty and mild-tasting corn fungus that is considered a delicacy in Mexico.

**Jitomate** Tomato.

**Lechuga** Lettuce.

**Limón** A small lime. Mexicans squeeze these limes on everything from soups to tacos.

**Lomo adobado** Pork loin cooked in an adobo.

**Masa** Soft dough made of corn that is the basis for making tortillas and tamales.

**Menudo** Soup made with beef tripe and hominy.

**Milanesa** Beef cutlet breaded and fried.

**Molcajete** A three-legged mortar made of volcanic stone and used for grinding. Often used now as a cooking dish that is brought to the table steaming hot and filled with meat, chiles, onions, and cheese.

**Mole** Any variety of thick sauce made with dried chiles, nuts, fruits or vegetables, and spices. Variations include *mole poblano* (Puebla style, with chocolate and sesame), *mole negro* (black *mole* from Oaxaca, also with chocolate), and *mole verde* (made with herbs and/or pumpkin seeds, depending on the region).

**Pan** Bread. A few of the varieties include *pan dulce* (general term for a variety of sweet breads), *pan de muerto* (bread made for the Day of the Dead holidays), and *pan Bimbo* (packaged sliced white bread).

**Panuchos** A Yucatecan dish of *masa* cakes stuffed with refried black beans and topped with shredded turkey or chicken, lettuce, and onion.

**Papadzules** A Yucatecan dish of tortillas stuffed with hard-boiled eggs and topped with a sauce made of pumpkin seeds.

**Papas** Potatoes.

**Parrillada** A sampler platter of grilled meats or seafood.

**Pescado** Fish. Common ways of cooking fish include *al mojo de ajo* (pan seared with oil and garlic), *a la veracruzana* (with tomatoes, olives, and capers), and *al ajillo* (seared with garlic and fine strips or rings of *chile guajillo*).

**Pibil** See *cochinita pibil.* When made with chicken, it is called *pollo pibil.*

**Pipián** A thick sauce made with ground pumpkin seeds, nuts, herbs, and chiles. Can be red or green.

**Poc chuc** Pork with onion marinated in sour orange and then grilled; a Yucatecan dish.

**Pollo** Chicken.

**Pozole** Soup with chicken or pork, hominy, lettuce, and radishes, served with a small plate of other ingredients to be added according to taste (onion, pepper, lime juice, oregano). In Jalisco it's red *(pozole rojo),* in Michoacán it's clear *(pozole blanco),* and in Guerrero it's green *(pozole verde).* In the rest of Mexico, it can be any one of these.

**Puerco** Pork.

**Pulque** A drink made of fermented juice of the maguey plant; most common in the states of Hidalgo, Tlaxcala, Puebla, and Mexico.

**Quesadilla** Corn or flour tortillas stuffed with white cheese and cooked on a hot griddle. In Mexico City, it is made with raw *masa* folded around any of a variety of fillings (often containing no cheese) and deep-fried.
**Queso** Cheese.
**Res** Beef.
**Salbute** A Yucatecan dish much like a *panucho,* but without bean paste in the middle.
**Sope** Small fried *masa* cake topped with savory meats and greens.
**Tacos al pastor** Small tacos made with thinly sliced pork marinated in an adobo and served with pineapple, onion, and cilantro.
**Tamal** (Not "tamale.") *Masa* mixed with lard and beaten until light and folded around a savory or sweet filling, and encased in a cornhusk or a plant leaf (usually corn or banana) and then steamed. "Tamales" is the plural form.
**Taquitos** See "flautas."
**Tinga** Shredded meat stewed in a *chile chipotle* sauce.
**Torta** A sandwich made with a *bolillo.*



## English-Mayan Phrases

Mayan vowels are pronounced as they are in Spanish. Double vowels are pronounced like their single counterparts but are held longer. The "x" is pronounced "sh," as in "ship"; the "j" sounds like "h," as in "home." Consonants that come before an accent (') are glottalized. Though the difference is hard for a newcomer to discern, glottalized consonants have a harder, more emphatic sound. Accents in Mayan words usually fall on the last syllable (unlike Spanish, which emphasizes the penultimate syllable unless an accent mark indicates otherwise). Plurals in Mayan are formed by adding the suffix -ob.

| English | Mayan | Pronunciation |
|---|---|---|
| Hello | Ola | ***Oh**-lah* |
| How are you? | Biix a beel? | **Beesh a bell** |
| What is your name? | Bix a k'aaba? | **Beesh ah k-ah-*bah*** |
| My name is . . . | In k'aaba . . . | **Een k-ah-bah** |
| So long | Tu heel k'iin | **Too heel k-*een*** |
| Goodbye/Take care | Xi'ik tech utsil | **Shee-*eek* tech oot-*seel*** |
| See you tomorrow | Asta sa'amal | **Ahs-ta sah-ah-*mahl*** |
| Okay (fine, well) | Ma'aloob | **Mah-ah-*lohby*** |
| Yes | He'le' | **Hey-*leh*** |
| No | Ma' | **Mah** |
| I don't understand | Min na'atik | **Meen na-ah-*teek*** |
| Thank you | Dyos bo'otik | **Dee-*yos* boh-oh-*teek*** |
| You're welcome | Mixba'al | **Meesh-bah-*ahl*** |
| Stop | Wa'alen | **Wah-ah-*lehn*** |
| I'm hungry | Wi'hen | **Wee-*hehn*** |
| I'm going home | Kin bin tin nah | **Keen been teen nah** |
| Bon appetit | Hach ki' a wi'ih | **Hach kee ah wee-ee** |
| Let's (go) | Ko'ox (tun) | **Koh-osh (toon)** |
| Where is the beach? | Tuxan há? | **Too-*shan* hah** |

## Mayan Glossary

**Ah kin** A high priest.
**Aktun** Cave.
**Atl-atl** Spear-throwing device.
**Bacab** A class of important gods.
**Balam** Jaguar spirit that keeps evil away.
**Cán** Serpent.
**Cenote** A natural waterhole created by the collapse of limestone caves; corruption by the Spanish of the Mayan word *dzonot.*
**Ch'en** Pool.
**Chilan** A soothsayer or medium.
**Chultun** A bottle-shaped, underground cistern.
**Corte** Indian woman's traditional full-length skirt.
**Há** Cacao seed.
**Huipil** A traditional Maya wraparound, woven cotton dress, worn leaving the shoulders bare.
**Ka'a'anab háal ha** Beach.
**Kayab** A turtle-shell drum.
**Kayem** Ground maize.
**Kin** The sun, the day, unity of time.
**Ku'um** Pumpkin.
**Manta** A square of cloth, used as a cloak or blanket; still worn by the Maya today.
**Milpa** A cornfield.
**Muxubbak** Tamale.
**Nohoch** Important, big.
**P'ac** Tomatoes.
**Palapa** Traditional thatched-roof Maya structure built without nails.
**Pok-a-tok** A Maya ball game.
**Pom** Resin of the copal tree, used for rubber, chewing gum, and incense.
**Quetzal** A rare Central American bird, now almost extinct, prized by Maya kings for its long, brilliant blue-green tail feathers.
**Sacbé** Literally "white road," a raised limestone causeway linking Maya buildings and settlements.
**Xibalbá** The Maya underworld.

# Index

See also Accommodations and Restaurant indexes, below.

## General Index

### A



### B



### C

## D



## E



## F



## G

## Accommodations



## Restaurants